AMONG THE PILGRIMS

Journeys to Santiago de Compostela

Mary Victoria Wallis

National Library of Canada Cataloguing in Publication

Wallis, Mary V. (Mary Victoria), 1951-
    Among the pilgrims : journeys to Santiago de
Compostela / Mary Victoria Wallis.
ISBN 1-4120-0796-8
    1. Santiago de Compostela (Spain)—Description and
travel. 2. Santiago de Compostela (Spain)—History.   I.
Title.

DP402.S23W34 2003   914.6'11   C2003-903882-3

TRAFFORD

This book was published *on-demand* in cooperation with Trafford Publishing.
On-demand publishing is a unique process and service of making a book available for retail sale to the public taking advantage of on-demand manufacturing and Internet marketing. **On-demand publishing** includes promotions, retail sales, manufacturing, order fulfilment, accounting and collecting royalties on behalf of the author.

Suite 6E, 2333 Government St., Victoria, B.C. V8T 4P4, CANADA
Phone   250-383-6864   Toll-free   1-888-232-4444 (Canada & US)
Fax   250-383-6804   E-mail   sales@trafford.com
Web site   www.trafford.com   TRAFFORD PUBLISHING IS A DIVISION OF TRAFFORD HOLDINGS LTD.
Trafford Catalogue #03-1164   www.trafford.com/robots/03-1164.html

10   9   8   7   6   5   4   3

TABLE OF CONTENTS

ACKNOWLEDGEMENTS

One of the loveliest tasks as I finish writing *Among the Pilgrims* is to thank all those who have helped me: first, my deepest gratitude to Scott, who had raised the idea for this book even before we set out for the Camino. Scott created an initial outline for me and later spent many hours designing the layout and cover and arranging the photographs. Then, with a combination of love and brute force, he got me through the writing with unfailing confidence that, someday, I would finish.

Many thanks to Brian and Marie Rose Northgrave, Suzie Slavin, Cathy Vance, Doug Malcolm, Jacquie Hunt and Marc Richard, for their useful editorial comments, willingly offered despite their busy schedules. Thanks to Louise Knight, Carol Myers and Marlow Roberts at Trafford for their prompt and cheerful help whenever I needed it.

I thank my mother, Gene, for giving me her zest for travel and her excitement for meeting new people in faraway places, and my father, Gilbert, for his abiding pride in me (sometimes undeserved) and his wisdom about the how and why of life in this world. I am very grateful to Neil, my lifelong friend, who kept reminding me I had a voice; and to Kjell, a fellow pilgrim during my second trip, who carried my gear on his bike when my shin splints were hard to bear, and whose conversations enriched my understanding of pilgrimage so much. I thank Errol, wherever you are, and all the other Camino travellers I met along the way, for their words and songs and smiles. Finally, I remember with gratitude the priests, volunteers and Confraternity members who care so much about the Camino, for welcoming me - and all of us - so warmly into their *refugios* and for providing endless support and assistance with our journeys.

On the meseta, a well equipped Camino pilgrim.

1

PILGRIMAGE

Our age wishes to have actual experiences in psychic life. It wants to experience for itself, and not to make assumptions based on the experience of other ages. Yet this does not preclude its trying anything in a hypothetical way - for instance, the recognized religions....

  Carl Jung. *Modern Man in Search of a Soul*

A serious human life, no matter what "religion" is invoked, can hardly begin until we see an element of illusion in what is really there, and something real in the fantasies about what might be there instead. At that point the imaginative and the concerned begin to unite.

  Northrop Frye. *The Great Code*

We are here on the planet only once, and might as well get a feel for the place.

  Annie Dillard. *In the Jungle*

Santiago de Compostela · Arzúa · Palas de Rei · Portomarín · Triacastela · Sarria · Villafranca del Bierzo · El Cebreiro · Molinaseca · Ponferrada · Rabanal del Camino · Foncebadón · Hospital del Órbigo · Astórga · Mansanilla de las Mulas · León · Sahagún

*Beside the trail, a doorstep decorated
with scallop shells, emblem of Santiago.*

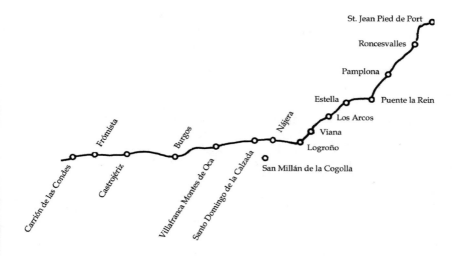

The pilgrimage trail known since the Middle Ages as *El Camino de Santiago* makes a shallow loop across northern Spain like the chipped edge of an antique dish. As are all antiques, it is a compromise of materials and illusion: part earth and asphalt, part story. It comes out of southern France, a little road that climbs up over windy passes in the Pyrenees, then slips down the south slopes onto the farmlands of Spanish Navarra. At Puente la Reina, the Camino turns west, more trail than road now, to cross La Rioja and the high, horizonless Castilian plateau. At Burgos, it bears slightly north; after León, it rises and drops over two thin spurs of the Cantabrian Mountains, then all but disappears into the eucalyptus forests of Galicia. Days later, less than twenty miles from the Atlantic Ocean, the trail from France makes its way up onto the broad crest of Monte de Gozo, the Mount of Joy. Below, shining in the sunset or, more often, glistening in the rain, are the steeples of the old city of Santiago de Compostela.

Santiago is an heirloom in granite. Like the trail that leads to it, it is built as much of legends and lies as of earth and stone. Even the weather is an accomplice in the artifice: mists drift like souls along the walls of buildings; raindrops dance on sunbeams among church spires. The dark, rectangular paving stones of the main square, the enormous Plaza Obradorio, hold the reflection of lowering clouds like the image of a dream.

On the east side of the Plaza, a Baroque staircase rises like a follies stage set to the doors of Santiago Cathedral. High above, in the nooks of the church's grand façade, winged statues pose triumphantly. Each one proclaims the Camino's illusion: here, in this Galician city at the end of the road from France, lie the bones of St. James the Great, friend of Jesus, missionary apostle, Spain's patron saint, and hero of the Reconquista.

James, whom Jesus nicknamed a Son of Thunder, died in Jerusalem in 44 AD, beheaded. After this gruesome death, say the legends, his body was gathered up by a few disciples and taken to Spain in a stone boat. He was buried in Galicia, in a tomb mostly forgotten until a local bishop discovered it again in the 9th Century. In the centuries since that crucial find, people have come to Santiago from all over to worship at James' shrine. During the golden Camino years between 1050 and 1200, pilgrims made their way through the streets of Santiago by the thousands. They crowded in thick streams through the doors of the cathedral to kneel, smelly and fervent, beneath its incense-inflated arches. Their prayers fluttered toward the saint like the outstretched hands of the starving, as they begged, in an age that awaited miracles the way we hope for an overdue telephone call, for a cure, a son, an end to famine and strife. At the very least, they sought solace for their burdened souls and a promise of paradise to take home to their faraway villages.

After the Protestant Reformation and the Renaissance, the great medieval pilgrimage drifted into the margins of history. But there were always a few people every year who went to Santiago, even after Napoleon's army had wrecked nearly everything along the route. And in the 1960s, with the blessing of Spain's Generalissimo Francisco Franco, the Camino began a dubious reincarnation as a modern pilgrimage trail. In 1987, it was declared the first European Cultural Route by the Council of Europe. Today, it is Europe's longest and most authentic historical itinerary, a designation that rankles those who feel that history and culture are for tourists, and that tourists are not pilgrims.

One spring in the late 1990s, I bicycled *El Camino* from the Pyrenees to Santiago - some eight hundred kilometers - in a little over two weeks. In August of the next year, I crossed it on foot in about a month. Those journeys now seem more like orbits than separate trips from one side of Spain to the other. Over two seasons, I passed through the same towns, the same landscapes, even drank from the same fountains. But as if my path had become an inward spiral, I saw all of these the second time from a new perspective, at an altered speed and with a different emotional frequency. The weather was spring fresh the year I bicycled and summer hot the year I walked. The clouds, fat with rain the first time, had thinned away to nothing the second; and the green fields of May were, in August, a wispy yellow, dry almost to disappearing. As for me, I went from being restless one year to something approaching contemplative the next.

Over two seasons, I fell in with a long line of other Camino travellers: cycling pilgrims, walking pilgrims, bus, car and motorcycle pilgrims, and many people who weren't pilgrims at all. Our days revolved around the Camino of the past. Crossing the threshold of medieval churches, resting beside ancient waymarks, simply by being where so many others had walked over the centuries, we became part of the old pilgrimage ourselves. We tried, sometimes awkwardly, to pay homage to the pilgrims of an old, outlandish-sounding faith; inevitably, we were kept aloof in the present by the centrifugal pull of time.

We were also travelling, I found, on the hopes and nameless dreads of our own times, enacting a peculiarly modern Camino history. In a 1993 book about the pilgrimage, I came across the statement of an eighteen-year-old boy: "Now no one can say I am worthless," he wrote. "I have done the Camino de Santiago."

Like the Camino itself, my trips extended beyond the road into the world of words. I wrote about the Camino before I left home, piecing together some intentions for the journey. I wrote while I was on the road, scratching notes and questions in my diary over chunks of bread and cheese, or curled beneath a shaky light in a pilgrims' *refugio*. Back home in Canada, I kept writing, trying to see past the prism of nostalgia to what the Camino really had to tell a skeptical age. I wondered whether I, or anyone today, had an authentic role to play in the stories and evolution of a medieval road leading to a dubious reliquary in Galicia. I was a medievalist by training, somewhat metaphysical by nature. But I earned my living in the health sciences, and the pragmatic, research-trained part of me was also drawn to the story of Santiago. I probed beyond the Camino of the coffee books, lovely as it is, for its hidden histories, its contradictions and fakery, and I wrestled with a hydra of a question: what is the spiritual traveller from a world of irony and iconoclasm to *do* with a medieval Christian pilgrimage route?

The Camino is history alive. It lures you, captures you in its tangled stories. A few cities with familiar names are located along the path - Pamplona, Burgos, León - places that were busy with trade and the affairs of church and state when the pilgrimage was at its peak in the Middle Ages. The cities have monasteries, museums, civic buildings, the tombs of Queen Eleanor, El Cid, St. Isidore. You are pulled into their cathedrals like a bee into a flower.

Between the cities are dozens of low-slung towns and wispy villages where you can fill your water bottle at an ancient fountain and rest in the shadow of a ruined wall. When you bed down for the night in a Camino *refugio*, you imagine the whispering ghosts of all the pilgrims who, over the span of a thousand years, have laid down their weary bodies in this same spot.

Camino geography takes you back and forth between the reality of physics and discomfort, and the perennial availability of joy. The weather is notoriously awkward. In 1997, spring storms turned some of the trails to porridge. There was a heat wave in 1998. The mountains make you sweat as you pick your way up through the trees, the endless roads leave you blistered and aching. But the light of the Camino is a balm, a translucence like a weightless wind upon the Spanish landscape. You see it playing in its oceans of wildflowers in the spring and its ripe, golden fields in the fall. Summer sunshine brightens the emptiness of the pancake plateau and cheers, ever so slightly, the solemnity of its mountain passes. In the forests of Galicia, light flits like a pianist's fingers among the eucalyptus trees, causing not sound, but scent, a sonata of resins, to play around your face.

In the dappled landscapes of the modern Camino, the old pilgrimage mystique may catch even the casual traveller off-guard. Though the Camino was forgotten by the world for centuries, its ruined buildings still exude confidence in the idea of pilgrimage. The smell of an old Christianity waits in the gapped walls of roofless monasteries that, even in their abandonment, have never lost their dignity. Faith lingers along the curving roofs and strange grotesques of Romanesque churches, and inhabits the arches of old stone bridges. The hopeful echo of prayers hangs by wayside crosses from the 14th Century.

The old pilgrim's confidence lives on in the people of the Camino today. I saw it in the friendly faces of believing pilgrims, felt it in the gentle hands of hostel volunteers as they cared for my blisters, and heard it in my conversations with the bright young priests in t-shirts I sometimes met in the churches.

But many strands of worldly life - a violent past and a welter of concocted myths, along with the tendrils of art and music and folklore - are braided into the *Camino de Santiago*. You discover these strands in ancient road markers, in gaunt old castles, Visigothic churches, foundries and prehistoric fountains, in old mines, menhirs, and stone fences separating worked and reworked farmlands. Parts of the Camino were already here when the Romans arrived in the 3rd Century before Christ. And since the time of Augustus Caesar, who got sick on the way west from León, the road has always clattered beneath the hooves and wheels and boots of travellers unconcerned with pilgrimage: Roman soldiers, Roman gold miners and villa owners, choppy waves of Germanic barbarians, Moors and Arabs from the deserts of Africa, the great French armies of Charlemagne, slave merchants, Jewish traders in wine and olives and silver, French churchmen, young men of promise heading to Burgos or León or Salamanca, crusty farmers, English whores, hardened criminals, vagrants from nowhere, Napoleon's imperial troops, Spanish royalists and revolutionaries and rebels and melancholy refugees. And now, the modern threads in the Camino: tourists with day packs up for a weekend from Madrid, vans delivering Coca-Cola, sport cyclists in shiny shirts and skin-tight shorts, farmers slouched on John Deere tractors, and women with scarves and stout legs goading a few cows with a stick.

In the Middle Ages Santiago was, after Jerusalem and Rome, the most important pilgrims' city in the western world. For five hundred years after James' tomb was discovered in the 9th Century, the faithful trudged into Spain from around the Christian world. All year long, but mostly in summertime, their walking sticks tapped the trail, engraved on its buckling surfaces their hopes for a glimpse of paradise in that far-off Santiago crypt. And even when the Protestants (my own spiritual ancestors) coldly stared it down and the rationalists explained it away - a shiny silver box of somebody's bones in a church floor - the bright allure of the tomb simply slipped out to become the allure of the Camino itself. An earthen road had metamorphosed into a good story, but like all good stories, it can change how you think.

My first journey to Santiago began in Canada on a May morning in 1997. My plane roared up off a Calgary runway, then tilted and slowly swooned to the east. The city's downtown towers retracted into a set of metal cubes in a giant plate of farmland. The planet receded backward. Clouds came wafting past my window, and before I knew it, I was adrift in airline hum and a white-bottomed sky.

In a few days from now, I would meet Scott, my husband and travelling partner. My flight this morning was the first step in a sequence we had worked out over months. He was finishing a work contract in Nigeria and already had our gear; I was bringing the mountain bikes. Converging like vectors, first one from Canada, then the other from Africa, we would arrive in the south of France two days apart and meet at a hotel in Biarritz. On the third morning, we would take the bikes by cab to the town of St. Jean Pied de Port, where the *Camino francés* begins. From the base of the French Pyrenees, we would pedal up over the pass into Spain and down into Roncesvalles. Then for the next couple of weeks, we would be heading west, past Pamplona and Burgos, across the meseta to León, then over more mountains into Galicia and down to Santiago.

Our plans sounded casually, almost insolently modern. Studying our Michelin maps, we had looked only at Spain, barely noticing the trans-Atlantic flights and shrugging away the French connection without a comment. The distances we would travel, Scott from Africa, I from western Canada, were both ten times the medieval journey, accomplished in perhaps a hundredth the time.

For many medieval pilgrims, the Spanish portion of the journey would have been like the last act of a play that had already gone on for weeks, even months. Trickling down from their villages and towns in Russia, Scandinavia, Germany, the Low Countries and Normandy, they had swelled the fan of roadways through France before funneling into the pass near St. Jean Pied de Port. English pilgrims sometimes took the old Roman salt roads in the West Midlands through unknown places like Droitwich and Stone Orchard down to the docks at Bristol. There they boarded ship for a bilious week-long journey to Spain. Coming ashore in the Bay of Biscay, usually at Coruña, they banded together with other English pilgrims landing from Southampton or Plymouth for the final leg of the trip to Santiago. Pilgrims from Italy and Byzantium trekked over the Somport Pass into Aragon to join the incoming northern pilgrims on the *Camino francés* at Puente La Reina. Others came from the south of Spain along the *Via de la Plata* from Sevilla, through the old Roman town of Mérida and the city of Salamanca to pick up the Camino at Astorga. Still others arrived in Santiago from Portugal, having scrambled through the unforgiving interior highlands or plodded up the Atlantic coast with their heads bent against the rain. For some, the return journey to St. James' shrine and back took well over a year. Many never made it home.

My flight - completely without incident - landed in Toronto. I had a few days' stopover before leaving for Europe. After a night at my parents' home, I took a bus to Ottawa to visit friends. I had been tired leaving Calgary and it cheered me to see the capital city ablaze with red and yellow tulips and the leaves an early, determined green. Behind the single spire of the Parliament buildings, bright clouds swung in a sky of robin's egg blue. Ottawa was the city of my birth. Near here, by the dark blue waters and rocky, tree-humped shorelines of the Canadian Shield, I had felt the first joys of being outdoors, had learned to swim and canoe, pitch a tent and hop fences. Later, living here as an adult, I had cross country skied and snowshoed in winter and hiked and biked, kayaked and windsurfed in the brief, exquisite weeks of summer.

I had gone to graduate school in Ottawa and, when I wasn't on my skis, had written a thesis on wisdom poetry in Old English literature. It was at this time, almost twenty years before I would go to Spain, that I first heard of the *Camino de Santiago*.

I had been reading a lot of Anglo-Saxon poetry and prose, but three works in particular, it turned out, affected me much more than I knew. At the time I studied them, they had sent only the gentlest ripples down my spine, unexpected and soon forgotten. Only later did I grasp that all three had been written by people who saw pilgrimage as an authentic way of being in the world, and that something within me, not academic or even intellectual, a question, or maybe just a space, a nameless curiosity, was reaching out for what they had to say. I was on my way to the Camino before I knew anything about it.

One piece was a poem of about a hundred lines, written in Old Englsh around the 9th Century, the same time (though I did not know this then) that the tomb of St. James was attracting its first visitors in Spain. The work had no title; later scholars named it *The Seafarer*. It had been included in a volume of verse donated by a Bishop Leofric in the year 1072 to the library of Exeter Cathedral, where it stays to this day.

The Seafarer is about a man in a small boat at night on a stormy sea, who sings his "true song" of hardship as the waves toss and the rocky cliffs on shore loom nearby. His friends on land have no idea, as they drink the night away, of his fear and loneliness. But as he burrows deep into his pain, a spark of insight erupts in the Seafarer's soul. What is the use, he asks, in longing for the empty, pleasure-hungry life of the ordinary man on shore? To move forth through God's world is the only free and authentic life. Amid the spiritual darkness of a storm-tossed sea, his decision almost makes itself: as soon as it is spring, the Seafarer will leave this world of pain and desire, and go into exile in a distant land, where he will wander in freedom and faith.

Here is the central and ancient idea about pilgrimage: our life on this earth is a journey. For a Christian, the path leads away from the material world, with all its folly and pain, to God. To be in but not of the world is the human condition; to embrace this reality with the faith of the Seafarer is to be a pilgrim.

During my time in graduate school, I spent many evenings reading what the Buddhists had to say about the spiritual path. This could be summed up in two phrases: *Attention! Attention!* and *Walk on!* In both the Eastern and the Christian view, pilgrimage was never an escape from woe but rather an observant walk amid everyday reality, with faith in God - or, if you are Buddhist, in the Dharma - as your refuge. The Seafarer had an eerily ascetic turn of mind, I thought, but like the Eastern masters, he knew that the authentic life could be lived only by keeping your heart on your faith and your feet, literally, on the ground.

The Christian ideas behind the Seafarer's pilgrimage first appear among the early hermits of the 3rd Century, people like St. Anthony, who sought out the deserts of Egypt, intent on giving up all comforts to live as close to God as was humanly possible. In later centuries, Anthony's desert idealism travelled north, up the Atlantic coast, past Gibraltar and Galicia and France to Ireland,

14

where it became part of the craggy seascape of Celtic Christianity.

From Ireland, the notion of a spiritual exile into the world went to England with sea-going Irish missionary monks of the 6th Century. Pilgrimages to far-off places caught on. Several are described in another book donated by Leofric to Exeter Library, the Venerable Bede's *History of the English Church and People*. Bede wrote his *History* in a Northumbrian monastery during the prosperous and relatively peaceful early 8th Century. It never lost its appeal. On an impulse, I bought my first copy, a soft-cover Penguin edition, in Toronto when I was eighteen. I read it in one sitting, often mystified, but kept going by Bede's genial personality. Many men and women, Bede wrote, high-born and low-born, clerics and laity, voyaged from England to Ireland or the Continent, expressing their faith in God through a life of exile. Some lived as solitaries, others as missionaries, others as monks. Many simply wandered from place to place, relying on the good will of the townsfolk they met for something to eat and a place to sleep.

Bede especially admired pilgrims who went to Rome. In the 7th Century, he tells us, King Ine of Wessex abdicated his throne and journeyed to the city of St. Peter "to spend the time of his earthly pilgrimage near the holy places, whereby he would receive a warmer welcome from heaven's saints." The handsome Prince Offa of Essex also gave up his claim to the throne and, in a move guaranteed to frustrate his pragmatic courtiers, "left his wife, his fields, his friends and country for Christ and the Gospel." Like Ine before him, Offa made his way across the Channel and down through France to Rome, where he ended his days as a monk. If he had wanted to, Offa could have carried on from Rome to Jerusalem, for the way was still quite safe and the two cities shared the honour of being the most important pilgrim destinations in the Christian world.

Before James' tomb was unearthed in 9th Century Spain, not many pilgrims travelled as far as Ine and Offa did from England to Rome. But short, even day pilgrimages to local shrines were a regular occurrence. From Christianity's earliest days people in the Holy Land had ventured out to worship at the tombs of the apostles. In the 2nd Century, they were venerating the remains of martyrs too. In time, these cults were carried into Europe. The worship of relics often replaced pagan rites as missionaries converted tribe after tribe to Christianity. In the 3rd and 4th Centuries under the Emperor Diocletian, a bloody wave of persecutions swept through the Roman world, producing hundreds more Christian martyrs. Objects that had belonged to these stalwart men and women, or bits and pieces of their bodies (sometimes the same bit but in different locations: there were two heads of John the Baptist in Constantinople in the 5th Century, and another one showed up in Central France in the 11th) - all these holy articles were drawing pilgrims from every corner of Europe.

In a world that offered precious few other ways of fixing life's woes, a saints' shrine - with its tomb, or chapel, or fountain, or its miraculous grotto - offered blessings galore. But in their writings, Bede and other chroniclers also hint at the seamier side of pilgrimage. The missionary Boniface sent letters back to England from the Continent worrying about the morals of naïve pilgrims faced with new temptations on foreign roads. Then there were the practical concerns of those left behind. Around 720, the English Abbess Eangyth, herself eager to head to Rome, was mightily irked when her devout but not so brotherly kinsmen took off to visit "the shrines of Peter and Paul and other martyrs, virgins and confessors," leaving her unprotected.

Reading about these pilgrimages showed me the freshness and vigor of the Christian faith in its early years in Europe: here was the earthy new religion of a crucified man-God, a religion of hope and solace, its gritty history flecked with the blood of martyrs and saints whose relics would save us from the evil within ourselves and in our world; it was a liberating, enlivening myth that called men and women forth into the world; it was still not completely sorted out (nor would it ever be): still a little pagan, it was splendid in how it brought the natural and the supernatural together into a reverberating, living unity. It could be crude and puerile, inconsistently preached and inadequately grasped. It had all the gangliness and sudden, unexpected magnificence of youth.

The Seafarer and Bede's *History* had been written in England during the 8th and 9th Centuries, just as the far-off forces that would spark the pilgrimage to Santiago were reaching their climax. The situation in southern Europe looked grim: by 750 AD the Moors had overrun most of Christian Spain. Few could have foreseen the events of the next century. Around 830 AD, a priest named Theodemir would uncover a tomb in a little place called Iria Flavia in northwest Galicia; the body of St. James would be discovered there; miracles would occur; the great Apostle would rise on the clouds over Christian battlefields and become Spain's dual saint of pilgrimage and the Reconquest. As the Moors retreated, and then for the next five centuries, millions would toil over the Pyrenees and across Spain to worship at his shrine.

My thesis supervisor in Ottawa had been Ray St. Jacques, whose title, Professor, belied his pleasant informality and boyish enthusiasm for medieval literature. "Everybody knows," he told a lecture audience one evening after receiving a teaching award, "that nothing could possibly be more useless nowadays than to study Anglo-Saxon poetry." He shrugged and laughed with his audience. The talk he gave, a merry, scholarly excursus on *Beowulf*, captivated us all. Useless or not, some things, you could see, were just fun to think about. Later, when people asked me why I studied medieval literature, I thought of Ray and answered with the incomplete but unbeatable argument: "For the sheer pleasure of it."

It was an off-hand comment that Ray made in a seminar on Middle English dream poetry that was my third encounter with pilgrimage. We were studying a poem called *Piers Plowman,* a work that mentions Galicia and St. James. "Those are my favourite parts, you see," Ray told us, amusement flickering around his mouth, "because my name, of course, is St. Jacques, which is French for St. James. Santiago is the Spanish: Santo Iago. You know the dish Coquilles St. Jacques? The casserole made with scallops? It's named after the scallop shells that pilgrims wore when they went to James' shrine at Santiago. "

Ray had an appealing style of teaching, but *Piers Plowman* was the most difficult and the most serious poem I would ever come across. Its 7,000 lines had been penned by William Langland, an English cleric from the West Midlands near Malvern, not far from the pilgrimage route that led to the docks at Bristol. A tall, imposing man who usually wore a long robe, Langland was a poet of great talent who divided the last twenty-five years of his life between London and the English countryside making his living in a line of work now extinct: he was a professional singer of Psalms for the souls of the dead.

Langland's century was a time of plague, war and moral decay. In the five hundred years since Bede's *History*, Christianity had been tarted up to suit the worldly whims of a wealthy, much racier Church. Pilgrimage had changed too, gotten superficial, become a cynical trade in indulgences and a contest among churches all over Europe - by now more of a supernatural autopsy lab - for prestige over who had the best relics. A sort of spiritual one-upmanship gripped the towns, high-stakes competition for those wondrous, hideous relics - chunks of forearm, heads, pieces of wood from Christ's cross, (enough, said one wag at the time, to make a forest), a toe, a few rusty corpuscles of blood, some drops of the Virgin's milk. Pilgrimage was show business, with all its underhandedness and tacky advertising. Shrine visits were histrionic events; reading about them made me think of Graceland.

Like a highly displeased mother superior, Will Langland ranted against the sleaze that had become the bread and butter of Christian Europe: manipulation and bribery among pilgrims and clergy, abuse of indulgences, traffic in false relics, not to mention the frivolous adventuring and drunkenness and blousy sex that followed the pilgrim routes. Hermits, he wrote, piously take up the pilgrim's hooked wooden staff and then troop off with their wenches in tow. Reason, one of Langland's allegorical figures, declares that a pilgrim should go only once to Galicia, at the end of his life, and stay there in perpetual exile the way the Anglo-Saxon nobility had ended their days in Rome. Better anyway, says Reason sarcastically, for those who seek St. James to stay home and seek instead St. Truth, for only he will save them.

Langland was a better poet than reformer; he could not stop the decline in Europe's religious life. It would go on for almost two more centuries after his death. Pilgrimage would eventually gutter out almost completely in the storms of war and religious strife that swept over Europe after the turn of the 16th Century.

In *The Seafarer* and Bede's *History*, I had seen the ascetic beginnings of pilgrimage in Europe. Langland showed me how it had faltered and gotten melodramatic. But I still knew little about the heyday of European pilgrimage. Of Santiago de Compostela I had read only what Langland and a few others had written. Geoffrey Chaucer's most famous character, the red-cheeked, gap-toothed Wife of Bath, had made the trip to Santiago five times. But I came across little else in my reading about Compostela, and the St. James pilgrimage was, and oddly enough still is, relatively unsung even in general histories of medieval Europe.

Soon I would be arriving in Spain to uncover for myself those remarkable years between the discovery of James' tomb in the 9th Century and the Reformation in the 16th. As early as 830, the royal court from neighbouring Asturias had visited the tomb in Galicia. The first known foreign pilgrim to Santiago was a certain Bishop Gotescalco from Le Puy, who led a group of the faithful there in 951. And as the Moors were beaten back to the south of Spain, the tide of visitors to James' shrine swelled for the next four centuries.

But the sweetest memories of the Santiago pilgrimage come from within a shorter parenthesis of time. Between about 1050 and 1200, the Camino was given its ultimate boost by a series of church reforms - a fresh vision of Christian life - that was moving through Europe. The new enthusiasm ran like dye along the Camino and gave it much of the look it has today. Kings and clerics built roads and bridges, opened hostels, had churches put up in the new Romanesque style, turned monasteries into way-stations for pilgrims, and made every effort to welcome those who brought their faith - and a good deal of spiritual prestige - to Santiago de Compostela. When we speak now of the medieval pilgrimage to James' city, we usually mean that long line of men and women with walking sticks, tattered capes, and an undivided assurance in an ordered universe, determinedly making their way on the rough road across Spain in the 11th and 12th Centuries. This is the Camino that shines for us now. It is a coffee-table book image, the Camino of two bright, busy centuries. Its story is interesting because it tells us about pain and piety and hope, and, as we walk among its monuments, about ourselves.

Before leaving Ottawa, I had dinner in the market with my friends Judy and Alex. I ordered bouillabaisse, a rich seafood soup served with scallops and mussels still in their shells. I had extracted a chunk of succulent scallop meat with my fork, and was about to set down the empty shell when I stopped.

"I need a scallop shell to wear in Spain."

Judy and Alex looked at me. "A what?"

"A scallop shell." In pagan religions, the scallop symbolized life and fertility. Botticelli's Venus rising from the sea on a scallop shell is perhaps the most famous example. As Ray had told us, pilgrims received shells as souvenirs once they arrived in Santiago. Today pilgrims on the Camino still wear shells on their hats, around their necks or tied to their backpacks.

Judy and Alex looked dubious, and I tried for more convincing evidence. One day in Galicia sometime in the 1st Century, there was a wedding. During the festivities the groom's horse suddenly startled and bolted, taking his rider with him into the sea. The guests despaired, thinking both had drowned. A boat appeared, headed for shore. In front of it was the horse, rising from the water with the groom still on his back. Both were covered with scallop shells.

"It turned out that the boat was bringing St. James' body to Galicia. The rescued bridegroom offered to bury the body on his land. The shell was a sign that he had been miraculously rescued by James and that he should become a Christian."

Alex took a sip of wine. "Uh-huh?"

"Yes." I soldiered on. "So the shell, you see, was proof of the power of Christianity, and a sign of the new faith - a religion of baptism and rebirth - arriving in Galicia."

"It's a stretch," said Judy.

I saved two shells from dinner and the next day asked another friend, who was handy with tools, to bore a hole in each one so I could hang them on strings around my neck. They were not large and they seemed fragile, so I kept one aside in case I broke the other. At the end of my second trip in 1998, I would give the one I wore to a pilgrim-friend I met on the way. The other still hangs on the wall above my writing desk.

I took the bus from Ottawa back to Toronto and spent another two days with my parents. My mother drove me to the airport the night I left for France. Things had gone well. The bikes were safely aboard, the flight was on time. Over the Atlantic, with the Milky Way foaming across a velvet sky, I thought of Scott getting set to leave Nigeria and about all our preparations and expectations for our journey across Spain.

Scott and I had known one another for decades, and the natural world was the scaffold of our best memories. We hiked and biked everywhere we could. Scott taught me to windsurf. We taught ourselves to sea kayak. We were known for taking friends on dubious adventures: snowshoeing at midnight looking for a local bobcat, running rapids in a leaky canoe mended with duct tape, backcountry skiing in the Rockies at twenty-five below. So our early thoughts about the Camino were of placing ourselves, once again, among nature's challenges, of cycling for days along trails that wound through convoluted mountain passes and remote forests.

Scott's father was of Portuguese ancestry. The history of Iberia and the culture of the Moors attracted him in a way that seemed as much personal as intellectual, as if some atavistic and hereditary force was pushing his attention. As for me, I had a persistent curiosity about what is often called, blandly, "the medieval mind," with its airtight faith (supposedly) and cheerfully illogical ways of organizing experience. I suspect, though I am not positive about this, that my attraction to medieval thought grew from a feeling of moral imbalance in my life, of never quite being able to figure out my priorities. The more I studied it the more I doubted that a medieval outlook was any more valid or helpful than anything else; sometimes the more I understood it the crazier it seemed. But its eccentricity also made the fixations and delusions of my own world stand out more clearly. And after bending my mind around medieval theology for so many years, I wanted to go to the Camino with my body, feel and see for myself the physical ramparts of that distant mental universe, set it next to the Now of my own life. And I wanted to find out where an old Christian pilgrimage route could take a science-minded skeptic with Buddhist leanings. If anywhere.

Scott and I debated whether we were really making a pilgrimage at all. In the end, we decided we were, but we differed on how, and neither of us was clear about how pilgrimage might look in a pluralistic, secular society. I had read about Buddhist and Hindu pilgrimages. I liked the idea of sacred travel, but I was wary of spiritual fads. I had no Christian beliefs, and could not presume to know what my motives might be on a Christian route, other than to relive the old Camino road out of respect for the faith of our unknown European ancestors.

There is no way that this self-gratifying, exploratory outlook on the Camino would have made any sense at all a thousand years ago. For one thing, Scott's and my motives were private; apart from polite, sometimes puzzled, curiosity, our friends and family had no stake in what we were doing. But in the densely intertwined social milieu of the Middle Ages, the state of your soul was everybody's business. Your trip to Santiago was a religious act of huge public interest that touched and, if successful, blessed everyone in your community.

Still, I am sure that for many eager souls, the trip to Santiago must have been a welcome release from the round of everyday life. It was a claustrophobic age. The church calendar had pretty well mapped out your whole life for you in advance. Pilgrimage was a chance to see the world beyond the parish. True, it was a dangerous journey, but many pilgrims must have been as excited as we were now by the idea of seeing places they had only heard about. There would not have been much talk about the beauties of nature on the trip however, and none at all about the joys of good outdoor exercise. There was nothing personal here, no cult of the body or private quest for self-fulfillment in nature. Pilgrimage was an overtly religious deed, and in going to Santiago, you were simply playing your part in a spiritual theatre where the same script was shared by everyone.

In the winter months before the trip, we gathered information about the Camino from libraries and the web: updates, maps, reports from pilgrims, reading lists, information on trail conditions and recommended tire sizes. We ordered guidebooks from stores in Britain; when they arrived we would grab the nearest chair and finger them from back to front in the first flush of interest.

As winter became spring, we trained on our bikes near our home in the foothills of the Rocky Mountains. Two or three times a week, we ground up and down the long roads that divided the ranch lands and pastures of Alberta. One day we took a break at the bottom of a shallow hill between grazing lands on one side and a forested slope on the other. We sat by a fence that bordered on the garden of a retreat centre run by an order of Franciscan monks. The signs by the gate said: Peace and Love to All. Retreat in Progress. This is a Nuclear Free Zone.

I thought of a book I had seen somewhere about "green pilgrimage," which involved "a Gaian solution" to modern spiritual woes. By this was meant the ecological equivalent of the search for religious faith. Could this be?

Could the pleasant, right-minded science of ecology do for human beings what religious faith, at its best, had done? What did eco-tourism have to do with the daring venture into spiritual transformation? I wondered how pilgrimage might change a polluted world, and how adventure travel or eco-tourism might work as a spiritual journey. Or was it that eco-tourism and pilgrimage were, at best, parallel activities and at worst, natural competitors?

As I read about pilgrimages taken by other people, not just in Spain but in India, China, Southeast Asia and South America too, I saw the traditional idea of sacred travel pulled apart into unheard-of strands: from being an act of faith in something already believed, it seemed to be becoming a search for personal identity, a communion with nature rather than a trial by fear in alien lands.

I detected a tug of war between purists and innovators. In the eyes of some Camino writers, even going by bike instead of walking to Santiago made us suspect. (In the Middle Ages, some people felt that going on horseback was a little too luxurious.) Putting together our gear - mountain bikes outfitted with cordura packs and combination touring-trail tires, Gortex raingear, light-weight fleecies, Thermarest sleeping pads, my new odometer purchased at the last minute at Mountain Equipment Co-op - we found ourselves up against the first intellectual trap for people travelling the Camino to Santiago: the nagging concern with authenticity, the sheepish comfort, and the feeling of somehow cheating the medieval pilgrim and missing the spiritual point of it all by riding along the path on 18-speed mountain bikes.

To feel guilty about being modern seemed silly to me. But I knew I wasn't imagining this bias in Camino literature when I read a book by one Fray Juan Antonio Torres Prieto. *Tu Solus Peregrinus: Viaje Interior por El Camino de Santiago* was the most riveting account I had come across of the pilgrimage from St. Jean Pied de Port to Santiago de Compostela. Prieto had travelled the Camino more than once; his last trip had been in the early 1990s. He does not say much about his former life; he may have been a lapsed or a careless Catholic, his vast knowledge of Church history made me think he had been an academic, perhaps a medievalist like me. And like me,

...perienced the Camino on a bicycle. But whatever his past, Prieto's pilgrimage across northern Spain that summer left him in a state of spiritual longing. Some time after arriving at Santiago, Prieto the pilgrim returned to a monastery at Silos, just south of the Camino at about its midway point. There, he signed himself in and took the permanent vows of a Benedictine monk.

Prieto had some none too sympathetic remarks on the motivations for "pilgrimage" to Santiago. There were three bad reasons for taking the Camino, he claimed. First, cultural interest: the pilgrim (so-called) wants only to amuse the intellect, and turns the sacred Christian symbols of the route into mere cultural curiosities. The second reason is ecological: this, as Prieto put it, is modern man's wish to escape his own pollution. The Camino is a nice place for a walk, he agrees, but you have only an illusion of inner harmony if you by-pass the religious messages that lie at the heart of the Camino. Prieto's final bad reason is that the Camino is a good place to meet interesting people. Here he notes our modern fear of solitude; social activities on the Camino can undermine the spiritual purpose of the route. Trying not to sound grouchy, Prieto does allow that these bad reasons are legitimately pleasant off-shoots of the journey; but, he says with a touch of the convert's zeal, they must not interfere with the central purpose of pilgrimage: the search for God in one's heart as one follows the sacred path to the Shrine of St. James.

The monk's perspective was a no-nonsense, dead serious one; it was not ridiculous and I understood his argument. But when Scott and I first began to talk about taking our bikes to Santiago, we had precisely Prieto's three bad reasons in mind. The question for us was not so much how to travel the Camino in the old pilgrimage spirit, but how to use the old route to take us to the heart of some of our modern realities: a love of beautiful landscapes and physical challenges, eco-awareness (whatever that meant), religious pluralism, an unsatisfying materialism. Like the Seafarer in the Old English poem, I saw the Camino pilgrimage as a conscious journey into life lived now, with all its messiness and wrinkles. For neither

Scott nor me could it ever be an affirmation of a single religious vision.

Over the Atlantic Ocean, I downed a hefty Scotch and made a rambling entry in my diary, then wedged my shoulder into a pillow between the armrest and the window and hoped for sleep. My mind wandered, pointlessly going over our equipment, thinking once more of Scott in Lagos. Was he going to get out ok? Had it been silly to try to meet this way in Biarritz? I squirmed in my seat, looked with unfocussed eyes out the window towards the stars.

In the Europe of a thousand years ago, pilgrimage was a death-defying deed that was not always done by choice. Often it had been a penitential act for offenses against church law. Many church officials ended up on pilgrimage this way, having bedded their better-looking parishioners and gotten caught. After the 12th Century, pilgrimage came to be imposed (if you weren't hanged first) as penance for civil crimes: murder, theft, and that most disastrous of medieval felonies, arson.

Pilgrimage could also reduce the time you spent in Purgatory, for even though confession absolved you of your sins, your soul was barred from heaven until the price for those sins had been paid. Purgatory, an old idea that became dogma only in the 16th Century, was the place of final cleansing reserved for the backlog of debts that remained after you died. But the fires were said to be hot, and it made sense to try to work off some of that time with a hard but generally cooler walk to a saint's shrine.

Preparations for your departure revolved around rituals marking your transition from an ordinary citizen to a pilgrim. First you needed permission from your spouse, your priest and your feudal lord, the order depending, I supposed, on questions of relative power. In the days after your pilgrimage was confirmed, a hollow, doomed feeling might creep into the space around your heart. The Camino was risky. Chances were good that you would never come home, but be left for burial somewhere along the route. You made a detailed will that included provisions for your family if you failed to get home, and sometimes even a contract indicating how long after your deadline for return your spouse was to wait before remarrying.

To die with your sins unforgiven or without forgiving others was, in the Middle Ages, the worst of all fates, a sure ticket to hell. So before you left, you made a full confession to protect your body and soul from Satan's ovens. Mass was also customary; afterwards, your priest ceremonially presented you with a walking stick, a *bordon*, with a hooked top and a little ski pole-like spear of iron at the bottom. The *bordon* would make walking easier. You could use it against attacks by animals and humans too. Just as important was its symbolic meaning as the cross of Jesus Christ and the soul's defense against the devil. Handing you your staff, the priest intoned a blessing:

> Receive this staff that it may be a support in your walk and your travail along the path of your pilgrimage, that you may overcome the devil's troops and arrive safe at the feet of St James. After your journey, may you come home to us with joy, in the knowledge of the true God.

Many pilgrims also received a purse, called an *escarcela* or an *esportilla*. Here too, a spiritual idea inhabited the physical thing. The purse was made of "the hide of a dead beast," usually a deer, as a reminder to the pilgrim to mortify his flesh (already shamed by sins and evil desires) "through hunger and thirst, with much fasting, cold and nakedness, with hardships and travail." The purse was narrow and flat, not much good really, but its uselessness was an unfailing reminder of your utter dependence on God's grace. It was to be kept unfastened at all times to advertise your need for alms as well as your readiness to provide for others.

The day of your departure. The longed for, dreaded time is here. The townsfolk gather round you by the church in the square offering last minute advice, a jovial slap on the back. Your neighbour hands you a tart from her oven to start you off. Within the busy, boisterous chatter of the moment, lie a rough, pious dignity and an ominous melancholy. Savagely, wordlessly, you embrace your wife, your eyes clenched tight against your tears. Your heart skips a beat as you lavish kisses on all your children, hold in both your hands their little faces dripping with tears and snot. You bid farewell to wetnurses, cousins and grandchildren, servants, friends, drinking mates, pet dogs, and maybe send a last sad, or sly, look to a renounced mistress. The long wave (but not long enough) before you turn to catch up with your fellow-pilgrims waiting impatiently down the road. The moment of separation: the vacant, forced laughter as the company sets out, the bravado burst of pious song while the heart, quivering painfully again in that hollow, dropping space, cranes backward to the ones just left.

These feelings abide in our lives too, but we do not feel them like this when we leave on vacation, not even on a pilgrimage. We fully expect to come back; there are earthly agents everywhere who can help us. On our side too are the gods of telephones, airline computer systems, and credit cards. We are confident, for these are, if not wiser, at least more predictable than the God of the Middle Ages.

I wriggled again into my pillow, finally drowsy; my thoughts broke away, leaving me to sleep.

There was something about the monk Prieto's pilgrimage that impressed me much more than his religious certitude. It was the athletic discipline of mind that he applied to his walk across Spain. His story resonated with an important event in my own life about eight years before my Camino trip, that had nothing to do with books or seminars or medieval poems.

Just after I had finished my thesis, I was invited by a friend to a meditation centre in the eastern United States. The brick building where I would spend the next nine days sat on the edge of a few acres of Massachusetts countryside. The place, a little ramshackle at the time I was there, had once been a Catholic seminary. Now the Buddhists were in residence. Our daily routine was:

sitting meditation, walking meditation, housecleaning, eating and sleeping. Nothing more. No writing, no reading, no talking.

Walking meditation was the most difficult. For forty-five minutes at a time, in a rectangular room with a polished pine floor, off-white walls, and windows looking out onto the front lawn, we walked with reptilian slowness, eyes lowered, back and forth from wall to wall. The mind was to be riveted to the sensations, felt through the body and in the mind, of weight on the feet, the smooth floor, the shift of muscles as we stepped slowly, mindfully, across the room. Inevitably, my awareness would drift away to the smell of lunch cooking, the cars in the road, the colour of someone's T-shirt, before awakening once again, over and over, to the contact between the floor and the soles of my feet. I skipped many of these sessions. Not because this was an idiotic way to spend my time, but because of fear, an uneasy boredom, and more deeply, a wariness about intimacy with my own life that boredom is a shield against. But I did understand, though I could not impress this on my reluctant body, that making steps was important, that the simple act of thoughtfully walking across a room on a gleaming wood floor was worth noticing as singular statement of our presence in this world. Walking meditation was simply walking, I saw, but it called for immense centripetal effort, a gathering of attention, concentration, insight, and affirmation. Through it, we were united with our movement in space and time; eventually we would come to see the absolute lack of anything still or unchanging in our existence. Walking meditation was a demonstration of impermanence, and of the fact that, in the most radical sense, we are nomads in time and in space.

Most religions have grasped this insight that life is action, a verb, not a noun. Many have turned it into an occasion for awakening and self-assertion. It is not possible to reject our captivity in time and space. Instead, the religious imagination plays a sly trick, turning movement and change in time into an object of contemplation. Prieto's pilgrimage was something close to walking meditation, an application of intention and will, discipline and direction to a journey, not just through a literal landscape but through his life as well. After the Camino, Prieto kept on walking, through the doors of the Monastery of Silos into a new life of, he says, spiritual joy. But even a less dramatic result than Prieto's has meaning; pilgrimage is not necessarily rebellious or aversive to the everyday world; one's life amid family and work can be a pilgrimage.

The rebellion of pilgrimage is in its goals, for these are identified not with ordinary successes and failures but with a deepening understanding of our movement through life on earth. This is perhaps its defining characteristic: pilgrims watch where they are going. To go on pilgrimage is to make distinctions, to see what is on and off the path, to call our wandering into question, to take each of our steps as if into a new land. Pilgrims often veer from the norm, go around differently, scramble to a new lookout. They cut across the fields, hop the fences, take the roads less travelled, or cross the roads instead of following them. They may even take the roads *more* travelled, but they "go" differently. The word *peregrinus*, from which the English "pilgrim" is derived, is one of those intriguing, so-called dead metaphors that, in an artful illustration of the primal intercourse between language and act, means a going forth *per agros* or through the fields.

In April, a few weeks before our departure, our Pilgrim's Passes arrived from the Confraternity of St. James in London, England. The Confraternity was founded in 1983. By 1997, 1500 people around the world had signed on, people who felt some kind of attraction to the revival of pilgrimage in Europe. There are Confraternities, or Friends of the Camino, in several countries - France, Holland, Italy, Switzerland, Belgium, Canada, and of course, Spain - all involved in promoting the Camino, restoring its historical monuments and running hostels for pilgrims. The English Confraternity publishes a newsletter several times a year. Even with limited office resources, volunteers have covered every aspect of pilgrimage in publications, a slide library, route updates, web sites, lecture programs, outings, musical productions and bursary programs. The Confraternity library is located in the still seedy Southwark district of London, at the Tabard Inn, where Chaucer's pilgrims had gathered to begin their pilgrimage to the Shrine of St. Thomas in Canterbury.

The Pilgrim's Pass is the modern descendent of the medieval safe conduct pass or letter of introduction. Scott and I needed ours as proof of our "pilgrim status". In the Middle Ages, such a letter was meant to ease rough encounters with authorities. It could protect you against harassment and theft, sometimes it was a ticket to more comfortable lodgings. Now, it was our entry to the pilgrim hostels that sat along the Camino every ten to twenty kilometres. The hostels, *refugios* in Spanish, were, as they had traditionally been, free for pilgrims to use; most people left a donation of few dollars. In some, a modest fee was charged. At each one we were to present our mimeographed yellow Pass to be stamped with the seal of the parish. The stamper was whoever had the stamp, the custodian at the hostel, an official at the town hall, or the bartender behind the counter at the local watering hole.

The Pass was a daily reminder of the investment of the Catholic Church in the Camino; the Pope had called for European unity from Santiago in 1993. It was to be taken seriously therefore as proof of our intentions about pilgrimage, a testimony to our resolve to earn, as honest-hearted pilgrims following the path and spirit of all former pilgrims, our blessings and indulgences at the shrine of St. James's. Once in Santiago, presentation of our stamped Passes would earn us the "Compostela," a photocopied certificate in Latin, stamped and signed, that would prove (in case anyone asked) that we had indeed completed the route "out of devotion" to St. James. Traditionally, prayers and confession in Santiago Cathedral automatically give the arriving pilgrim half-time off purgatory; in Holy Years, special Years of Grace granted by the Church in years when the Feast of St. James, July 25, falls magically on a Sunday, pilgrims receive a dizzying lifetime pardon for all sins. Not long after the Passes arrived, I expressed some reservations in my diary about becoming this kind of pilgrim.

I was born into a long line of Presbyterians and Methodists and I carried a mistrust of Catholicism within me like an internal organ. My father had grown up on a middling prosperous Southern Ontario farm. My grandfather was a man of kindness and easy faith, and working alongside him day by day, my youthful father learned to recognize the hand of a divine designer in the breeding and birth that occurred in the barn and in the fields. My grandmother was of a sterner nature. She is known to me only from pictures, where her hair is coiled neatly above her pale brow, and her eyes, betraying nothing, look at me through rimless glasses. When my father was a child, she had forbidden him to wander along the next concession line because, as she had flatly reasoned, "that was where the Catholics lived."

My father, with his own father's common human sense, outgrew the severe lines of this rural prejudice. Still, in devious ways, it had shaped how he understood the world. When I was growing up in the 1960s in Northern Ontario, he often repeated a story, as if trying to clarify something to himself, about a successful lawyer who had made a thousand dollar payment to the local priest so that on one particular Sunday of the year, he could skip Mass and spend the weekend at a hunt camp with my father and his friends. For that thousand dollars, he could also eat venison on Friday. My father would laugh with a contemptuous snort telling this story. "God's not *that* stupid," he would say, or "That priest otta have his head read," to which I once retorted that I didn't think it was the priest who had the problem.

It had been exactly this kind of Protestant scepticism, with its impatient dismissal of saints and indulgences, that had reduced the traffic of pilgrims along the Camino in the 16th Century. The same reforming spirit contributed to the decline of the pilgrimage in later centuries. It was still at work in the 19th Century, when the English Protestant George Borrow arrived in Santiago. An Evangelist on a mission, Borrow sold Bibles along the Camino, making a little money for himself as he tried to pull the Spanish people from the grave of their worn out Popery. Borrow was offended by the gewgaws in Santiago Cathedral and said so. He is not the most attractive figure, but sad to say, his tradition was mine: a rebellious religious individualism and an aggressive hostility to superstition, which meant images and the prayers you uttered to them, and the idea that you could exchange favours with God.

Without realizing it, I had imbibed the dowdy rationalism of the Protestant. It was all I knew. But one day when I was twelve years old, I stole away after school with my friends to North Bay's big Roman Catholic cathedral. Acting as if we weren't nervous, we walked up and down the aisles, avoiding the front altar but gaping and tittering at the statues that startled us from recesses in the dark stone walls. All I had known of churches was the comfortless air of Calvin Presbyterian Church. But *this*, I thought, was nearly as good as Madame Toussaud's Wax Museum at Niagara Falls. Without realizing it, I had discovered religion's sensuous side. The high, shadowed sanctuary was thrilling, gothic, somehow forbidden, and made only more lurid by the exquisite grossness of rural Catholic iconography. The gushing crucifixes and simpering saints with their plastic flowers sickened me like awful pictures in the news tabloids, as repugnant as the high arches were marvellous. This tension of attraction and revulsion never left me, the one driven by the need, largely denied to the Protestant, for a mystical, sensual spirituality, the other reinforced by that old relentless logic about magical thinking, a dislike of melodrama, and something I had heard referred to as simple Protestant good taste.

Those visits to the cathedral left me with a vague and, at the time, unnamable curiosity about how the mythic imagination and the rational mind accommodate each other. Much later, studying Anglo-Saxon literature, I encountered the bizarre geometry of medieval Christian doctrine. Suspended like a three dimensional spider web, medieval theology explained nature and the physical world, the life of the emotions, and all the orders and ranks of society together under one spectacular, utterly airtight and therefore more or less psychotic myth of fall and redemption. But it also accounted for the interior movement of every human spirit towards that which is whole and good, and towards mystery. I read the 14th-century *Cloud of Unknowing*, then other works of Christian mysticism - Julian of Norwich, Hildegard of Bingen, Meister Eckhart, the sorrowing John of the Cross. In these books, I found the contemplative traditions that nobody in Calvin Presbyterian Church had ever heard of. The mystics showed me an inward path past the self to the Other, and my heart lept at the discovery. There *was* another way to order and measure one's life! Intellectually, Christianity would remain unbearably awkward for me; inevitably I moved to Buddhist teachings which, while more radical and demanding, at least did not make me feel as if I had to sacrifice my sanity in order to believe.

As I was preparing to leave for Europe, I sometimes pulled out my Pilgrim's Pass to look it over. Considering my eccentric religious progress, the thing seemed destined, for better or for worse, to be demoted from a rite of passage to a souvenir. Perhaps I was an inappropriate pilgrim. Except that I was bringing something else with me on this first trip to Santiago, something that I did not especially want, but that would turn out to be the key to how I would eventually interpret the Camino for myself.

In the months leading up to my departure, I had been in the grip of what a medieval analyst of the soul would call *acedia*. I was captivated and then immediately bored by everything. I was discontented and indecisive. Nothing seemed worth an effort. I often felt tired. At work, I was edgy. I was too lazy, too fidgety for any meditation practice. Even in planning this trip to Spain, I resisted the idea of an inward journey. In other words, I was the perfect candidate for pilgrimage: a distracted and restless soul in need of an anchor, a practice, a refreshed vision. James and his shrine were invitations to a journey. The journey was not to them in any other sense than the geographical, but as the day came to leave, I realized that the Camino - the road followed over the centuries by people in search of inner peace - offered something important: a meeting with the restlessness and fear that was consuming me, an exercise in disciplining my mind and taming its wild ways so that I could be clear and hopeful once again. I was after the same thing as the pilgrims of the Middle Ages: a cure.

I landed in Paris, then flew to Biarritz, a place I had never seen. In the remnants of my girlish imagination, Biarritz meant pretty, unknown princesses from the pages of European glamour magazines, a young Jackie Onassis, expensive sunglasses. Walking from my hotel through shop-lined streets to the beach, I was returned from popular fantasy to an ordinary world. Tentative, early season tourists milled around the entrance to the big casino. I wandered through a maze of hillside paths above the sea, past blossoming heaps of red and yellow flowers. I ventured out on a rocky promontory to *le Rocher de la Vierge*, a top-heavy rock hunched like Rodin's Balzac, overlooking the Atlantic. Turning back, I could see a thick strip of outdoor restaurants lining the beach. Polite, automatic waiters with black ties and white aprons angled over tables balancing trays of bread and seafood and tall drinks.

At one of these places, I sipped iced tea and stared out into the bright day. On the sand in front of me, the first sunbathers of May lay still and stoic under the cool afternoon sun, bikinis flattened like dark maple leaves against their pale skins. Beyond them, surfers in black wetsuits mounted lace-lined waves, hung like gorillas, then writhed in the air before toppling into the water's sloppy embrace. The gleaming surface of the sea stretched like a silver tray into the horizon.

I would wait two extra days in Biarritz for Scott to get out of Lagos, where a diplomatic incident had temporarily closed the airport. I sat in various cafés along the beachfront drinking tea or Perrier and lime. I wrote my diary and read the three guidebooks I had with me. One was the Everest publication, *A Practical Guide for Pilgrims*, which was thorough and aimed at active people with a cultural interest in the Camino. Then there was Alison Raju's handy *The Way of St. James*, with its sincere, matter of fact respect for Camino traditions, and its cheerful, impossible English pragmatism. ("Consider joining your local rambling club at least six months in advance and go out with them as often as you possibly can.") But my favourite book was *The Pilgrim's Guide to the Camino de Santiago*, by Elias Valiña, a parish priest from the tiny mountain-top hamlet of El Cebreiro in Galicia. Over a lifetime of archival research and active restoration of the Camino, Valiña almost single-handedly reconstructed the old route and made pilgrimage to Santiago possible again after decades of neglect. His *Guide*, with its photographs and special sections on cultural history, is a masterpiece of dignified simplicity and clear-eyed practicality. We used his book often during our journey, always with pleasure. Valiña died in the 1980s. By the time we reached El Cebreiro, where he is buried, he had become a good Camino friend.

Guidebooks and diaries run like reinforcing cables through the history, fractious myths and mystical hope that make up the Camino. The very first Camino guide, a medieval Latin text known in English as *The Pilgrim's Guide to Santiago de Compostela*, is one of five books bound in a formidable 12th-century tome called the *Liber Sancti Jacobi*, or the Book of St. James. Several copies of the *Liber* are shelved in libraries around Europe, but the most famous and complete belongs to the archives of Santiago Cathedral. At the end of the *Liber*, a letter claiming, falsely, to have been written by Pope Innocent II states that the entire volume was donated to the Cathedral sometime in the middle of the 12th Century by one Aimery Picaud. It is generally held that Aimery was the author of the *Guide*, though nobody knows for sure.

Little more is known of Aimery than that he was a native of the French town of Parthenay-le-Vieux. He may have had musical talent since he seems to have written a hymn found among the musical compositions that are placed after the *Guide* in the *Liber*. But above all, he was a travel writer. With an angle.

It is clear that Aimery wanted to be helpful to his pilgrim public as they set off on the road to Santiago. But he was obsessed uncontrollably by a patriotic desire to glorify every one of the Camino's French connections. Aimery made no secret of his Frenchman's distaste for Spanish ways. In this he was simply writing to the times. The Camino was to a very large degree a French invention, co-opted here and there by Spanish interests. There were French settlements, French monasteries, French merchants and soldiers and thousands of French pilgrims all along the Camino, which was also called, not without reason, the *Camino francés*. There were French contenders for the thrones of Castile and León, French influences in the Cathedral at Santiago. French literature was on the circuit too, making unrepentantly wild claims: Charlemagne, France's hero king, had dreamed of James in his tomb before it was even discovered, had been the first to the tomb, had cleansed the Camino of Moors to protect innocent pilgrims.

Aimery fed the biasses of his French audience as he told them what he felt they should know about their Camino. But he was a better propagandist than orienteer. The *Guide* contains inaccuracies that must have flummoxed its early users, if they were using it as a guide at all. Early on, for instance, Aimery sensibly gives a time and distance breakdown for the Camino so that pilgrims might estimate their travel expenses. Then, without a trace of self-doubt, he allots a single day to the nearly hundred-kilometer trek from Jaca to Monreal - towns situated along the route from Aragon over the tough Somport Pass into Navarra. He divides the other route, the one Scott and I would follow, from France over the Ports de Cize Pass to Roncesvalles and on to Santiago, into thirteen quick days, some 750 kilometers. Many of Aimery's day trips run well over fifty kilometers on tough terrain - empty stretches of glaring hot meseta with awkward river crossings, the long pass into the Bierzo, the stony tracks through Galicia's forests - impossible feats even on a horse in those days, and hard even now for fit Canadians on aluminum alloy mountain bikes. As Scott would dryly remark one day in Navarra, Aimery had trouble handling his data.

Still, Aimery's travelogue rings true and we couldn't help but view our own Camino through the words in his *Guide*. He must have had a good meal at Estella, where we would have a picnic by the river, for he speaks with enthusiasm about its excellent bread and wine and plentiful meat and fish. Sahagún was prosperous in the 12th Century; today it is shabby. Carrión was and still is a well-managed and industrious little town. Aimery alerts his readers to the practice of washing one's entire body, but especially one's genitals at the aptly named River Lavamentula (or Wash-Penis River), just two miles from Santiago. The spot has been obliterated by the new road, but we could still imagine pilgrims stripping in shivery excitement and washing up in a final burst of energy before entering the city of St. James. Santiago, Aimery tells us, is "filled to the brim with plentiful delights." His description of the Cathedral is lovingly detailed. Through it, we glimpse the ravishing dignity of the Romanesque before the fashions of the Baroque took over. It is a description written by a man for whom the goal - to kneel before the Apostle - was much more important than the journey.

Scott arrived in Biarritz late on the third morning. We were very glad to see each other, but three days of cycling were already lost so we abandoned plans for a romantic beachside lunch and left immediately by taxi for St. Jean Pied de Port. Our packs sat like a third passenger on the front seat beside the driver. The bicycles went into the trunk, more or less, and were fastened with a couple of shock cords. The driver was an amiable, trustworthy fellow. Animated by our delight in the French countryside, he drove with the doubly satisfied smile of a man enjoying the familiar beauty of his native land and the sight of foreigners discovering the same. The French Basques took great pride in their patrimony, he told us. As we approached St. Jean Pied de Port, the last French town before the pass into Spain, his pride swelled in the loveliness of the French Basque region. Then, on reflex, he launched into his mental image of utter dilapidation on the other side of the Pyrenees. Shrugging, pursing his lips, his head shaking in superior pity, he relished the second-rate living of the Spanish Basques, their untidy villages and their lack of interest in paint.

In his travelogue for French pilgrims, Aimery Picaud used a livid blend of hearsay and bigotry to portray the Navarrese and the Spanish Basques. The two groups, he claimed, were alike in their impiety and filth. They were ugly people; the Navarrese in particular were tainted with dark skin. They were all as malicious as Saracens, drunk, disloyal, corrupt, slovenly in their dress. They spoke a barbarous language, were cruel to pilgrims, and would kill a Frenchman for small coin. They had revolting, canine manners in eating and drinking. Their sexual habits were disgusting: it had been said, Aimery reported, that when aroused, Navarrese couples displayed their private parts to each other; men kissed the vulva of women ... and mules; they had intercourse with beasts and kept their favourite animals safe from other Navarrese with the use of animal chastity locks. When they robbed pilgrims, he informs us, they also "rode them like asses" - thus adding sodomy to the catalogue of Basque-Navarrese horrors.

Eight centuries separated our taxi driver from Aimery de Picaud. Time, together with recent years of peace between France and Spain and a change in how we talk about foreigners, if not in how we think about them, had taken the most colourful items, with the exception of slovenliness, off the crime list. Aimery's piercing malice had burned out; what survived in its shell was the dismissive condescension of a taxi-driver. When he dropped us off in a St. Jean Pied de Port parking lot near the Camino trailhead, he agreed to meet us in three weeks in Irun, just across the Spanish border, and return us to Biarritz. He gave us two business cards, in case we lost one.

*On a pillar at the Monastery of Silos, the prototype
of Christian pilgrims, Jesus with his followers on
the road to Emmaus.*

2

THE TIME BEFORE

My map absorbs me with what it does not reveal.
Each time I gaze upon it I am captivated by what so
far has not been included within its margins.
  James Cowan, A Mapmaker's Dream

Vast emptiness and nothing holy in it.
  Bodhidharma, First Zen Patriarch in China

So our muscles are force specialists, and our bodies
compensate with distance-amplifying internal levers of
tendons and bones. That makes our appendages
distance specialists......
  Steven Vogel, Cat's Paws and Catapults

42

*The Roman road and bridge at Ciraqui are still
in service for pilgrims on the Camino.*

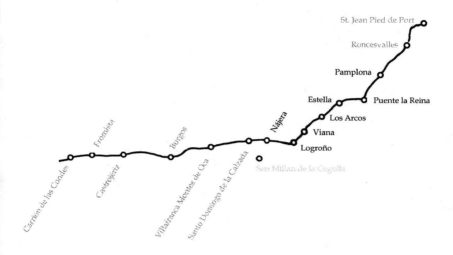

I
t was afternoon when we left St. Jean Pied de Port. We would need some luck to get over the Pyrenees into Spain and down to Roncesvalles while it was still light. But it was worth the risk; two days were already lost in Biarritz and the inviting blue sky was afloat with summery white cumulus.

We rode our bikes to a low, stone wall at the bottom of a hill where a large sign was posted: *Chemin de Saint Jacques de Compostelle*, it said, and underneath, in larger letters, *Route de Ports de Cize* and *Summus Pyrenaeus de la Voie Romaine*. A Roman highway then, heavily travelled long before it became the *Camino francés*. The sign pointed up a narrow paved road that disappeared into a turn behind the lush greenery of trees. We turned to our bikes, tightened the straps on our packs and realigned our mirrors. A breeze dabbed at our shoulders while crickets shrieked from foliage behind the fence. Leaves everywhere made a sound like distant cheering, as if nature was already celebrating the act of pilgrimage while we, the hard-working crew, prepared for the serious task of getting over the pass to Roncesvalles before nightfall.

In 1673, an Italian pilgrim from Bologna named Domenico Laffi came through St. Jean Pied de Port on his way to Santiago. Like us, he had departed the town, which he called San Giovanni de Piedeporto, while "the sun was still high in the sky." In his diary he wrote:

> We walked all the while between precipitous mountains, which are terrifying just to look at. They seemed as if they were always about to fall on top of you. Night fell while we were still among these precipices. We were getting desperate lest we fail to find a house to shelter in.... At last we saw a light far off among the steep hills and made our way toward it as best we could. [In the morning] we kept on climbing the very high and rugged hills for a stretch of seven leagues. It was a frightening and dangerous journey.

Today the spring landscape looked anything but frightening. Only later did Laffi's words came back to us, when we heard of some foot pilgrims a few days ahead of us who had been forced by heavy snow off the pass and back to St. Jean Pied de Port. A group leaving the week after us was drenched with rain during their ascent and spent eleven hard hours getting to Roncesvalles.

Laffi had been right about the uphill part too. After days casually strolling in Biarritz and the lazy cab ride to St. Jean Pied de Port, the road up from the Santiago signpost was suddenly, shockingly steep. My legs pushed hard against the incline, but the effort was enormous. After a minute and a half, my bike reached a kind of equilibrium of forces and stopped dead on its own, like the conclusion of a physics experiment.

Scott came up beside me, breathing hard. "Seven hundred ninety-nine and a half more kilometers to Santiago," he said, "but only seventeen to Roncesvalles. We'll take our time. It's not a race. We're ok as long as we keep moving."

We began to walk our bikes up the hill. I could feel my rear wheels wobble obesely under the weight of my pack. Working up into the pass, we would ride a few kilometres, then dismount and push, leaning into our handlebars, past the hedges that lined the road. In the fields, stout sheep nuzzled the grass, bunched together in woolly clots the colour of chalk. Hearing us, they startled and shook apart, bobbing and bleating. On the other side of the road, brown-flanked cows nosed through low bushes, half hidden, their bells tinkling like Tibetan chimes. Above them, the hills rose steeply out of sight.

The road curved on, rising, and we laboured to keep up. The flanks of the Pyrenees began to gather like ocean waves, swelling and undulating beside us. Long, green slopes poured soupily into shadowed valleys. Cultivated fields dropped briefly, then flattened and flowed sideways like a flood of lime juice into thickets of trees. Further off lay still pastures, pegged by fenceposts to the banks of hills, yellow green in the sunshine. Just past their corners, partly hidden by a veil of shrubbery, immaculate farmhouses sat in a netting of dark grass.

We stopped for a drink where the road curved west across the face of an open incline. By now, my muscles felt warm and well oiled. I had gotten used to panting, felt as if I'd been panting all my life. The bulging hillsides were behind us now and from this height, the green slopes that beside us were so deeply textured began to seem faded and compressed. Long trays of yellow-green meadow stretched into the north, holding sheep like tiny, upside-down teacups. Blunt ridges of land, shadowy crescent valleys studded with the glinting roofs of far-off villages, pallid fields and dark forested slopes rambled towards the eastern horizon. A line of mountains, treeless it seemed, made a gray smear between the last of the hills and the sky.

I looked at my bike where it leaned against a roadside marker, at my packs full of stuff, at Scott studying the mountainside, water bottle in hand. So far, our trip was a negotiation between mechanics and poetics, between vectors and kinetics and the rotund bulges of a voluptuous landscape. For hours my awareness had rotated from my labouring legs and the rigid feel of my bike, to my fingers bent stiffly around hard handlebars, to the crunching road, the tumbling hillsides, the wind that tossed the shrubs like hair, the clouds careening over us, then back again to my legs as they pushed my pedals down, down, over and down, over and down.

Until our departure from the sign in St. Jean Pied de Port, pilgrimage had occupied my mind in the wordy layers of metaphor. For instance, pilgrimage expresses the fact that we travel through this material world from a womb to a tomb. Looking at my pack now, I decide it is also a complaint: we go bearing burdens. Pilgrimage makes us feel the heaviness, the gravity, of our earthly life.

Pilgrimage is a statement of longing. This earth is an alien place and we are wounded by being here; we want, as a child in the hospital says, to go *home*!

It is also an act of faith, but an impatient one: we *know* that we will go home one day. And we are so full of confident desire that we start walking now, as if rehearsing our coming to the promised land.

More darkly, pilgrimage is a defense mechanism. We all know perfectly well how utterly we are embedded in this world. We are as atoms in a piece of iron. But this truth is hard to bear: restive and fed up, we lug our weight off somewhere else on earth - to a place every bit as solid as the one we just left - but we act as if it isn't. We cling to our delusions and allegories, pretend that earthly shrines of timber and stone are gateways to paradise, unable to concede that we are really trapped as deeply as we are in the world.

It has been said that pilgrimage is an instinct in human beings. Even the partisan Catholic Encyclopedia calls pilgrimage a custom that "arises spontaneously from the heart", an "instinctive movement in human nature", a craving that (I smile to read) God has satisfied by giving us Christian places to visit. But today I feel, as I labour up this pass into the heights of the Pyrenees, that pilgrimage is not instinctive or natural. It is an act of hopeless rebellion. So stuck and so resistant to being stuck, we strain to take flight from the stony runway beneath our feet, find a way out, a release, a salvation, only to discover ourselves still here.

Why not give in to being stuck? Abandon the metaphors of pathways and gateways and look plainly at our glued-on selves. What would pilgrimage be then?

When I was very young, my family took a holiday at a cottage on a rain-soaked island in Georgian Bay. The forest was a sea of wet leaves the afternoon we arrived, and as my mother unpacked the groceries, my father had put his hand on my shoulder and said, smiling, "Go get your raincoat and let's have a little look around, shall we?" On this first day of our trip to Santiago, pilgrimage felt more like that: an excursion into the here and now. A look around.

After more hours of hard work, we arrived at the tree line, where we stretched out to rest on a rough mat of grass. The wind charged us from every angle. We squinted through it back to the northeast. The farthest hills had receded into monochrome humps. We could still see the sheep and the shrubs and the green cascading slopes, but it all seemed altered. Everything had the look of something remembered.

I rolled onto my side and looked at Scott. "Is your water handy?"

He yanked his bottle from the holder for me, then got up to gaze back over the ridge we had just crested, planting his legs against the wind and hugging his fists to his hips. He stared a while before returning to sit beside me. He stroked his beard, thinking.

Two thousand years ago, this was a Roman route for tin and soldiers running from Burgundy to Spain. Before the Romans, the Celts migrated through here, and after the Romans came the Germanic barbarians. In the 700s, it was King Charlemagne's Franks heading south, looking for a fight. Eleven hundred years later it was Napoleon and his men, after the same thing.

"And in between, all the pilgrims. Pilgrims travel where pilgrims have already travelled."

I thought about this. I had started peddling today with a personal view of pilgrimage: who was here before didn't really matter; what mattered was that I was here now. But Scott was right: it takes pilgrims, plural, to make a pilgrimage road. People, a lot of them, one after another, walking their hopes and pains into this trail, pressing their stories upn it.

We looked at the sky and the bright chubby clouds. Still ahead of us was the pass identified by Aimery as the Ports de Cize, so high, he says, that it seemed to touch the sky. Charlemagne had cut his way through that defile with "axes, hatchets, pickaxes and other implements." According to one of Aimery's unreliable sources, the king erected a cross on the height of land, knelt and prayed to Santiago, then marched his army into Spain to crush the Moors who were terrorizing the westward highway. Nowadays, says Aimery, all pilgrims on the Ports de Cize remember the king's prayer by planting their own cross there and praying as he had, with their faces turned toward Galicia.

We were hours from Charlemagne's peak. The sun was already well into the west. "We'd better high tail it," said Scott.

There was a meaningless sign where the Camino veered off the road. After some confusion, we dragged our bikes over a heap of bedrock onto the pale green ghost of a trail. Pushing against the wind no matter which way we turned, we twisted over rocky outcrops and across scruffy pastures where grass lay flattened by wind and dotted with animal droppings. Suddenly there was no land above us. I felt abnormally high and exposed, as if I was walking on the roof of a penthouse. Far away in the east, the mountains drifted like entropy along the horizon. There had been people here, thousands upon thousands over the centuries, but you would never think it now: we were eternal, solitary pilgrims, two shadows against the sky.

We soon discovered that this was a false summit, one of many mounds of land that rounded up and away like the slope of the moon and left you on top with nothing else in sight than the sky. But then, a few steps further on, another even higher slope appeared across a wet saddle of mushy grasses choked with bands of gravel. The Greeks believed that the hero Heracles had come through here on his way from the Underworld. Behind him he left the lovely nymph Pirene, who loved him ardently, and whose tears became the rivers and streams and springs that trickle from the mountain heights.

Leaving one summit, our bikes accelerated suddenly down a patch of shiny grass and mud to a stone marker. France was behind us; Spain was ahead. I took a picture. In the eastern sky, the tight cumulus clouds were starting to look vague and spread out. The air was moist, cooler than before.

Our descent through spring-fresh Spanish forests was refreshing, but when we arrived at the flanks of Mt. Aztobiscar, the trail swung up again. I heard myself sigh. My muscles were soggy and my heart, as if swollen to fill my whole chest, seemed to be crowding out my lungs. When we came to a paved road, I began an internal chant: "I have reserves, I have reserves." I glanced ahead. Scott was coming back down to me from the top, yelling into the wind that Roncesvalles was in view.

I shoved my bike up the hill and stopped beside him. Fatigue seeped through my limbs like a narcotic, but with it came the narcotic's gifts of exhilaration and satiety. This must have been Charlemagne's spot. No pilgrims' crosses now, but these were surely the views that Aimery had spoken of, over "Castille, Aragon and France." To the east, sweeping in front of a wall of gray clouds, a rainbow plunged thickly into low-slung forests. The Romans had worshipped the sun from this crest. Now, in the west behind towers of cumuli, its evening rays were elongating in swaths of pink and orange. The road below us dropped in hairpin turns into a broad valley where, in the dusk, roofs and church spires were going opaque and the forest shrank into inert patches of dark gray. It wasn't far now; we knew we had made it. Soon we would head down, but for a while, in the day's last lingering moments, we settled on the grass with our arms around our knees.

In the Middle Ages, most pilgrims took the Ports de Cize - the pass we were on - into Spain. Although it was longer and more difficult, it was for those same reasons safer than the lower alternate way to the west. That other route, now Highway N133, jogs south through the valley of the Petit Nive River from St. Jean Pied de Port to Valcarlos, before a steep final pass to Ibañeta and Roncesvalles. In the summer of AD 778, a military incident occurred along this route somewhere between Roncesvalles and Valcarlos. As battles go, it was relatively minor, but it was considered worth recording by the Frankish historian, Einhard, who was King Charlemagne's biographer.

Einhard had been a student of the English schoolteacher, Alcuin. Alcuin, whose own teacher had been the great monk Bede, had left England in 781 to become what we would call an education minister at the court of Charlemagne in Aachen. His Frankish pupil Einhard was a man of notable ugliness - it was often remarked upon - but an agile and far-sighted intellect was at work behind that lamentable face. Alcuin admired him greatly. Einhard's *Vita Caroli*, or Life of Charlemagne, is a gem of medieval biography. In it, we learn what happened near Roncesvalles in 778.

Moorish potentates are squabbling over their new Spanish homelands while Christians in the northeast flounder in political chaos. Loyalties are running in all directions. The Moorish Governor of Barcelona, Sulaiman ibn-al-Arabi has asked Charlemagne to help him against his enemy Abd al-Rahman I, emir of al-Andalus, in return for a few Spanish cities. Charles agrees. But while besieging Saragosa, the king is called home by a Saxon uprising in the Rhine valley. On his way through Pamplona, where Basques had driven out an Arab garrison a few decades before, he destroys the city walls. Einhard chooses not explain this, though it is likely that Charles intended to stem a Basque rebellion there.

It is August 15, Einhard tells us, late in the day. Charlemagne has been leading his men back to France in a thin column through a narrow defile in the Pyrenees. The ground is uneven, the men are encumbered with arms and gear. Charlemagne is at the head of the line. (Later versions put him near Valcarlos at the time of the incident, well into a game of chess with the treacherous Ganelon.) The rearguard trails behind near Roncesvalles, unaware that from high on a ridge over the pass they are being stalked by a band of lightly armed, fast moving Basques. While the king (we imagine) strokes that famous beard and moves his knights and bishops over a magnificent enameled chessboard (on view today in the Roncesvalles museum), the Basques, Einhard tells us, descend on the unsuspecting rearguard, force them into the valley, kill everyone, strip their baggage, and disappear into the dusk. Revenge is impossible "for the nonce," says Einhard, because nobody has the slightest idea where the nimble Basques have scattered to. Einhard also mentions that in addition to Anshelm, the Count of the Palace, and Eggihard, the king's steward, a certain Roland, Lord of the Breton Marches, is killed in the skirmish.

Just over a thousand years later, in 1835, a Frenchman named Francesque Michel comes across a small Anglo-Norman manuscript which he publishes in Paris under the title *La Chanson de Roland ou de Roncevaux*. Unremarkable in appearance, the manuscript eventually makes its way to the Bodleian Library at Oxford, where it is ignominiously catalogued as Digby 23. But the story inside Digby 23 is one of literary history's most celebrated discoveries. Its author, an 11th-century writer whose name was probably Turoldus, had taken Einhard's account and turned it into what would pass in the Middle Ages for a Hollywood blockbuster, a brilliant twist of propaganda and popular entertainment. Inside the covers of Digby 23 was France's first and greatest epic, the seed pod from which a thousand Camino legends would grow.

Turoldus preserves the shape of Einhard's story: Charlemagne is returning from Saragosa; his rearguard is attacked in the pass; Roland is killed. But in Turoldus' hands, the Basque aggressors become Moorish infidels, or Saracens, and Roland a mighty French count. Treachery is afoot in the Christian camp, for there is enmity between Roland and his step-father, Ganelon, who bears him an unknown grudge. Ganelon betrays Roland and his rearguard to the Saracens. The ambush takes place in Valcarlos Pass: Roland's men are deafened by a thousand bugles and blinded by the piercing sunlight reflected off Saracen shields. The infidel attack, when it comes, is terrible. But Roland refuses to blow his famous horn, the oliphant, for help, preferring to protect Charlemagne's army himself and his own honour in the doing.

The battle goes badly for the Christian Franks. Roland's friend Oliver is killed, and then all the others until only Roland himself and the king's Archbishop Turpin are left. Roland at last raises the oliphant to his lips, signaling to Charlemagne that help is badly needed.

The Saracens flee as the sound balloons into the valley - a frightful noise, half honk, half howl. Near death and with his ears gushing with blood from the force of his blowing, Roland tries to break his sword, Durandart, against a rock so that "no man who flees in battle" should have it as a prize. But for all his hacking, it is the stone, not the sword that cleaves. Watching it shimmer in the sun, Roland recites its deeds in the service of Charlemagne: it has conquered Anjou, Brittany, Poitou, Maine, Normandy, Provence, Aquitaine, Lombardy, Romania, Bavaria, all Flanders, Burgundy, Apulia, Constantinople, and (to our surprise) Scotland, Ireland, England.... So many lands, he sighs. No, Durandart must not be left in pagan hands. Unable to destroy his weapon, Roland staggers to a nearby tree. Lying down upon his horn and his sword, wracked with agony of mind and body, he turns to face Spain and submits himself to God. Charlemagne has heard the oliphant's cry, but arrives too late to save either Turpin or his beloved count.

The king fumes in his grief and plans revenge. The ensuing battle plays out along Old Testament lines. God gives Charlemagne a time advantage over the Saracens by extending the daylight hours, just as He had when Joshua fought the Amorites. And even as Pharaoh's army perished in the Red Sea, so the Saracens drown while retreating across the River Ebro. When the terrible Baligant, leader of all Islam arrives with reinforcements from Babylon, St. Gabriel comes to the rescue and Charlemagne slays all. The king returns to France, where Roland's fiancée dies of a broken heart, and Ganelon, convicted of treason, is ripped to pieces by four horses. At the end of *Le Chanson*, Charlemagne wearily contemplates more battles against the Saracen foe.

In the two hundred years after Charlemagne's defeat at Roncesvalles - the unadorned one recorded by Einhard - there were more Basque rebellions, more wars between Franks and Moors, and a succession of feuds that flamed like little volcanoes on the placid plains running south from the Pyrenees. In between came the first pilgrims heading to James' tomb in Compostela, drawn as if by a divine thread across the traffic of soldiers and mad rebels and loose-living adventurers. They must have been caught in the cross-fire sometimes, murdered as suspected traitors, robbed, raped, taken hostage. They were adventurers themselves, travelling on rumours and faith into an uncharitable land.

We looked back towards the pass, then turned to stare over the plains of Navarra. The wind seemed preternaturally hushed, a eerie draft of time that had blown all that history into the air.

Nowadays the Ports de Cize is also called the Route de Napoleon, though Napoleon himself spent only a couple of months in Spain during the war that bloodied Iberia and left *El Camino de Santiago* in ruins between 1808 and 1814. It was Napoleon's Marischal Murat who crossed through here in 1808 on his way to invade Madrid. In no time, Murat had taken the towns guarding the Pyrenean passes, and his troops were flooding into Spain by every possible route. Soon after, the Duke of Wellington landed in Portugal and began moving a British army supported by Portuguese and Spanish guerrillas eastward against the French. By 1812, Wellington had liberated Madrid; in the summer of 1813, he won the Battle of Vitoria - north and west of Pamplona on an old northerly Camino route - and drove the French north over the Pyrenees. A year later, Wellington would invade France from the sea and take Bayonne, near Biarritz, as well as Toulouse and Bordeaux. In the same year, 1814, Napoleon would abdicate, and the terrible Peninsular War, known in Spain as the War of Independence, would come to an end.

Assisting Wellington as he pushed the French back to France was a Portuguese aide-de-camp, a guerrilla fighter named Samuel Antonio Xavier Burgos. He had been born in 1792 in Tres Montes, Portugal, to Emmanuel Burgos and his German wife, Mary Welch. For his services in Wellington's entourage, Samuel was rewarded after the war with land in Ireland. Sometime later, he was stationed with the British in Canada. He fell ill, was quarantined near Quebec City and missed the boat back to Ireland. Somehow, he managed to swap his green and rolling Irish farmland for a dense swatch of southern Ontario forest. This he cleared and farmed. He married young Mary Clapp, native of Elmwood, Ontario, who bore him several children, among them a daughter, Emily. In 1869, two years before Samuel's death, Emily married a William Drewery. Among the grandchildren was Harold Drewery, who studied engineering at the University of Toronto, married a brown-eyed beauty named Helen McNamara, and moved to Deep River, Ontario. Sitting here beside me on this crest overlooking Roncesvalles, was Hal and Helen's second child, Scott Tiffin.

The Burgos side was a rough and ready kind of family, blunt, intelligent, sturdy folks, with their share of drunks and characters. You could see the Portuguese in Scott's father Hal, in his olive skin and high cheekbones. Right up until he died, he had a peppery, let's-get-on-with-it disposition. Looking at him, I had thought I could just make out his feisty guerrilla ancestor, Wellington's aide-de-camp.

In the *Chanson de Roland*, Charlemagne and his French soldiers had been styled as liberators when they pushed over the Pyrenees to rid Spain of the Moors. But the French were not always welcome in Spain. The Camino towns harboured resentment like vermin, and the situation only worsened when French settlers arrived and lorded their high-flown ways over the locals. In the centuries to come, things would often turn nasty; there were skirmishes, rebellions, outright war. The storied Camino eventually shrank back into a dusty everyday track as the Peninsular War swept through Spain and Napoleon's men ransacked the last of its treasures. By 1814, when Samuel Burgos was helping Wellington chase the French out of Spain for the last time, pilgrimage was probably the furthest thing from his mind.

Samuel lies now in Reid's Cemetery, Thurlow, Ontario. As we thought of him here on a dusk-shrouded flank of land over Roncesvalles, the irony seemed extraordinary. He was our closest personal connection with this pass, a distant uncle, a Portuguese guerrilla fighter against the French. Staring over the lands that had taken the weight of Charlemagne's men and Napoleon's men, and all the pilgrims in between, we felt more connected, through Samuel Burgos, with the end than with the beginning of the *Camino francés*.

Such a silence now. The wind was reduced to a sulky mutter. In the east, the rainbow faltered against the clouds. The western sky was a loose pink, rippled like a tossed blanket. The air had a chilly nip that reminded us of our hunger and fatigue. Far below were the spires and stone buildings of Roncesvalles. Past them, the Camino disappeared into a dark welter of farms and forests.

Scott stirred beside me. "Time to go down?"

"Yeah. I'm freezing."

"It'll be colder still once we start down this hill. Take my vest. It's handier than yours. It's on the top there." He gestured with his chin; his beard looked damp. I rummaged a moment in his pack, pulled out a vest and a pair of gloves. Tentatively we let our bikes down the long switchbacks, our brakes screeching like maddened vultures. In fifteen minutes we were on the main road into Roncesvalles. We passed a small chapel built, they say, by Charlemagne for Roland's body. The sky was murky with clouds, then suddenly black with night. We could smell rain in the east.

In the bliss of exhaustion, needing food and a bed, we checked into the first place we found, not the hostel but a new two star inn, *La Posada*, around the corner from the monastery. It smelled of pine, had simple, rustic décor somewhere between Swedish and French Canadian. We were alone in the dining room for supper. It was the kind of rich, plain feast we would come to know well: vegetables in broth, a plate of well salted pork ribs, rashers of bread, a bottle of red Spanish wine, cheaper than water and tastier than anything, and for dessert, an apple on a plate with a knife. Later, we slept in a room silent as a tomb.

It was raining lightly next morning. After breakfast, we visited the Collegiate Church of Santa Maria, a 13th-century creation of the French Gothic, all pillars and pointed arches and streaks of light from on high. The 14th-century Virgin of Roncesvalles sat on the altar, framed from behind by a gorgeous blue stained glass window. Her face, famous and reproduced in hundreds of guidebooks, is turned toward the Christ child in her lap, an expression of wonderment in those slightly oriental eyes. The child holds an apple and playfully reaches with his other hand for his mother's breast.

We walked around the church cloister, then took shelter from the drizzle on a stone bench. The cloister walls were open to the sky and luminous with moisture. Above them, slanted tile roofs shone against the spiky treetops of a fairy tale forest. The air dripped with liquid silver. Roncesvalles was the imagination's town. As soon as the *Chanson* came out in the 12th Century, pilgrims were here worshipping the weapons of Roland - now unofficially a saint - as if they were holy relics. Around 1127, Alfonso I of Aragon, a few of his nobles, and the bishop of Pamplona had a pilgrim hostel built "at the peak called Roncesvalles near the chapel of Charlemagne." The hostel, founded on the strength of the legends, became a monument to Christian charity. A 12th-century Latin poem says it gave shelter and Christian care to thousands of pilgrims, "sick and well, not only Catholics, but also pagans, Jews, heretics and vagabonds." Roncesvalles basked in royal and church support from all over Europe. Wealthy pilgrims left huge donations. The town grew plump with Christian prestige; its pulse - the pulse of money and myth and good religion - could be felt all the way to Santiago.

The soft-mannered parish priest at Roncesvalles appeared in a raincoat. He invited us to his office, where he stamped our Pilgrim's Passes. "People come to the Camino for various reasons," he said thoughtfully, his shy eyes slightly averted behind his glasses, "some for cultural reasons, others for spiritual ones." He shrugged and seemed resigned to the first reason, like a man who, having heard every conceivable confession a thousand times, has learned to leave the judgment of God's fallen world to God Himself.

It must be asserted categorically, wrote the monk Prieto in *Tu Solus Peregrinus*, that the Camino was born as a *Christian* pilgrimage. It was *not* the result, he emphasizes, of druidic or orphic or gnostic spirituality, nor was it an extension of ancient Roman or Celtic civilization. Prieto would brook no argument to the contrary. I wondered how he could be so sure.

There is no evidence of a pilgrimage route running west from Roncesvalles earlier than the 800s, and the Camino now is a completely Christian affair: all its shrines and churches were built by and for Christians as spiritual checkpoints in the pilgrim's progress to Santiago. The Camino has been called "a pious invention" of the 9th Century. An allegory in geography. A singularly Christian pilgrimage. But this made it sound as if there was no spiritual ground here before, as if the Camino had been plunked down on a *tabula rasa*.

I have a sympathy for second stringers, for the things that stand mostly ignored beside the main attraction. Travelling along the Camino, we saw remnants of other histories: an ancient fountain, an overgrown hilltop fort, pre-historic arrowheads jumbled and forgotten in a cabinet. These aloof remnants strewn around the Christian trail make up the interstices of that "allegory in geography." They are the vestiges of the earliest inhabitants of Spain, and they belong to the same tissue on which the Camino was woven. They were made by nomadic hunters, shamans, farmers, witches and healers, priests, astronomers and seers. Like all humans stuck in a landscape, these people used the topography of their land, chill streams, shadowed forests, drumlins, eskers, mountain cliffs, and caves, to overcome the mind's blindness and enter into union with large and numinous truths. I wasn't sure what, if anything, their practices - the adoration of weather gods, dances around trees, sacrifices at springs, the hacking out of stone tombs - had to do with the Christian Camino, but surely there were sacred spaces here long before there were any Christian pilgrims.

Even the raw geography of northern Spain can jar and arouse the psyche. It is beautiful, but beauty is not its defining feature, and it is rarely a benign beauty. An eerie indifference lies under the sweet, sunny landscapes of the

the land can turn on you quickly, owes[1] you nothing, will caress you one moment and bake your bones the next.

Behind the coastal areas near Emporium, where Spain and France meet on the Mediterranean, and where Phoenicians and Greeks once had trading colonies, a modest line of mountains runs into the southwest. Behind it, an elevated tableland stretches like the pitiless face of a planet across the centre of the peninsula. This is the meseta, a terrain pocked and eroded, indifferently sprouting contorted tufts of yellowing grass amidst its stones and soil. In the spring rains, its surface turns to gluey mud, then desiccates to bone hard chunks under the blind sun of summer. To the north, the meseta butts against the mountain ranges of Cantabria, whose abrupt slopes, though not particularly high, have been gouged and roughened by millenia of glaciers and erosion. To the west, two spurs of the Cantabrians divide the meseta from the spongy Galician uplands. Here, a millenium before Christ, a few lucky Phoenicians found mineral deposits. The air drips with fog. It can pour for days, but when summer sunbeams pierce the mist dribbling from debilitated clouds, the hills turn into humps of glistening dark green wool. The uplands extend west to the coast, where the land ends like a torn hem in fjords and craggy black granite: Finis Terrae - the end of the land. Facing into the setting sun, it was, in the old view, the gateway to the underworld, to wisdom or death.

Embedded in the flanks of the Cantabrian cordillera that lies due west of Roncesvalles and some hundred miles north of the Camino are about a dozen paleolithic cave sites, some as old as 30,000 years. Altogether, these caves lying like hearts' ventricles inside the mountains make up the Spanish arc of a twisted crescent of caverns that has its northern end in Central France at Lascaux. Some years ago, Scott and I had visited the French caves. But the most famous caves in Spain, the ones at Altamira, are now locked to amateurs because the "white disease" that fades the markings on the walls is carried on the breath of all those who enter.

Around 14,000 years ago, in an Age named, attractively, the Magdalenian, the spent ice of the last great freeze was dripping over a Europe slowly recovering her forests and animals. The annual hunting round was once more bringing paleolithic nomads north to the Cantabrian ranges. Somehow, using knowledge that had already endured for 15,000 years, the nomads found their way back into the caves. Balancing their charcoal pencils and pots of goo under the flames of their torches, they squeezed their bodies into interior galleries and painted the impeccable beings of their world on mottled walls: bison and red deer, horses and boars, shamans and gods. They lined the figures up, or stacked them one on another, left some overlapping and others upside down. Among their painted masterpieces, they made kindergarten-style handprints with paint and drew curious, priapic stick men with enigmatic markings whose meanings will never be recovered.

Their obsession was the cosmic hunt; the divine beasts that ranged across these walls and ceilings had their earthly counterparts in the herds that were the nomads' sustenance. The physical requirements for food and warmth coalesced with spiritual instincts for creativity, worship and petition. On the walls at El Jugo, east of Altamira, and to the west at Tito Bustillo, the deer is mother of life; at Altamira the boar is beast of death, devouring the vegetation god; elsewhere are the bird goddess and the fish god. Presiding over the hunt is the Divine Goddess, all-giving wet-nurse and terrible slayer.

Nobody knows what sacrifices, chants or prophecies took place under the watch of these magic creatures. The pictures of them seen in books have no story that you can make out, though you sense that there is one. You feel a tickle of recognition, too remote to grasp. It is absolutely certain that you are looking at something healthy. The perspective is perfectly rendered, conveys an utterly sane balance between the visionary and the worldly, unmediated, or at least unobstructed, by consciousness. It is good human work: mineral pigments mixed with animal fat; the mind on display, unashamed, expressing its hunger, its natural humility, its playfulness. You sense, perhaps with envy or a disconcerting streak of grief, a reciprocity between the imagination and the powers of the material world. They knew something you don't. This was not an Eden, nor a Golden Age. It may or may not have been peaceful, though there is no evidence of a warring consciousness. But for perhaps 25,000 years, human creativity seems to have danced lightly on that meticulous point between terror and confidence, succumbing to neither.

You don't need to know about Altamira and the other cave sites of Spain to understand the Camino today. In the Middle Ages nobody had the slightest idea they existed. But from certain sections of the Camino, you can see the mountains of Cantabria to the north, and if you think to turn your head in that direction, and imagine the animals roaming through those silent vesicles, you might feel stirring in yourself the same twin compulsions that drove the nomads to these caves: the one for petition that does not cost you your dignity, the other for celebration that remembers greater forces than yourself. You may also be cheered by the continuity of your pilgrimage with the deepest human past: how different is it, really, from that of the worshippers in these torch-lit grottos, who travelled along paths and river valleys behind their life-giving herds, then scrambled on their bellies through slim, rocky arteries into the holy of holies.

We set out on a paved road from Roncesvalles just as the drizzly sheen in the air began to evaporate. Now that they were over the shock of yesterday's climb, my legs felt ready to move. We headed south to Puente la Reina on N172, an alternate route that the parish priest, whose hands looked as if they had never touched a handlebar, had told us was better than the pilgrims' trail for cycling. He had been right. We pedaled easily, gently downhill through a narrow gorge on a tree-fringed road. One or two cars passed us with a hush. On our right, a river bubbled in the brightening day. Tall cliffs rose from the far bank, great grisly walls of granite studded with dark-leafed shrubs and contorted trees trunks twisting defiantly toward the sun. On the flat cliff top, straight trees stood looking out across the gorge like a scraggly line of sentinels. Our route kept to the country, by-passing Pamplona and turning onto N121 to join the Aragonese portion of the Camino at Campanas. There was more traffic here, and we were ready to stop for a break.

A medieval chapel in the modern town of Campanas is dedicated to San Nicolás of Bari. Nicolás lived in the 4th Century in Asia Minor, a bishop who some say was slain during the persecutions of the Emperor Diocletian. Perhaps because he had a protective affection for travellers, Nicolás was a well-known saint along the Camino. At times he even rivaled St. James in popularity. There are chapels dedicated to him in the big cathedrals at Burgos and Santiago, and a whole church at San Juan de Ortega. He is the patron of children, sailors, and oddly, pawnbrokers, as well as of countless European towns, counties, cities, and countries. We knew San Nicolás of Bari best, however, as Saint Nick, or Santa Claus.

After Campanas, the land opened out. We cycled vigorously towards Puente la Reina among the broad, shallow hills of the Robo River valley, arriving at the town late in the day. We checked into El Meson, an "art-hotel" decorated with sculpture, paintings and furniture from every period and place, all delightful, the possessions of a collector with a taste for the flamboyantly, merrily discordant. The restaurant was posh: post-modern post and beam, with a private dining room like a medieval hall. "What kind of a pilgrimage is this anyway?" I wondered out loud over sherry and escargot.

Puente la Reina, or Queen's Bridge, is named for the royal lady - probably Doña Mayor, wife of Sancho III of Navarra - who ordered a pilgrims' bridge constructed over the Rio Arga at the west end of town, where the Calle Mayor, or Main Street, becomes the Camino. It is a romantic bridge of tawny stone. Every pilgrim crosses it, while car traffic takes the industrial metal contraption further downstream. We visited it after supper, and returned there the next morning for a picnic breakfast on the riverbank, watching as its six arches loomed into six magic circles in the mirror-still water. Before cycling away, we walked over the bridge twice. We paused a long while at the midpoint of its arc over the Arga, staring into limpid tree-lined waters, wondering if there was any possible way to make a river prettier.

The paleolithic cave temples, some hundred and fifty in all, lie in a boomerang-shaped belt of land that swings down out of Central France and west at the Pyrenees into Cantabrian Spain. Superimposed on this swath of sacred art is another much larger group of sites ten thousand years younger than Altamira. In Spain, this new zone forms a horseshoe starting at the Pyrenees and sweeping west from Roncesvalles, Pamplona, and Puente de Reina, out along the Cantabrian mountains, then down the Portuguese coast to Gibraltar and east again across Spain toward Valencia.

These are the territories of the megaliths, rocks of unimaginable tonnage arranged on wind-swept fields of grass: blunt stone tombs hulking above the ground, and tall, stiff pillars - part phallus, part ghost - standing alone or gathered in groups like a petrified cocktail party. East of Vitoria, close to the Camino by a Roman road, sits the Dolmen at Aitzkomendi, a roofed structure set in a depression of land. It is beetled, low-slung, and crude looking, like a house of stone slab cards. Further west in Galicia near the town of Melide is the famous dolmen of the Fox, the Pedra de Raposo. On the coast at Noia, due west of Santiago, a collection of dolmens waits in the fog on Mount Barbanza. To the north, near La Coruña on the Bay of Biscay, a few kilometres from a church dedicated to Santiago, are the Dolmen of Dombate and the Pedra Cuberta, a tomb with an enormous, six metre chamber.

The megaliths stand at odd angles under the sky after centuries of weather and gravity. Some are 6000 years old, which puts them just inside the Neolithic, when nomadic life was disappearing and people were settling in villages and learning to till the soil. Some say that the annual Paleolithic hunt across Spain's oceanic landscapes was replaced during the Neolithic by rituals marking the agricultural seasons of growth and decline. In other words, nomadic movement itself moved into the imagination, became a *metaphor* of journey and return that was played out, year after year, on a permanent itinerary signposted with dolmens and tombs. Travel between these sacred sites was perhaps the original metaphoric pilgrimage, a journey through symbolically enhanced topography to that place where death opens into life. For these gray structures, introspectively silent in the fog, and always cold to the touch, are "the tomb that is also a womb."

Possibly, the upright dolmens had been built as observatories; many are arranged in wide circles and are said to be oriented to the sun's rays at various times of the year. To me they looked like a group of fossilized surgeons standing around an invisible operating table, pondering with deep, dark enthusiasm the workings of birth and death. Spirals are incised on some of them, galaxies in small, tiny mirrors of the Big Whirl, the ultimate symbol of the voyage through death into the centre where life springs forth again. I could imagine people dancing in the shadows of these stones: the initiated, the graduating shamans, the freshly circumcised, the newly scarred and enlightened, the visionary poets, the saved, the ones who had sought out the other side and returned.

Christianity is sometimes described as a cult of death and rebirth. If it is, it is also much more than that. But you can't help but make a connection between the megalithic cults of the tomb and the womb and the worship of Christian relics. The Santiago pilgrimage itself shows the same form as these megalithic rituals: a journey through a charged landscape to a sanctuary where visible mementos offer the life-giving power of those who live now on the other side of death's door.

Minutes after leaving Puente la Reina, we were on a rough strip of reddish-brown earth cluttered with fieldstones, twisting across small hills and gullies, more or less following the highway towards Estella, Viana, and Logroño. Earlier in the spring, the track had been washed and cut by streams of rainwater, then mashed and moulded by tractors, horses, cows, and people. This morning it was dry, a skinny trail of petrified mud lumps in a scruffy landscape. On our bikes it was slow going; often we had to get off and push, not, as in the Pyrenees, because of the wind and the long steep climbs, but because of stones and ridges of dried mud that brought our wheels to a dead stop on the little rises. Three or four foot pilgrims plodded past us, greeting us solemnly as their legs scraped over the stone-studded clods. When the track ran close to the main highway, we switched over. The asphalt surface was suddenly smooth, like an airplane just after take-off.

There were few vehicles at this hour and the wind was light. In a few hours we came down a final hill onto the bridge at Estella, where back in the 12th Century Aimery had so enjoyed the food. We sat for our lunch, which was fresh and delicious, on a low stone wall that separated the town from the river. A grassy lawn stretched back to the Church of San Miguel. Beyond the church was a maze of little streets and stone buildings. It was a relief to idle over our bread and cheese and watch the shallow river rippling in the sunshine. The local kayak school was out, young people in yellow and red helmets practising Eskimo rolls or dabbing their oars in the little currents by the shore. A few yards from us, three French pilgrims had just finished their lunch. As they swung their loaded packs high against their shoulders, they seemed to sink like fenceposts into the ground.

I had loved reading about the earliest inhabitants of Spain, and in 1998, on my second trip to the Camino, I would go to Soria, a town in Castile southwest of Estella. The Numantine Museum here was known for its collection of Stone Age artifacts. I spent most of an afternoon in the company of Man the Tool Maker; first, Homo Erectus, hunting here between ice ages some 300,000 years ago; then the Neanderthals and Cro Magnon. They had all slept in caves. They knew about fire and how to cook. Dumbly, I looked into glass cabinets that displayed their spearheads, arrowheads, scrapers and cutters, my mind groping in the mists of human memory for links, a sense of descendency, something more than simple information about tools.

The next morning, I returned to the Numantine to look at the Iberian and Celtic collection. The Iberi, as the Romans would call them, began arriving in Spain around

1600 BC, likely over the Pyrenees. They headed south, avoiding for the most part the manic-depressive meseta and the drizzly northwest. They liked cities and as they settled the fertile hills of Catalonia and the mild eastern coasts, they built well fortified townsites with swanky downtowns. The Iberians had a written language, still undeciphered. They were superb artisans. Their figurines and pottery had a smart, urban stylishness. Feeling like a customer, I pored over ladies' jewellery dreamed up by designers two thousand years ago. They were the kind of things I'd have bought for myself in an upscale Iberian market.

Around the middle of the 8th Century BC, tribes of Iron Age Celts entered Spain, hauling their weapons and cauldrons and iron tools down the same Pyrenean slopes. The Celts were more rurally inclined than the Iberians, though just as war-loving, possibly more. Undaunted by climate or topography, they settled with their slaves and thick-haired women and kids on the hilltops and riverbanks of the meseta, erecting big rambly forts that also had houses and markets. They infiltrated Galicia all the way to Finisterre. They were attracted to megalithic sites, which they sometimes reworked, incising upon them their own swirls and whorls: the Celtic spirals and labyrinths at Mogor, a fishing village west of Santiago, are said to be the most important in Spain. They also gouged out shelves in the old megalithic walls for their cult emblems. Skulls, for example. They seemed an irrational, unsympathetic race to me. They apparently should be thought of as colonists in Spain, but the word struck me as too benign. In pictures I had seen, the remains of their forts, once moated and pallisaded with wood, slouched on the flat-topped hills like a pack of unfriendly dogs. They relished violence; they worshipped trees and rivers with human sacrifices.

I tried at least to respect them. In our travel books, Scott and I had seen pictures of their *pallozas*, stone huts with pert thatched roofs, clustered together in settlements. Later on our cycling trip, we would visit the *pallozas* in the mountain-top village of El Cebreiro, a village just inside Galicia, on the highest peak of land along the Camino, with views east and west over two oceans of green hills.

Perhaps 1500 years ago there had been a Celtic settlement at El Cebreiro; in the late 1960s, its stone huts had been reconstructed, complete with thatching. Some of the restored *pallozas* were now hostels and bars. The Romanesque Church of Santa Maria stands on the site of a long gone Celtic temple. We wandered up to see it in the early evening. Its metal cross made an ink mark in the dusk sky. It was impossible to imagine how the original Celtic temple had looked, but in the moonlight, you could almost hear the sounds of a rough and passionate religion: hoarse incantations, the choking gush of sacrifices, children whispering, drums and horns, women humming, the sing-songy voices of old story-tellers, the sound of a hundred hands clapping, the wind snapping up over the hill crest; and over all, the silent coal-black skies revolving with stars and planets. The Romans reported that the Celts danced frenetically under the full moon, that they exposed their dead to vultures. I was struck by this; it wasn't such a ghoulish idea: in the Middle Ages these ugly recyclers with their hunched black wings were still viewed - even in theological circles - as the bringers of life out of death.

At El Cebreiro we would also visit a Celtic "model home." It was beetled with thatch on the outside but surprisingly high and spacious inside. I sat on a bench in the sooty kitchen, writing my diary on a hinged table that a Celtic housewife, or maybe a slave, would have lowered from its upright position against the wall. Fire tools were within easy reach near the fire pit, and a seriously blackened cooking pot swung over the flames on a long arm. Meat could be hung to smoke over the fire, suspended from the ceiling on hangers that looked like over-sized lampshade frames. To my left on a stone ledge was a concavity for washing things, and a narrow drain that slanted through the wall to the outside. I could see straw beds from where I sat, next to a sturdy wooden storage chest. The place was ingenious, the solid invention of people who intended to stay around. I could imagine a family of Celts hunched at this table, wolfing down grilled venison and berries by the fire. Surviving. With a little more effort, I might have grown to like them.

After lunch in Estella, we cycled to Viana, arriving at the pleasantly simple pilgrims' *refugio* in the early evening. Only a few people were staying the night. We walked through room after room of neatly lined-up triple bunks, feeling as if we had arrived at a party on the wrong night. Here and there, a pilgrim lay dozing on top of a sleeping bag, her blistered bare feet splayed out on a pile of clothes. I did some laundry and hung it on the springs of the bunk above me. In the night I awoke to find socks and a t-shirt dangling close to my face like the leftovers of a dream.

We had met a friendly young woman from New Zealand in the evening and the next morning in the communal kitchen, we chatted while Scott washed some dishes left on the counter. The New Zealander was tall and frail, with long blonde hair in braids and a delicate, heart-shaped face. She said she had quit her job in Wellington (she called it Willington) to make this pilgrimage.

"Is Spain a Cetholic country?" she asked me. The question surprised me. How could you not know that Spain was Catholic? Later on, I would think the question had some interesting angles.

Heading from Viana toward Logroño, we avoided the pilgrim paths and kept to the highway to make up time we had lost at the start of our trip. When the highway and the Camino happened to converge, we often stopped to chat with foot pilgrims. I hoped we might have met the New Zealander again, as she had left Viana before us, but she never appeared. The countryside was hilly, green with the coming of summer, stretched taut like upholstery with vineyards and fields.

We were in full-blown Celtiberian country now. The Celts and Iberians had intermarried; the resulting tribes were a blend of moody war-hunger and urbane aesthetic sensibility. They had kept mostly to the east of a line running diagonally across Spain from the Pyrenees down towards Mérida. We had already stopped at some their towns: Estella and Ciraqui, then Los Arcos, which was called Curnonium by the Romans, who resettled it. Ahead of us were Logroño in La Rioja, then, further out on the meseta, Frómista and Carrión de los Condes. All Celtiberian, once.

Approaching Logroño, we passed the hill where the town of Varea had once stood. In Celtiberian times, Varea had been a regional capital, but was sacked in 76 BC by the Roman general Pompey. The Celtiberians liked places such as this: safe hilltops overlooking broad, fertile plains close to commercial routes and waterways. No Celtiberian temples exist; probably they held religious festivals at natural sanctuaries. Like all pagans, they petitioned, cajoled, bribed and worshipped forces in the natural world: mountains, trees, rivers; the sun and the moon.

Between Varea and Logroño, we crossed the Rio Ebro, a sultry swath of water sidling southeast from Cantabria to Saragoza and the Mediterranean. We paused on the stone bridge, balancing our bikes between our legs. The legends say that the Ebro was the home of Lusina, or Melusina, the goose-footed water goddess of fertility. Her consort was the mighty Lug, Celtic god of the arts, after whom the Galician city of Lugo is supposedly named. The goose and the cryptic figure of the goose's foot can be seen all along the Camino. The word *oca*, Spanish for goose, is tucked into place names such as the Montes de Oca, a band of high land marking an old boundary between Navarra and Castile. Here, by a 1936 memorial to those who died in the Spanish Civil War, is the Pass of the Pedraja, in whose name the Celtic word for goose shows up: *Jars*. Elsewhere - for instance, at the Anso River and the town of Ganso - the goose is recalled in its Latin form, *anser*, or its Visigothic, and Spanish alternative form, *ganso*.

In France, "to spin the goose" meant, for reasons I didn't grasp, to speak in the secret language of the builder's guild. The goose's foot was the emblem of the masons who called themselves the Hijos de Maestro Jacques, or Sons of Master Jacques. It is said that the town of Jaca, at the far east end of the Camino near the Somport Pass, takes its name from these masons, the Jacques; the cathedral there is the first piece of Romanesque architecture in Spain. Several weeks away, deep within the Montes de Oca in the Church of San Nicolás at San Juan de Ortega, you again find the sign of the goose's foot carved into the masonry, the mark of the brotherhood of masons.

The Camino's goose roots may reach far back in history in another direction too. The goose is thought to be the European version of the Egyptian ibis, the serpent-fighting bird sacred to Isis, the mother goddess. Isis' main temple had been at Philae on the Nile near Aswan, and her worshippers were the black-skinned Nubians. Isis was also venerated in various Roman sects up until the 3rd Century. She may have gotten to Spain. Her Christian descendant along the Camino, so the argument goes, is the dark-faced Virgin, miracle-worker and friendly healer. There are black Madonnas at Los Arcos, Estella, Ponferrada, Salamanca, and Soria.

Apart from its medieval quarter, I found Logroño a dour, tedious city. Even the laundry looked sad as it flapped like soggy leaves beneath the windows of gray apartment blocks. We registered at an unremarkable little posada just off the old town. Coming back out to the street to take our bikes to the posada storage room, we greeted another cycling couple stopped by the doorway. Before long, they too had registered and, as it happened, were given a room next to ours.

Heinrich and Else were from Germany. Like us, they were bicycling to Compostela, but had started at Roncesvalles. Else had large bones, blond hair cut short, and a smile that crinkled warmly over her face. Heinrich was a little shorter than his wife. He had a very round, bald head and a barrel chest, but there was something about him that made me think of squares. He gave an impression of reliability and discipline, as if he had a set of cabinets in his head into which, with cheerful obsessiveness, he fitted the world.

Both spoke perfect English. An international businessman, Heinrich had gone to school in the United States in the sixties. Else was a nurse, had worked in Australia for a few years after she graduated, "to use my English." That explained her accent, a combination of Teutonic precision and Aussie brassiness. Against her beatific smile and her joyful manner, that voice was like a neon light announcing an alpine meadow.

We became friendly immediately and arranged to have dinner together. The restaurant was a humdrum place on a street near the hotel. We ordered our meals and in a few moments, a huge bowl was placed unceremoniously before us with enough vegetable soup for an army. I ladled the steaming broth into four bowls. Scott passed bread. Else and Heinrich were not drinking wine, and we declined too this evening, though Riojan wine was cheap and good. Before long our meals arrived, landing like tossed hats on the table. *Guiso* - meat stew - accompanied by potatoes and bread. Simple, hot, good.

We talked about our journeys. Else and Heinrich had kept to the highway all the way from Roncesvalles. "The traffic is quite noisy," said Else, smiling as though recalling a flower garden. They liked the idea of some off-road cycling on the Camino trails, but Heinrich wasn't sure their old, three-speed bikes could take it. The Everest Guide had good suggestions for cyclists, we told them. We ourselves were thinking of trying the small country roads near the main highway when the Camino trail was too awkward for a bicycle.

Heinrich and Else were going to Santiago as pilgrims but had toured Spain several times before. "I enjoy the north because of the Camino," said Heinrich, "but scratch the surface anywhere around here, and you're looking at Rome. I'm interested in religious history and the Roman missionaries."

Scott looked at him, interested. "There must be a lot of Roman remains here in the northeast because of the tin road coming down from France."

Scott was a natural historian; as far back as I could remember, he could recite dates and events like the days of the week. He loved to find patterns in historical processes, but was even more intrigued by twists of personality and geography and chance that sent history in unexpected directions. In Heinrich, he had found a kindred spirit.

"The Phoenicians were actually at the mines first," Heinrich was saying, "going after the tin and copper and silver on the west coast."

Else poured us all mineral water while he talked. "The Romans came to Spain for the mines too," he went on, "but it was really the war with Carthage that got them here in the first place."

"Yes!" said Scott. "When Mary and I were in Sicily a few years ago, we spent an afternoon in the town of Messina. That's where the decisive battle in the First Punic War happened. Right there in the harbour!" He looked as if he could still hardly believe it. "Rome beat Carthage in a sea battle and took Sicily and Sardinia.

Else laughed. "I could never keep those Punic Wars straight at school. They didn't seem important to me."

"You've got think of how they shaped the world you live in," said Scott, "I'm not that interested in history that doesn't take me anywhere toward understanding things now."

"So what happened next?" asked Else.

"Carthage tried to cut its losses by moving into Spain. They did well economically and Rome got worried about a Carthaginian power base here. In 218 BC, they started fighting near the coast at Saguntum. That was the Second Punic War, and the start of Rome in Spain. It took about thirteen years to get the Carthaginians out of here. The Pyrenees were crawling with troops."

"Was that when Hannibal took his elephants over the Alps?" said Else.

"Yep, thirty-seven war elephants through the snow."

"Did they make it?"

"They think made it all the way through to Rome."

"Did they go over the Pyrenees by the pass we took?" I asked.

"I don't think anybody really knows."

Carthage pulled out of Spain in 205 BC, and Rome started in on the mines. But now they had trouble with the locals. The Celtiberians had played both sides during the Second Punic War, had fought for Romans or Carthaginians, depending. Now they were faced with the Romans alone, who wanted them down and out. The brutality was terrible; even the citizens back in Italy were shocked to learn how the so-called civilized Romans treated the Celtiberians. They broke treaties, betrayed their allies, massacred thousands whenever they felt like it. But the Celtiberians were nothing if not tough; it would take Rome two hundred years to put down all the rebellions.

The most famous revolt, lasting twenty years, was at Numantia, near present day Soria. It is said that Roman soldiers fighting there were unhappy at the prospect of going back to Rome. To draw out their stay in Spain, they made only weak attacks on the city. But in 133 BC, the Romans finally destroyed Numantia and either butchered its citizens or sold them into slavery.

Heinrich began to wrap up his Roman history. "It still took nearly a century for Rome to take all of Spain. Julius Caesar had everything but Galicia by 45 BC, just a year before he was assassinated in Rome. Then in 24 BC, Caesar Augustus campaigned in Iberia and began the occupation of Galicia."

"That's when he became ill and nearly died on they way west to Astorga." I said.

"So you could say," said Heinrich, ignoring the footnote, "that the groundwork for the story of St. James is laid during the wars with Carthage. No Roman Empire, no Roman Church, and no Roman Christian mission in Spain. Else and I believe that Christianity would still have been around, but it wouldn't have looked like it does now. And if Rome hadn't taken Spain, the whole Camino would have been totally different, if it had even existed at all."

We were given dishes of ice cream for dessert. Then the bill, which was staggering. Heinrich was miffed, but Else told him to let it go. We continued talking over our ice cream. "Six missionaries arrived from Rome in the early first century AD," said Heinrich. "And there's a legend that James himself came to Spain from Jaffa sometime before the year 40. He was beheaded in Jerusalem in 44," he added parenthetically. "That much, we know. The legends says he went to Saragoza and then on to Galicia."

"But his mission was a flop," said Else, with a gay smile, "he only converted nine people!"

"Have you been to Saragoza?" asked Heinrich. "It was originally an Iberian city, then Roman. There is a story about James at Saragoza too. As Else says, he wasn't a successful preacher, but in Saragoza, he was praying with his companions by the river when the Virgin Mary appeared to him on a pillar, with lights, angels..." Heinrich waved his right hand in circles, "and so on. She ordered James to build a chapel where she could be worshipped. That's the origin of La Virgin del Pilar."

"You can see her in the big basilica now, on her pillar," said Else, "but it's really just an image from the 14th Century."

"So the first Christian shrine in Northern Spain wasn't built for James, it was built *by* James, for the Virgin." I said.

"When you think of it," said Heinrich, "there are a lot of saints other than James whose names are woven into the Camino - Nicolás of Bari, for instance, and then further west, you have San Millán and San Martín."

"But there's no chance that James was here at all, was there? He didn't preach here and he isn't buried here either."

Heinrich closed his eyes and shook his head dismissively. "Oh no, no, no, of course not. But there is a tradition, which may be true, that St. Paul was in Spain preaching to Jews who were living on the south coast at the time. In the Letter to the Romans, he promises to visit Rome on his way to Spain. And in the Acts of the Apostles he says he was commanded by God to "be a light of the Gentiles, that thou should be for salvation unto the ends of the earth, meaning Finisterre."

"You know the Bible well," I commented.

"We're Lutherans," beamed Else. "We belong to a Bible study group in our church."

Later we strolled back to the hotel along the Ruavieja, Logroño's "old street," a pleasant haven away from the drab and tinny modern city. Its famous bodegas were just starting to come alive, and now, I thought, it would have been nice to share a bottle of Rioja wine. Instead, we chatted outside our rooms in the dim hotel hallway. The faint scent of cleaning liquid drifted like a ghost along the walls. Scott produced the Everest Guide and our Michelin map and together we examined possible cycling routes until the warm weight of fatigue came over us all, and we said goodnight.

Getting ready for bed that night, I thought back to our dinner conversation. Before the Romans, it was as if the Spanish landscape had occupied the people, and not the other way around. Land was an instinct, something that a bison hunter or a megalith builder or a Celtic shaman would have understood without even having to feel it, like a pulse, or breathing during sleep. The Romans must have disrupted that implicit mysticism when they clanked off their ships onto the Mediterranean shore. Now there were soldiers and miners and slave-drivers in Spain, and a new geographical idea - the province. Under the Romans, Iberia became a political unit and a commodity, something you could measure and divide and parcel out. Over three centuries, the peninsula turned and bubbled within its boundaries like a fertilized egg inside its sac: first it was two provinces, then three, and then, by 297 AD, five. In the northwest, Galicia remained where it had always been, while Tarraconensis ran across the north and northeast chunk of the peninsula. South of it, ballooning out to the east coast from a wedge in the meseta was Carthaginensis, whose name reminded me of those world-changing battles of nearly five hundred years earlier. To the west, where Portugal is now, was Lusitania; in the southwest corner was prosperous Baetica.

No one at dinner had mentioned Spain's Roman roads, but we ourselves had been on one only two days earlier. Just west of Puente de Reina on the way to Estella is the hilltop town of Ciraqui. Once a Basque place called, ominously, Town of Vipers, Ciraqui gazes with benign solemnity upon the soft farmlands of Navarra. When its 13th-century church is open, which it wasn't, you can apparently see a Roman votive altar stone on display. We bought oranges and some packaged flan in a signless little store nearby, then took our bikes onto a bumpy road a short distance down the hill toward the main highway. The stones of the old road, pocked and misplaced now, made rough riding. But Scott was jubilant. A Roman road! And as if that were not enough, in only a moment, we were on a Roman bridge: a single arch like a huge wheel fallen from an ancient piece of heavy equipment. The bridge had a dismembered look and was in ruins on one side; we had to dismount to get onto it. But you could still see in its well engineered lines the reassuring pragmatism of Roman technology.

We had eaten our snack on that bridge, our legs dangling over the wrecked stone arch. I watched the road wobble disjointedly to the modern highway and disappear up a small hill on the other side. Roman roads, I thought, seemed so rational, a deed enacted by the brain's left hemisphere to organize the marvellous Spanish landscape. Against the aesthetic and spiritual, the roads stood for the pragmatic and the material. I had seen schematic diagrams of a Roman road: first the U-shaped channel dug in the track after the road bed had been surveyed, then the *statumen*, big stones that filled the bottom of the U. Next came a shallow row of smaller stones mixed with lime and sand, the *rudus*, and then the *nucleus*, finer, like gravel, something you could really skin your knees on. The top layer was called the *summum dorsum*: blocks of cut stone the size of big bricks and covering the whole road in a slight arc to drain water to the ditches.

As soon as they arrived in Hispania, the Romans had set about building a network of highways for getting soldiers and supplies around the peninsula. In a land where rivers were few and not easily navigated, it was the Roman road, doubtless trailing earlier informal roads of the Celts and Iberians, but improved beyond recognition, that would be the crucial link among people of the peninsula for nearly two millenia. Along them would travel not just soldiers, but merchants and slaves and settlers. And missionaries. Christianity. Islam. Crusaders. And pilgrims.

The highways were relatively safe during the first two centuries of Roman rule. There were postal and relay stations, and the routes were marked every few kilometres with *milenaria*, tall stone pillars that looked a little like dolmens, but gave only mundane information about distances and who had built the road. Cities sprouted along the highways, though these were few and modest: there was nothing much between Pamplona and Astorga, and only León, where the only Roman legion in Spain was stationed, had military importance.

A list of the roads in northern Spain reads like an anatomy of the circulatory system, complete with Latin and vernacular names. One highway began in the west, leaving Brigantium (Coruña) on the Atlantic coast for Lucus Augusti (Lugo) and Legio (León), then running, at times a little off the present Camino, to Pompaelo (Pamplona). At Pompaelo, it joined the tin route coming over the Pyrenees from Burdigala (Burgundy) in France. A road coming in from the southwest at Caesaraugusta (Saragosa) continued on through Ilerda (Lérida) on the way down to Tarraco (Tarragona) on the Mediterranean coast. A shunt ran north from Caesaraugusta to Pompaelo. In the west of Spain, another artery wiggled up from Gades (Cádiz) on the coast to Hispalis (Sevilla), through Augusta Emerita, (Mérida) and Salamantica (Salamanca) all the way to Asturica Augusta (Astorga). A route in Portugal left Olisipo (Lisbon), carrying supplies north all the way to Iria Flavia. In fact, most of the roads in the west came in at Iria Flavia on the banks of the Rio Sar. Sometime in the early years of the Christian era, the body of St. James would come ashore near here, in a stone boat all the way from Jerusalem, accompanied by angels.

As Heinrich had put it, the Camino was the result of a chain of events that began when Rome had branded its culture onto the religious landscape of prehistoric Spain. What defined the Camino, he had said, agreeing completely with the monk Prieto, was its Christianity. But in Spain, that Christianity was many centuries in the making. "A lot of things needed to happen before the Camino could ever be conceived," Heinrich had said, "and only a few of them had to do with James."

The Romans had brought their state religion with them to the peninsula: rituals celebrating the institutions of the Empire, including the Emperor himself. For many people, this kind of state-engineered religion was too meaningless to take seriously. More imaginative sects attracted the disenchanted, the disenfranchised, the bored, and the intellectually frustrated. These were cults that promised salvation, esoteric understanding, inner transformation: the cults of Osiris, Mithra, Attis, Demeter, and the cult of the dead and risen god from Palestine, Jesus Christ. Heinrich had mentioned six Roman missionaries who were known to have preached in Spain. These, I later learned, had arrived sometime in the first century, and begun their work in the southern province of Baetica. Their names sounded more like rivers or instruments of torture than missionaries, but there they were, inscribed in the 8th-century Mozarab liturgy of the Spanish Mass: Torquatus, Indalecius, Euphrasius, Cecilius, Ctesiphon and Hesichius.

Christianity crept north from Baetica along Roman roads through Sevilla, Córdoba, Mérida, Toledo. It appealed to city folk mainly. Considering that over ninety-five percent of Spain was rural at the time, the number of Christians was not large. But the new faith, with its uncompromising message, took Rome by surprise. Like all revolutionary religions, which it was at the time, it threatened the imperial order. Between 285 and 305, Christians were tortured and executed with heart-sinking regularity by Emperors Decius, Valerian and Diocletian. The slain were at once transfigured into martyr heroes. Christian communities laid claim to the relics of their own special victims, or else stole them from somewhere else: the 12-year old St. Eulalia in Mérida, Spain's only virgin martyr, "scorched by fierce flame" as Bede puts it; Saints Vincent and Valerius, martyred in Valencia, but taken over by Saragosa; St. Saturninus, tied by the neck to an angry bull and yanked to his death in Toulouse in 250, later claimed as a patron by the city of Pamplona, where he had briefly preached. The young St. Zoilo was put to death in 301 in Córdoba. Seven hundred years later, his relics were brought north to the monastery named after him in Carrión de los Condes. The pilgrim hostel connected with that monastery was one of the most eminent on the Camino, mainly for its impressive Córdoban relics.

The persecutions hit Catalonia very hard. Here Christianity had a more sophisticated style; many Christians were cosmopolitan slaves and merchants with connections to Italy, Gaul and Africa. Drawn by this intellectual cultivation, and by its deliciously lugubrious martyrs' history, the church in Spain little by little shifted its centre of gravity north. Christian communities spread out along the roads from Catalonia to Astorga and León. They had bishops in Saragosa and Astorga before 4th Century, and a Church Council was held in Saragosa in the 380s.

The lamps of the church were lighting up every town in its turn along the highways of northern Spain. By the time Emperor Theodosius the Great, himself of Spanish origin, outlawed paganism in the late 4th Century, Christianity had seeded itself in the protoplasm of Spanish culture. It had a peculiarly passionate inflection; despite the large number of true scholars it produced, it was a faith of devotion, not intellectual argument. Spain was on its way to becoming tenaciously, combatively, perhaps unthinkingly Christian.

Our discussions with Heinrich and Else reminded me of the story of the Asturian priest Priscillian and his strange, slightly repellent Gnostic heresy. Gnosticism was just one of many cults in Spain that competed with the new Christian religion. In 1878, a gnostic carving of the sun and moon over a temple facade with an open hand was found at Astorga. On it is inscribed: *Eis Zeus Serapis Iaw*, or Zeus, Serapis and Jahweh are One. Gnostic ideas were eastern: there was no shortage of esoteric views circulating among the ranks of eastern mercenaries on assignment in Northern Spain, or among Asturian soldiers just home from Egypt. Priscillian may have picked up some of his ideas from an obscure Egyptian Gnostic named Marcus.

Priscillian's heresy is only slightly clearer than his sources, but in its broad strokes, it shows the future face of Spanish religion: tender devotion mixed with sadistic fanaticism, harsh toward the body, oblivious to pain, attracted to the mystical. Priscillian, who apparently was a vegetarian, preached a dramatic asceticism and a highly personal, emotional relationship between the Christian soul and the Holy Word. He believed that matter was evil in origin, that astrology was true. Oddly perhaps for a man of such extremes, he seems to have been an attractive figure. His instruction, a blend of Christian melodrama and Gnostic severity, fell on fertile ground. He was of course considered dangerous by the orthodox. His teachings were condemned and he was beheaded in Treveris in 385. In one tradition his body was taken to Astorga; in another, it lies in the wall of an old Celtic temple near Lugo, taken over by the Romans and in the 4th Century, turned into the Chapel of Santa Eulalia. A third tradition holds that it is really Priscillian who was found at Iria Flavia by Theodorus in the 830s and whose bones lie now in the crypt of Santiago Cathedral.

Between Estella and Viana, Scott and I had stopped at the Monastery of Irache, said to be on the site of an old Visigothic religious centre. A community of Benedictines has resided here since 958. Irache is a quiet place set against the flat-topped cliffs of Navarra. It was sunny as we pulled up. I could hear the heat in the dry twist of our tires on the driveway leading to the building. Beyond was a park full of trees. The monastery, whose walls had the colour and texture of a nutmeg, was impeccably simple, with tile roofs, a few small round windows here and there, and a low tower at one end. The bell tower, which stood higher, was square and had a military austerity. Built into a side wall of the monastery was a fountain with a coat of arms above it. We had read about this in our guidebooks: a wine fountain. I held my water bottle to the spigot, and out poured an excellent red wine, a gift that had been offered by the monks to pilgrims since the Middle Ages. This was our introduction to the generosity of Camino *hospitaleros*, men and women who instead of going themselves to Santiago, made it their business to provide for the well-being of those who did.

We toured the monastery briefly, then sat against a tree in the park sipping our wine. A Dutch tour bus had pulled into the parking lot, and tourists were streaming from its door. Squinting into the sunshine as if they had just wakened up, they followed one another in a line to the monastery entrance.

If Irache really was Visigothic, then its history goes back almost to the 5th Century. The Visigoths were on the end of a wave of Germanic invaders who had already been tearing at Europe for a hundred years. In England, it had been the Angles, the Saxons, and the Jutes. Here in Spain, it was the Vandals, the Alans, and the terrible Suevi, who were the worst of all, and who settled in Galicia.

Before leaving for Spain, I had tried to get through a history of the Germanic tribes in Spain. They were, I learned, forever squabbling among themselves, and the Romans were quick to play one off against another. After a while, I was turned off by the utter pointlessness of knowing who attacked whom, knowing that eventually they were all going to go down anyway. But I did remember that by 448, the Suevi, expanding southward, held almost all of Spain, including Mérida and Sevilla. It was at this point that the Visigoths entered Spain from Gaul, invited by Rome to help them against the Suevi. The Visigoths defeated the Suevi at Astorga in the 450s. The defense bases that were established in Spain over the next fifty years were the beginning of the Visigothic presence in the lands around the future Camino.

Eventually, the Visigoths eliminated both the Romans and their own Germanic rivals, though the Basque, Cantabrian and Asturian tribes in the north would remain every bit the headache they had been for the Romans. By 569, the Visigothic King Leovigild held most of Spain from his base in Toledo. In 574, he sacked the Celtiberian stronghold of Varea, the hilltop town Scott and I had passed just east of Logroño. It took Leovigild until 585 to beat back the Suevi in Galicia, and he never got Cantabria. But by now Roman power had vanished, though Roman culture had not, and Visigothic Spain was as unified as it was ever going to be.

It was a theological problem that the Visigoths faced now. Although they were Christian, they diverged from orthodox Roman doctrine because they did not believe that the Trinity was formed equally of the Father, the Son and the Holy Spirit. Instead, they held that the Son Jesus was subordinate to God the Father.

"I can see their point," Scott had said when we talked about this. "Sons are not the same as fathers. Did it make any difference to how they behaved? I mean are you a better person if you believe that the Son and the Father and the Holy Spirit are the same thing?"

I said it didn't seem so.

In Spain, the two churches - Trinitarian Roman and the Arian Visigothic - eyed each other warily; occasionally there was hostility. In 589, Leovigild's son, Recarred, converted himself and his nation to the Trinitarian side. Reccared also founded the monk Prieto's monastery of Santo Domingo at Silos, which has thrived or endured, one way or another, over the centuries. Today it is known for its Christmas recordings of Gregorian Chant.

Recarred's reign was the beginning of a united Spain that would last two and a half centuries. Celtiberians, Carthaginians, Romans, and all the misfit and leftover Germanic settlers like the Suevi and the Alans, were now one, at least in name, under the Visigothic court. Over the next two centuries, the Visigothic kings would patch up many of the big holes in the Christian fabric that lay over Spain. It was also during these years that Spanish Christianity, which always had a fervid, mystical tone, began to show signs of belligerence and intolerance. It was tightly organized, noticeably anti-semitic, and highly disciplined.

The Dutch tourists were returning from their visit to the monastery. We were approached by a man from the group who had seen our bikes and wanted to ask us about cycling on the Camino. He was delighted by what he was seeing from the bus windows, but wanted to see more of the Camino outdoors. He doubted he would have enough time to walk the whole route. Scott showed him our Guides and maps, and we gave him the email address for the Confraternity of St. James.

"I'm sure there's a confraternity in Holland too," Scott said.

"Sanks for ze advice," he said, waving and smiling as he returned to the bus. "Next year, for sure, I come back!"

By the 7th Century, the Visigothic Church was Spain's weightiest social institution and its biggest landowner. Bishops were accumulating land; there were constant quarrels over rents and taxes. Small villages along the remote Roman roads in the north now had their own churches. Several of these would later be rebuilt as Camino cathedrals.

In the spring of 1999, I would make a brief journey to Spain to walk along a portion of the *Via de la Plata*, the pilgrimage route that ran north and south between Sevilla and Astorga. Near the town of Alcuéscar was the Visigothic church of Santa Lucia. To get there, I walked two and a half kilometres along a dirt road on a forested hillside. The church was set into a wide clearing in the forest. A rough lawn ran around the building. In front were a couple of wildflower bushes, a pile of sand, and a mobile cement mixer. I took a picture of the east end of the church: it was a blocky affair with three grated arched windows, and a roof redone in galvanized steel. Overall, the place had a pleasant sturdiness, like a friendly old bulldog bitch. This season, it was being restored. Birdsong, an incessant, chirpy little bark, hung on the hollow sound of tapping hammers.

I stepped through the church doorway into a cool bath of dust and must. At the end of the narrow nave were three chapels under simple horseshoe arches. There was no altar. Chunks of plaster were peeling from the stone walls. A little light leaked in through small, high windows. Now and then, a pair of wings beat tremulously above me like a shiver down the spine, and a thin peep streaked briefly in the dusty air under the ceiling. The church was dry, primitive, confident, a little argumentative perhaps, as if transfixed in some perturbation about the Trinity. It would be easy to worship here, if you were a straight-laced believer.

Stone, earth, a bit of light: Santa Lucia had traces of the illogical splendour of a painted cave. But sitting there, I had a boxed in feeling, as if something had been attenuated. Likely, I was imposing upon this church the impression I had gotten from my reading, that Visigothic Christians were bent on erasing, or at best, masking earlier religious culture in Spain. For all its success in the royal court, Spanish Christianity was still a small planetary system in a pagan universe. The Visigoths had to work hard to replace old magic with new religion and to plow ancient spiritual grounds into respectable Christian landscapes. The most important Spanish book of the period was Paulus Orosius' *Seven Books of History against the Pagans*. In the 6th Century, San Martín of Braga could be heard fussing about his heathen parishioners. And even a century later, the Council of Toledo had to make rulings against the worship of trees and stones. Visigothic Christianity made me think of canned soup: the label says beef, but most of it is broth from something else.

Sam Keen says in *Apology for Wonder* that when Christian theologians announced that God could not be known in natural events but only in special miracles enacted in history, they destroyed the presence of the holy at the heart of the everyday. Reciprocity with nature's flow and rhythm, the sense of eternal movement in the spiral, the cycles of birth and death, were replaced by different views: God was to be sought in the history and in the intellect of his people, not in the rhythms of nature, in the Scriptures and liturgy rather than in the forms of the land. The worship of the divine in nature, on hilltops, in caves, by fountains, shifted to the veneration of human beings: Christian martyrs and saints. Visigothic monasteries, like monasteries throughout Europe at the time, began to produce saint's lives by the hundreds, while the original spirits of the fountain, the grove, and the mountain peak were fading like ancient cave paintings exposed to air.

James the Apostle was not a highly visible saint in Visigothic Spain. The early Spanish Church never went in for having its own apostle the way that Rome had St. Peter. But St. Jerome, that brilliant theologian-grouch who lived in Palestine in the 4th Century, claimed that James had preached in Spain and was buried there too. And an old text from the 5th Century, the *Breviarium Apostolorum*, translated in the 6th or 7th Century from Byzantine Greek into Latin, gives a list of where the apostles preached. James, the son of Zebedee and brother of John, it says, preached in Spain "and the West." Back in Palestine, it goes on, James was beheaded with the sword during the reign of Herod and was buried in a place called Achaia Marmárica. It may have been Jerome's comment, along with the odd and unreliable *Breviarum*, that gave rise to the belief that James preached in Spain. Wherever it came from, the idea got around: Aldhelm, the English Bishop of Malmesbury who died in 709, believed that James had converted the Spanish nations.

There is only one Visigothic reference - interpolated by an unknown writer - in San Isidore's *On the Birth and Death of the Fathers*, from around 650, that says James preached and was buried in Spain. But in the same century, a Bishop Odoario established a Church of Santiago de Meilan in Lugo. Then there is the very odd "Letter of Pope Leo," forged but supposedly written by the Bishop-Patriarch of Jerusalem and sent round the Western Roman Empire sometime around 500 AD. Leo, we are told, was visited by four of James' followers who had just returned from Galicia. Their report: after James was beheaded in Jerusalem, his body had been gathered by several disciples and placed in a boat. The boat made a seven-day voyage to the western coast of Spain. Near Iria Flavia, the saint was buried with two disciples "*in arcas marmoreals.*" Leo's letter advises all Christians to go to the tomb, "for verily there lies hidden St. James."

This *arcas marmóreas* has caused confusion. In the *Breviarum*, it may have meant a place, perhaps the Greek city of Marmarikes. But texts get slippery when they are copied one from another. Scribes make errors, miss a line, distort a context, or change passages with new facts. And so *arcas marmóreas* slithered like a chameleon around the manuscripts, appearing as *achaia marmárica*, *arce marmarica*, *in arcis marmaricis*. In some sources, the place name was turned into an architectural term, leaving James buried somewhere *sub arcis marmaricis* - in a marble sarcophagus - perhaps under (*sub*) an arch.

On the eve of the arrival of Islamic armies at Gibraltar, the Camino was still just another Roman road, leading west through towns, estates, occasionally a city, and dotted with a few churches and semi-Christian holy places. Along it travelled powerful churchmen, ruminating about doctrine, planning their next land takeover, deciding a dispute. With them went arrogant nobles, uncouth even in their relative wealth, wary, well-to-do Jews, and slaves from all over. Then there were all the farmers, with their skinny wives and grimy kids, feeling the hard Roman stones under their feet and the weather on their backs. The road ran past Celtic fortresses, abandoned Roman *castros*. It crossed rivers with their magic dribbling away, and detoured around mysterious stone markers and bands of grass strangling old tombs. It passed the hunting grounds of the old cave dwellers. In the distance were the mountains, still home to resistant tribes, where, inside and unknown to all, divine bison silently roamed the walls. The land danced with spirits and demons, and believers of all kinds crossed themselves and uttered charms at haunted places to make sure Jesus, or some deity of their own devising, took care of them. Some prayed to Jesus' disciple, the good St. James, whose named floated here and there like a whisper over the landscape.

Before leaving Logroño, we ate breakfast with Heinrich and Else. They would spend the day exploring the churches of the town, so we parted at the hotel door. We bought lunch fixings in a cluttered little shop, then set off through modern Logroño along an endless downtown street, past gas stations, the dump and what the Everest Guide euphemistically called an "industrial estate."

The Camino to Navarette was an easy ride beside rolling fields. The limpid landscapes were tossing with morning birdsong and laced with sunshine and a few rainclouds. Big pillows of wildflowers, scarlet and saffron and lavender, nestled in the grasses beside the trail. In the rain that inevitably fell, their colours had brightened like blown coals.

By Navarette the sun was out again. We sat on a bench in an elevated square by the Church of the Assumption and unpacked our lunch: cheese, meat, bread, olives, avocados, strawberries, pears, cakes and chocolate. We ate with an addict's euphoria. Afterward we rested in the sun, watching the locals mill around the fountain in the centre of the square: an old round woman walked her dog; four boys skiddered by on skateboards; a couple of old men gossiped on a far bench.

Coming outside after seeing the Church, we were greeted by two young women filling their water bottles at the fountain. They were from Belgium, were walking all the way from there to Santiago. In France, they had trekked twenty-five kilometres a day with one day in every ten for a break. Their backpacks were taut like sacs of flour. They were tanned and fit and very thirsty on this sunny afternoon.

"Where did you stay when you were trekking down through France?" Scott asked.

"In our tent," said one. "We didn't have enough money for anything else in France. In a field or under some trees. In Spain we stay mostly at the hostels. Sometimes we still camp, though."

Scott asked if they were planning to walk home.

"Probably not all the way; we have to go back to school in the fall. We'll walk back as far as we can, and if we run out of time, we'll take the train."

"Why are you doing this?" I asked. This was not good Camino etiquette. Reasons for pilgrimage are private, and it is considered rude to be inquisitive. But their journey was so ambitious that I wanted to know what was behind it.

I needn't have worried about etiquette, for the answer was simple enough. "We love to hike and camp," said one. "We enjoy the challenge. The landscape has been very beautiful everywhere."

The other smiled merrily, lifting her eyebrows. "*C'est magique!*"

I watched them walk together off the square. The taller one stopped to adjust the strap of her pack, hoisting the load with a heavy jerk toward her shoulders. She quickened her step to catch up, and they both disappeared around the corner out of town.

We packed up our bikes to leave. The sun's rays were piercing, and they glanced around the stone square as if in search of something. I was mulling over "*C'est magique!*"

"I wonder what those two think about what they're doing," I said.

"It's what they told you. They like hiking and camping. It's just natural. They don't *have* to think about it. Most natural things are unthinking. I mean not self-conscious or overly analytical. Walking, for instance, the way they do, it just flows out of your body. Isn't that where a pilgrimage really starts? In your body. It knows it wants to move, so off it goes. You don't have to get fancy. Ask a paleolithic nomad. He's confident; he just goes. It's your mind that gets confused about what to do and where you're going."

I watched Scott shove one foot into a toe-clip, and then, gliding his bike into the square, toss the other leg effortlessly over the seat. I joined him and side by side we coasted to the corner, swung right and headed out of town. In a few moments, we caught up with the Belgians. They had hit their stride by now. As they sashayed down the road, their legs swung like pendulums under their backpacks. They grinned and waved when we passed them.

That night we slept in an expensive *parador* in the town of Santo Domingo de la Calzada. We were, we had realized after Navarette, carrying too much gear; if we stayed at the *parador*, they would let us leave some of our things in storage there. We would pick them up in a couple of weeks on our way back from Santiago by car.

Twisted column in the cloister of Monastery of Silos, carved by a Christian acculturated to Moorish styles or by a Moorish emigree. Arabic tradition inserted imperfections into artistic works to show that man could not attain the perfection of Allah.

3

MOORS

*Therefore, the quiddity of things, which is the truth of
beings, is unattainable in its purity; all philosophers
have sought it, none has found it, such as it is; and
the more we shall be profoundly learned in this
ignorance, the more we shall approach truth itself.*
Nicholas of Cusa, <u>On Learned Ignorance</u>

*The inescapable conclusion is that the true location of
the world, of its countries, mountains, rivers, and
cities, happens to lie in the eye of the beholder. Only
there does (sic) its individual features partake of that
dream quality that one associates with invention.*
James Cowan, <u>A Mapmaker's Dream</u>

*What is the imagination if not the transformation of
experience into knowledge?*
*Carlos Fuentes. From a newspaper interview
read while waiting for a train.*

*Ruins of a Moorish castle west of Vega del Valcarce,
guarding the pass to the summit of El Cebreiro.*

My second Camino journey began in August of 1998. I would be alone for this trip, walking instead of cycling. My plan was to start for Santiago from Pamplona, the city Scott and I had by-passed the year before. After Pamplona, I would be going through the same towns and cities I had seen in 1997, but keeping to more of the narrow Camino paths than we had with our bikes. I had a feeling of familiarity with what I was about to see. It was the walking that was new.

I had been in the air a long time, having flown from Toronto across the Atlantic to London the day before. This morning I was heading towards Madrid over a crystalline landscape. To the northwest, a range of mountains receded on earth's barely perceptible curve into the horizon. Directly below me, a patchwork of farmlands moved north with deliberate slowness, brilliant rectangles of green and ripening autumn yellow slashed with rivers of magenta and silver. We came in over the meseta, a high plate of land the colour of bleached deer hide, home only to bugs and scorch-resistant grasses, horizontal except where its flat top gave way suddenly into clawed-out valleys. In the distance I could see Madrid, a cluster of metallic cubes in an enormous petrie dish of meseta, dense in the centre, with thinning colonies extruding into the land around. The city's high-rise towers grew larger as we descended, and their windows winked in the noon sun's glint.

Madrid was in the middle of Spain, north of the Rio Tajo and a good distance south of the Duero. Under the Romans and the Visigoths, major settlement never got much further north than this. North African Berbers, those moody, underdog tribesmen used by the Arabs for their invasions in Spain, sometimes ended up here, having been contemptuously tossed these bleak chunks of land in payment for a grudging loyalty. But mostly, the land that stretched up from Madrid to the Duero valley was where, between 711 and 1492 AD, Christians and Muslims had fought it out for the soul of Spain. Looking down on the meseta now, I could just imagine Moorish troops riding northward in pools of dust, their horses' heads rocking over the pale earth and the sun's rays darting off their shields.

From Madrid, I took a bus to Soria. A weather sign near my hotel said the temperature was 42 degrees Centigrade. That night I slept ten hours, and when I wakened my nose felt dried crisp. I bought a litre and a half of water and boarded another bus, an immaculate, ultra-modern affair, for Pamplona. We jiggled out of the city and picked up speed on the highway, with the acoustic guitars of Pink Floyd wailing on the sound system. Beyond the windows, the meseta passed in slow-motion, desiccated and littered with low, boxy hills. The yellow fields had all been shaved to a spiky brush-cut; gaunt groves of timber stood along their borders. On a silent video screen mounted by my seat, Cindy Crawford gunned her way through a violent movie. I wanted to keep my eyes on the scenes outside, but the grisly scuffles kept triggering my attention like a recurrent dream.

I was coming into Basque lands. Basque place names are bizarre - Lizarra, Iturgaíz, Egozkue, Iroz - and give no clue to the origin of this odd, defiant race. Wherever they came from, the Basques seem to have had a hereditary talent, a twist of DNA as contorted as their language, for setting everybody on edge. They arrived here before the Celts and were already well-known trouble-makers when Pamplona was founded in 75 BC. The Romans were never really able to manage them, though like an exasperated high school teacher, they did pound a little Latin into them. Pamplona had its own bishop by 589, but Visigothic preachers were sorely tried, and the Basque conversion to Christianity was sketchy. Rebellions were a constant headache. The Visigothic King Rodrigo was here in Navarra fighting Basques the day the Moors landed at Gibraltar in 711.

The Moors inherited the Basque problem when they took Spain, getting themselves thrown out of Pamplona in 740 and defeated in other battles over the next few years. Charlemagne and his Franks had no more luck than anybody else and finally resorted, in a pique, to destroying Pamplona's walls, for which it is thought, though Einhard was not specific on this point, the king was attacked by Basques at Roncesvalles. Charlemagne's son, Louis, had some success in 806 when he took Pamplona. But the Basques continued to make a royal pest of themselves. In 824 there was a second battle at Roncesvalles when they again crushed the Franks. Later, a Basque Pamplona became the headquarters of a small independent kingdom under a Christian king, Inigo Arista. In the early 10th Century, the region fell into the hands of another local, who became King Sancho Garcia I. This was a lucky turn in the royal line. Within a hundred years, Pamplona was flourishing under Sancho III as one of the premiere Navarrese towns on the Camino.

During the pilgrimage years, Sancho promoted French immigration to Pamplona. Among the newcomers were ambitious French entrepreneurs and artisans, some of them former pilgrims who, piety aside, couldn't help but notice the business opportunities in the area. Sancho set aside two districts of Pamplona for the French: San Cernin and San Nicolás. But the very success of the project became a problem: the two upstart French colonies squabbled with each other and with the Spanish-Basque old-timers. The mood was tense, and no doubt many innocent pilgrims, walking wearily through the city at dusk in search of a hostel, were caught in the crossfire of gang wars and brawls.

Pamplona was a moneyed city, but snappish and prone to conflict. Disputes even plagued the sweet-tempered Franciscan friars here. When St. Francis arrived on his way to Santiago in the 13th Century, he was asked to mediate among the factions. A statue in the old town was erected to honour his peace-making efforts, but the quarreling went on until the 15th Century.

In 1521, during a spate of religious warfare, Pamplona was once again attacked by the French. A certain Inigo López de Loyola, son of a Basque nobleman, was seriously wounded in the fighting. During his convalescence, Inigo immersed himself in books and found himself drawn to the lives of Jesus and the saints. Later he dragged his war-lamed leg on a pilgrimage to Jerusalem. He returned with a missionary's zeal and moved to Paris, where he studied theology and planned a trip to Palestine to convert the Muslims. But new wars prevented the journey. After consultations with the Pope, Inigo, or as we now know him, Ignatius Loyola, founded the Society of Jesus whose members, the Jesuits, would eventually take Christianity around the world.

Among Loyola's first disciples was the great missionary saint of south India and Japan, Francis Xavier, also a Basque, born near Pamplona in 1506. His body lies now in Goa, in the Basilica of Bom Jesu, where pilgrims arrive daily. Every ten years Xavier's relics are placed on display and the pilgrimage goes wild: throngs of Indians, Christianity draped like a new cloak on their Hindu souls, press into the nave of Bom Jesu to pray - for reasons great and small - to the corpse of a Pamplonan saint.

It was an interesting pattern: Xavier, the missionary saint from a Basque family, disciple of the great Basque Loyola, gone off to an utterly pagan land and buried there; the big church built for him, the motley pilgrim throngs. Change the names and countries and you have Jesus' disciple James, a Jewish Christian, arriving from Jerusalem in far-off Spain, buried there in a pagan landscape, attracting pilgrims from all over.

Pilgrimage has its own inconclusive logic, cares not a whit about historical or even theological coherence. Shuns it, in fact, and requires instead, in order to happen at all, a fertile chaos of faith and landscapes and human remains. We go forth "through the fields" pulled by an open-ended imperative far more artistic than logical. If pilgrimage were rational and made absolute sense, our legs would never move.

It took a long while to find the pilgrims' *refugio* in Pamplona. I asked an elderly man on the street where it was, and by way of reply he took my arm and led me there himself. But the place was already full. I was given directions to the alternate *refugio*, through the parklands of the old Ciudadela and into a modern district where high-rises stood like missiles in the hot pavement. The hostel was in a building that resembled a 1960s high school. A woman at the registration desk casually gestured me into a cavernous gymnasium lined on one side with bunk beds and on the other with mattresses. Outside, the air had been heaving with sunshine; now I was suddenly chilly. Only a few pilgrims had arrived so far today and the place had a tinny, echoing silence. Choosing the floor over a bunk, I picked a foam mattress from the pile, unrolled my sleeping bag and organized my pack. I took a tepid shower, then went outside once again, up the long road past the monolithic apartment blocks and across the Ciudadela to the old town.

Like many medieval pilgrims, I went first to San Cernin's, a fortress of a church dedicated to the 3rd-century martyr of Toulouse who had preached for a time in Pamplona. A bronze plaque by the church marks the well where he had baptised new Christians. Cernin had a missionary friend named Honestus, who was the tutor of Pamplona's first bishop, a St. Firminus. Firminus is said to have returned to France and been martyred in 287 at Amiens, but Pamplona still claims him. It is on his feast day every July that dumb, hell-bent bulls and foolhardy men chase each other through the streets of old Pamplona.

I stayed a long while in the Church of San Cernin. Its air was cool, its darkness translucent like ice on a dark river. Slender candle flames sent shadows shivering up the walls into the nave. Around me were many statues, one of St. James. A priest in street clothes crossed to the pulpit and began, silently, to rehearse his sermon. I watched him mouth his words and gesture for emphasis, then lean over his notes to scribble in some changes. I had never seen a priest rehearse a sermon. It was like watching a magician practise a technique. I kept my eye on that priest, feeling vaguely as if I was in on a secret, as if he was revealing something he shouldn't. In a while, he stopped his silent sermon and gathered his notes, peering steadily at me over his half-frames as if he had overheard my musing. Then he walked to the centre of the apse and knelt low toward the altar. I looked away and when I looked back, he had vanished.

San Cernin shares patronage of Pamplona with Our Lady of the Camino. One day long ago, an image of the Virgin vanished from a church in a distant village, only to show up in Pamplona at San Cernin's. Our Lady was carted back to her village home several times but always managed to return. In the end, a chapel was built for her in San Cernin's, and here she has remained.

Nowhere else along the Camino is the Virgin so venerated as in Navarra. In Pamplona Cathedral, some streets away from San Cernin's, she stands on the high altar as the Virgin del Sagrario, patron saint of Navarra. To the west in the nearby town of Gazólaz is a Romanesque church dedicated to Our Lady of the Candles, who is honoured every February 2 in the Feast of the Purification. Before the Christian conversion, this site likely saw action in Roman festivals for Demeter and Ceres, and even, some guess, in megalithic rites honouring the Great Mother.

Down the street from Pamplona's four-tiered wedding cake of a town hall stands the Museum of Navarra, in a building that in the 16th Century had been the Hospital of Our Lady of Mercy. I arrived half an hour before the place closed and went in at once. I was in search of one object: an ivory reliquary made in a workshop near Córdoba early in the 11th Century.

It sat in a glass cabinet in the middle of an almost empty room, a rectangular chest just under two feet long, covered on all sides with lacy white ivory and glittering like an artistocrat's eyes. A Moorish craftsman had made it whose name was Faray.

I walked around the cabinet, peering at the chest through the glass. Along one side, Faray had carved a nobleman with servants and musicians in the gardens of his palace; on other panels were dueling elephants, a jousting tournament, hunting scenes with hounds and falcons, animals and birds, lions felling a deer. Around these scenes were devotional sayings and blessings. Here too Faray had inscribed the name, in Cufic, of the person to whom the casket was dedicated: Abd al-Malik, a man about whom I would later learn much more.

Whatever Al-Malik had used this casket for - rich garments, jewels, books - when it came into Christian possession (however that happened) it would house nothing less than the Holy Grail itself - that great goblet adorned by angels with the emeralds flung from Lucifer's forehead as he tumbled out of heaven, the very cup used by Jesus at the Last Supper, and by Joseph of Arimethea to collect blood from His side as He hung on the cross. As everyone knows, Parsifal, great Knight of the Round Table, had recovered the Grail, but who, I wondered, knew that it had been placed in Faray's ivory chest? For years, grail and chest travelled around Europe, passing through many pious hands before arriving at the Benedictine monastery of Leyre, just east of Pamplona. Astonishingly, at this point, the Grail was lost track of. But the chest was chosen to hold the relics of two Christian sisters, Nunilona and Alodia, beheaded at nearby Huesca in 851 during the reign of Abd al-Rahman II. Eventually it went with its martyrs' relics to Sanguesa. In 1836, it was taken to Pamplona Cathedral and in 1953, on a steep final descent from the mystical to the touristic, it landed, without so much as one holy bone inside, here in the Museum of Navarra.

No one else was here at this late hour. The light from the window was fading. In the silence, I looked at the casket once more from the doorway. Its ivory shone with a sly brightness in the dimming room.

Outside, the streetlights in Old Pamplona hung by the buildings like big white dots. A breeze was awakening a town that had been paralyzed all day with heat. The locals, glad to be out, ambled along cobbled avenues. I heard what sounded like a medieval shawm blaring over the firecracker tap of a drum. In a small square near the

Church of Santo Domingo (an important Camino church, according to my Everest Guide), a parade was gearing up for Domingo's festival. Two men were playing horns while a lady with a creased brown face and a bright kerchief energetically whipped her tin drums. Little girls danced with small, clownish puppets. Four huge paper maché mannequins sat on stools at the edge of the square, each one dressed as a church official in a skirt and lace surplice and, on its outsized head, a gold-painted mitre. Suddenly four plump boys in t-shirts, shorts and running shoes hurried to the stools, effortlessly lifted both stool and puppet onto their shoulders, and began dancing in a circle. Now the mannequins were taller than ever, twirling and tottering around the square to a cacophony of drums and horns.

I sat on the plaza steps. Pairs of Adidas jig-stepped beneath the puppets, whose skirts flared like the robes of dervishes. The breeze, catching the skirts, lifted them higher to reveal a set of wooden stool legs. One bishop came unbuttoned at the back, and the body of a little boy, his head hidden by the stool, appeared inside like an internal mechanism.

I followed the puppets as they danced into the street. Out of their huge immobile faces, unsmiling eyes thickly rimmed with some kind of ecclesiastical eyeliner stared into the air over the crowd, deaf to the raucous music.

I left the parade and turned in the direction of Pamplona Cathedral. At a cross street, a new melody met me: the nimble notes of Scarlatti. I bought food in a store nearby and hurried back to where buskers, two women on violins and a man on a cello, were well into a dance by Dvorak. I sat in the street beside a crowd of teenagers, leaning against a wall with my drink and a little carton of flan. The group, classically trained, was excellent. I stayed until they packed up their instruments, then handed them a few coins and left the old town to walk back in the dusk to the hostel.

I felt cheerful. Pamplona's violent past seemed to have been refined and diverted into theatre and artifice of all kinds. I had seen what had always fascinated me: not just the shows themselves, though they were good, but the mechanisms underneath, the parts that are supposed to be kept out of the way. If I am looking for the truth in things, I wondered, do I look at the face of the product or at the contrivance by which it is made?

At least seventy people were bedding down for the night when I got to the hostel. It was strange to lie on a piece of foam on the floor in this hollow cave of a gym. So many people, yet I felt insulated and private, enclosed in a world the size of a mattress. I barely dozed at first, kept awake by the rustle of sleeping bags and the onset of rumbles and snores. At 4:45 the next morning I awoke to new noises: plastic bags and backpack zippers, heat-wary pilgrims getting ready for a few hours of walking before the sun roasted the world. By 5:45, I was out the door myself, walking in near darkness towards Puente la Reina, some six hours away. This was my first day of walking the Camino. A shimmer of freedom angled in the shadows before me. A gift. All I needed, I had in my pack. Under its weight, I felt my shoulders relax. I felt relief, though from what I wasn't sure.

My cycling trip with Scott in 1997 had been a pilgrimage with an outward focus - so outward in fact that I sometimes wondered if you could call it a pilgrimage at all. But pilgrimage is a form of meditation, and that trip had two characteristics of meditation: intense concentration, and receptiveness without bias. We had paid attention, had investigated the feel of the Camino, the presence of strength and physical challenge, the intensity of travelling together as partners.

That trip had been full of irregularities and contradictions. Our mode of travel put us at odds with what purists would call true pilgrimage: we were going too fast on our bikes; sometimes we stayed in hotels, which made us self-indulgent and kept us apart from the pilgrim community; we were skeptics about the historical Camino; worst of all, we often seemed to be on the Camino, unapologetically, for the sheer fun of it. But it was good to be on the margin. From there we had looked upon the Camino with both naïve honesty and thoughtful receptivity.

There were times, especially when our bikes were bumping over long ropes of rough dirt track, when I told myself I would never, ever walk this route. It would be too slow, I thought, too tedious, too distracting talking to other people all the time. I was slightly offended one day on the meseta when I stopped to chat with a foot pilgrim from Ireland. He asked me darkly if, while on my bicycle, I had been able to hear the meadowlarks. It felt my spiritual credibility was being called into question. I loved the meseta and everything on it. But I had never heard a meadowlark in my life, and I definitely hadn't heard one there. That single, annoying incident stayed with me: the pilgrim's unkindness was hurtful, but I was goaded too by my own defensiveness. By the time we had reached Santiago, I was hearing an inner call to return. I would walk the Camino for the meadowlarks, or for whatever the voice of the meadowlark stood for. Maybe I also wanted to prove something to the Irish pilgrim, though he would never know it.

Navarra this morning was a land of broad slopes and asymmetrical angles, elusive in the shadows before dawn. The night's coolness hung in the air even as the first tepid wash of sunshine spread behind me over the eastern sky. Ahead of me was the moon, going down on the same axis as the sun's rise. Before long the two hung opposite each other in the sky and I was walking an arc between them. My steps had a flat, opaque sound that made me secure, so that even though I was moving, I felt attached by sound itself to something solid. As the sun illuminated the hill slopes, they too became solid and dense. The moon eased itself into the horizon. When it disappeared, the sky ahead became a huge bright blank.

About thirty kilometres northwest of Pamplona lies a range of mountains, the Sierra de Aralar. Within this range is a dense forest of beech and hawthorn haunted by the sound, half moan, half growl, of a subterranean river flowing under a cavern into an interminable lake. In a nearby grove of yew trees hulks an eerie assembly of megalithic dolmens and menhirs - the largest in Spain. On one peak in the Sierra de Aralar stands a more recent religious site: the Sanctuary of San Miguel in Excelsis. I had come across a story about this San Miguel in a book by José Arenas, a professor at the University of Barcelona. The story interested me for it took place on the eve of the arrival of the Moors in Spain, before James was found, and before the Roman road across the north was ever conceived of as a Christian highway.

During the reign of the Visigothic King Witiza (who will die in 710), a Navarrese gentleman named Don Teodosio de Goñi lives near Aralar with his wife Constanza, a lady of noble descent and unspotted virtue. Teodosio is called away to fight somewhere, and Constanza invites her husband's parents to stay with her while he is gone. Returning some time later from his mission, Teodosio is beset by a terrible storm. Though he is close to home, thunder and lightning force him to take shelter by some rocks. Crouching there, he is approached by a hideous old man in a black robe. The spectre brings Teodosio the worst of news: his wife, the lovely Constanza, is at this moment being unfaithful to him. He himself has seen two people in her bed and if the good noble will go home now, he will see for himself. Furious, Teodosio makes his way through the storm to his home, slips into his bedroom and finds two people sleeping. Swelling with anger in the shades of the darkened room, he plunges his sword deep into their bodies. But alarmed by his own rashness, he creeps back outside to decide what to do next. A door opens and his wife cries out with joy to see him. Teodosio is aghast. The poor man has stabbed his own parents to death.

Teodosio makes a pilgrimage to Rome, where he grovels before the Holy Father and begs a penance to atone for his terrible crime. The Pope orders him to wear a heavy chain about his waist until it falls off on its own. Teodosio walks back to Spain to lead an anchorite's life in the Sierra de Aralar. Seven years pass. One night, the noble, his waist still encircled by his chain, is set upon by a dragon. Terrified, he calls upon Michael the Archangel to help him. The skies open at once and the figure of the Archangel appears, waving a cross triumphantly over his head. Michael addresses the dragon (in perfect Basque according to one source) and the beast falls dead. At the same moment, Teodosio's chains drop from his waist and clank upon the ground.

St. Michael left an image of himself and his cross on the mountain top at Aralar. Teodosio built a stone chapel to house them. The peak is still one of the most venerated spots in Navarra, though the chapel is said to date from 1098 and was plundered by French Basques in 1797. The statue - its helmet emblazoned with a cross, and its face replaced by a glass globe - is carried in procession to nearby towns each year. At the Feast of Corpus Christi, pilgrims climb to the top of Aralar to pay homage to St. Michael the Archangel.

I liked the theatricality of this tale, its Lear-like storms, operatic rage, innocent love, its pope and dragon and sky-mounting saviour. Even with all this fantasy, it had a certain realism: people going about their business as they always had, travelling, fighting, looking after in-laws, even lending them the master bedroom. It was the pre-Camino world; pilgrimage meant Rome, not Santiago. If you were in danger, you called on the Archangel Michael. This was the landscape - as much a fable as real trodden earth - where the Camino would be born: already drenched in weird legends and haunted by unworldly beings who spoke your language.

The Aralar story showed me a Camino landscape without the Camino, reminded me that the Camino, both the literal trail and the Camino idea, was an issue - and a tissue - of history. Had it not been for the mines, the wars, the Romans with their roads and then their crosses, the Moors with their sabers, had it not been for the land itself, poised for epiphanies, the Camino might not have existed at all. Everyone knows this, of course, but it was important for me to notice it again, because it was one key - of many - to my own pilgrimage. I live in a world of the intellect, of opinions and arguments, a world made of thoughts that wobble and billow like loose tents in the wind. In such a world, history, even memory itself, can shift in a second to blow the other way. The past is unstable, depends on your point of view. There are contradictory aspects of history that we simply can't help but know. That is the modern pilgrim's reality.

I was on a pilgrimage through a time and a space that have always been in a process of deconstruction and reconstruction. This is a modern way of putting it, but the problem is actually a very old one. It is the Zen riddle. What one *thinks*, says Zen, is not what *is*. *Not this. Not this!* Going around the mind's inventions, Zen finds the knowing that precedes concepts and opinions and histories. It is a spiritual exercise akin to the Christian Via Negativa, the path of the mystic who denies words, even - *especially* - religious language, in order to sharpen the awareness of the unnamable presence behind the words. When I saw how pointless it was to seek a consistent truth in the historical Camino, when I relaxed my attempts to make sense of all its contradictions, and to fit my square peg of a self into its roundabout stories, I discovered I was truer to myself as a pilgrim. *Not this! Not this Camino!* What, then? *There* was the *real* journey.

Things I couldn't help but know: When King Witiza died, the succession to the Visigothic crown fell into dispute. A certain Rodrigo was chosen by the nobility over Witiza's supposed son, Agila. But the realm was still agitated: at the halfway mark in the year 711, gangs of Visigoths were still beating each other up with one hand and slapping at Basques with the other.

At the same moment, on a little tooth-like protrusion of land in North Africa, where the mouth of the Mediterranean opens onto the Atlantic, a Berber named Tariq ibn Zaid stood squinting northward across a fourteen-kilometre esophagus of water. Tariq served the Arab governor of North Africa, Musa ibn Nasayr, and on this stifling July day, he was on business for Musa, readying himself to cross the strait to a matching knob of land on the other side, a place that would later take his name: Gib al-Tariz, Gibraltar. The crossing was straightforward. Once he got to the other side, it is said, Tariq burned his boats to show his intention to stay. The Berber gathered his men and headed inland. Word of his coming spread quickly. King Rodrigo was forced to quit his wrangling with Basques and make an emergency trip south to the banks of the Guadalete River, somewhere between Jérez and Algeciras. Here, he and his Visigoths were wiped out by the Moors. His body was never found.

Tariq's boss, Musa, was delighted and joined his man in Spain. The two headed north. Córdoba, almost completely defenseless, fell at once. Toledo was next. There was much confusion and devastation: in the fracas the archbishop of Toledo, head of the Spanish church, deserted his post and ran away. In 713, we find Tariq north of the Duero Valley, mowing his way into the Cantabrian foothills and west to Astorga. Only in 714 does he return to Toledo.

Carmona fell, then Sevilla and Mérida, where there was some hard resistance. Musa and Tariq (I had the impression from my reading of a couple of madcap adventurers on the loose) went on to Tarragona, Barcelona, Saragosa, and, back in Galicia, to the old Celtic town of Lugo. After some time, the Islamic dynastic headquarters in Syria called, unamused. The pair were summoned to Damascus, and their reception apparently was not warm. Neither would return to Spain. They quarreled, and disappeared from the map of history.

Damascus sent its own commanders out to Spain, though a contingent of self-styled rulers - one of them Musa's son - had already made themselves at home in "al-Andalus." Before long the Moors had spread through Spain and were now slipping through the Pyrenean passes into France. In 732, exactly a hundred years after the death of Mohammed, they met Charles Martel "The Hammer," grandfather of Charlemagne, in a battle that would mark their northernmost advance. In the 1960s, every Canadian high school history teacher made you remember this crucial event in the history of western Europe: the Battle of Poitiers.

It is surprising to discover your own tracks along the wobbling highways of history. This Spain under my feet had been crossed and recrossed by Moors who had fought at Poitiers, a place I had contemplated only briefly as one distant fact among many, from the other side of the Atlantic, thirty-five years ago. Pilgrimage, it seemed, was helping me locate my own existence in the circuits of history: like an electron jumping among the orbits of all possible events, I actually show up here, for a flicker of a life.

While the Moors had ravaged Spain to the south of the Duero, the mountain ranges of Cantabria and the damp hills of Galicia were, after 711, sitting pretty much as they always had: in the hands of Basques in the east and various clans of Cantabrians and Asturians in the west. In Roman and Visigothic times, these groups had been only vaguely Christian, and were never unified. But as the Moors chomped north like a swarm of locusts through the meseta grasses, the scrappy mountain settlements began to pull together, bullishly defensive. Visigothic refugees arriving from the Duero Valley helped to fill in this rag-bag of alliances, particularly in Asturias, making the north cohesive enough that when the Moors got to a Cantabrian village called Covadonga in 718, an army, united under a Visigothic noble named Pelayo, was well and truly ready for them.

The Spanish Reconquest began here at Covadonga, in a hollowed-out pass near the Cave of the Most Blessed Virgin, by a gorge gushing with clear water and flanked with timber-covered mountains. The Legend of Covadonga is found in the Chronicles of Alfonso III. Here we learn to our surprise that the Moors were accompanied to Covadonga - perhaps escorted - by the Bishop of Seville, a certain Opas, one of the sons of King Witiga. The voice of compromise or capitulation, depending on your point of view, Opas tried to deter Pelayo from fighting, needlessly pointing out that he was pathetically outnumbered, and shrewdly suggesting he make friends with the obvious winners. Pelayo, we are told, retorted that the Kingdom of God was like the moon, disappearing and then returning in its full glory. "We trust, therefore, in God's mercy," he went on, "that from this little mountain will return the salvation of Spain." Opas went back to the waiting Moors. "We fight," he reported, and the battle began. When it was over, a handful of Christians had slain 300,000 Moors. It is said that the womenfolk helped by throwing stones at the invaders. In another version, stones fired at the Christians reversed their direction in mid-air and flew back into the Moorish troops, causing much personal injury.

The Battle of Covadonga was Spain's Battle of Poitiers, the turnaround of Christian fortunes in Spain. The fighting would go on for an astonishing seven centuries, but the Moors would never get any further north than this. The Sanctuary of Nuestra Señora de Covadonga became a pilgrimage site of great fame, visited by pilgrims on their way to Santiago from the boat docks on the Cantabrian coast.

From the start of the invasions, the Visigoths were unsure how to respond to the Moors. Some, like the pragmatic Opas, saw the advantages of coexistence with a conqueror who, as anybody could see, had the upper hand not just in military might but culturally too. Many people chose to settle down and live alongside the invaders. These came to be called the Mozarabs. Others remained intransigent resisters: not just Pelayo and his band of rebels in the outback ranges of Spain, but even educated Visigoths at Toledo and Sevilla. All felt the natural resistance of the underdogs, but those with learning could also sense the greatest danger to coexistence with a superior and powerful culture: the infiltration of ideas.

Reading about the Moors in Spain, I could see that, even more than battles and soldiers, my journey to Santiago had been shaped by ideas, and by a long bout of squabbling about those ideas. The most troublesome idea was the Christian Trinity, something I had once found interesting as a kind of theological Rubic's Cube. In 8th-century Spain however, the Trinity was not a game.

In these early days of Moorish ascendancy, the Jews were fairly easily tolerated as fellow monotheists and People of the Book. But the Christians, with their notion of the Trinity, bothered the Moors terribly. Often, they just didn't get it: if you were a monotheist, why would you want to divide your perfectly good God into three persons? Would this not sink you to the level of a common polytheist? And if they did grasp the subtleties of the

Doctrine of the Trinity, perhaps they wondered - as I did - why something so important as salvation would depend on something so hard for ordinary people to keep straight.

The fascination with ideas is a bond among open-minded believers of any religion, even competing ones. In Spain, inevitably, there were dialogues between Christians and Muslims, with the ominous result that a few Christians began to rethink their Trinity. Coincidentally, an old Nestorian community was hiding out in southern Spain, and the eastern teaching, long ago condemned, that Jesus had two natures, one divine and one human, was reincarnated under Islamic influence as the Adoptionist heresy. Jesus was a hundred percent divine, said Elipandus, the new Archbishop of Toledo. So far, so good. Then the archbishop tossed in a zinger of a qualification: in a physical sense, Jesus was merely the adopted son, not the natural son of God. This watered down Trinity - an Islamicized Christianity - made the hair on orthodox heads stand up. Adoptionism became Spain's hottest intellectual issue. Much ink was spent on the controversy. The great educator Alcuin wrote a fiery treatise against the teachings of Elipandus. Pope Hadrian struck out at the *Error Hispanicus*. As for King Charlemagne, he had to play his cards right with certain Moorish allies, so while staying supportive to the cause, he was rather less vocal about it.

The mightiest weapon against Adoptionism - and against Islam and the theological mess it brought with it - came from northern Spain. The monk Beatus of Liébana was among the fiercest opponents of the heresy. In his *Commentaries on the Apocalypse*, written in 776, we are reminded - for the first time in a hundred years - that St. James, the disciple of Jesus Christ, had preached in Spain. We see too on Beatus' brilliant world map with its endearingly drunken lines, a picture of James' head located, tellingly enough, in Galicia. Some years earlier, at the court of the Asturian King Alfonso II, a hymn in homage to the king's predecessor, Mauregatus, had appeared. *O Dei Verbum Patri*, it was called: O Word of God the Father. The fifth verse praised the Sons of Thunder - the name given by Jesus to the hot-headed brothers James and John. The tenth verse was dedicated to James himself: Resplendent golden head of Spain, it said, our patron and defender. May he protect the king, the clergy and the people, preserving them from injury and illness, so that with his help they may achieve final glory.

So here I was, on pilgrimage to the shrine of a saint who, back in the 8th Century, rose to fame not only in response to Moorish marauders, but to fight a kind of religious infection within the Christian camp. I was walking in Spain because of a theological squabble over an issue that was even more unfathomably remote from my world than the idea that James could heal my woes. I couldn't help but wonder, shouldn't the history of a pilgrimage resonate, even just a little bit, with the pilgrim's own life now? Perhaps even this was too much to ask of the old Camino.

This King Mauregatus of *O Dei Verbum Patri* hymn was the seventh in a meandering line of Asturian monarchs going back to the rebel Pelayo. A "Duke" Peter of Cantabria appears in the chronicles out of nowhere and marries Pelayo's daughter. A series of intermarriages take place - Basque and Galician brides are hinted at - sprouting various little dynasties that eventually coalesce into a royal house dominated by a long line of Alfonso's. The first, Alfonso I, pushes the Moors south into the Duero Valley and gets back León, Astorga, Braga and possibly Salamanca. While lopping off Muslim heads, he also rounds up Visigothic inhabitants of those towns and resettles them in the north to strengthen the Christian presence there. Emboldened by numbers, Alfonso makes treaties through marriage with Basques in the east and moves his influence into Galicia in the west.

Alfonso II comes to power in 791. Already something of a francophile, Alfonso easily grasps that what would help him most in his battle against Adoptionism (and Islam) is not Rome, nor is it the Visigothic capital, Toledo, which is moribund. It is France. Roncesvalles was only thirteen years ago and Charlemagne is still active in Navarra. The Franks seemed interested in Galicia too, for Charlemagne's campaigns around Pamplona have made him notice Asturias. For the Asturian court, which seems to have depended upon him,

Charlemagne is a kind of royal role model, the protector of orthodoxy against the heresies that are raging through the Islamic south. The courtiers at the Asturian city of Oviedo - the new Toledo, head of Christian Spain - scan Old Testament scriptures and find reason to reinvent themselves as the New Israel, elected by God to form a new covenant. Shining now with both the lustre of French interest and a strong Biblical back-up, the nucleus of the anti-Moor resistance solidifies. With the protection of its Apostle James, Asturias will carry the banner of orthodoxy for the Spanish Church.

Christian tradition prefers that patron saints make an actual appearance in their assigned territory, to show they approve of the cause. James' presence in Spain was still only a dream on a few pages of obscure history. But Asturias was now the only Christian muscle that twitched in Spain. James was badly needed; somehow, Asturians would have to get their hero home.

I got to Puente la Reina after six hours of walking, tired but overjoyed with the freedom I felt in the bright air of the Camino, and delighted too with Navarra and the pilgrims I had talked to on the way. In the *refugio*, I met Deidre, a biologist from Scotland. We shared my laundry soap and draped our wet clothes together on a steel fence by the road. She told me she had come to the Camino with a friend to walk for about ten days. The friend hadn't been able to take the heat and had gone to Madrid, so Deidre would be walking alone from here on. Like several people I met, she had intended more of a walking tour than a true pilgrimage. Later, I met others who had time only for a short visit to the Camino, but considered themselves pilgrims all the same. Several were completing the walk in one week stages over four years.

Puente la Reina was as pleasant as when Scott and I had cycled through the year before. I took my time seeing things that in our haste to catch up on lost time, we had had to forego. I sat for a long while in the Church of the Crucifix, writing my diary and examining the wooden crucifix for which the church is famous. Its crosspieces extended upwards on an angle from the near the centre of the vertical, giving the whole thing the shape of a large goose's foot. The body of Christ hung suspended from arms raised high, his head sagged heavily over the bare chest. The body was graceful in suffering, the legs curving from the folds of the loincloth down into the feet with its big single nail. In the Middle Ages, this *Crucifijo* had esoteric connections. It may have been brought by grateful pilgrims from a town in Germany that had been rid of the plague. Another tradition says it was left by a German pilgrim who enjoyed the hospitality he received at the hostel in Puente la Reina.

I wandered from the Church of the Crucifix into the convent nextdoor and found myself in a sunny cloister. Along its walls, shaded from the sun, were half a dozen cabinets with glass windows in their doors. On their shelves, scattered as if they had been tossed there, were a large number of pre-historic and Celtiberian artifacts. I stared with my usual dumb interest at the arrowheads and spearheads, straining to catch some message - a smell of animal blood, a sound, a "hello!" - from the old life.

The walls of the cloister were covered by popular religious posters. There were calculated scenes of poverty, empty faces of black and Asian children staring out at me from an odd angle, pictures of endangered wildlife, deforested lands. One caption said: The Holy Scripture is, with the divine Eucharist, the food of our spiritual life. On others I read: The Cross is the gift of Jesus. If the Kingdom comes, life will come. *Human Rights* in big green slanted letters. The Ozone Layer. Pollution with a picture of garbage. I liked this quote: Charity and truth are the two grand passions of my life. As I was leaving, I realized that the only people I had seen in the seminary - some ten or twelve - was a group of mentally retarded young people, purposefully, if awkwardly going in and out of the doors of the cloister, and looking brightly and inquisitively at me as they walked past the cases of ancient tools.

In the morning, I left Puente la Reina along the Calle Mayor, passing under old-fashioned street lamps and balconies dripping with red geraniums. At this hour the flowers were a muted, drowsy red; later in the day, they would give off a brilliance like fat rubies in the sun. My boots scraped along the road. On Doña Mayor's lovely bridge, I paused, as Scott and I had last year, to admire the limpid waters of the Rio Arga. Then I turned and walked off the bridge onto the Camino trail.

In the village of Villatuerta, I had a rest at the little parish Church of the Assumption, lying on a bench in the alcove by the door. I was tired and my feet ached. A Spaniard, two Brazilians, and two women from Denmark came by and took shelter in the shade beside me. In a while, the priest joined us, a young, casual fellow wearing a black t-shirt, a cross, and a bright grin. We asked him what Villatuerta was famous for. He hesitated, smiling, and said he was new to this parish. "I don't know the history very well yet," he added as he walked away. A few moments later, he was back, holding a book. We stood and huddled around him as if we were completing a drug deal. The book had pictures of the local religious iconography, complete with a torrid battle scene: frothing horses, tumbling men, swords akimbo, a shining crucifix. I asked the priest what this was. "The Victory of the Cross over the Moors," he answered. I thought, what else? The priest's eyes met mine. His smile was guileless, but I think he almost winked.

The air was churning with hot sunshine. On the way out of Villatuerta, I drenched my pant legs in the fountain to stave off the raging heat. Later, I ran into the two Danes in a forested area where the path narrowed. We joked pointlessly in a mixture of English and German about the weather. Under my pack, my back was slippery with hot sweat.

The word *invention* is one of the quirks of the English language. You think of the light bulb or the steam engine, or, as the Oxford English Dictionary might put it, something devised or produced by mental activity or original thought. *Invention* comes from the Latin word *invenire*, which can mean to devise or construct, but was used by the Romans mainly to express the notion of finding something out, discovering or coming (*venire*) upon something. Thus we have the Invention of the Cross, when Helen, mother of Constantine, uncovered Christ's Cross in Jerusalem, or the Invention of the Tomb of the Apostle James in 9th-century Galicia. Most of the older English meanings for *invention* carry this sense of finding something that is already there (the act of coming upon or finding) or - and this is the curious part - of making something up. Not a machine that works, like an artificial heart, but a story or a piece of literature or music, or an out and out lie. What all this says about how our human brains once perceived perception, I don't know, but it can't be an accident that the idea of discovering a thing is captured in the same word as the idea of making a thing up in your mind, as if the act of seeing creates what is seen.

It is sometime in the 9th Century, perhaps 825. The location is a neglected and overgrown copse in western Galicia. Close by, at the intersection of a north-south Roman road and a westerly one leading to a disused Roman necropolis, is a small village. Possibly, this is all that is left of the old city of Asseconia, built by the Romans over a Celtic fort. The town of Iria Flavia is not far away, with its Church of Santa Eulalia, the only bishop's seat in the north of Spain that had not been attacked by the Moors.

A local hermit named Pelayo is out for a walk in the wooded area that some would later call "Libredon." The place, we might imagine, is a little weird, filled with the rustlings and creaks, streaks of light and creeping shadows that always turn a collection of trees into a forest. Pelayo startles, looks up. A spangle of lights showers through the foliage. Songs of angels burst from the night sky. Pelayo can't believe his eyes or his ears. The neighbours say they too have witnessed such lights and sounds hereabouts, more than once.

Theodemir, the Bishop of Iria and a man of common sense, is informed. His flock is impressionable, he knows, and he has the intelligent cleric's wariness of apparitions. Theodemir fasts for three days, filling his spirit with divine grace before approaching the forest. Braced now, he leaves the road and steps in among the dark-barked trees. The underbrush crackles under his feet. In the heart of the forest, he comes upon a small stone building. Inside he finds a chamber decorated with marble. Bruising his hands in the excitement of discovery, Theodemir sees, under the ruined mosaic floor, three tombs, one large, two lesser. This, he realizes, trusting to the clarity of perception afforded by prayer and a three day fast, must be the tomb of St. James and his two disciples. Where else would they logically be, he reasons, his heart feeling moist and beginning to throb, but here in the only untouched orthodox enclave left in Spain. Just when we need him most, our patron, the resplendent James, bestows his presence upon us. Oh happy hour! Oh mighty faith!

Two hundred fifty miles to the northeast, Alfonso II holds court in Oviedo. Informed of the find, he hastens with his entourage to Iria Flavia, where as "patron and master" of all Spain he becomes the first official pilgrim to pray at James' tomb.

The king is cunning as well as devout, and he knows he has to act fast. The Franks are also on the look-out for a fresh patron and will snap James up the way a dog grabs a bone if the Spanish don't get him first. The king orders a rectangular church built without delay over the tomb. He places all the land within a three-mile radius of it under the authority of Theodemir's Church of Santa Eulalia at Iria Flavia. This land donation of 834 is the nucleus of the future city of Santiago de Compostela.

Word gets out locally and pilgrims begin to trickle in from nearby hamlets, from fishing villages on the coast, from farms in the Galician hills. Alfonso sends a letter to Pope Leo III. Rejoicing at a discovery that would unify his fractious Christendom, the Pope sends a letter in bad Latin, still available in three slightly different versions, to bishops east and west announcing the invention of the tomb. The letter goes to Milan, Constantinople, Antioch, Jerusalem, Alexandria. The old 5th-century Letter from an earlier Pope Leo - forged by goodness know whom - starts making the rounds again, proving how James' body had gotten to Spain.

At first, the cult grows slowly. One chronicle from the time of Alfonso III doesn't even mention Santiago.

e plenty of other saints in the area with their own claims to fame. St. Martin of Tours for instance, famous for his opposition to Priscillian's heresy and, after his own death, for ridding Galicia of leprosy. Then there are the saintly virgin couple Julian and Baselisa, and as always, the Blessed Virgin. But by 860, July 25 is officially the day of the "Nativity of St. James [whose] sacred bones, borne to Spain and buried in its western regions, towards the sea of Brittany, are the object of celebrated devotion by those people." In 899, Alfonso III, the Great, will build a basilica with three wide naves on the site of the earlier Alfonso's modest church and the future of the cult of St. James is secure.

The events at Iria Flavia, which took place sometime between 812 and 834, are found in an official document known as the *Concordia de Antealtares*. The *Concordia* was written in Compostela around 1077, by which time the cult of St. James was in full swing, and legend and fantasy had grown into it like Galician moss. What the monks of Antealtares most wanted you to remember was that James had preached in Spain in the 1st Century, that his message had been spurned by the Galicians, that his cult had fallen into neglect, that Theodemir had recovered it in the 9th Century, and that they - the Benedictines of Antealtares - were the authorized custodians of the St. James shrine. In laying claim to the story, the monks assumed the rights to the cult of St. James and to the Church at Santiago; that meant land donations, contributions of money and relics, income from pilgrims gifts, souvenir sales, and church maintenance fees, and prestige galore. The *Concordia* - a literary invention about a 9th-century fantasy-discovery (who knows how Theodemir's mind actually processed the details of the stone tomb) became official history, retroactively legitimizing the cult of St. James and its owners at Santiago.

So what about all these legends and forgeries and histories rewritten? I asked other pilgrims whether they felt any dissonance between their purpose as pilgrims and this weird tangle of history and myth. Very few cared.

"Why does it matter?" said Deidre when we had talked over laundry at Puente la Reina. "I just do this for myself anyway, and I take what I can from it. It's the symbolism that's important, not the facts - what it means to me now, not how it got this way."

But it wasn't that I wanted the stories to be true, it was that I was still trying to find my place in a world of contrivance and illusion. Since I was here at all, I was creating my own role in Camino history; yet a private mythology that ignored what didn't fit my scientific or historical temperament seemed isolating and exclusive; pilgrimage may be a walk through your own story, or a walk to find your own story, but the notion of a shared human vision also seemed important. Pilgrimage was about community too. I had to recognize my distance from traditional Camino history. But I had to avoid drifting into a made-up symbolism that set me apart from what I witnessed on the Camino. My pilgrimage had a new angle now: it was a walk through the floating tissues of history, getting used to being in and being out at the same time.

I stayed at the *refugio* in Estella that night. There was no problem finding a bunk. I chatted with Anya, a German woman I had seen on the trail, who had arrived on the Spanish Camino over the challenging Somport Pass. "It vass completely empty," she said. "und so beautiful mountains. I vass ze only vun until Puente la Reina. Zer, ach, alza people! But my feet.... ach...". I glanced down. If those were feet on the ends of her legs, they were first ones I'd seen that looked like footballs. She swung them up onto her bunk as if they were filled with water. I leaned over. "Don't touch zem!" she shrieked. "Plees."

"It's ok," I said, "I used to be a nurse." Inwardly, I thought, "Those feet aren't going *anywhere*."

But Anya was determined. She was relying on a pair of German-made retractable walking sticks that looked like ski-poles. When I caught up with her the next day on the way to Los Arcos, she was bearing down on them as if they were crutches.

Anya was tall and big-shouldered, had short cropped hair and an almost defiant look in her eyes. In Germany, she was a social worker, now out of work after a year of cutbacks. It had been nerve-wracking. On this pilgrimage she would reassess her life, she told me, and make a decision about where to go next. But her biggest concern at the moment was how to get those pigskin feet to the next hostel. Feeling that she might need some moral support, I walked with her towards Los Arcos along the side of a flat-bottomed valley. After an hour of trudging, we rested in the spindly shade of a grove of pines. Across from us, through a haze of heat, broad, triangular hills marked the other side of the valley. Near the top of one was an old church - I could just make it out with my binoculars. I turned and lay on a bed of pine needles with my head lower than my feet, feeling extreme relief in my legs as my blood flowed heavily up into my thighs. We talked idly, compared notes about social welfare systems in Canada and Germany. We drifted and dozed, until Anya abruptly announced she was ready to go. I was surprised by what I suppose was some kind of Teutonic *animus*: she had an almost masculine obliviousness to discomfort. I tried her walking sticks for a few minutes, but they felt awkward and superfluous. Later, I would sincerely wish I had a pair myself.

In Los Arcos, we waited with other pilgrims for the hostel to open. A long line curled through the courtyard. A good-looking Spaniard with a red kerchief on his head was behind me. As we waited, he burst out singing in a spontaneous, Pentecostal kind of way. He had a wonderful voice and I asked him if he was a professional singer. He laughed and said he taught physical education in Valencia.

We were four to a room at the hostel at Los Arcos. Anya and I were assigned to a cubby-hole with the Spaniard and his elegant Spanish girlfriend. "I love her, but she is very stubborn," he told me in English, as she dabbed an expensive face cream onto her cheeks. "I know what she needs. She needs somebody to draw a line for her." He smiled confidently. From what I saw that evening, she seemed to enjoy whatever lines he had set for her, but they had a fight later in the trip and she went back to Valencia.

For supper, I made myself a fruit salad at a table on the veranda. I met Errol, a South African with a long ponytail and a thick red beard, who told me, as all South Africans are condemned to tell everyone else in the world, about apartheid, pre- and post. I met Duncan, native of England, who ran a language school in Sevilla. Travelling with him were his niece, Virginia, who lived in, of all places, Niagara-on-the-Lake in Southern Ontario, and his mother, Martha, a wide, frizzy-haired woman with a ruddy face and a sturdy English pleasantness. "I'm very slow, dear," Martha told me with matter-of-fact honesty. "Two things hold me back: my age and my weight."

I chatted with Bernardo, an architect from Madrid, who reminded me of Canada's famous Prime Minister, Pierre Trudeau: somewhat effete, highly intelligent, patrician in aspect. As I talked, his eyes followed my words around my face. I imagined women would like him. He was accompanied by a strikingly beautiful one, an old friend involved in development work in Mozambique. The two had coincidentally run into each other on the Camino. I liked her and the next day I was pleased to see her in Viana. She was alone this time, disconsolate and in terrible pain. "I can't do this," she told me tearfully. "My feet can't take it. I'll stay here a couple of days and see if they get better. If they don't, I'll have to go home." Unfortunately, I would never see her again.

While in Los Arcos, I visited the Church of Santa María, a cathedral built in the 12th Century but full of glitter and frou-frou from the Spanish Baroque. Near the back of the church, its lush reds and golds and blues leaping from the wall, hung a stunning Flemish retable with Old Testament prophets and scenes from the life of the Virgin. The characters, taken from life, were magnificently painted. Looking at them, I felt pulled into their midst; they seemed to stand around me in the clarity of a prophetic dream, their calm, living faces brilliantly alert, looking intently everywhere but at me.

Mass was reaching full throttle, and I turned to peer over the round heads of the crowd into a blur of gold and incense. The organ's shriek sprang joyfully into every arch, every curve of the church. Choir voices tilted on the air above us. The sermon was strong but tender, almost intimate, as if the priest knew, but chose only to love, the details of life in Los Arcos. There had been a funeral this morning, someone told me, and recently, much illness in the community. This Mass, in honour of the Virgin, was sung today for the sick and bereaved of Los Arcos.

I wanted to stay afterwards to see a slide presentation about the Virgin, with poetry and music. But as the fanfare of the organ ended, exhaustion seeped through me. Back at the hostel, I fell asleep on my bunk before I had even zipped up my sleeping bag.

The ivory chest in the Museum of Navarra had been on my mind during my solitary walks west toward Los Arcos. It had been Scott, with his passion for Moorish culture, who had first read about it. "It tells a whole other story," he told me. "There's hardly a trace of high Moorish culture anywhere along the Camino. Just a few architectural flourishes, and that's it. If you kept only to the Camino, you'd hardly know the Moors had even been to Spain, let alone fought Christians from one end of the road to the other." So much Moorish art and learning had passed over the Camino into France and northern Europe. "It's incredible! The memory of that richness is almost completely obliterated now. You have to see the ivory casket to get an idea of what the Moors were really all about."

It was the ivory itself that had struck me when I had first seen the casket up close: a polished ivory, but not too shiny; a sultry, moony off-white with creamy shadows, veined here and there with tiny black cracks. The raw pieces had come to Spain from East Africa or possibly India, carried in caravans by Moorish traders using the pilgrimage routes to Mecca. Religion and trade have always travelled together; after the 9th Century, the *hajj* to Mecca had boosted commercial traffic throughout the Middle East, just as Santiago pilgrimage had, though less so, across Northern Spain.

The Moors craved luxury goods: silk, paper, glassware, fine metalworks, enamelled pottery, gold, rich carpets. Córdoba was the artist's Mecca; here could be found, as now in New York or Paris or London, the best workshops and couturiers. There were once 13,000 top-notch leather and silk workers in Córdoba. Faray had made his ivory casket just outside the city in the palace of Abd al-Rahman III at Madinat az-Zahra. After Córdoba fell in the early 11th Century, the workshops moved away to safer places. But if you had enough money, you could still get whatever you wanted: swords from Toledo; linens from Saragosa; Sevillian cotton. Even farmers were buying, everything from copper and iron to raisins.

Moorish goods came in a respectable trickle to the hard-up Christian north. Markets were pitched in the griddle-hot church squares of Camino towns, and pilgrims mingled with traders and middlemen - Christian, Moors and Jews – who carted their wares along the Camino or through the river valleys: farm implements, seeds from new strains of wheat, irrigation devices, and a few luxuries: slaves, olive oil, wine, ivory, leather and fine jewellery.

Few ordinary pilgrims of the Camino years could have dreamed of the Muslim world that glittered south of the Duero. What they knew of the Moors was propaganda about howling turbaned armies, of a vicious race with spears poised to disable God's kingdom and ruin the Christian's soul. Shuddering thoughts. But there were other pilgrims, whose numbers grew as the century wore on - clerics with a little book learning, illiterate but well-connected nobles - men who hunched over bread and cheese at the long inn table among sharp-eyed merchants and crudely muscled soldiers, musing over what they had heard, that down south beyond the Rio Duero shone the arabesque courtyards and splashing fountains of a dozen swaying, mystifying, alluring, Christless cities, metropoles dedicated to arithmetic and books, to baths and poetry, quivering with music, whose airs were redolent with the scents of oils and spice and jasmine, and where the charcoaled eyes of undulating women, it was whispered, promised all.

If they bothered to think of them at all, the Moors generally regarded the Spanish Christians as childish barbarians. The religion of Jesus was simply a primitive form of Islam, surely expendable now that the final revelations of the matured faith had come. With unblinking superiority, the Moors sniffed their noses at the Europeans, regarding them as the unwashed roughnecks they pretty much were. Their attitude was best summed up by the comments of the 10th-century Arab geographer, Masudi, a lively writer who, rather than stooping to religious bigotry to explain the pathetic state of European man, objectively drew on the best anthropology the times could offer:

> As regards the people of the northern quadrant, they are the ones for whom the sun is distant from the zenith, as they penetrate to the north, such as the Slavs, the Franks and those nations that are their neighbours. The power of the sun is weakened among them, because of its distance from them; cold and damp prevail in their regions, and snow and ice follow one another in endless succession. The warm humour is lacking among them; their bodies are large, their natures gross, their manners harsh their understanding dull, and their tongues heavy. Their colour is so excessively white that they look blue; their skin is fine and their flesh coarse. Their eyes, too, are blue, matching their colouring; their hair is lank and reddish because of the damp mists. Their religious beliefs lack solidity, and this is because of the nature of the cold and the lack of warmth. The farther they are to the north, the more stupid, gross and brutish they are..... those who dwell sixty odd miles beyond this latitude are Gog and Magog. They are in the sixth climate and are reckoned among the beasts.

Reading this, I couldn't help thinking that if the word Neanderthal had been around in the 10th Century, Masudi would have used it.

If Christians and their religion were beneath contempt, the Moors could scarcely be bothered with Christian learning either. Aristotle had long been available in Arabic; so were Persian astronomy and Hindu mathematics. The Moors were nothing if not inventive; they devised navigational tools, the abacus, irrigation methods, breeding methods, astronomical gadgets. A list of their interests reads like a modern university syllabus: botany, geography, mathematics; theology and philosophy; medical diagnostics, surgery, pharmacology.

Many Mozarab Christians knew everyday Arabic; a few were even translators, though this was mostly in the hands of the Jews, who knew every useful language there was and made superb diplomats. But mostly what the learned Mozarab had on his shelf was nostalgia: musty writings from the Visigothic past, recopied over and over in a kind of cultural repetition compulsion. Of scientific scholarship there was nothing. In the year 1000, when only about a thousand people each lived in León, Astorga and even Santiago, most of the royal courts were illiterate. You could hardly blame the Muslims for their indifference.

What erudition did come to northern Spain arrived only to leave. True, the Monastery of San Millán, just off the Camino, had in its possession a good collection of Arab mathematical treatises. But most Arab learning travelled east along the Camino and disappeared over the Pyrenees into France. There, in the 12th Century, it would steer Western theology and philosophy in a sharp new direction, and lay the intellectual groundwork for modern science and medicine. Eventually, Arab notions of experimentation and data collection would change in the most profound way our relationship with the physical world.

In the Los Arcos hostel, Errol had told me he had heard of three pilgrims from Morocco who were walking the Camino. Nothing was known about them and I never did meet anyone who had seen them. It was a pity. But the absent Moroccans were the perfect metaphor for what

Scott had called the "invisible Moorish presence" on the Camino. They were the other half of the Camino story.

It was dark and cool when I set out from Los Arcos, after a stand-up breakfast of packaged rice pudding and a muesli bar in the yard of the hostel. Some meters ahead of me was a pilgrim carrying a small light that made the trail just visible. I followed for about a kilometre, then stopped to adjust my pack. Another pilgrim surprised me from the shadows, where he had just finished urinating. Thus I met Alfredo, a fast-talking Spaniard who fell in with me as if we had always known each other. We walked; he talked. As the sky grew lighter, I struggled with his non-stop, rapid-volley Spanish. At Sansol, I grasped that he wanted to find a bar for some breakfast, and to the relief of my exhausted ears and brain, we parted by the church.

Sansol, post-Alfredo, was quiet. I walked into the church portico, hearing only my own footsteps. This church once belonged to the monastery at Carrión de los Condes. The town's name, Sansol, is a linguistic twist on St. Zoilo, the Cordovan martyr whose body was brought to Carrión in the 4th Century. Last year, here in this portico, Scott and I had wolfed down a picnic lunch while overlooking, from a low wall where we had set our food, the moist spring fields of Navarra. Now, on this hot day, the landscape seemed parched and overused. But out on the plain just a kilometre away, Torres del Rio, all in light brown stone against the brightening sky, looked exactly as it had for centuries: the perfect, tidy, compact, pleasingly proportioned medieval town.

I descended the steep trail to Torres with bushes scraping my legs like the nails on parched, ghostly fingers. Last year, the town had been active when we arrived. I had bought water in a little shop. In the small, round church, a German tourist had played medieval music on a recorder, which I had enjoyed. Today, at this early hour, the streets of Torres were empty. I felt I was in a town from which even legend had departed, whose quaintness had ossified. Its dessicated walls were as still as reptiles in a desert.

I walked alone for the next ten kilometres through stony landscapes with sparse trees, fields of grapevines and hay stubble, and smaller plots with long squat rows of mauve lavender bushes. The sky was clouding over. The trail rose and dropped, became narrow and even stonier. On the brow of a high ridge, I stopped for a drink, staring out upon a wide valley spread like Mother Nature's banquet table with groves of oak, fields like earth-toned placemats, and rocky outcroppings topped with shrubs. In the distance under the clouds was Viana. Scattered needles of lightning pierced the hills around the town. Slowly I picked my way down long switchbacks into the valley. The acrid odour of pig manure curled through the air, high-pitched, like sugar gone off.

In Viana, the most westerly town in Navarra, I rested for an hour in the busy square, eating cheese and apples and taking pictures of the street life. A few kilometers later, I was in the province of La Rioja, heading to Logroño past the old Celtiberian stronghold of Varea. The rain had never gotten around to falling, and the sun was blazing again. Foolishly, I had bought only sweetened juice at Viana, and drinking it dehydrated me. Late in the afternoon, I staggered through the door of the Logroño *refugio*, desperately thirsty and dull with fatigue. I saw an arm reach out to help me off with my backpack. I was given a chair and told I could rest before registering. Someone brought me water, and when I had greedily sucked it back, another was brought to me. After I signed in, a man came upstairs with me, smiling quietly as he carried my pack. I followed him through a large room crowded with bunks and gear, twisting around doorways, dodging the legs and backsides of pilgrims busy unpacking. In a back corner of the dormitory, he found me a top bunk and helped me up before leaving with another wordless smile. I lay immobile on my back, cherishing with every cell of my overheated body the cool draught of human kindness.

Later I cooked myself a light supper in the hostel kitchen, did my laundry, and returned to bed. The dormitory was full, but people were tired and quiet. Beside me were a father and daughter, Ana and Luis, settling down amid a last rustle of sleeping bags. In the bunk below me was Evy, whom I had met in the kitchen, an energetic Brazilian living in Italy, with an ear-to-ear smile.

Evy had gone out after supper to a bar, and had come back just as the room softened and grew dark. We barely greeted each other before he vanished into his sleeping bag.

For perhaps ten seconds there was silence. Then, beginning with some tentative sounds like a guitar being tuned, first from Evy below and then from Luis, the wheeze of noses and the thrum of adenoids began to fill the air. Like a band of violins, each with a different note. Like a pack of coyotes answering and amplifying each other's ragged howl. Many years ago, I had been the night nurse on a male surgical ward, but I had never heard anything like this.

My bunk was beside the window. Cars passed in the street; mothers called to their children; motor scooters went by like long, loud zippers. The garbage trucks arrived. The metallic clanking of trash and glass was hollow, inhuman, endless, a sound from a tin can factory over the growl of trucks waiting in the alley. I was too tired to roll over. The words of some 12th-century mystic came to me: "Live welcoming to all." Spaniards do. They never go to bed. A dog barked with energy. A gang of young men went by arguing and laughing, their voices thick with hormones. The garbage trucks revved to a pitch just past tolerance and moved on to the next barrel of refuse. I think that rather than falling asleep, I was simply knocked out cold by the sudden, explosive noise of a garbage truck taking off. When I awoke in the morning, it seemed as if the racket had only just stopped.

In the 17th Century, the Italian pilgrim, Laffi passed through Logroño. The place had given him pleasure. "It's a rather large city, situated in a plain," he wrote in his diary, "very beautiful, rich and convenient, and abundant in all things.... There is a beautiful cathedral which is large, well-maintained and with good offices. .... After visiting various convents of monks and nuns - most beautiful - we arrived at a large portal that took us out of the city."

I didn't find Logroño as attractive as Laffi had. Visiting here last year with Scott, I had disliked the city; the stained concrete walls of the modern city had reminded me of a grimy squash court. The place had nearly the same effect on me today. But the people in the hostel had looked after me with great kindness - it wasn't their fault there had been a snorers' convention on garbage night. And in the old town there were sights of interest: the Church of Santa Maria la Redonda, with its Baroque twin spires called *Las Gemellas*, the Church of San Bartolomé, whose medieval tower shows Moorish influence, and the Convent of San Francisco, built by a grateful nobleman whose son the saint healed when he came through Logroño on his way to Santiago.

In the early morning, I walked slowly in a light drizzle down the Ruavieja, the "old street" that had seen pilgrim traffic since the 11th Century. Last year I had walked with Scott, Heinrich and Else down this same street after dinner, past the doors of bodegas from which music had spilled like wine. This must have been where Evy the Brazilian had had a few drinks last night. Now on this gray morning, the bodegas were only mute signs over closed doors. I stopped for a moment at the Pilgrims' Fountain, a lifeless shrine-like shelter with a couple of taps, built in the 16th Century and now wedged below ground level between the street and a drab apartment block. Here I made a slight curve onto the Calle Barriocepo. Before long, I reached my first destination: the Church of Santiago el Real.

Santiago el Real had a cloak and dagger elusiveness, didn't stand as much as hide beside the street, masked with the gray of a shadowless mist. Its tall facade was stretched and flattened against itself as if it hoped you might miss it. I nearly did, in fact, then happened to notice two small doors shrinking under a plain arch. I tried them but they were both locked.

For a better look at Santiago el Real, I turned into a perpendicular street just in front of the church doors. But from wherever I stood on this side street, I could see only part of the facade at a time, wavering in the rain like a partial image from a dream. Above the doorway, set within an arch, stood a figure of St. James in the pose and dress of a pilgrim. Higher still, above this figure, and dominating the scene from a deeply indented arch, was another James, this one astride a white charger in mid-gallop. His cape rippled in the wind behind him as he leaned forward; one hand held his standard with its flag straight out while the other was flung valiantly back, brandishing a sword. Along the base of the sculpture were Moors, their heads about to be trampled to dust. Santiago Matamoros - the Moorslayer - a kind of Obi Wan Kenobi riding across the landscape of Reconquista Spain.

They say this 10th-century church stands over an earlier one built in the 9th Century by the son of Alfonso II, King Ramiro I of León. Ramiro had erected that first church in honour of a battle near the town of Clavijo, some twenty kilometres south of Logroño in the direction of Soria. The Battle of Clavijo, which never took place, is the cornerstone of the Spanish version of the Reconquest.

The Clavijo story begins in 8th-century Asturias during the Moorish invasions and the reign of King Mauregatus. The Moors have not only plundered Asturias thoroughly, but exacted from the king a terrible and humiliating tribute: a hundred Christian virgins annually for the gloating gratification of the Cordovan court. The tribute would be paid out, with great anguish, for over fifty years.

Ramiro is the first Asturian king to deny the Moors their Christian girls. Not a man to have his pleasures mocked, Abd al-Rahman II - father of 45 sons and 42 daughters - gathers a large army and rides north from Córdoba to Clavijo. Ramiro awaits him, but his troops are a sorry lot and the odds look bad. On the eve of the battle, the king hunches gloomily in the royal tent. Suddenly startled, he looks up to see St. James standing before him. "Do you not know that I am the patron and protector of Spain?" says the Apostle. "Fear not! Tomorrow, I will assist you in battle."

Next morning, on the plains by the hilltop Castle of Clavijo, as the Moors confidently begin their rampage into the trembling Christian ranks, the clouds tear open. Out charges St. James, his sword darting and flashing like lightning as he spurs his white steed onto the battleground. Emboldened, full of rejoicing, the Christians fight gloriously with their hero at their side. When it is all over, on the 23rd of May, 844, 70,000 Moors lie slaughtered on the plains of the River Ebro.

The Clavijo story - backdated to just after the Invention of James' tomb - was written down early in the 12th Century. It has been bluntly called a "gross historical fake." Who knows how it happened. Maybe someone - a local madman? a reliable fellow like the butcher? - saw a mirage in the distant sky and with a florid spurt of invention over a pint of beer turned that vision into a news story. Or maybe a committee, set to debate propaganda measures, reviewed recent military events and invented Clavijo to suit their political needs. Or was it, after all, a wholly impersonal process, an involuntary action of the imagination we all share, the mind bubbling with myths from a place we don't yet know about, that would burst into a hundred, a thousand, minds at once?

The Spanish Reconquest had begun as an attempt to get back stolen land. But the Christians soon recognized that a Moorish war was a holy war, a *jihad*, a soldier's rite of initiation into Muslim heaven. Just like the Crusades in the Holy Land, the Reconquista became the mirror image of the *jihad*; by the late 11th Century the whole thing had the look of a true religious war, and Clavijo was invented or imagined to fire up the Spanish Crusade.

An important political fact was also at work. In the 9th Century, Alfonso II had welcomed Frankish military support and Frankish culture into his beleaguered Asturias. But by the mid-12th Century, with French settlers in their comfortable homes and prosperous shops all along the Camino, resentment was festering. The French were the subject of grumbling debate in the council halls of Spanish castles, the butt of snide and sullen remarks in the local taverns. They made more money than the Spaniards, flaunted their *savoir faire*, wore ridiculous and extravagant clothes. But it was the glory stories about St. James that really rankled Spanish ears: gusts of propaganda blowing along the Camino from the francophilic councils at Santiago. France's King Charlemagne was stealing all the good Camino stories. It was neither Pelayo nor Theodemir, but Charlemagne who according to the *Liber Sanctus Jacobi* had first learned of the whereabouts of James' tomb. It was not King Alfonso, but Charlemagne who was the first pilgrim to arrive at Iria

Flavia. It was always Charlemagne, James' favourite hero, riding into Spain, fighting his way across the country, stabbing Moors into the dust. How humiliating that the great patron of Spain needed somebody from away, somebody from France no less, to save his own country.

So Clavijo was used by the hispanophilic fringe to publicize the battles of the kings of Asturias and Castile and León against the Moors. The story had an unbelievably long and tight hold on the Spanish imagination. At the same time it was written in the 12th Century, another document from the days of Ramiro was dug up and falsified to prove that a religious tax was due annually to the Church at Santiago as a thank-offering for the victory at Clavijo. The income from that donation was not small, and continued to be paid until it was abolished in 1812.

But the Clavijo mystique lived on. In a book called *Santiago Apostol, Patron de España*, published in Madrid in 1940, I came across a lament about that day in 1812 when the so-called Vow of Santiago, the tax of gratitude for Clavijo, was done away with: A new era began that day in Spain, I read.

> Now, the cry "Santiago!" was no longer heard in the battles that Spaniards still had to fight. Here began the great decline of spiritual and terrestrial values. Spain would lose her colonies in America and, in the last days of the century, the last rags of an Empire that had come together under the patronage of the Apostle.

A soft dirt path took me along the Camino from Logroño towards Nájera. Fields stretched away on both sides. Ahead of me, I saw familiar pilgrims from the hostel, the ebullient Evy, snorer par excellence, among them. I walked slowly, enjoying the breeze and birdsong and the feel of the ground under my freshly rested feet. The rain had stopped and the sun was making cheerful threats about baking us all to a crisp.

I had climbed a steep embankment into a little stone village and paused for a drink of water when Evy turned. Seeing me, he beckoned and grinned. I waved back, he waited, and when I caught up, he fell in with me. Walking together was a sudden release from the inwardness of the day's journey so far. I laughed hard at Evy's crazy jokes. I missed the scenery, even tuned out the sting of a new blister. I forgot pilgrimage altogether.

We came to a small village where we stopped at a bar to rest, sitting outside in a shaded porch on white plastic chairs with our bare, blistered feet draped over our boots like specimens in an anatomy lab. The South African Errol was there, also Alfredo of the light-speed Spanish. Before long, Bernardo arrived, hobbling. I met a curly-haired Italian, Martino, who was travelling with a French friend who worked in a library in Paris. I gave some Tylenol to a Spanish pilgrim with a very sore knee. I sat between Duncan, minus his mother who was lagging behind with Virginia, and the father and daughter pair, Luis and Ana. I was introduced to an unsmiling, heavy-set massage therapist from Madrid; this was her fourth and, emphatically, her *last*, Camino pilgrimage. The cheerful custodian of the hostel at Logroño came by in his car to see how we were doing. We bought him a beer, and he leaned casually against a pillar on the porch as he discussed the details of the day's route with Luis and the young Ana.

My conversation with Duncan turned into a friendly debate about James the warrior. "That alter-ego of the Moor killer isn't quite as nice as the pilgrim image," he said as he poured me some mineral water. "It shows how much the Camino's about violence. Spanish Catholicism is colourful and passionate," he went on, "but not deep. It's fueled by drama and bloodshed. So's the Camino."

"There *is* a softer side," I replied, thinking of the priest's loving sermon in Los Arcos. James was, after all, a pilgrim's saint, the gentle figure standing below the Matamoros on the facade of the Church of Santiago El Real, a healer who was so identified with his pilgrims that, like no other saint in the Christian calendar, he was most often shown dressed as one of his own pilgrims, as if he himself were making his way with them to his tomb. In the Church of Santiago at Puente la Reina I had seen the most attractive of these images of James: a robed pilgrim resting the fingers of one hand over a walking stick and holding a book in the other. On his hat was a fat scallop shell. His darkly tanned and weather-beaten face was strikingly oriental; this was St. James "the Black," with his slanted, faraway eyes and half opened mouth.

"That's as romanticized as the warrior saint," replied Duncan, swigging his beer. "Only in the other direction. It's either too vicious or too sentimental for me."

Later, I read a story that reminded me a little of Duncan's cynicism. It was from the *Historia Silense,* a 12th-century chronicle kept at the Monastery of Silos in Galicia. In 1064, a pilgrim from the Holy Land arrives in Santiago Cathedral. He overhears other pilgrims praying to James: "Santiago, good knight", they implore, "liberate us from present and future evils." The man is annoyed, sarcastic. "Santiago," he harrumphs to himself, "was not a knight, he was a fisherman." That night (as he dozes, we suppose, in his pilgrim hostel) Santiago comes to the man wearing the whitest of knight's outfits and girded with a sword that flashes like the rays of the sun. In one hand he holds a set of keys.

"Who told you I was not a knight?" demands James. "I stand before you in this guise to prove that I fight as God's champion in His service. I protect all who love me and call on me, in every danger. Behold these keys. King Fernando has besieged the Moors at Coimbra for seven years. Tomorrow, I will open the doors to the city. When Fernando enters, Coimbra will fall into his hands."

Which apparently it did. After an angry diatribe against the Franks, the *Historia Silense* goes on to tell the Coimbra story as another piece of anti-French propaganda: King Fernando of Castile is beleaguered by the Moors at Coimbra - a Leonese outpost in what is now Portugal. James appears dressed as for Clavijo and the Moors die in droves.

As the Reconquest went on, Santiago Matamoros eclipsed James the pilgrim saint. Pictures like the one I had seen in the priest's book at Villatuerta were hung in churches all along the Camino: a mounted Apostle leaping from glowering thunderclouds into battle amid armoured chests and swooping swords. And under everything, a layer of gape-mouthed, turbaned heads.

On the Camino to Santiago in August 1998, I was walking in a rare, narrow trough of time where peace was all around. A few years before, Basque separatists had gunned down a high-ranking government official in the streets of Sevilla. There were outbreaks of Basque violence in 1997, and it had crossed our minds, when Scott and I cycled through last year, that we might see some violence in Navarra. In León, there was another kind of hostility, the old animosity between León and Castile. We had seen graffiti for a separate León: *Puta Castile!* in dripping red paint on the roadside rocks after Astorga. Castile the Whore!! But on this hot, still day, in the company of my easy-going fellow-travellers, it seemed more likely that, if anything, I was under the watch of the gentle pilgrim James.

Abd al-Malik, the original owner of the casket I had so admired at the Museum in Pamplona, was the son of one Abu Amir Muhammad ibn Abi Amir al-Maafiri, "the Victorious One," or as he was usually known, al-Mansur, Scourge of Christian Spain. Al-Mansur was the quintessential usurper, had risen to power in 10th-century Córdoba by manipulating the weak and challenging the strong. His story is not surprisingly a violent one, but it is played out on a stage of immense, if fragile, elegance and sophistication, beginning at the court of Abd al-Rahman III.

In 912, after putting down a series of rebellions among Arab upstarts and sulking Berbers, Abd al-Rahman III seized power in Córdoba, first as Emir, then as Caliph. Al-Rahman's standing army numbered 30,000; his harem, 3,600. Under his rule, the Córdoban court glittered. He was the first to issue coinage using African gold. His palace at Madinat az-Zahra was a paradise arched with coloured marble and ebony, streaming with gold and sparkling with gems. When the huge doors were swung open to the sun, it was said, crystals and bright ivory blinded the eyes.

It was Abd al-Rahman's great grandfather, Abd al-Rahman II, whose troops were trampled by Santiago Matamoros at Clavijo in 844; Abd al-Rahman III had his turn at a real battle at Simancas in 939. He must have been sure of himself as he joined battle with King Ramiro II of León. His arms factory at Córdoba was producing 20,000 arrows a month and 3000 tents a year. From the stud farms near Sevilla came his most splendid cavalry horses. But as the battle progressed, the clouds began to boil. Santiago made another of his lightning appearances (white charger, cape, sword) and the Muslims were clobbered. The Caliph had not noticed Santiago in the sky; believing instead that treason had cost him the fight, he swiftly rounded up the suspects and had them crucified.

Abd al-Rahman III had a son, Hakem II, an astute warrior like his father, also a patron of scholars. His library held 400,000 manuscripts. (The best stocked Christian library ran around 4000.)

Hakem's heir, Hisham, was the son of his favourite concubine, the alluring Subh, a Christian Basque taken as a captive to Córdoba. A weak loop in the Córdoban net formed around the concubine and her son, and it was here that al-Mansur saw his own fortunes in the making.

He came from an established Arab family in Algeciras. He was well educated at Córdoba and had succeeded through plain ability and a good deal of cageyness in penetrating the labyrinths of the bureaucracy of al-Andalus. His first break came early in 967, when he was appointed to look after properties that had been given to Subh by Hakem. In time, Subh was sharing with al-Mansur both her properties and her bed.

The unfortunate Hisham was only eleven when he came to power. The lad barely knew what was happening: al-Mansur formed a regency with two other men, one a minister of the caliph, a Berber much disliked on racial and personal grounds; the other a general. In time, the Berber minister was murdered. As for the general, he died in a fall from his horse. By now - the year was 981 - the young Hisham was of age. But al-Mansur kept him diverted by the delights of the harem as he set himself up as "mayor of the palace."

On his own at last, and with an enormous standing army of 50,000, al-Mansur turned his sites to Christian Spain. There was a second battle at Simancas with Ramiro III of León. This time, Santiago Matamoros was not available and the Christians took a bad beating. In 985, al-Mansur was tearing at Barcelona; in 987, Coimbra; in 988, León and the monastery at Sahagún. In 995, he took Carrión and Astorga, and captured Count Garcia Fernandez of Castile, who died of his wounds in Córdoba shortly after.

By 997, al-Mansur was in Santiago de Compostela. The general wrecked the city and set about destroying the cathedral. He levelled the south aisle but left the apse and James' bones alone. It is said that he presented the Christian nobles who accompanied him on his mission with 2,285 pieces of silken fabric called *tiraz*, in a multiplicity of colours and patterns. It is also said that he let his horse drink from the baptismal font, which made the animal vomit. Perhaps unsure about what this meant, al-Mansur withdrew, but not without taking back with him to Córdoba a hefty souvenir: the cathedral bells.

In 999, the general was back in Pamplona; in 1000, Burgos. Before his death in 1002, on the way home from burning the Monastery of San Millán to the ground, he had completed no less than fifty-seven campaigns. Though he posed as a strict and devout Muslim, (he was never without his Koran), *jihad* was not much on his mind; like the Vikings who were hacking away at the rich monasteries of northern Europe, al-Mansur was after plunder, treasure, tribute, livestock and captives. When they heard of his death in Córdoba, they cried: "Our provider of slaves is no more!" The Christian chronicles, downplaying the fact that al-Mansur had used plenty of Christian mercenaries for his raids, reported that the "scourge" had been "seized by the Devil and buried in Hell."

Abd al-Malik, the first owner the ivory chest in the Museum of Navarra, carried his father's ambitions further: 1003, Catalonia; 1004, Castile; 1005, León; 1006, Aragon.

After León, he was given the epithet "Sword of the Kingdom." But in 1008, "the Sword" died unexpectedly of a heart attack.

In spite of military success, al-Andalus was, by the time of al-Malik's death, a mess. Long on the downhill slope of indolence, overspending and in-fighting, the caliphate was now teetering on the edge of anarchy. Al-Malik's son (by another Basque concubine) was murdered. The Guadalquivir River flooded. There were outbreaks of plague. The Berber tribes, always the restive underdogs and now positively seething with spite, trashed Córdoba and massacred its citizens. They plundered al-Hakam's gorgeous libraries. The playboy Hisham disappeared. By 1031, al-Andalus had reached rock bottom. The power of Córdoba, or what was left of it, shrivelled and disappeared while the Berbers carried on a reign of terror in the countryside.

After 1031, small statelets began to take shape on the scarred landscape of al-Andalus. These "taifa states," as they were called, were independently governed by small-time, self-styled emirs, the "taifa kings." Now more than ever, Muslims and Christians would mingle, on the battlefield as enemies, but often as allies: in protection rackets and assassination schemes; in workshops and markets and taverns and around the tables of scholars and translators; in each other's homes and beds, sometimes even in each other's place of worship. Officially they hated each other; in practice, their emotions must have run the gamut: envy, admiration, mistrust, love, pity, and no doubt a wish shared among many for simple, peaceful co-existence.

I left Duncan at the roadside bar working on his third beer, and headed to Nájera with Evy, Errol and Alfredo. We trooped bravely through the heat: a slim, aquiline Spaniard, now strangely subdued, a quiet South African with a flaming ponytail, a brilliant Brazilian-Italian Dionysius, and me. We walked amid a galaxy of low-flying hills weighted with grainfields and vineyards. In the distance, church spires stood above red-roofed villages like rockets ready for take-off.

In 1142, Peter the Venerable, Abbot of the French Benedictine Monastery of Cluny had travelled here on a fundraising tour to the court of Alfonso VII. In Nájera, he met two scholars, one a German, the other English. Both were searching for Arabic books on mathematics, astronomy and astrology, which they were going to translate into Latin. Peter talked them into collecting Arab religious texts while they were at it. Eventually the Englishman, Robert of Ketton, made the first known Latin translation of the Koran. But Peter the theologian cared not a hoot about the merits of Islamic learning; what he wanted from a Latin Koran was ammunition to fire at what he liked to call "the abominable heresy of the Saracens."

Now here we were, walking in the footsteps of three medieval men of ideas to Nájera. Our conversation was a word salad: Italian and Portuguese, fire-cracker Spanish, and that soft, unplaceable South African English. We debated world affairs, we teased each other, told jokes I didn't always get, took pictures, shared food. In a few weeks, we would all be gone from the Camino, taking our new thoughts somewhere else. But today, for a few fleeting hours, we were part of that traffic of human thought that has always crossed the porous membranes of the Camino.

Roland battles the Moorish giant, Ferragut, on this carving on a church column in Estella.

4

STORIES

Mew, meadows, steppes, bear still the fabled kings
Long after roofless courts are left to chalky whirring
things.
      Margaret Avison, Unbroken Lineage

We are going to a place where
Things are only what
they are. Or, with the barest exception, something
else, but only just something else, hardly. Words
are not allowed at all.
      Robert Kroetsch, Excerpts from the Real World

The long bridge at Hospital de Órbigo,
site of a famous jousting tournament in 1434.

It was a very long way to Nájera. In the late afternoon, I was still walking, or by now plodding, with Errol, Alfredo, and Evy along a flat track down the middle of a pie plate of a valley. Far out on the perimeter, a rim of low hills wrinkled wetly in the heat. We had run out of conversation, sung every song we knew. We made attempts at *Mr. Tambourine Man,* but none of us could remember the words. Tired, suddenly too hot, we fell silent. Even Evy was pensive, watching the ground as if he was counting stones. My left shin was becoming sore and I felt as though I had a headache in my left hip.

When we came to a wooded area on a shallow bluff, Errol said quietly, "I think I'll sit down and read my book a while." Errol carried five books in his backpack. He often lent them to people, joking that it reduced his load. I had borrowed his copy of *The Buddha in Everyday Life,* which I was reading at night.

A little further on, I thought about sitting down too, but Evy perked me up. With just the trace of an effort, his face brightened. "Come o-o-on, baby," he crooned. He cocked an eyebrow at me, then launched into *The Girl from Ipanema,* jigging down the trail like a street dancer at carnival. I found him very funny. Alfredo snickered mirthlessly and looked across the hills into the horizon; the cool, cerebral Spaniard seemed to feel diminished beside the free-wheeling Brazilian.

The outskirts of Nájera were shabbier than I remembered. Scott and I had liked this town. We had good photos of its pert, sand-coloured buildings, its narrow streets with flowers, the Rio Najerilla peacefully winding under the town's bridges, and the big, dome-topped cliffs at the far end of town that had given Nájera its name: the Arabic *Naxara*, "between two hills." The dingy, ramshackle dwellings on the way in had vanished from my memory.

Evy spied a *heladeria* - an ice cream shop - that opened onto the street between two dust-caked buildings. Inside, the air conditioning was severe and the bright metallic lights made me think of an operating room. We slouched on white plastic chairs licking sweet, cold, Kool-Aid-coloured balls of ice cream. Outside, framed by the doorway, a few cars went past, then a handful of pilgrims looking hot, a couple of cyclists, and an old lady with a cane and a bent back.

"Have you seen any pilgrims on a horse?" Alfredo asked in a split-second streak of Spanish. I processed the question like a slow learner while Evy shrugged, his mouth full of ice cream.

The Everest Guide says you can cross the Camino by foot, bike or horse, but I couldn't imagine how you would care for a horse here. In the Middle Ages, most pilgrims would have been on foot, too poor or penitential for the luxury of a horse. But hoof-marks and manure and the strong, sweaty flanks of horses snorting in the dust - these would have been everyday sights along the Camino. Rich locals owned a variety of horses: palfreys for regular use and pack-horses for servants and baggage, though mules used less water. Then there were the war-horses, for which Spain was renowned. Training such an animal was difficult, and so cruel I could barely read about it, but the finished product, a horse that insolently tossed its mane and pranced so its polished tack glared in the sunshine, now *that* was something to see. To dusty, foot-sore pilgrims, those sleek creatures with their straight-sitting, grim-mouthed riders must have looked menacingly glamorous.

I tried to picture equestrian nobles prancing haughtily through Nájera on the way east to Catalonia and Aragon, or west to Castile. The more chivalrous among them might greet pilgrims along the road kindly, offer alms or protection. Some would have asked for a prayer at Santiago. But while the pilgrims headed due west to Galicia, many of these nobles, along with their bodyguards and soldiers, would eventually turn south off the Camino to Madrid, Toledo, Granada, the Portuguese border, Sevilla. Their purpose was to fight Moors and, almost as often, each other.

There is a good story from Nájera. Sancho III, King of Navarra is called away on royal business, but for some reason does not take his favourite horse with him. Instead, he entrusts the steed to the care of his wife, Elvira, who remains at Nájera. Their son, Garcia, begs Elvira to let him ride the animal. She flatly refuses. He nags. The horse-keeper advises her: don't let that kid on the horse. Elvira holds firm. The lad is furious, plans his revenge. When his father gets home, he will say that Elvira has slept with the horse-keeper. Garcia gets his brother Fernando to go along with the ruse, though at first Fernando is reluctant. Sancho comes home, learns of his wife's adultery, has Elvira imprisoned and calls a judge. The matter will be decided by a duel between Garcia and Sancho's bastard son, Ramiro, who is the only one brave enough to take on the queen's defense.

In the meantime, the boys have repented and confessed to a monk from a local monastery. The monk reports the confession to Sancho. The duel is called off. Elvira is returned from jail and agrees to forgive Garcia on condition that he will never inherit her homeland of Castile. And so on Sancho's death, Fernando gets Castile, Garcia gets Navarra, and the bastard hero Ramiro, who dared to defend the innocent queen, gets Aragon.

There is a curious twist to the end of the story: in a public ceremony, Elvira formally adopts Ramiro as her legitimate son. As he kneels before her, she covers him with her dress, then lifts it from him, thus ritually giving birth to him herself. The story was likely written by a minstrel at Ramiro's court in Aragon as a praise piece to the bastard king, whose claims to the throne needed all the support they could get.

Stories like this streamed across Spain from the Pyrenees to Galicia. In them, the gross elements of Camino history - envoys, raids, battles, coups, murders and marriages - were transmuted into tales of brightest valour and darkest evil. Some were amusing vignettes about local thugs or glamour boys like Garcia and Ramiro; others were giant sagas, true epics with complex and fatally gifted heroes.

At school, I had lumbered through most of the big old European epics - *The Iliad, The Odyssey, Beowulf, The Song of Roland*: huge masculine chronicles of heroes and their deeds, their weapons and their noble friends, of their horses, their numberless, nameless soldiers, occasionally their women. Epics were thick with strategy, treachery, violence, insolence, and bloody death. They were wide and theatrical. "Vast is the plain and broad the countryside," says Turoldus in *The Song of Roland*. But they could also be intimate and immensely tender. When Charlemagne breaks the news of Roland's death to his betrothed, the beautiful Aude, she falls dead at his feet.

> The king thinks she has fainted.
> The emperor feels pity for her and weeps;
> He takes her by the hands and raises her up.
> Her head is drooped over his shoulder.

A melancholy wisdom lies within the epic, expressed in the tears of old men and mourning queens. Epic heroes strive to be good in the only way they *could* be good and still survive in a bad world. Some are too good, and die. Others are not good enough, and also die.

On the page, epics can seem stilted and repetitive. They were composed to be recited though, or chanted to music. Because they were oral, few epics are known from before the 12th Century, for it was only then that scribes, usually literate clergy, began to copy them into manuscripts. In Spain, where epics were as common as anywhere else, only a few fragments of the old Visigothic ones are left. The tales connected with the Camino were written down only after 1100. Most were spin-offs of *The Song of Roland*, in which Christian heads, most of them French, shine like golden globes over the swarthy Moors. Or as Turoldus puts it his *Song of Roland*:

> The helmets glitter with their gold and precious
>   stones
> And the shields and saffron byrnies
> And the spears with their ensigns attached.
> The bugles sound, the notes are clear and loud.

Although it was made to look that way, historical truth was never really the point of an epic. What you got was a point of view decked out as history. *The Song of Roland* was straight-up Christian chauvinism; Turoldus would do whatever he must to history, as long as he could ignite the crusading spirit of the Europeans against the Moorish invaders, and sell a good story while he was at it. Here are Roland and his friend Oliver realizing they have been trapped in an ambush at Roncesvalles:

> Lord Companion, I think
> We may have a battle with the Saracens.
> Roland replies: And may God grant it to us.
> It is our duty to be here for our king:
> For his lord a vassal must suffer hardships
> And endure great heat and great cold;
> And he must lose both hair and hide.
> Now let each man take care to strike great blows,
> So that no one can sing a shameful song about us.
> The pagans are wrong and the Christians are right.
> No dishonourable tale will ever be told about me.

In my darker moments, I saw this kind of epic, with its martial virtue and its crude Christian morality, as vulgar, simplistic rabble-rousing. The best epic was much more than that, but it never stopped being easy propaganda. It travelled like blood along the arteries of the Camino.

On our way into Nájera, we had passed a modest hill called the Poyo Roldán that lay between the Camino and highway N120. In the *Codex Calixtinus* there is a story, a short tale that thinks it's an epic, about the Poyo Roldán.

The giant Ferragut, of the lineage of Goliath, has arrived in Spain "from the lands of Syria, sent with 20,000 Turks by the emir of Babylon." Outside Nájera, he meets Charlemagne. It is agreed that the giant will take on the king's best men in single, mounted combat. The fights commence. Charlemagne watches, frowns as Ferragut lays low one French hero after another. Roland, "the champion among equals," asks to go next. His eye narrowed, the fair young knight rides towards the beetle-browed hulk. The giant lifts Roland from his horse with his right hand and, leering like King Kong, dangles him beside his horse's great mop of a mane. The horse begins to gallop toward Nájera; Roland reaches up, grabs the giant's beard. With a mighty tug, he flings Ferragut and himself to the ground. Ferragut tries to remount. Roland slices his horse in two, then knocks the sword from the giant's hand. Ferragut swaggers forward, aiming his punch. Roland ducks. A fat fist lands on the brow of Roland's horse. The animal falls dead. The two men square off now, planting their feet to fight it out with fists.

At three in the afternoon, they take a breather and, relaxing under a tree, fall into a religious debate. Like hulks anywhere, Ferragut is really an amiable fellow, and beneath all that flesh, as dumb as a post. A Moorish witch, he tells Roland, has cast a spell to keep him from Christianity. Then, in a regrettable moment of confidence, Ferragut lets slip that his body is vulnerable in one spot only: the umbilicus.

The oaf has a bright idea, and proposes the following deal: whoever loses the next round will accept the winner's religion. More fighting ensues. Roland finds himself hopelessly wedged between the hard ground and a mountain of brute muscle. Knowing he is nearly done for, he appeals to the Son of the Blessed Virgin Mary, who (thanks be to God, says the author) helps him to twist a little under the giant's weight. Just above him, he spies the vulnerable navel funneling like a black hole into the giant's gut. He plunges his dagger in. Ferragut slumps. Roland wriggles out from under, thus proving the superiority of Christ over a Moorish witch. As he dies, Ferragut converts to the true faith. In another version of the story, Roland finishes Ferragut off by hurling a rock at him. And that rock, says the legend, is the small hill I had walked past with Evy and Alfredo, just this side of N122.

The Roland and Ferragut tale was written in the 1100s and is included in a book of other such tales entitled the *Libri Turpini*. Supposedly, the *Libri* stories were the eye-witness accounts of that Archbishop Turpin who had fought with Charlemagne and Roland in Spain. After escaping the Basques at Roncesvalles, so the story goes, the Archbishop returned to Vienna. There he recorded his adventures for the glory of Charlemagne and the *Camino francés*. More likely, the stories were not written in Vienna at all, but in France, by someone whose name was not Turpin.

Over a hundred copies of the *Libri* stories survive. In them we find almost all the lore about Charlemagne that was making the rounds at the time. The tales may have been meant as serious works in Latin rather than popular entertainment pieces. Some scholars believe they were written to inspire the clergy to preach the crusade; others, that the stories were a set of reading exercises for teaching Latin to rambunctious schoolboys. Whatever their purpose, the Turpin accounts of Charlemagne's exploits in Spain gave enormous prestige to the Camino. And they had the support of those many churchmen at Compostela who looked with approval on the French presence in Spain. Turpin's collection makes up Book IV of the *Codex Calixtinus*, coming just before Aimery's *Guide*. And like the *Guide*, it exalts everything French about the Camino.

This was what so irritated the Spanish. James may have saved Spain, Turpin or whoever he was implies, but he couldn't have done it without the French. In fact Turpin rewrote the history of the *Camino francés* in his *Dream of Charlemagne*. He begins the tale in France, as Charlemagne undertakes to fight the Moors. James' tomb is utterly unknown. But for several nights running, the king's sleep is disturbed by a vivid dream in which the thick arc of the Milky Way sweeps across the Spanish sky into Galicia. He is visited in his dream by the Apostle James, who informs him that it is to his - James' - own tomb that the starry path leads. The king is still perplexed. What does the dream mean? James patiently explains that Charlemagne has been chosen to open the road to his hidden burial place. The king and his valorous men will banish the Moors from the road west so that pilgrims may safely travel to the shrine at Santiago.

Charlemagne heads first to Pamplona. The city walls are impossible to penetrate. After three months, Christ and St. James are called on for a Jericho-like feat of wall breaking. The Christian success at Pamplona makes news at the Moorish strongholds along the Camino; the king marches on to Galicia, freeing occupied cities along the way and collecting tribute and booty from the now docile Moors. He arrives at James' tomb, the saint's first pilgrim. (Never mind about Alfonso II and his court travelling down from Oviedo in the 830s to the forest crypt uncovered by the fasting Theodemir.) Today no one knows if Charlemagne was even alive when the tomb was found. Einhard says nothing about it. But every August 6, a Mass is still said in Santiago Cathedral for Charlemagne's soul.

On the way back from Santiago, Charles meets the Moor Aigoland for battle near the meseta town of Sahagún. The king's soldiers camp in a meadow on the eve of the fight. Before they sleep, they drive their lances into the ground. In the morning, those who will die as martyrs for Christ's cause find their lances alive with bark and leaves. Though they cut the lances down for the battle, the roots remain in the ground and eventually grow into beautiful trees. Aimery does his level best to confirm this story: at Sahagún, he writes in his *Guide*, choosing his words carefully, "there is a meadow in which, as it is reported, the sparkling spears of victorious warriors, planted for the glory of God, were once blooming."

The battle with Aigoland at Sahagún is indecisive; Aigoland pulls back into León while Charlemagne withdraws to the east. There is more fighting at Pamplona. The action then comes to Nájera, where Roland meets Ferragut. On the way back to Gaul, Charlemagne finishes off Saragosa and two Moorish kings, Marsirus and Beliguandus. Then Turpin's story glides back into the familiar territory of Roncesvalles. Roland dies in the Saracen ambush, and Charlemagne returns with a few survivors, including Turpin himself, to France.

Of all of these tales, it was Roland's fight with Ferragut that everyone liked the best. Back at Estella, on the wall of the palace of the kings of Navarra, I had photographed a carving that depicted that confrontation. Later I would see more images, almost identical, at Villamayor de Monjardín, then just outside Navarette, and again at San Juan de Ortega. In the Middle Ages, that image of Ferragut and Roland going head to head was a key to the meaning of the Camino. On this very road, Roland had trounced Ferragut, just as David had once beaten Goliath, and Christ had vanquished the devil. The war with the Moors that ran the length of the Camino was not only the struggle of Christendom against its heathen foes, but the battle of the pure Church of Christ against Satan's mistress, the Whore of Babylon. And just as importantly, these recurrent images of the knight facing the brute were a reminder to *you*, that your pilgrimage was a struggle within yourself between good and evil, and that your faith, like Roland's, would see you through.

We arrived at the *refugio* in Nájera around six in the afternoon. My hip felt strained and tired; a pain in my right shin was bothering me. Evy and Arnaldo were still strong and decided to carry on to Azofra. In the doorway, we laughed and hugged farewell, still teasing each other affectionately. I didn't feel sad. I was sure I would see them again. Unfortunately, I never did.

On the main floor of the *refugio* was a reception room that doubled as a refectory, with oak panelling and a wooden eating table polished to a warm gold. Here I found Duncan, again without either his mother Martha or Virginia, and Anya, whose feet were slowly healing. Errol materialized on the steps down from the dormitory, holding a book. Deidre was there and the curly-haired Italian, Martino, drinking coffee with his French friend.

Before long, Bernardo limped in from the street where he had been smoking. He sat down with me at the table. I commented on the lovely room.

"Those are the original beams up there," he said, tipping his head toward the ceiling.

"How old's the building, do you think?" I asked.

"No idea." He looked with a casual, practised eye over the ceiling.

"It's not the original 11th-century hostel, is it?"

"No, but it's old," he said, shrugging, "maybe Renaissance."

The *refugio* custodians assigned us to bunks upstairs. The plank steps were shined slick and we were instructed to take our shoes off before going up. The dorm was a large, bright room with neat rows of new bunks. Mine was at the back, over Errol's. I went through what was becoming my late-day ritual, beginning with an inspection of my blisters and ending with a pile of clothes to launder. I heard a conversation at Bernardo's bunk and went over in my bare feet. Bernardo was lying down, with his feet arranged under a gray shirt. I asked to have a look at them but he said they looked disgusting. I told him I was a nurse, but he was still self-conscious. "They're like something from a butcher's display case," he said, nodding toward the two inert bumps under his shirt.

Bernardo had been talking to Duncan and Errol about teaching the history of architecture.

Errol turned to me. "Aren't you were a medieval professor or something?"

"Well, I have a PhD in medieval English," I said. "I make my living in health care, though." I had explained my career so many times, and to my relief, nobody today seemed interested in asking for details.

"The PhD's a frill, is it?" said Duncan, mockingly.

"I guess you could say that."

"Sometimes," said Bernardo, smiling, "the frill makes all the difference."

I told Bernardo I wanted to take a detour by cab the next day to see the monastery of San Millán in the Montes de Cógolla. "You're an architectural historian." I said, "Why not give those feet a rest and come with me?"

A community of Christian hermits had founded San Millán sometime during the Visigothic period in the 5th or 6th Century. The place was a little south of Nájera in a confusion of hills near the margin of the Camino world. Spanish literary historians call San Millán the medieval birthplace of Spanish literature. It had also been a hornet's nest of political and religious squabbles that in a couple of curious ways, had involved the cult of St. James.

"Good idea," Bernardo said. "I've never been to San Millán. I'll see how I feel in the morning. If I rest my feet tonight and only walk a little tomorrow, maybe I'll be able to carry on to Santiago. If I can't, I'll probably go back to Madrid." This, I could see, was a disappointing prospect. Despite his feet, Bernardo was enjoying his time on the Camino enormously. Whenever I had seen him, he was busy talking with other pilgrims, with local shopkeepers, with tourists. Later at dinner, he treated us all to tiny lettuces he had bought, that looked like Lilliputian Romaines and were eaten with sardines and olive oil.

That evening after a rest on my bunk, I left the hostel and went around the corner toward the Church of Santa Maria la Real. Nájera was cool and opaque now that the heat was off. A few rain clouds hung slack in the sky as if they were off duty, and the sky itself was a soft, dense blue. The rounded, sand-coloured church towered like a fortress as I approached; at intervals, thick bulging vertical welts ran in half cylinders up the height of the wall.

This church, late gothic, was put up in the 14th Century on the site of an earlier one from the 11th. That first church had an odd beginning. In 1052, Sancho's son Garcia, boyhood liar, scourge of his mother Elvira, and now a grown-up King, was out hunting nearby when his falcon and the dove it was chasing disappeared into a cave. Garcia went in after them and found the birds sitting peacefully together by a vase of lilies at the foot of a statue of the Virgin. Garcia had the Church of Santa Maria la

Real erected over this cave, where Mary with her flowers had soothed the enmities of nature.

Garcia was an avid relics collector. He had in his possession the remains of St. Vincent the martyr and of Prudentius, Bishop of Tarazona. He had gotten the Pope to send him Saints Vital and Agricola from Bologna, along with a few body parts belonging to St. Eugenia. He once presented his new church with a gold cross inlaid with the teeth of the first Christian martyr, St. Stephen. I understood relics and why they are important to faith, but I couldn't help myself: the character of King Garcia of Navarra gave me the willies.

The custodian was unlocking the door to the upstairs choir stalls just as I entered the church. I went up immediately. The rich, dark wood stalls lined the chamber like a panel of straight-backed judges. Each was carved with figures of life in a sinful and demon-infested world. I wandered from chair to chair. On one was carved a human back, minus a head but with huge hanging genitals: the unholy grossness of carnal desire. On another were two children, one pulling the other's hair: discord. Here was a man with leprosy, which was often confused with gonorrhea and thus had a built-in reference to debased sexuality. I saw a stomach with a face in it: gluttony; a dog licking its hind leg: animal desire. There were other horrors: human buttocks with skin sores; a froggy demon with his head on backwards. Presiding over all was an impressive carving of Garcia himself, whose weird relics would be the antidote to all the monstrous vices of this world.

As well as the choir stalls, I had wanted to see a certain sarcophagus in the pantheon of the Church of Santa Maria la Real, a "very fine example," my guidebook said, of Romanesque sculpture. The church had been locked when Scott and I came by in 1997. I had written in my diary: "Church closed unfortunately; skinny little streets to get there, and a pause by the doors to rest and get our bearings before moving on." But over the next year, my attraction to the Romanesque grew, and the tomb continued to interest me. So did the person for whom it was carved: the unfortunate Blanca of Navarra.

The genealogy of northern Spanish kings is a bewildering, many-branched tree of Sanchos and Alfonsos. It is easy, for instance, to confuse Sancho III of *Navarra*, husband of Elvira of Castile, the maltreated mother of Garcia, who died over a hundred years earlier, with Sancho III of *Castile*, who married Blanca of Navarra in 1156. This Blanca of Navarra, who was also the great grand-daughter of El Cid, had died, age twenty-one, giving birth to her first child, a son. In a mere two year's time, her grieving husband would also die and her son become King of Castile: Alfonso VIII, toddler.

I had expected Blanca's tomb to be spectacular but I passed it twice without even noticing it. Finally, someone pointed it out to me: it consisted of a thick, dusty stone lid. I looked again with surprise across a black security chain: the thing was a chipped slab, indelicate, hacked off at both ends. I laughed at my own amazement and wondered, though I never found out, where on earth Blanca and the rest of her tomb were.

Blanca's death, like the death of every important, beautiful woman, had stunned those who shared her world, admired her, loved her, placed their hopes in her. Looking over her tomb lid, I thought about the ways we struggle to repair these terrible losses, when meaning comes loose from our everyday life and pain disconnects us from the world we think we understand. Blanca's death had ruined the family hopes of Sancho III and sent a tremor through the lands outside the castle. I looked again at the lid. It was the sculptor's task (he was very good) to lay Christianity's great truths like a skin graft over this metaphysical injury. The carvings on Blanca's lid were a tapestry of analogies, resemblances, repetitions, associations, homologies, emulations and sympathies - all the mental tricks that held the medieval psyche together. The result was a theological showpiece: Blanca's death seen in a cosmic mirror, made intelligible *sub specie aeternitatis*, in the light of eternity.

I crouched to look across the chain at a relief carved on one panel of the lid. Blanca lies on her deathbed. At her side her husband Sancho mourns. Two angels are above her head protecting her soul as it leaves her body to fly to God. It is a familiar, even homey scene of personal grief. What had it really been like? Perhaps she was serene and full of faith in her last moments; maybe she screamed, struggled in pain, bleeding and crying for her baby before passing out.

But the sculptor knew that for all its real anguish, personal loss was scarcely the point. Events like this, everyday, random and particular, were like a road sign in a desert without an arrow. Reference was essential; the world was held together by stories that stood like ladders across the planes of being from gross earthly life to the timeless vaults of God's heaven. So in the same frame with Blanca's deathbed, the sculptor shows a scene from the parable in Matthew's Gospel, of the wise and foolish virgins: Ten virgins go forth to meet their bridegroom. Five are foolish and carry no oil for their lamps. At midnight all the brides are summoned. Needing to trim their lamps, the foolish virgins ask the well prepared ones for oil. "Buy it yourselves!" say the wise but not especially generous virgins. And while the foolish girls dash off for oil, the bridegroom arrives and takes the five wise ones inside, shutting the door forever on the others.

Here the sculptor asks me to ponder Blanca's story: was the oil of eternal life ready in her lamp? Or was she foolish, careless of her soul, caught up in court dalliances, motherhood, power? Blanca's fate will one day be mine, and even more than Blanca, who is dead and gone, the sculptor means this scene for me. I too (I gather) must watch, for as the parable says, "ye know neither the day nor the hour wherein the Son of Man cometh." Like Blanca, I may be summoned when I least expect it. So I must be prepared, says the sculptor, and keep my oil well stocked.

I walk around the lid several times. Dominating the whole work is a carving of Christ in Majesty. The great Judge looms, warning us, awaiting us at the end of time when our eternal fate is sealed. On one panel are the Three Kings visiting the Infant Jesus in the manger. This story had always been popular in Spain: the first known Spanish drama is a good piece called the *Auto de los Tres Magis,* of which unfortunately only a tiny portion remains. Here on Blanca's tomb, these static, regal figures mutely holding their gifts stand for the submission of foreign monarchs to the Christian king at his birth. The sculptor has lined up the birth of Alfonso during the wars against Islam, with the birth of Jesus Christ, the King before whom all nations would one day bow. I look again, missing Blanca; baby Alfonso has centre stage now. The feminine experience - of birth, motherhood, loss, death - has vanished.

There is a New Testament scene on another side of Blanca's lid, the slaughter of the Innocents by Herod. This sets the birth of Alfonso during the Moorish occupation beside the birth of Jesus during the reign of an evil king. Further along the lid is an Old Testament scene: Solomon judging the two women who both claim an infant as their own. This is Solomon the wise king, whose authority and just judgment is a sign in earthly history of the ultimate king, Jesus Christ.

Would the infant Alfonso fit into that scheme of wise kingship? It turned out fairly well for him overall. When he came of age in 1169, he married Eleanor, daughter of Henry II of England and Eleanor of Aquitaine. His life must have been full of worry. He sometimes got on badly with other Christian kings in Spain. He faced continual wars with the Moors and was terribly beaten at Alarcos in 1195. In 1212, he undertook the battle of his life. With soldiers mustered in Navarra and Catalonia, along with allied troops from France, he headed south to Andalucia. On July 16 he moved through the steep Despenaperros Pass to Las Navas de Tolosa. His men were seriously outnumbered. Their single and critical advantage was their war-horses. The Muslims (on foot, oddly) were routed. In the long view of history, Las Navas de Tolosa would be a turning point in the Reconquista. But Alfonso was dead only two years later, leaving his realm, despite his triumphs, pretty much the way it was when the sculptor was carving the lid for his mother's tomb.

I studied the carvings on Blanca's lid for a long time. The sculptor had shaped into one flawless, reliable pattern the death of a queen in childbirth in a little kingdom in Spain, the fulfillment of Old Testament prophecies, the holy war with the Moors, the eventual triumph of the Church, and even the last moments of earthly time, with Christ in Majesty standing over all.

Everything fit, everything related, everything referred to something else, aligned in a hierarchy whose summit, hidden in the clouds, was God. It seems impossibly contrived for most of us now; still, it was true holism, something we yearn for in our atomized, dissected world.

I wondered what this kind of story meant to ordinary people like Blanca's courtiers, or how a miller or a milkmaid would labour over such a cerebral scheme - a semiotics of salvation - to explain their hard-bitten lives. This way of organizing the scattered events of history into a cosmic portrait was a scholar's method of association, but it drew on a magical way of thinking that everyone shared in some degree. It was endlessly seductive, unfalsifiable. It worked because language, that most potent, most charming of human gifts, could create a place for everything.

"We have a deal," Bernardo told me the next morning. "I'm going to San Millán with you." I was doubly pleased; Bernardo was good company but he knew a lot about architectural history too.

"It'll be nice to have a personal guide," I said.

He shrugged with his cigarette. "It's not really my period. But we'll see."

We walked slowly towards the Nájera taxi stand next to the hotel. "How are they this morning?" I asked, looking at his feet.

"Not good, but if I can get from here to a bar for a coffee and a smoke, I'll be fine." He laughed his wheezy, hearty laugh.

Outside the hotel, a cab driver was polishing his car; we negotiated a fare to San Millán. The cabbie wanted to have his morning coffee before leaving, so Bernardo and I went to the hotel bar for breakfast: cups of black coffee, croissants and cigarettes for him, juice and half a croissant for me.

The paved road south to San Millán passed though landscapes that surprised me again and again with a beauty I couldn't have imagined. I looked out the taxi window onto broad valleys that swam with trees, soft hillsides striped with terraces, and in the distance, higher, bald hills. It was like turning the pages of a coffee-table book: one exquisite shot after another and no lapses into the ordinary or the dull. This beauty all around me could not have escaped medieval travellers either, must have inspired them too to contemplation and pleasurable thoughts. But for us, as it was probably not for them, such vistas set a standard of spiritual perfection. If we are at home in these landscapes, we like to think, we are at home in ourselves. In picture books of the Camino now, the most sublime meanings of pilgrimage are carried in the scenery.

Our cab went up a twisting, leaf-lined road to San Millán de Suso. The term "suso" comes from the Latin *sursum* for "above." There are, in fact, two monasteries at San Millán. This one, the older, is tucked into a fold of high hills called the Montes de Cógolla. And as if seclusion in the crease of a hill was not enough, Suso seemed, as we approached it, to back even further into the thick leaves that lay plump and verdant on the hillside.

The area around the Montes de Cógolla abounds in caves that were likely used long before any Christian hermits discovered them. It was to a cave at what would later become San Millán de Suso that the hermit Millán himself retreated in the late 5th Century. His life story, or *Vita*, was written in Latin only a few decades after his death by one Braulio of Saragosa, whose brother, Fronimiano, had been a disciple of the saint.

Until he was twenty, Millán was a shepherd in the nearby village of Berceo. He was apparently an excellent flutist, though sometimes he is shown with a stringed instrument. One day, forgetting his flocks, absorbed in his tunes, he sleeps and dreams that his pipe has turned to a quill, and that he is gazing upon God. At that same moment, the emptiness of worldly life is revealed to him. He is left with a single desire: to flee the world of men and undertake the solitary, stationary pilgrimage of the hermit monk. He seeks instruction in the contemplative life from a local master, Felix, and retires to his cave. He becomes famous for his devotion and wisdom, and is given charge of the parish of Berceo, on the mistaken assumption that piety means administrative talent. Before long he is relieved of his duties for giving away the church goods to the poor. Returning to Suso, Millán spends the rest of his hundred and one years praying, receiving spiritual seekers, healing, and instructing his small flock of hermits. When he dies, his tomb immediately becomes a shrine.

Millán was not well-known outside of Spain; I couldn't find him in either of my dictionaries of saints. But in being here, I was following thousands of pilgrims who for two centuries before James was found in Galicia, came to lay their pains and hopes before the gentle Millán.

Bernardo sat on a stone fence smoking with the cab driver while I climbed a short, steep hill behind the monastery. The view was spellbinding. Directly below me were the motley tiles of the old church roof and its squared bell tower. Any moment it seemed, the bells would begin to swing and dong. To my left and to my right, the hill bulged into the air before dropping to the plain below. Further out amid a swath of trees on the valley floor sat the newer monastery. Cultivated fields swept away from it in all directions. To the east lay hump-backed hills, densely forested, looming, persistent as a shadow over the bright ripe fields. Looking out from this high point, I felt almost dizzy in the arching emptiness of the air. The things in the valley - monastery buildings, crops, trees - were small, finite, bound, under light that seemed to go up forever. Earth, under the aspect of eternity.

"Watch out for the loose stones," said Bernardo as I skiddered back down the slope. Ever the gentleman, he offered his hand as I hopped onto the gravel parking lot. Then he lit a cigarette and we walked along the squared monastery walls observing with my binoculars the decorative patterns on the outside capitals.

"Mozarab," Bernardo told me, "although those sun-wheel motifs go back through the Visigothic period into antiquity." He shrugged. "You find them everywhere." The angular belfry stood up stalwart against the soft hillside forest. The eaves of the shallow tiled roof were constructed in three tiers.

Bernardo dragged on his cigarette. "That's Mozarab too".

The church was closed for *obras*, but in a while a man drove up who had a key. After Bernardo introduced us, he consented to unlock the northeast door for us. We entered a gallery with several arches that faced into the valley. The brickwork, we were told, was from the 1930s. Catching the sunshine through the arches were seven tombs topped with flat stone lids. At the far end of the gallery was another tomb. "*Una tumba Romana*," said the man, who was an archeologist. He pointed to where its pagan symbols had been chiselled away. A Christian was in there now.

The rest of the church was roped off and not even the archeologist could allow us to enter. Instead, I stood by the door from the gallery and peered into an interior that seemed to contain dust and stone, but no air. To the right was the nave of the old church from the 10th Century. To the left was an addition ordered by Sancho III of Navarra a hundred odd years later. It had an irregular shape to accommodate the hillside bedrock it had been cut into. Looking through the gorgeous arches (Cordovan, said Bernardo) and past the nave, I could just glimpse San Millán's oratory, which until 1030 had also been his burial chamber. In it was a black alabaster effigy of the saint.

"Spooky," I said to Bernardo, sniffing the musty air.

"Like a catacomb. It makes your hair stand up. Look over there to the walls opposite." Behind the workmen's barrier I could just make out hollows in the rock like eye sockets in a skeleton but weirdly elongated. "More caves where the monks lived, if you call that living, hunched over, meditating and praying all the time. Later those caves were used as burial places."

I took a picture of a pilaster that had been squared into a round pillar. It was the only colour in the whole place, a patch of blue mosaic tile. Near the top was a small rectangular opening. I could not see it, but the archeologist told us that the piece of wood that lay inside was San Millán's most remarkable miracle. Workmen building a granary in the neighbourhood had cut a beam of wood too short. Millán was informed and withdrew to his prayers. Returning to the men, he instructed them to carry on with their work. When they lifted the beam, they discovered that it was now more than one full hand longer than the others. They cut it to fit, and the trimmed piece was placed in this blue tiled pilaster.

I bought one of the guidebooks the archeologist showed me. I wasn't sure how I was going to carry it in my pack, but the pictures showed me much more than my own eyes could have in all the dust and grime of the fenced off repairs. I flipped through the pages. With photographic lighting, the place looked less like a dungeon and more like a haunted stone mansion, its shadows split by bands of yellow-orange air. In a sturdy, sincere way, it was almost elegant.

The monastery had been prosperous. When the Navarrese kings took La Rioja back from the Moors in the 10th Century, they moved their court from Pamplona to Nájera. The kings were generous to Millán's monastery; it grew in wealth and size to become the economic and cultural hub of the area. It had an outstanding scriptorium. It was here that Arab mathematical texts had been collected. But looking around now, it was hard to imagine any scholarly activity. The building seemed to have forgotten itself, like a hard-limbed old man whose memory has departed, a mere body now, all ossified and blank.

Around the time that the Navarrese court moved to Nájera, the Asturian court in the west moved from Oviedo to León. Thereafter, the kingdom of Asturias was known as León. The lands of Castile had been included in this kingdom. But there was dissatisfaction in Castile with León's handling of the war against the Moors. Castilians were - by nature it was claimed - restive and rebellious. They were also, it seems, forward-looking, and maybe just plain bored with Leonese conservatism. A separatist movement emerged. And that separatist movement needed a patron saint. León had James but at this early date the cult of Santiago had not spread very far east. In La Rioja, folks were devoted to their own sage and miracle worker, San Millán. They called him "Father-Patron." Before long, Millán had become Castile's spiritual counterweight and competitor to León's St. James.

The Spanish epic *Poema de Fernán González*, a work from the 13th Century, tells of the independence movement in Castile. At the heart of the story is Fernán González himself, Castile's advocate and an effective fighter of Moors in his own right. Even through the murk of legend, he appears to have been a man of charisma and perspicacity. But Castile needed more than one good man for its founding tale. So at the Battle of Hacinas, in the heart of Castile near Santo Domingo de Silos, with Moors on the offensive and Fernán's Christians in severe danger, who breaks from the clouds but San Millán, decked out as a warrior on a white charger. It was a nice piece of pro-Millán propaganda. For two hundred years, James and Millán would compete on the battlegrounds of Castile for patronage of Spain.

To leave San Millán de Suso, we had to pass once again through the gallery where the stone tombs sat in the sunshine. Three tombs on the inside wall belonged to Navarrese queens and were unremarkable. The ones along the window side, however, held the decapitated corpses of seven Castilian brothers; the free-standing one at the end had their tutor.

The story of the Seven Brothers - *Los Siete Infantes de Las Salas* - is long and grisly. It was copied into the *Chronicles of Alfonso X*, which were begun around 1279, but the events took place in the mid-10th Century, an uncouth time in northern Spain, before the civilizing effects (relatively) of Church reforms, Arab learning and the Santiago pilgrimage.

A wedding is being held in Burgos. One Ruy Velasquez is marrying a noblewoman, Doña Lambra. Guests arrive from Galicia, León, Portugal, Aragon, Gascony, Navarra. The festivities go on for weeks. One day, a tournament is held which ends in a bad argument, nosebleeds, broken jaws, and a death. The new bride, Lambra, is insulted by the youngest of the seven sons of Velasquez' brother-in-law, Gonzalo Gustios "the Good". A long feud ensues. Velasquez betrays Gustios to the Moors - to al-Mansur, as a matter of fact, who knows Gustios and likes him, so only throws him in jail rather than killing him. Velasquez then slaughters Gustios' seven sons in an ambush. To their father, still in jail, he sends the head of each son, along with that of their illustrious teacher, Nuño Salido, who has died at their side. Gustios remains in prison and is visited by al-Mansur, who is the picture of sympathy and generosity. He brings his sister to keep Gustios company. By her Gustios has another son, Mudara, who eventually has vengeance upon Velasquez, travelling to his home and running a sword through his body. Mudara then has Doña Lambra burned alive. The bodies of the sons, the seven "flowers of Spain" are laid to rest in the monastery at San Millán alongside their patron saint. The heads are taken to the Gustios' home village of Las Salas de los Infantes. (Heads and bodies, said my new guidebook to San Millán, were successfully matched in the 16th Century, in the presence of many witnesses.)

We stepped from the monastery into a dappled afternoon, leaving behind the headless corpses, the dead queens, the miraculous, worm-eaten piece of wood, and the dusty mysticism of the caves beyond the arches. Bernardo lit a cigarette. I squinted into the sunlight that flashed through the valley, watched it catch the copper green spire of the second monastery of San Millán. The tile roofs looked flat and humorless, as if refusing to reflect the eager sunbeams that showered playfully over them. As our taxi drove away from San Millán de Suso, I turned to watch the church walls recede into the forest. Al-Mansur had burned this monastery to the ground in 1002. By 1030 it had been rebuilt. In 1053 King Garcia decided to add the remains of Millán to his relics collection in Nájera. But the king's plan fell afoul of the divine. The story is told in the *Translatio Sancti Aemiliani*, an account written some 160 years after the event. Not far from the monastery, we read, the animals hauling the cart with Millán's body (what remained of it after nearly four centuries) stopped in their tracks and, under the command of the saint, refused to go further. Garcia recognized the problem at once; this was the typical signal of dead saints who did not wish to have their body parts taken to new homes. So Garcia built a second monastery on the spot of Millán's refusal. We were driving there now: San Millán de "Yuso," the monastery below.

I had come across several stories of saints intervening from above to stop people from taking their relics to new locations. In his *Pilgrim's Guide*, Aimery tells similar tales about Saints Martín, Leónard and Gilles, and even James. Usually, the tale was a cover for the political squabbles of rival monasteries or rival cities.

Under San Millán's failed *translatio* lies a rift, or perhaps a fault line, between the conservative monks of Suso with their Visigothic traditions, and the Romanizing forces of new church reforms being ushered into Spain from France by the Benedictine monks of Cluny. The reforms are supported by Spanish royalty, who see them as a move into the big leagues of European culture. But there is resistance throughout Spain to the homogenizing, politically correct usages that would tie everyone to the Roman Church. Even the idea of a unified state under one church is foreign and suspicious. The monks of San Millán de Suso are divided. The pro-reformers, who move down to Yuso, seem to be opportunistic realists. But the conservatives on the hill see the reforms as a humiliating submission to the political agenda of the aristocracy. With all their might, they fight the imposition of the Benedictine Rule on their age-old monasteries: they balk at banning mixed monasteries, for Suso has always had both monks and nuns; and they deplore the new subservience of monks to bishops, who are often nothing more than arms of the state.

The battle is hard fought: there are heated words, vitriolic letters, civil resistance, violence. Some of the dissidents are banished. In the end, the Romanizing forces win. Millán's body finds a permanent home at Yuso and the old, conservative monastery on the hill, though it lives on for a while, eventually declines into ruin. Nowadays, Yuso is run by the Augustinian Recollects, a Benedictine order that has been here since 1878.

Our cab left us in a wide plaza. Coming from Suso nestled in the hillside forest to Yuso spread among the trees and field of the valley was a bit like travelling in time between the Seafarer's world in Anglo-Saxon England and the world of *Piers Plowman* in the 14th Century. The older monastery on the hill stood for a simple but not simplistic faith, where men and women wrestled with their desires and sought in the uncompromising way of the cave and the altar to live as children of God in a hard-bitten world. The new church was jowly and self-satisfied, every bit the complacently grandiose church of the wealthy establishment. Where Suso had seemed archaic and introspective, eerily old like a leather-skinned mystic with faraway eyes, Yuso was extroverted and unapologetically worldly.

"I don't know how much I want to walk," said Bernardo as he lit a last cigarette before going in.

"No problem," I said. "You can sit down wherever you want; there's no hurry."

We walked slowly, both of us limping as we looked around. I thought La Rioja's "Escorial," as my tourist brochure called it, lacked dignity. Its basic lines, Bernardo said, were Romanesque, but he showed me where, over the years, gothic, neoclassical, baroque and rococo elements had appeared like overwrought legends embellishing the truth. It said all the right things about Spain and God, but for all its curlicues and flourishes it seemed to both of us rather vacuous.

Suso and Yuso were famous for their scriptoria, where for centuries monks had copied and recopied manuscripts in that wonderful hand called Carolingian miniscule. A document from AD 992 still exists, the *Codex Emilianense de los Concilios*, or San Millán Codex of the Councils. It is of interest for its historical information, but it is the little notes and scribbles made by the copyist in the margins of the text that interest most people. In the Mozarabic monasteries of Islamic Spain, monks usually wrote marginal notes in their spoken language, which was Arabic. But here in La Rioja, next door to Castile, we see notes for the first time not only in Castilian, or more properly perhaps, the closely related dialect of Navarrese, but also in Basque, the first written examples of vernacular languages in Spain. Thus the *Codex Aemilianense*, on the basis of a few hand notes in a language that people had been speaking for years, is considered by Spanish language historians to be the "cradle of the Spanish language."

Three centuries later, around 1200, a local priest named Gonzalo de Berceo wrote a translation of Braulio's

7th-century Latin biography of San Millán. Gonzalo was a frank, cheerfully mediocre poet with what seems to have been a likeable personality. He was born in nearby Berceo and lived all his life at the Monastery of San Millán de la Cógolla. He was still alive in 1246. He wrote a great deal of verse - mostly saints' lives - in Castilian, partly, as he says, because he wasn't very good at Latin. But he also thought it was important to teach his parishioners in their own language. For this, he wrote entertaining tales about Millán. His *Life of San Millán* is the first known work written wholly in the Spanish vernacular.

Berceo also wrote, or translated in his own way, three works dedicated to the Virgin. One of these I almost wished I hadn't read. A monk much corrupted with sin decides to undertake a penitential pilgrimage to Santiago. The night before he departs, he has a last fling with his girlfriend. He does not confess his sin. Three days into his pilgrimage, the devil, disguised as St. James, appears before him. "You have offended the Blessed Virgin by not confessing your crime," says the apparition. "Your punishment will be first to separate yourself from that member which performed the fornication, and then to cut your own throat." The man obeys, removing "that member," then putting a knife to his own neck. Suicide being a mortal sin, demons arrive at once to cart him off to hell. The real James appears now and blocks their path, for the monk has been unjustly tricked by Satan. An argument ensues over his fate. The case is put before Mary, Queen of Heaven, who mercifully rules that he be returned to life. He makes a clean recovery, as Berceo notes:

> The wound that he had from cutting his throat
> One could barely perceive the scar;
> He was relieved of suffering, and all stinging pain,
> Everyone said: "This man had good fortune."

Glad to be alive, thanks to the Virgin, the man continues to Santiago. But "regarding his organ which he had cut off, it did not grow back a bit, it remained as it was." And, Berceo adds, with unflinching voyeurism, "in order to make water, he had only a hole."

Bernardo and I took the group tour of the Yuso monastery. Our guide was a tall, nervously thin theology student who I later learned conducted manuscript research here. Today his every cell was buzzing with enthusiasm for San Millán. Hastily he herded us into the exhibition room, impatient to talk about Millán's reliquary chests. First the old chest, stripped of its ivories and jewels and gold by Napoleon's soldiers in 1809. All that remained of it was a wood structure and a piece of Arabic cloth lining the bottom of the box. Our guide pointed with his stick - identical to the ones used by my school teachers in northern Ontario - at various points of French desecration. Fortunately, he said, the chest had been carefully described before 1809, and a replica was made based on that description and on copies of the some of the stolen ivories that showed up in later years as far afield as St. Petersburg, Berlin, Florence, and New York.

When excited, our guide rolled his r's in long, rippling cadences. "Aqui tenemos la rrrrrrréplica," he announced, leaning over us, trying to push us without touching us as he hurried to the ivory-laden casket in the middle of the room. "Una rrrrréproduccion marrrravillosa," he triumphed. With his stick, he pointed to the carvings that told the saint's life. My eye was on that stick; it was a little like watching the puck at a hockey game: Millán's miracles here, and here, Millán performing an exorcism. And here, San Millán with his disciples, father and master, dressed like a Visigothic priest. Millán was motionless in this last scene, the very image of godly stillness. Those staring eyes evaded the stick with a mystic's concentration as it veered to the death scene: "La muerrrrte de San Millán!" The r's were a study in pathos.

At the end of the tour, Bernardo and I thanked the guide, for his talk had been impressive. As we returned to the ivory chest for a last look, I watched him from the corner of my eye. He was a good listener and his answers to the tourists' questions were serious and detailed. I could just see him as an 11th-century monk, bustling through the monastery on his way to the scriptorium, irrepressibly eager, with a scholar's easy dedication to his manuscripts, not noticing how the other monks smirked.

During the church reforms, I expect he would have gone with the traditionalists. But he seemed the kind of person whose love for his work went beyond the partisan and the petty, someone concerned with what was right and just, who would have pressed his theological resources to the limit to figure out where he would make his stand.

"I've got to get out of here," Bernardo whispered to me, touching my arm. I didn't know if it was his feet or the sudden need for a cigarette. "I'll see you outside." He nodded and lifted his eyebrows, then walked away painfully.

I returned to the Yuso church to look again at a painting the guide had pointed out to us behind the altar. It was very large, showed a white steed charging, a bearded man in a black robe that billowed out behind his upraised arm, a sword like a gilded snake held high, and bodies and turbans collapsing under the horse's feet. James Matamoros? Not at all! San Millán at the Battle of Hacinas, riding out of the sky to help Fernán González. Mild old peace-loving Millán, who spent his hundred-and-one-year life in search of God's peace, had been yanked from his rest and sent off down the road from Cógolla onto the field of the Reconquest. All so that León's St. James for once wouldn't have the upper hand.

That evening I would read more about Millán the warrior in my new guidebook. Written by an out-and-out Millanite, the book had the odd defensiveness I had noticed in other works by Spanish historians. The painting of Hacinas, whines the author, giving vent to what was almost a personal grudge, "remains a silent protest to those who deny [San Millán] his well-earned patronage over Spain."

I found Bernardo sitting on a bench in the courtyard of the Yuso monastery. He flicked his cigarette ashes onto the pavement. "Seen enough?' he asked as I approached him. I was glad to sit down for standing was almost as hard on my shin as walking.

We talked about what we had seen. Bernardo was tactful but direct. "It's interesting to look at for a while," he said, squinting at the monastery walls through the sunshine, "but really, compared to so much else in Spain, it's second rate, bordering on third rate. There's nothing wrong with it. No real grammar mistakes. It's just self-conscious and mediocre. I was a bit bored."

We took a cab to Azofra, a tiny town with square buildings baked solid in the sun. There had been a pilgrim hostel here in the 12th Century. Today the place was almost devoid of people. We found a bar where Bernardo treated me to a drink, half beer, half lemonade, which was palatable. Then came *bocadillos*: salami, fatty beyond eating, good cheese and bread. We exchanged stories of our lives, in my case much edited. Bernardo was more open, told me of his family, his divorces. It was mostly about women. I looked at him over our plates and glasses: the clever, easy scholar, a superb teacher, a romantic patrician, not at all arrogant, wanting to be liked, wheezing heavily at his own jokes, cheerful and sure of himself but aging with sadness. He seemed a little lost in the curl of his own life.

We waited at the Azofra bus stop while the sun broiled us like an oven element. Once aboard the bus to Santo Domingo de la Calzada, I was chilled to the bone by the air conditioning. I huddled in my seat and stared out over lands made famous by El Cid.

"Spain's all-time hero," said Bernardo.

"Did you see the movie? With Charlton Heston and Sophia Loren."

"Years ago," said Bernardo. "It was ridiculous. But it had the blessing of Pidal, and who could argue with that?"

"Menendez Pidal? The one who wrote that book about El Cid?"

"Hmm, the Spanish literary historian. He died in 1968. The book was *La España del Cid*. He was the historical advisor for the movie when he was in his eighties." Bernardo paused to look out the window at Navarra's sun-baked farmlands. Pidal, he said, had greatly advanced the study of Spanish literature and philology. "But some of his ideas were crazy. He was romantically in love with Spain. When we were going through a bad time politically, he made the Cid into a national hero. That was in the 20s."

Bernardo glanced at me sideways and smiled. "Of course, Spain has always been going through a bad time politically." He looked out the window again.

"Pidal thought El Cid stood for something great in the Spanish character, something that defined it, had always been there. He couldn't see that legend and history weren't the same thing. But the Americans bought it. They like big heroes like that, the Charlton Heston types. It was just after the war."

"The thing the Americans went for," Bernardo went on, "was that El Cid was just an ordinary fellow, a self-made man, not a king. He stood for democracy, the rise of the little man. They also liked the rebelliousness of the Castilians. Alfonso the king comes off like a fool in the movie. Which he wasn't."

Rodrigo Diaz, otherwise known as El Cid, or My Lord in Arabic, was not that ordinary a man. His family was aristocratic and held a sizeable portion of land at Vivir, a few miles north of Burgos. He is born in 1040. From boyhood, he is trained in the skills of a soldier. He serves in the Castilian court of Prince Sancho, son of Fernando I. His first battle is in the Pyrenees in 1063. He works his way up in the court. Fernando dies; Sancho becomes King of Castile, while his brother Alfonso gets León. Sancho is murdered. It looks as if Alfonso has done it. Rodrigo goes to Alfonso's court, though the two do not get along very well. Rodrigo marries a little above his station, in what was probably the marriage of the year. Maybe Jimena looked like Sophia Loren.

Something goes wrong with Rodrigo's career at Alfonso's court. Parting from Jimena and his two daughters, he goes into exile, arriving at Saragosa where he fights as a mercenary for the Moors. He returns after five years and is reconciled to Alfonso. In 1079 he is in Sevilla, collecting tributes from the Moors for the king. But time and again, Rodrigo runs afoul of Alfonso. He attacks Moors when he shouldn't. He keeps tributes that were meant for the king. Finally, while Alfonso readies to invade Valencia and have it out with Rodrigo, Rodrigo invades Castile.

From the bus, I could see more or less where Rodrigo had done his battling. Nájera was badly hit. The story is told in the *Historia Roderici*, a Latin work that turned up in the library of San Isidore in León in the 18th Century. Likely, it had been copied in the 13th Century, somewhere in eastern Castile or La Rioja, from an 11th-century manuscript:

> At length, Rodrigo left Saragosa with a very great and innumerable army, and entered the regions of Calahorra and Nájera which were in the dominions of King Alfonso and subject to his authority. Stoutly fighting, he took both Alberite and Logroño. Most savagely and mercilessly through all those regions did he lay waste with relentless, destructive, irreligious fire. He took huge booty, yet it was saddening even to tears.... He altogether stripped it of all its goods and wealth and riches, and took these for himself.

Finally, with the Moorish Almohavid troops at the door to Spain, Rodrigo takes Valencia from the leaders of a Moorish coup and becomes master of huge territories to the east of Castile. He is joined by Jimena and the children. He has only five years to live. His governance is said to have been extremely cruel. He had his opponents burned alive.

That is the historical version. The legend in the great Spanish epic, *El Poema de Mio Cid*, begins with Rodrigo's exile from the court of Alfonso and his parting from Jimena (as the nail from the flesh, says the poet). The tale is embellished beyond recognition. There is an invented account of the marriage of his daughters to two brothers from Carrión. Despite their high station, the brothers turn out to be low-lifes who dishonour and abandon the daughters just after the wedding. Much of *El Poema* has to do with putting this situation to rights. The daughters finally marry into the royal houses of Aragon and Navarra.

El Poema del Cid is the elegant story of a crafty, honourable, clean-living adventurer, quite a different tale from the wild and wooly *Siete Infantes de las Salas*, and different too, in its moderate tone and lack of flamboyance, from the *The Song of Roland*. It was probably written close to 1040, around the time that the *Codex Calixtinus* came out with the Charlemagne stories, and some decades after *The Song of Roland*. In fact, the author of El Cid had read *The Song*, and he knew the old legends of Castile and León and all about the battles with the Moors. Gerald Brennan, in his book on the history of Spanish literature, says that El Cid is a local story. Unlike *The Song of Roland*, it resists the urge to fly off into the heights of religious passion, feudal loyalty and cosmic battles with evil. It is a pragmatic tale: our hero is interested in land and money. Perhaps this is what Pidal liked so much about the figure of El Cid in *El Poema* - a plain, balanced realism, an earthy wisdom that he wanted to think was a Castilian trait.

And perhaps it was. My impression of the Castilians who lived along the Camino was that they actually *were* Cid-like, in the poetic way: slightly formal, dignified, even ceremonious. They looked at you directly; they answered you with courtesy and confidence. They seemed fair and in control. They understood the emotions but they were not sentimental.

A month after I got home from the Camino, I sent a picture to an old man, a farmer I had met in Castrojeriz, who had walked with me out of town along the Odrilla River. The valley floor that day was an almost featureless carpet of hay-yellow. Ahead were the steep hills rising from the valley to the meseta plateau. The old man and I talked intermittently of crops and harvests, the weather, the Camino. At times I didn't understand his accent. The picture, taken by Anya, who was walking with me that day, was of the two of us, laughing, against a very blue sky. I did not expect to hear from him, could barely imagine my letter getting through to such a tiny place as Castrojeriz in the first place. But within weeks, I had received a reply, addressed to Mari. "What a thrill you gave me when I received your card and of course the photograph," he wrote in phonetic Spanish, scrawled with the intense care an old man gives to something unaccustomed. "I send an affectionate greeting from this brief companion on a portion of the Camino. Mari, I hope from my heart this letter arrives in your hands so you will know that I received the photo and showed it to my wife and she was thrilled too. I hope you understand this letter and if some time you return, ask for me and I will welcome you with great affection."

Reading his words, I almost cried.

In a short while Bernardo and I were in Santo Domingo de la Calzada. On our way to the *refugio* we passed the five-star Parador where Scott and I had stayed last year, a low-looking building on the main square near the cathedral. It was built in the 12th Century as a pilgrim hostel by the Santo Domingo whose town this is, and who had also put up a hermitage and a bridge for pilgrims over the Rio Oca.

Compared to the elegant stillness of the Parador showpiece, the pilgrim hostel was a dark hive. The entrance was cool, smelled like a stone garage. It had black walls, a floor of small black stones, and a table where two cheerful young men sat to register pilgrims who were arriving for the night. On the second floor was a narrow kitchen. A few people were making meals; three pilgrims were perched on a third flight of stairs inspecting their feet. Up those steps was a large dormitory with rows of beds separated by low walls. At the first available bed, Bernardo laid down at once, groaning. His feet were no worse, but far from better. My own leg had not gotten much better either. I saw that Duncan's mother, Martha, had arrived. I sat on her bed to chat, conscious of the pain in my shin. She was exhausted. "It's my size, dear," she said.

Martha told me that Virginia was in the yard doing laundry, so I gathered up my bundle and went outside. The yard was a grassy, walled-in rectangle; at one end, shirts and socks hung like notes on a musical staff of clotheslines. Bicycles leaned against another wall. A few pilgrims were reading guidebooks or writing their diaries in the meagre shade of a couple of bushes. There were deep enamel tubs near the back door of the hostel where you could wash your clothes. Virginia wasn't there, so I milled around in a loose line-up with the others, holding my pouch of filthy clothes, my bottle of biodegradable soap, and my clothespins. Ahead of me was a tanned Spanish woman I seemed only to meet at hostel laundry basins. In Los Arcos we had joked, while negotiating space for our clothes on a small rack, that even if you only got the smell out, you would have at least the illusion of cleanliness. We laughed now to discover that here we were once again, on another laundry detail in a hot and dirty world.

Standing near me were two men I had met a few times on the trail. They were an unusual couple; something had struck me about the shorter one, how he said hello gruffly as he strode past me, then bounced off down the trail on calves that seemed to have rubber balls for muscles. He had a long, gray beard and a swollen, aggressive face. His stocky physique seemed restless. The energy of the couple was concentrated in him; his clean-cut friend seemed evanescent. They were like the body and the soul come apart.

I asked in English where they were from. "Ve haff come all ze vay from Hollant on our feet," said the restless one. "All ze vay. Sirty kilometres a day." He nodded his head as he spoke. "I feel tventy-fife again! Ha! Ha!"

I asked how long it had taken. "Two months. All ze vay from Hollant sru France." Clearly, it was a triumph.

"What do you do in Holland?"

There was an unexpected pause. On parole? I thought to myself. The friend looked on placidly.

"I vas social verker. In ze street. It vas so hard verk."

"Lots of people with drug problems?"

"Everyzing, it vas hard verk."

"So this pilgrimage is a chance to recover your energy and relieve the stress?"

Another pause. But his voice was a little softer. "I'm not allowed to verk now."

"Burn-out?"

"Burnt out." I could tell there was more to the story, and thought that perhaps "on parole" hadn't been that far off.

"Sirty kilometres a day. And getting faster. Up at 5 o'clock."

It was my turn at the tub. The Dutch were next to me, sharing a tub and discussing, with quiet but passionate intensity, the process of washing thirty kilometre a day clothes. I took my time, letting the cool water dribble over my hands as I wrung out my t-shirt. Why wasn't it this simple to do everything in life, even the complicated things?

I hung my clothes in the sun, then went into the shade of the building to do some yoga, hoping this would ease my leg pain. A cyclist I had noticed putting his bike against the wall came over.

"Do you speak English?" he asked me hopefully. He had very shy blue eyes that floated softly away from mine when he spoke. His voice was low and full.

"Yes," I answered, trying not to stare at his eyes. "I'm from Canada. Where are you from?"

"Finland," he said, catching my eye briefly with a look of amused hopelessness before looking away.

I said something inane that implied that Finland was a very exotic place to be from.

Kjell was a journalist with a radio network in Jakobstad, a small town that lies, we later figured out, at about the same latitude as Coppermine in the far north of Canada. A priest friend of his had written her master's thesis on the Camino. He had become intrigued, was taking a month's sabbatical in Spain. When he went home, he would make some radio programs and write a few newspaper articles on the Camino. He had bought a bike in Pamplona. "But I'm going too fast," he told me in excellent English. "I shall arrive in Santiago too soon and I can't afford to stay many nights there. I want to talk to more people too, but it's hard to find anybody who speaks English, or at least an understandable English. Nobody, of course, speaks Finnish." He said he had been glad to hear me speaking "a vunderful English" at the wash tubs.

I told him that Scott and I had gone by bicycle to Santiago the year before. He wanted some suggestions, he said, and pulled the Everest Guide maps from his bike pack. Together we sat on the grass. "You can take an alternate route into Burgos," I told him, pointing to the route. "They say the highway is terrible, full of trucks and really dangerous. Everybody we talked to last year said it was "hell." But the ride on the meseta is fabulous if the weather is good - all the way to León, it's flat and fast, although you may get a head wind."

I felt I was babbling, but Kjell listened closely, studying the map. "And the mountain passes? What about those?" He had a journalist's attentiveness.

I was about to show him the road from Vega Valcarce to El Cebreiro, when Duncan came by. "I hear you're writing a book," Duncan said to me in a tone of challenge. I had not mentioned this to many people. "Tell me," he said with a cagey wink and a tone of mock exasperation, "why does everybody on the Camino want to write a book about it?"

I paused. "It's a good question," Kjell interjected, speaking to me. "That friend of mine, the priest in Finland, her thesis was about people's experiences on the Camino. She got most of her information from a Spanish magazine called *Peregrino*."

"What did she come up with?" asked Duncan.

"I haven't read it yet. I didn't want to come with someone else's notions. I'll read it when I go home."

"You must have read a lot of articles and books before you came to Spain, right?" Duncan asked me.

"Quite a few."

"So are you going to say anything different?" he asked, in a tone that assumed the truth would be no, no matter what I said.

"Probably."

I said that putting any experience into language helps you find an authentic response to it that you may not be consciously aware of. "You can grasp what your pilgrimage is about intuitively, and *feel* you understand it," I said, "but to *know* you understand it, to make it real enough to make a difference in your life, you sometimes need to write it down. At some point too, even the most private pilgrimage will beg to go out in words for others to hear."

Kjell said, "One guy I read said pilgrimage was about community. That means, as far as *I* understand it, that on a pilgrimage, people can get around the roles they play in their normal lives. They can be in more direct contact with themselves and with other people."

"You're perhaps more honest on a pilgrimage," I said. "You have nothing to show except yourself, and when you discover a true voice in yourself, you also find that it wants to be - is meant to be - shared with others. Maybe that's why people write about their pilgrimage. They need to tell a true story about themselves."

"But that's not why you're writing for your newspaper, is it?" said Duncan, still digging, looking at Kjell.

Kjell laughed. "No. It's my job. I like it, it means a lot to me. But it's to sell a newspaper with interesting stories. The Camino is a different way to travel. People like to hear about something new."

"I came here mainly because I wanted to meet others," he went on. "To talk to people. Pilgrimage, conversation, writing about it too, you exchange ideas. You make a real community that way."

It was getting cool. Kjell wanted to find a tobacconist's shop. He was calling his wife every couple of days, but his phone card had run out. I went for a walk with him to find one, but nothing was open. The streets were nearly empty now, cool and dry as dust. The sky was deepening to dark blue. When my leg began to hurt again, we parted and I limped back to the *refugio*. After cooking myself some supper in the kitchen - a can of baked beans and a can of corn - I wrote my diary. Later I slept on a bed with an abyss like Ferragut's navel in the middle.

In the morning, Bernardo told me he was going back to Madrid. "I can't keep walking," he said, shaking his head at his feet, "it's going to take them a couple of weeks to heal." I was disappointed. He had been an excellent companion at San Millán. We said good-bye in the alcove of the hostel, and I watched him head off to the bus station like a man walking on nails.

Kjell was in the kitchen eating breakfast when I returned inside. Soon he would be off on his bike. The Dutch had been gone since 5:15. Before long, I was on my way too, heading slowly for Grañon, wondering how long my leg would hold out. I crossed the bridge over the Rio Oca. In the Middle Ages, a pilgrim spending the night by this bridge had been killed by rocks that fell from a cart when the oxen drawing it became unyoked and panicked. Santo Domingo de la Calzada himself had restored the pilgrim to life.

It was early when I crossed that bridge but already the heat was gathering like oil in the air. On either side of me lay hilly fields of barley and hay dotted with dark green trees. Grañon, a single street town at the end of a long hill, was only six kilometres away but it was nearly two hours before I got there. As I limped in, the stone walls of houses stood straight up off the street like a row of blank pages from parchment manuscripts.

I sought some coolness in the church, which looked small from the street but was gothic and cavernous inside and very pretty. I was distracted by a statue of the Virgin, more doll than statue, a triangle of creamy satin heavily brocaded with gold thread. She wore a silver crown that bulged like a lamp under her galactic halo. The halo was trimmed with what seemed to be silver poplar leaves.

Grañon stood at the frontier between La Rioja and Castile. The lands around here had been much fought over: Castile takes its name from the large number of castles found in these parts. Alfonso III had built one here at Grañon in the 10th Century. There were also two pilgrim hostels here in the 12th Century, one of which came under the jurisdiction of San Millán's monastery in 1189.

So many adventure stories had curled into Spain from France to hang over these war-torn Camino territories like banners: French flights of grandeur wafting over sturdy Spanish pragmatism. The relationship between French and Spanish had always been complicated, an infuriating feedback loop of dependence and resentment. During the Camino years many people, including the churchmen in Santiago de Compostela, knew perfectly well that the stories about Charlemagne in Spain were lies. But there was too much at stake. Santiago was getting rich; the Cathedral had a spectacular prestige. The glory reflected by Charlemagne on the Camino was not to be cast aside for the sake of a bit of honesty.

Actually, it didn't matter to the Spanish so much that the stories of Charles and James were lies; what did matter was that they were *French* lies. And it wasn't only the Charlemagne legends that maddened the Spanish, it was the invasion of fashion-conscious French settlers in the staid little Spanish towns, it was the French contingent of holier-and-smarter-than-thou church reformers; it was the new French trend to Roman ways in the Mass and the loss of the old, loved Visigothic rites.

One Spanish answer to all this was to create an alternative Camino mythology. San Millán had been part of this pro-Spanish thrust, so perhaps was El Cid, and of course, the Clavijo story. But the best literary attempt to assert Spain's independence from creeping French influence is a tale in the 12th-century Chronicles of Alfonso X. The story of Bernardo del Carpio was concocted from a stock of stories that over the years had been fattened as a counterweight to French hegemony. Whoever wrote it knew the French *Roland* well and wanted to right the balance, even if it took a complete fabrication to do it.

One version of the story: the Count of Saldana marries the sister of Charlemagne. The marriage is clandestine and when Alfonso discovers it, he imprisons the Count. But he does agree to raise the Count's rather promising son, Bernardo. Meanwhile, because he has no heirs, and is being harrassed by Moors, Alfonso foolishly invites Charlemagne to help him in his battles. In return, he will cede his reign to him. Charlemagne of course agrees to a ridiculously easy set of terms.

When his ambassadors and nobles hear of Alfonso's offer, they are outraged. The most vocal is Bernardo. Under pressure, the king revokes his offer. Now it is Charlemagne who is outraged. In a letter, he demands that Alfonso become his vassal. Bernardo collects his knights and heads of to join forces with Marsil, the Moorish king of Saragosa, to fight Charlemagne. Charlemagne invades Spain, is beaten back.

Returning to France, Charlemagne leaves his rearguard near Roncesvalles under the charge of Roland and other nobles. Alfonso, with Marsil and Bernardo seizes his chance to close the pass and attack the French, slaying Roland and routing the army. Charlemagne blows his oliphant to summon his forces, but when he sees them straggling, or dead, he abandons the battle and returns to

Germany to prepare for a later battle in Spain. The king dies before this can happen. His sepulcre is painted on all sides with scenes from his victorious battles, but on the side facing south to Roncesvalles and Pyrenees, where he had been vanquished by the Spanish, there is nothing but a bare wall.

Bernardo meanwhile learns that his father is in prison. He seeks his release, but Alfonso refuses despite Bernardo's loyalty to him in battle. There is a long series of battles and petitions. Bernardo builds a castle near Salamanca and goes to war with Alfonso (with the Moors once again as allies). Alfonso proposes to return his father in exchange for Bernardo's castle. Bernardo agrees. His father is brought forth on a horse from the prison, dressed in finery. Bernardo kneels to kiss his hand and finds it cold; looking up, he sees a lifeless face; the poor old man had died three days earlier. In a rage, Bernardo flies at the king, only to find himself once again exiled. He departs to the French court where he is warmly welcomed. He claims kinship with another son of Charlemagne's sister, but is repudiated by this half-brother. He leaves Paris, sacking what towns he can and in three battles, wipes out a large number of Moors. Finally he marries Doña Galinda, who bears him a son who grows up to become a mighty knight.

A good story, not a great epic, terribly confusing, but intriguing in its play of human emotion. For days, I had been walking through a land full of such odd tales, ill-fitting stories like old doors on sagging walls. Charlemagne slaughtering Moors on the way to Santiago, the soldiers' lances in the field at Sahagún, Blanca's death in childbirth, San Millán leaping from the sky, the nasty business with the Seven Brothers, the castrated pilgrim forgiven by the Virgin, Bernardo routing Charlemagne. Stories like these had kept the old Camino pilgrims entertained, but many, like the Roland and Ferragut tale, also kept them fortified, uplifted, spiritually on track. The best stories are always the ones that soften your hardship at the same time that they keep you connected to your path.

I stepped from the church at Grañon onto the street. The sky was threatening rain. My leg didn't hurt so much. I was pulling out my map when I heard a voice behind me. It was Errol. "I remembered the words to *Mr. Tambourine Man*," he said. We began walking together, and he sang for me, every word just right.

Suddenly, it seemed impossible to be happier.

The Camino passing through the town of Estella.

5

LANDSCAPES

Thoreau called us sleepwalkers. Have you ever found yourself walking along a path in the woods and then suddenly realizing that the whole forest around you has changed? You started out among conifers, but now you are surrounded by deciduous trees. Or you realize that the birds are active and noisy, and you don't know when the change took place. You have awakened. You let the smell of fern leaf wash through you. You realize why you were asleep. You were talking to yourself, caught up in an endless, familiar dialogue. What were you talking about? You can't remember!

Paul Rezendes. *Tracking and the Art of Seeing*

This is a new way of being-in-the-world, which consists in becoming aware of oneself as a part of nature and a portion of universal reason. At this point, one no longer lives in the usual, conventional human world, but in the world of nature.... One is then practicing "physics" as a spiritual exercise.

Pierre Hadot. *Philosophy as a Way of Life*

The trail after Puente la Reina.

A few unkind things have been said about his talent as a travel writer, but Aimery Picaud has the honour of being the author of the first known guidebook to the Camino de Santiago. His book appeared in the 12th Century, a compendium of places and stories and tips for travellers. We'll never know why, or whether he cared, that some of his information was utterly wrong. But Aimery understood his market well enough to recognize what all pilgrims need to know: first, the places they have to go through to get to Santiago, and second, where to stay. Nor did Aimery have any doubt about what mattered next to the practical pilgrim of his day: water. So, early in his *Guide* after his lists of towns and hospices comes a chapter (attributed for whatever reason to Pope Calixtinus) called: *The Bitter and Sweet Waters Found along this Road.* Aimery writes the chapter in the hope that pilgrims heading to Santiago "may strive to avoid unhealthy waters and may choose to drink from those that are good for them and for their mounts."

This was important information. Dozens, perhaps hundreds of rivers cut through that northern swath of Spain between the Pyrenees and Santiago. On days when

God's grace flickered in the summer air, the Camino rivers offered the pilgrim a sweet end to sticking thirst, a rinse for blistered soles, a catch of trout, or even, if you wanted to bother, a chance to wash a week's worth of sweat from your body. But when the clouds closed over the world and the demons were out, those lilting streams metamorphosed into the bearers of evil: snake bites and rashes, leg-buckling flash floods, slippery rocks, a twisted ankle, fouled waters, diarrhea. Then there were the human dangers: thieves biding their time under the bridges, and that most despised breed of Camino extortionist, the river toll collectors. "May their ferrymen be damned!" cries Aimery of the Navarrese boaters near the Pyrenees, who charge a coin even from poor pilgrims - "and for a horse they ignominiously extort by force four" - to cross the river in a boat "made of a single tree." If you drown, the boatmen "wickedly rejoicing" will pocket what they can from your belongings. "You will do well," Aimery advises, "in pulling your horse by the reins behind you, outside the boat, and to embark but with few passengers, for if it is overloaded it will soon become endangered."

In another of his anti-Navarrese fits, Aimery tells his own story of evil doings on the bank of the Rio Salado, just west of Ciraqui near Lorca. Arriving at the river, he and his companions meet two Navarrese rogues. The men assure the new arrivals (while sharpening their knives) that the waters are completely safe for men and animals. Two of the horses are allowed to drink; both fall dead and are skinned at once by the evil Navarrese.

One May morning some eight hundred years later on the way from Puente la Reina to Estella, Scott and I took our bicycles onto the double-arched, stone bridge at the Rio Salado. We stopped part way across for a photo. Through the lens, I could almost see those gagging horses and Aimery's wretched fury. And whether they were or not, the waters flowing sluggishly under the bridge, strewn with bits of garbage and leaving slimy white rivulets by the mangy bank, really did look insalubrious enough to kill a horse.

We crossed four rivers that day on the way to Estella. Between Estella and Burgos, there were almost a dozen and a half more. Camino rivers like these were seldom used as pilgrim highways. They were difficult to navigate and they usually flowed the wrong way, particularly those going through the meseta. The Rio Arlanzón, for instance, runs westward only a short distance into the meseta from the northeast. Then, along with its tributaries, including the Pico and the sinuous Vena, the Arlanzón turns into a fan of waterways that drains away from the Camino to the southwest. Almost all the other Camino rivers flow out of Cantabria and carve due south across the Castilian tableland.

On a map, these rivers lie across the meseta like careless lines of longitude. Where they intersect the Camino, towns and even cities are marked. Aimery's list of rivers whose "waters are sweet and healthy to drink" is really a verbal map of these meseta settlements:

> the Pisuerga, a stream that flows, to be sure, under the bridge of Itero; the Carrión that runs by Carrión; the Cea, at Sahagún; the Esla, at Mansilla; the Porma, under a certain large bridge between Mansilla and León; the Torio which flows by León underneath the encampment of the Jews; the Bernesga which flows by the same city, but on the other side, that is to say, towards Astorga.

Other streams also shimmer in the valleys that wobble south across the wind-beaten meseta: the Hornazuela, at Hornillos del Campo, where a high stretch of tableland rises like a coffin lid out of the river valley; the Sambol, leaking south through purest, sparsest meseta past the ruins of the San Baudilio convent; the low-slung Rio Odrilla near Castrojeriz, with its little pilgrim bridge almost buried in the grasses of the wide valley floor; and the willow and poplar-lined Uzieca, babbling beside the Camino as it heads north for a short distance from Villovieco.

Eventually, all the waters flowing through the remote valleys of the Spanish meseta disappear into the westward currents of the Duero. The Duero is one of very few Iberian rivers that manages to break through the mountains of Portugal to the Atlantic Ocean. Non-navigable in Spain, and embedded in Castile's most severe terrain, the Duero makes a natural boundary between the northern meseta and the south; during periods of migration, it was a landmark for settlers arriving from both directions.

Travelling through the limitless scrublands of the meseta, Scott and I could see the mountains of Cantabria running along the northern horizon in a low sawtooth ridge. Two centuries before Aimery wrote his Guide, an excess of farms had exhausted those fertile Asturian slopes. People began to head south for a better living, threading their families and piled-up carts and draught animals down the meseta river valleys. They went as far as they needed to in the direction of the Duero. Where they stopped, they cleared land and built villages and protective fortresses. They adapted their farming to a climate ever more extreme, where grasses heaved in the hot winds of summer and disappeared under the dead white snows of winter.

The Asturian settlers heading south were met by Mozarab emigrants heading north, driven like the Asturians by the need for land. Trucking their families and valuables northward into Christian river valleys, the Mozarabs arrived in the neighbourhood of the Camino with a full quiver of Moorish innovations; by the end of the century, the plough had replaced the hoe, and new southern cereals like hard wheat and sorghum were sprouting in the fields. The waterwheel was a common sight. Sturdy little burros imported from the south replaced water-guzzling, high maintenance farm horses. New mill designs freed up hands for more field labour. New irrigation methods meant you could cultivate lands lying further from the rivers. River valleys that had for centuries moseyed along beside empty grasslands and meagre farms gradually freshened up and got busy with merchants and entertainers and scholars from the Moorish south.

But St. James' pilgrims went west and east, and for them, the rivers were a way of staging the journey to Compostela. River crossings often promised a monastery or an inn where you could get some supper and a night's rest. Many riverside towns were known for their beautiful bridges. Cycling in 1997, Scott and I had discovered that one of the Camino's great pleasures is still its medieval stone bridges. The many-arched Puente Órbigo, for instance, at the east end of Hospital de Órbigo, is famous for its history of warfare and jousting. But what also interested me was why they needed such a wide bridge at all back then: torrential rains or heavy spring run-off in the Cantabrians could cause huge floods to gush into the Órbigo valley. The floods made the low, barely moving waters of the Órbigo boil up over four hundred metres of valley land, ruining the hopes of new riverside vegetation, and forcing the mink and muskrat snooping along its banks to scurry after higher ground. A smaller bridge would soon have become a useless island.

Sometime after the 1950s, the Órbigo was dammed upstream for irrigation. Tall poplars have grown over the old, once flooded banks, and as you lean and look down upon them from the parapets of the long bridge, as we did, eating apples, the trees whisper and shimmer, exquisitely graceful in the breeze, while a chastened river flows in a single narrow stream to the south.

The solemn city of Burgos sits towards the east margin of the meseta, with León poised as its brighter, airier western counterpart a hundred and seventy kilometers away and slightly north. At Burgos, the Camino runs parallel to both the Rio Arlanzón and the main highway, past the Hospital del Rey and the Monastery de las Huelgas. Near Tardajos the river disappears off into the southwest, and the highway veers towards the north, but the Camino keeps straight west along a paved road towards Rabé de las Calzadas. On the way it crosses another flood-prone river, the Urbel, coming down from the north. On high water days in the centuries before the road went in, luckless pilgrims found themselves sloshing to Rabé across a half league of soupy grassland. It is said that they sang this wry old ditty to keep their spirits up:

De Rabé a Tardajos   From Rabé to Tardajos,
ne te faltaran trabajos   you won't lack labour;
de Tardajos a Rabé   from Tardajos to Rabé
libera nos, Domine   Lord, spare us!

At Rabé, the Camino swings up onto another long, high weather-stricken piece of meseta. In Spanish, the meseta is synonymously called the *paramó*, a curiously restful sounding word for a landscape that nobody seems to like very much. All our modern books on the Camino regard the *paramó* as an endurance test; it is tedious, hard and bleak, desolate. Prieto writes, "Here you must make a real effort, for it seems as if the plains have no end." "There is no way," says Don Valiña in his *Guide*, "that it can be made a pleasing prospect."

But nine centuries ago, Aimery said this of the *paramó:* "There follows the land of the Spaniards, that is to say, Castilla or Campos. This country is full of treasures, of gold and silver." The land "abounds in fodder and in vigorous horses, and it has plenty of bread, wine, meat, fish, milk and honey. On the other hand, it is poor in wood, and," adds Aimery, never missing a chance, "full of evil and vicious people.

The sky was a translucent gray the day Scott and I cycled west across the *paramó* from Rabé de las Calzadas to Castrojeriz. The trail was wide and rough with stones and dry mud. There was no shelter from the endless sky. Eight kilometres out of Rabé, we stopped to chat with three plump, jolly francophone pilgrims from Canada. They would not eat today, they said, until they reached Castrojeriz. I gathered this was a spiritual practice, a type of renunciation, though they seemed awkwardly reluctant to say so.

As we talked, two German men came walking toward us. They gave us robust grins as they scissored by without missing a beat. Minutes later, we rode past them on our bikes. Walking in unison as if automated, they waved and grinned again. At Hornillos del Campo, they caught up with us, sitting down next to us as we prepared our lunch on the steps of the church. We offered them food, but the louder one, a biologist, laughed and said they were too tough to have to eat. Instead they rolled cigarettes with their elbows on their knees, and gulped bottles of warm beer.

In the 17th Century, Domenico Laffi had also met some Germans on his way to Galicia. "We joined them," he tells us, "walking together the whole day across the great plain." On that day, Laffi also reports, the meseta was scorched

> not only by the sun, but by swarms of locusts which had destroyed everything.... There were so many of these accursed locusts that one could walk only with difficulty. At every step, they rose in the air in clouds so dense that you could hardly see the sky..... It is pitiful to behold because not only people die of hunger but also beasts because they can't find pasture, all having been consumed by these creatures.

At Hornillos del Campo, the Hornazuelo valley turns almost due south and the Camino ascends a rough escarpment from the valley floor onto another slab of meseta. Leaving the Germans behind us, we lumbered with our bikes up the steep track. Suddenly we were on top, gloriously exposed as if taken up from the grave in the Rapture. We paused astride our bikes, inhaling a new, pure air. The meseta stretched away, eerie and alluring under the sky's diffuse light. Its grassy surface was dotted interminably with shrubs. The horizon was far off and very low, as if we were looking out over the curve of the earth. On our map, Hontanas was only ten kilometers away. From where we stood, it was invisible; going towards it across this ghostly terrain was an act of faith.

A freak wind from the east propelled our bikes over the hard, double track that lay before us. I felt it steady me as my wheels tripped on dry clods, lurched into furrows, then accelerated with a jerk over pads of smooth dry mud. We were lucky with the weather; one good rain would turn that solid soil to glue, gumming up bicycle gears and leaving foot pilgrims walking on impossible clay stilts. It never did rain, but all day the sky was coated with a steamy film. Indistinct clouds hid out along the horizon, curled over their white, wispy vapours. The only sounds were birds' cheeps and sporadic thuds of wind.

Altogether, the trail from Burgos to Castrojeriz went through thirty-eight kilometers of Spanish *paramó*. But those ten kilometers between Hornillos del Campo and Hontanas were beyond anything I had imagined. The land was dense with the colours of a spring you might see on another planet: greens abnormally green, greens coated with yellow dust, quirky beiges and rose, patches of bleached soil like fallen kites, scrappy, brown-twigged shrubs whose thin leaves were streaked with a milky silver. Limestone rocks were strewn among the grasses like big old teeth.

As it had so many times on this journey, physical effort sharpened my perceptions. If it is possible to grasp the pilgrim's movement at its most refined, abstracted even beyond the footsteps that are said to be its defining feature, it was here, riding rough and slow, our feet off the ground, across the *paramó*. Something in this overturned plate of a wilderness drained me of distraction and drove all my energy, all my attention, into that membrane we almost never notice, where the body meets the whatness of the physical world and bargains with its forces. Pilgrimage as a negotiation between mechanics and will, causing an overflow of kinesis into human time. Pilgrimage reduced to its smallest units, not simplifying, but revealing in all their fine complexity the forces that each moment weave us into our world: the precise articulations of bones, the power of will driving down the legs into the pedals, the see-sawing of the knees, the reassuring resistance of the ground, the crunch of tires felt in the balls of the feet, the wind compressing the flesh of the back, the sturdy torsion of arms over handlebars. Walking, I would never feel it like this, never know so intensely the intimacy between the laws of physics and our fathomless compulsion to "go forth through the fields."

Some months earlier, I had read Prieto's account of crossing the meseta. Now that I was here myself, I wasn't surprised that he had turned that trip into a religious experience. The meseta is the perfect intoxicant for those with the double craving for the ascetic and the sublime. I could see how Prieto would find a spiritual home in the otherworldly colours of the *paramó*, touched by its breezes out of nowhere, surrounded by its tousled pastures and its far-off circumference, staring up into its infinitely pale dome. He says it was a place of purification, opposed to the city with all its corruption. The meseta offered seclusion, where one "is absorbed in the mystery of God through the dialogue of prayer." He said something else that I wanted to understand better: the meseta is where solitude and silence meet, where an interior stillness occurs, not in blank mindlessness, but through active control of the imagination, and what he calls *fierce concentration* upon "a God who reveals himself in a thousand forms."

As his day on the *paramó* wore on, Prieto began to weary of the crushing sunshine, the endless track, the maddening locusts. He says he felt like the Israelites, whining in the wilderness on their sojourn to the Promised Land. His malaise made him think of the Christian hermits of 2nd-century Egypt who had fled the world's fleshpots to fight the demons of desire in deserts even more desolate than the Spanish meseta.

Those monks were well acquainted with this "ennui of mid-day." They called it *acedia*: the sickness of despair and spiritual fatigue. You have embarked eagerly upon the spiritual life. The glamour of the quest sustains you until, earlier or later, the brilliance becomes familiar, the routine dull, the landscape around you empty and unresponsive. I could see how the meseta would be a severe testing ground when the mirror of your longing and hopes clouds over, and you are just *here*, wandering drowsily among wind-swept grasses under an opaque and oppressive sky.

You don't need geography to feel *acedia*. In the weeks before Scott and I left for the Camino I had felt this same weariness of heart in my everyday life. I wandered from work to home and back without conviction, bored, groping for meaning but always resisting commitment to it. Nothing was clear, or even worth clarifying. The world was a smudged mirror. But it was still, after all, a mirror and what it showed me were my own shadows, a self shrinking from definition, vaguely aware that my sad, projected world was only that, yet unable to let it go. Here on this first journey across the Camino, I was still having dark dreams. I sometimes slept badly and woke up exhausted. I was tired of trying to inspire myself. For motivation, I relied on Scott, who moved effortlessly in and out of the Camino world, noticing everything new with delight, as natural as a dog sniffing shrubs in a new park. I didn't know what to do, and so I would simply wait it out, coasting on his enthusiasm.

But today, riding across the meseta, with Scott's athletic figure a few metres ahead of me, I felt no ennui. Everyone else, it seemed, had met with misery of one kind or another on this rough, endless track. But I was taken up into a pure and fearless present. The sky overhead, infinitely translucent, was as reassuring as the ground under my tires. I watched my knuckles bulge under my worn cycling gloves as my hands gripped my handlebars. I felt my forearms shudder on the bumps. On this high shelf strewn with grass and stones, concentration seemed the only option - part opportunity, part requirement. I had become fiercely involved. I was *in*. I hadn't earned these moments with years, or even days, of monkish or any other kind of discipline. It was a gift, a bright break in the clouds. Perhaps it was what is sometimes called grace.

Every Santiago pilgrim has to cross rivers. But in the Middle Ages, when geography danced lightly between maps and allegory, rivers also belonged to a spiritual terrain. They were part of the cartography of salvation.

The Church had always made much of the line between the profane and the sacred. Rivers, in this dualistic view, were an emblem of spiritual cleansing. Not rivers of life down which you travelled to a nirvana of oceanic unity, but rivers of transition that had to be crossed, where old sins were dunked away and a whitened soul climbed the far bank. To get from the wasteland of lost souls to the abode of the redeemed you had to "go over Jordan," just as the Israelites had on the way to the Promised Land. Rivers reminded the Christian that the soul going by way of earth to a celestial home must resist the world's folly and, washing away his defilements, cross over to a land of the spirit. River symbolism had a levering rhythm: captivity to release, fear to faith, danger to safety, repentance to absolution. Crossing rivers was an analogy with the movement of the soul: a mini-baptism, a ritualistic replay, or rehearsal, of redemption.

One night in El Burgo Ranero, three days from Castrojeriz, Scott and I had dinner with Thomas McCann, a tall, bespectacled medieval art historian from England. We had first met Tom in the church at Torres del Rio and were fortunate to run into him again here in Ranero, in a cavernous, mediocre restaurant across from the pilgrim hostel. He was travelling alone by car along the Camino, carrying out some personal research. Every two years, he led a tour group to Spain to study the iconography of Camino churches.

Our conversation had come round to an intriguing topic: just how different *are* the medieval and modern ways of explaining natural phenomena. Modern scientists, we had already agreed, take nature apart, reduce it to its smallest pieces and most basic mechanisms, then manipulate its variables and predict outcomes. If there is story-making in science, the plot lies in cause and effect as the scientist moves from one observable event to another.

Thomas poured us some red Rioja wine. "But medieval scholars looked at nature not so much in terms of cause and effect, though of course there was always some of that, but in terms of *meaning*. Rather than moving *across* the literal, their explanations ran *up and down*, from the literal to the metaphorical and mystical. They understood the natural world through expanding theological analogies, through categories of meaning from the lowest material things to the highest orders of intellectual and spiritual conception. They studied nature to find the divine laws that were carrying humankind towards its ultimate confrontation with the Absolute."

This is how we think an educated medieval mind worked: every physical thing that existed represented both its own being and a metaphysical reality that had its end in God. The natural world, animal, vegetable and mineral, was of some minor interest in itself, but what was most important to know was how every natural process fit God's salvation agenda for His created and fallen world. To truly understand nature was to grasp the transcendent truth to which the literal forms of things pointed, and thus to understand their *meaning* for human destiny.

Christianity, like Judaism before it and Islam after it, was a religion of the Book. Thus the final authority for interpreting the physical world was the Bible, the linguistic key to the universe. On its pages was the code, though an obscure one requiring much effort, for understanding the symbols embedded by God in His created world.

"It wasn't only the Bible, either, that was the key to salvation," Thomas continued. "As Hugo of St. Victor used to say, nature was the other 'book.' Nature's shapes and patterns also revealed God's plan for redeeming his prodigal world."

It had been the Greeks, especially Plato, who laid the foundations for this kind of thinking. But it was the monkish scholars of the early medieval period, beginning with Origen and the early Church Fathers, and especially St. Augustine, who built a Christian edifice on the notion that physical phenomena point to spiritual realities. Until the Renaissance, every educated mind in Europe based his - or her - study of the natural world on the Bible and these early Christian commentaries.

"And scientific inquiry went completely underground," said Scott.

"It *was* almost extinguished in the Middle Ages. Why waste time investigating nature for its own laws? That only leads you from one fact to another. You go nowhere but along the horizon. Better to extend your understanding upward into God's plan for his creation."

I had heard it said that Augustine single-handedly cast an entire millenium into an intellectual trance, but that was unjust. There were many brilliant minds at work in the Middle Ages. And most of them, from Augustine all the way up to Hugo of St. Victor, were saying with the authority of an Isaac Newton or a Stephen Hawking that the universe was a living compendium of salvation moments and nature was a book that showed the mystical pathway to a loving Creator God.

"You couldn't beat that," said Thomas. "It wasn't science, but it did have meaning, and for most people, explanations, which are a kind of story, exist for the sake of their meaning. Eventually however, Arab learning got to Europe, bringing Aristotle and rules for inquiry into how things worked, and Western European schools began to shift away from their metaphysical dream."

"It sounds like a collective psychosis," said Scott.

"It does sound psychotic to the post-Cartesian, post-Freudian mind. But I believe it fit with the overall way people thought. They lived in a magical universe that was kept together by references among signs. It's hard for us to imagine living in a world where the literal can instantly trigger a symbolic meaning." Thomas leaned back and crossed his arms. "But it would also be very wrong to think that medieval men like Aimery were any more or less in touch with literal reality than we are now."

"Like Freud's cigar, a river was also a river," I said.

"Hmmm." Thomas smiled vaguely.

I thought it was odd that Aimery, the practical 12th-century French cleric, showed no interest in the landscape symbolism of the Camino. But Prieto, modern monk, ex-lawyer and academic, sees almost nothing *but* allegory in his walk to Santiago.

Thomas emptied his glass of wine. "I think most pilgrims to Santiago were just concerned about getting through as safely as they could. They used whatever prayers and charms they had available to do it. I haven't read Prieto. I guess I should. It sounds as if he has personally bought into the mystical idealism of the Middle Ages. But we don't have access to all the cultural paraphernalia that went with that mysticism. That makes it look very pure and straight forward. In reality, there was a lot of magical thinking and intellectual confusion about, parading as religion."

Scott added with a smile, "Just like now."

The waiter arrived and surveyed our half-full plates with disbelief. "*Postre?*" he asked tentatively, but we declined.

"The advantage, though," said Thomas as we were leaving to return to the hostel, "was that everything and everybody had a place in the scheme. Nobody knew about molecules and bacteria. Death was everywhere. You could be drowned or murdered or eaten by wolves. But your church told you that your whole being was still accounted for in the divine plan. You fit in, you meant something. The Church even gave you access to salvation. We're like ships lost at sea in comparison."

"Are we?" I wondered. "Was it really that much better then?"

One year later, in 1998, I walked the meseta from Castrojeriz to Boadilla del Campo with Anya, the German social worker turned pilgrim. Her feet were still bothering her, but she had worked out a way with her walking sticks to keep pressure off the tender spots. My own leg was also very painful. When we met, she was going faster that I was. "How's your shin?" she asked me.

"Still hurts," I said. "Want to walk together? I'm pretty slow. If you want to go ahead, I don't mind." But she stayed with me, hobbling on her sticks beside me.

If the meseta cycling adventure had been a celebration of movement through space, walking it was to find oneself in time, or in the absence of time. Above our heads, the glaring August sun seemed to have stopped moving. Its yellowness spread like the wings of a giant eagle, blotting out the blue sky and casting golden reflections into the air that were too blinding to look at directly. The fields around us were hot and still: barley, wheat, fallow, rows of sunflowers with big silly faces, some pasture here and there. Every blade, every stalk looked as if nothing here had ever moved, not even the wind, since the beginning of time.

The original Camino was nearby; the small bridge over the Odrilla Rio had borne the weight of nine hundred years of pilgrims. Roads, field redistribution, the railway and the habits of new generations had buried much of the old route, but I don't think the land that morning was unlike what it was during the hey-day of pilgrimage. Then, agriculture was managed by community councils who divided the land into parcels for cultivation and fallow and, after a harvest, for pasture. Sheep were grazed throughout. Since land was held in common, fences were almost non-existent. Aimery had been right about the lack of forests - even by the Middle Ages, the land had been shorn of much of its timber, first by the Romans, never champions of the tree, and later by the Visigothic farmers. But Aimery saw more stands of oak than now, species that could thrive in the limestone and gravel sediment that made up the soils of the meseta. These were conserved as a ready supply of wood for fire and for building. Now, clear-cutting of the remaining forest stands has denuded the region, and in place of Aimery's rich groves of tall oaks, tangled patches of shrub sit in bunched heaps here and there across the landscape.

Around mid-day, Anya and I arrived at the Rio Pisuerga, an important waterway flowing through the meseta from the gorges of the Cantabrian Mountains. Like the Urbel and the Órbigo, the Pisuerga's periodic floods brought either blessed moisture and or a swirling disaster to the local farmlands. Between the little towns of Itero del Castillo and Itero de la Vega, the Pisuerga makes a U-turn. At the top of the U, the waters widen and grow restful, so river reeds and bushes grow abundantly. Here too sits the Puente de Itero, a sedate bridge made floodproof by eleven stone arches.

At Itero del Castillo, the world materialized like a kind of Central Station in the heart of the mystical, empty meseta. Here, the church, the marketplace and the military all met and mingled. In the 12th Century, Itero was a fortified boundary post between Castile and León. In 1174, a certain Nuñez Perez de Lara and his wife Teresa established a pilgrim hospice here. Nextdoor was a Cistercian monastery, which was taken over in the 13th Century by the Knights of the Order of Hospitalers. Until well into the 18th Century, the Knights managed large properties on both sides of the river. Downstream was a mill, and further west beyond the bridge was the town of Itero de la Vega, whose name means fertile valley. Looking over what remained of the villages, with their stone houses and towers, I tried to imagine the old hubbub at this Camino river crossing, as monks and soldiers, millers and farmers, traders and pilgrims had met, talked, traded, danced and argued year after year, as if life would go on forever.

Until the 1990s, a ruined church was all that was left of the hospice at Itero de Castillo. In pictures from earlier guidebooks, it is a roofless stone rectangle. Stones the size of skulls lie in heaps in the turf outside its cracked and gapped walls. A fallen wood door blocks the entrance. A picture of the interior shows a lawn of wild grass, and an arch unconquered by time rising over some steps into a perfectly proportioned apse. The slab of an altar, still horizontal, sits heavily on a crumbling support of stone blocks.

By 1997, the church had been transformed by the Italian Confraternità di S. Jacopo di Compostella from Perugia into one of the most delightful *refugios* on the Camino. The sky was overwhelmingly bright as Anya and I hobbled toward the building. The noonday air smelled faintly like dry spices. A ferocious bolt of heat came from the glaring walls near the door. But when we stepped across the threshold, we were immersed in a cool bath of dark air, a bliss enhanced by the pleasant decor of the long, rectangular church and the easy welcome of the Italian staff as they smiled and held out biscuits and coffee.

The nave had been reroofed and was lined on one side with a kitchen counter, a stove, shelves for coffee cans and spice jars, and a long braid of garlic. A table laid with a red and white plastic tablecloth ran up the middle of the room. On it were graceful bottles of olive oil and vinegar. A wrought-iron candelabra hung from a fat hook above the table. Light poured into the room from narrow windows set high over the altar. On the apse wall were a crucifix and pilgrims' purses of medieval design. Chairs had been set up around the altar. At the other end of the nave, beyond a screen, were beds for about sixteen pilgrims.

Martino, the curly-haired Italian I had met a few days earlier, sat smoking at the table with a quiet Swedish pilgrim I had not met before, who was drinking coffee from a ceramic cup. Smiling playfully as he rolled his own, the Italian mischievously discoursed on the joys of smoking, ending with a little flourish that made the solemn

Scandinavian, who said he had kicked the habit eleven years ago, burst into laughter and reach for another cookie.

I noticed Martino was without his companion.

"Where's your French friend?" I asked him.

"He had to go back to Paris," he answered. "A problem in the family. It's a pity. We were going well."

"I'm so disappointed for him." I said. "And for you. He had such a cheerful manner."

"Si, si. He did. I knew him a long time. We travelled much together. We met when we were Boy Scouts."

We all looked up at once. Two more pilgrims had entered the hostel, one a trim, smiling Spaniard with short hair and a silver stud in one ear, and the other more vision than reality, part angel, part vamp, all hair, platinum, and eyes, long and sultry. His body looked frail and sinuous under his jeans and t-shirt. Both men were happy and friendly, immediately likeable. The taller one, Victor, chatted and ate biscuits while the sex angel, José, smiled dreamily at everyone and caressed his coffee cup. They were from Madrid, out for a leisurely pilgrimage, and nothing in the world was going to take the pleasure of it all away from them. They had plenty of time, could always get another job waiting tables when they went back to Madrid. After a while, they left to have lunch, preferring, they said, to have picnics outdoors.

Anya's feet were starting to hurt again and she decided to stay here at San Nicolás for the night. Had it been later in the day, I too would have stayed at this most gracious of hostels. But it was only one o'clock; ahead lay more enchanted meseta, more quiet stone villages. I decided to go on to Boadilla del Camino, eight and a half kilometers away.

I paused once more on the Puente de Itero to peer over its perfect arches into the cobalt stream of the Pisuerga. At one time, mink and muskrat had streaked through the water by the bank; perhaps a few still did. I saw Victor and José eating their lunch on a blanket in the shadows by the river bank; they smiled and waved as I leaned on the parapet over them. Near where they sat, sparkling sapphire-blue eddies jitterbugged past the reeds and bushes.

The Boadilla hostel was a modern bungalow whose rooms rambled on one to another like subterranean tombs. A rectangular dormitory just off the entrance hall was lined with plain low cots. A dim sitting room on the other side of the hall harboured an ancient couch, a few frayed armchairs, and a small dining table and chairs. In the kitchen, as in all *refugio* kitchens, though arranged neatly this time, was an assortment of leftover food in cans and packages, second hand dishes and cutlery. A plastic bag of grainy looking cookies sat on a shelf over the stove.

I walked down the hall, finding no one else around. The place was dark and cool. I had been sweating outside under the sun, now I was almost chilly. I came to the most spectacular room in the house: an enormous lavatory with gleaming black tiles, several showers, a long tiled vanity with new sinks and tall, spotless mirrors, and a separate bathroom with a tub.

The idea of a warm bath was irresistible. In a few moments, I was stretching out in water that felt like a quilt of warm silk. I leaned back, closed my eyes, felt my Camino-hardened muscles dissolve.

There was a sudden knocking on the bathroom door, and a male voice shouted something about water and "el pueblo." It was hard to make out the sense of it; apparently I had angered someone by using a tub of hot water. Later, when I met the *hospitalero*, I apologised for having a bath and offered to pay him for costs. He was much more congenial in person; no problem, he said, with having a bath. He just wanted to remind me not to waste water, as it was a precious resource.

This *hospitalero* one of Spain's very few organic farmers. It was a struggle, he told me. There was little awareness of eco-agriculture and even less market for organic food. I don't know how he survived.

I asked him where I could wash some clothes. "There's a public laundry where the women go, across the road. The water is beautiful." He smiled as he handed me a thick bar of Castile soap. "You'll love doing your laundry outside, with the trees and the fresh air."

The laundry was a long, roofed shelter with concrete tubs that flowed with water diverted from irrigation canals. The tubs ran the length of the shelter, were slanted and corrugated on the side to make a washboard where you could scrub your clothes. I slopped and scrubbed my shirts and pants in the cool, tinkling water. Behind me, the trees rustled in the late afternoon breeze and birds chirped in the bushes. A colony of brilliant green algae had staked a claim at the base of the washboard just below the water line. A few had smeared over my shirt. Nothing a little Castile soap couldn't handle. I washed and pounded and rinsed and wrung.

In everyone's life, there are certain acts that are later remembered as landmarks of private history. Years ago in Pakistan, I had an icy shower, a cross between the Chinese water torture and a jet of hail, that will always be my defining experience of self-mortification and exultant absolution in the cleansing of my body. Once while camping in Afghanistan, I crawled out of my tent one night expecting to be sick. And I was, but afterwards I watched in rapture as the full moon rose like a god over the jagged shadows of the Hindu Kush. Never before or since have I felt so ill and so exhilarated at the same time. But the act of scrubbing my clothes with Castile soap on a cement washboard in the public shelter at Boadilla del Camino, August 1998, my arms swelling with the exertion and my hands growing clean and raw in the swirling water, will always be my supreme moment in personal laundry.

I was hanging my clothes on a line in the reflected heat of the hostel wall when more cyclists appeared: five French pilgrims, two of whom were women, and two very quiet young Portuguese men. They all wanted to wash some clothes, hesitated at first about the public laundry, but returned enthusiastic with their bundles of wet clothes to hang by mine.

That night we all bedded down in the big room with the cots, but as one man and then another began to snore, I knew that to remain would be death to another night's sleep. I dragged my mattress from the dormitory, past the bikes standing in the hallway and into the sitting room, where I went to sleep beside the coffee table. In the early morning, hauling my mattress back across the impenetrably dark hall, I knocked over a bicycle. That bicycle crashed immediately over another, then another went down, and another. I imagined a galaxy of metal parts and broken mirrors scudding over the tile floor. The entire hostel seemed to shudder. From the dorm came grunting voices and the startled rustle of sleeping bags. I found the light switch and to my great relief, saw that apart from being heaped over each other like scrap metal, the bikes were intact. I poked my head in the door to the room. "Lo siento!! I'm sorry! Pardon! ... I think your bikes are OK ... it was my mattress .... you all snored so much!!" Somebody laughed. I hauled my mattress to my cot as people scrambled out of their beds, smiling at me sleepily, unconcerned that I had knocked over their bikes. It was time to get up anyway, someone said. In a few minutes, the long gleaming bathroom, with its alarming mirrors and big soap dishes, was full of half dressed and towelled pilgrims washing up, quietly, as if you could create privacy by being silent.

The hostel superintendent had prepared a splendid breakfast: whole grain biscuits, mint tea, fruit and coffee. He told us he practised a type of touch therapy, moving his hands slowly over areas of negative energy to heal the body and the mind. I let him try to do something about my worsening leg pain. It was relaxing to lie on the couch. He focused and breathed, studying my leg with the palm of his hands held an inch or so above. I imagined I could probably do with a whole day of this, even without the attentions of the *hospitalero*. But he finally sat back, looked at me honestly and said he couldn't find any negative energy to extract. He accompanied me as I limped out the door to where the French and the Portuguese were taking group photos. We joined in, jostling and grinning and saying *Queso!!* in the warm morning sun.

The French gathered their bikes to leave. I asked one of the women how she was enjoying her trip. She looked at me with her head to one side and the smile of someone who is helplessly happy. "This is so much fun," she said in French. "I could do it forever." As she spoke, I felt her pleasure as if it were mine. Fun seemed a superficial word for it, but if it were possible to have profound fun, this would be the time; the taste - the gift - of pure, uncomplicated pleasure, enjoyed in every part of your being.

When you travel the Camino across the meseta from Burgos to Astorga, you encounter over fifty rivers and canals, varying in width and volume but all heading roughly north to south. The last river, the Tuerto, gurgling in a deep valley below the city of Astorga, marks with nature's grainy, meandering geometry the western margin of the Castilian meseta.

The Tuerto is the line of demarcation between two geographical regions; it is also the line between two spiritual landscapes. Behind you to the east lies the meseta, whose far-off circumference, longitudinal river valleys and tea-cup dome made it a sort of pilgrim's *mapamundi,* a piece of divine cartography that could, in the stark simplicity of its drama, turn your earthly journey into a cosmic quest. Once the Tuerto is crossed, however, the vectors of geography and faith peter out. The far northwest of Spain, which is the province of Galicia, will enclose you in a puzzle of mountains, lowlands, helter-skelter watersheds and basins. The northwest looks to the Atlantic, but before the ocean come steep, twisted valleys, huge hills of glacial waste, upended plates of rock, archaic mountains loaded with forest, and low, fertile plains. Water runs everywhere in hollows and gullies, and seems to go nowhere; there is no way to navigate a river back to the meseta.

Near Astorga, patches of sharp, dark stone begin to appear, outcroppings of quarzite, the first sign of the paleozoic rock formations that cover Spain's northwest all the way to the Atlantic. This plate, mostly buried but rising into view here and there in amorphous hunks, has been here for 600 million years. Over it lie Galicia's moist forests and farms. Human hands and machines have redecorated only its most superficial features.

In the land near Sarria, deep within Galicia to the west of Triacastela, there is a depression, visible from the air, that follows the direction of fault lines that occurred when Europe first separated from the American continents. That first pushing apart of the mid-Atlantic floor shoved slabs of bedrock up into a two thousand meter range that became the Montes de León, running southwest from the Cantabrian cordillera between the meseta and Galicia. The Montes today come down hard at the eastern edge of the Bierzo, a piece of sunken crust that separates them from a second more westerly range, the Ancares, with its pass through El Cebreiro. The west slopes of the Ancares descend into a confusion of high, green hills that, from the air, stretch like a mist-ribboned Eden across the rest of Galicia to the sea.

One night in 1997 after an exhausting climb from Vega Valcarce, Scott and I were asleep in the quiet old convent, now a hotel, atop the pass at El Cebreiro. All at once, from deep in sleep's blank abyss, came a heart-quickening dream, a sensation of mad trembling. The air itself seemed to be vibrating. Floating up, blinking, I gathered that our bed was banging against the wall, that the armoire was having hysterics, that something wooden behind the wall was knocking urgently on something else. I do not know how long it lasted. Afterward, I lay listening to my heart thumping hard and slow and tried to piece together what had happened. Oddly, the idea of an earthquake never occurred to me. But in the morning the bright-eyed, black-haired hostess of the hotel greeted me with a flurry of Spanish. "Did you feel the *terremoto*?" It was the sole topic of conversation at breakfast. The event had been exciting and harmless. In 1108, an earthquake a little further west had destroyed the entire town of Cacabellos.

Long before they were seen by human beings, the slabby heights and steep gorges of Galicia were shaved and manicured by the weather. Not the day to day climate of the Atlantic that today brings rain and lush growth to the northwest, but the drawn out, gradual climates of the Miocene, the Tertiary, and the Quaternary Periods. There was once a tropical climate here, then a bout of prolonged dryness when wind buffed the surfaces of rocks already polished with water. During the Ice Age, cold tongues of

ice penetrated and stretched the valleys, then r\
shrugging off mud and stones that now lie in heaps ⊥er
forests and farmlands.

No medieval traveller would have guessed at the
geological history that lay here under the Galician paths to
Santiago. Nature was God's one-time creation, all finished
in six days. To some, these tortured forms and harsh
passes were evidence of a fallen world, a world turned
upside down in the catastrophe of Adam's sin. But if
nature had been rent, it was still a gift, a solace, a
livelihood; the trials it forced on the pilgrim were
purgative, necessary tests of spiritual stamina. And many
believed that the redeeming power of Jesus Christ,
scheduled to show up on the brink of the millenium,
would restore the disgraced and disfigured land to its
Edenic beauty.

But for me, Galicia was an Eden even now, with its
graceful, oceanic topography. Aimery thought well of it
too, though he would never have called it an Eden.

> This country is wooded, provided with
> excellent rivers, meadows and orchards, and
> with plenty of good fruits and clear springs; on
> the other hand, it is poor in cities, towns and
> cultivated fields. Bread, wheat, and wine are
> scarce, but rye bread and cider abound, as do
> livestock and beasts of burden, milk, and
> honey. The sea fish is either enormously large
> or small. The land abounds in gold and silver,
> fabrics, the fur of wild animals and many
> other goods, as well as in Saracen treasures.

An Eden, but not without its challenges. If the
meseta tested your endurance with the heat of the fiery
sun, the Camino after Astorga presented the test of cold.
Warmth at night, warmth in winter, warmth enough to dry
out were the gifts for which one praised God in Galicia.
Rain blew in regularly and still blows in from the Atlantic.
A mere nine kilometers from Astorga at Santa Catalina de
Somoza, sits an imposing mountain named for a local
malevolent rain god. Marti Teleno is a type of thundering
Thor, a maker of storms and a general bringer of ill luck.

One of the deity's pranks is described in the Capitulary Acts of the City of Astorga from September 1846. Torrential rains had fallen for a day and a half. At dawn on the third day, people standing atop the town walls watched as a foaming front of water advanced from the west through the Jerga Valley, a glittering four meter band that had already covered the shelter over the Encalada Fountain. In the wide silver ribbon of its wake bobbed dead and drowning livestock, farm implements flushed from soupy barnyards, and the furnishings of wiped out houses. The water poured over fields of ripened grain, made the roads useless, and indifferently carted off the mills and bridges it found in its way.

Teleno must have been otherwise occupied the day in 1998, about a hundred years after the famous flood, when I left Astorga for Rabanal del Camino. I walked under a desiccating August sun on a narrow road that ran like a strip of fine charcoal through the yellow fields. Occasionally a car passed and someone would wave. The grass by the road was delicate like the soft fur of a yellow kitten. Further off where the plain sloped almost imperceptibly south, leafy trees in plump groves floated like cumulus clouds just above the ground. Beyond them the grass liquefied to a yellow sea and distant patches of scrub became squat islands. Then there were hills, humped over each other, cloaked in dark green. In the far distance lay the mountains, higher, but still looking like hills, big horizontal bodies whose hazy colour faded upward, as if they were trying without being seen to blend into the dim, milk-blue horizon.

I walked slowly. The only sound was the wind whispering to itself. Tiny birds perched soundlessly on the twigs of shrubs standing paralyzed by the road. A cricket rubbed its wings. It was so dry my nose felt light inside and nothing pressed my skin. But the scene was dreamily fluid like a transparent lake, a swirl of warmth and yellow grass, islands of shrubs trembling like water in the heat, rounded mountains vaporizing into the sky.

I stared across the plain. I was a visitor from the other side of the planet, almost from the other side of the millenium, a lone spectator in this theatre of time now bereft of its players and inhumanly quiet in the bright sun. There had once been a busy transport industry here, as poor farmers turned to carting to improve their living. Nearby roads would have echoed with carts and donkey's hooves. Gone too were the hawkers and local monks and farmwives greeting one another, the sound of axes ringing from nearby stands of oak, dogs barking up flocks of skittish sheep, farmers in dirty tunics hoarsely urging their oxen through the fields, kids bullying their sheep with sticks, and pilgrims in threes and fours, singing as they plodded past, their sticks grinding chalkily against the stones.

Anywhere from Astorga west through Rabanal del Camino, pilgrims who lifted their eyes from the gritty road before their feet saw small fields lined with shrubby bush and forest stands. They might have spied among the shrubs the pretty rock rose, fragrant bushes of wild thyme, pink heather, white broom, and golden chain. But except in the valley floors, the soil here was thin and under it lay an unsympathetic mix of schist and quarzite. This life could hardly have been called flourishing. But neither was it mere subsistence. The sheep and goats munching in the fallow fields would supplement income from cash crops. There were a few vineyards, as much as the careless climate and stony soil would allow; even today you can see white adobe humps over the caves, now mostly abandoned, where local wine was aged. Cows were raised mainly for labour in the fields, but sometimes a farmer could sell a little milk or leather or a couple of calves. I have read, though it seems hard to believe, that beef was not highly valued; the carcasses of cattle were often left to rot after the hide had been stripped; others would have died of disease or wild animal attacks. Then the oozing odour of a dead cow stiffly humped in the field would share the air with the high-pitched stink of stored manure, while overhead, vultures circled on the updrafts, eyeing their feast in the humorless, calculating way of the scavenger.

In the 19th Century, the Maragateria, as this area is now called, began an economic decline. Curiously, that decline beautified the landscape. Arable land, long abandoned, abounds in tall shrubs: white broom, yellow laburnum, various heathers. Tree stands that were once clear cut are coming back. Some fields, like the tiny one lined with a stone fence where I stopped to eat a chunk of dark chocolate and air my overheated feet, are filling in with groves of hawthorn and oak.

Seen from the plains of the Maragateria past Astorga, the Montes de León lope low along the south-western horizon, but after Rabanal, some hours further west, where I finally bought a walking stick, the rise in the land is suddenly under your feet and you are heading almost before you realize it into the Monte Irago pass. The Camino here is a ramp of highway tarmac swirling slowly up through a dilating landscape of humpbacked hills. On a bicycle it is arduous, as it is also on foot. Once you arrive at the crest of the pass, which extends from Foncebadón over to Manjarín, the land gives an impression more of width than height. The mountains lie to the south in heavy bulges, their old rounded shoulders draped in a haze of shrub.

Foncebadón is a wreck of a village, a collection of small stone buildings deserted centuries ago and disintegrating in the wind. Still, limping with my new stick along its single, stone-strewn road in 1998, I saw that a little grocery had opened. There were a few parked cars, recent models. People drive up by day to see the view. At night, the buildings crumble a little more, and local dogs piss in blackened doorways.

I sat in the sloping meadow beyond Foncebadón's one street. The grass was an uncompromising mat of bristles. But it was warm to sit upon, and the wind fondled my face. I stared out through humming hydro lines into blunt, textureless mountains whose grandeur seemed attenuated, as if they couldn't be bothered showing it off anymore. A man with a shotgun sauntered past me down the hill; beside him trotted a young German Shepherd mix, his tail curled ecstatically high.

In the 10th and 11th Centuries, the pass over Irago, or Mount Rabanal as it was sometimes called, was merely a long, uphill dirt path. Foncebadón and Manjarín (or Fonten Sabbatoni and Majorinus as the Romans called them) were one-lane villages clinging to life by a few spikey blades of grass. But it was the weather on the thousand meter high pass that has been imprinted on the collective memory of the Camino. From the beginning of September to the end of May, the thready fields and cowering stone huts were either flogged pitilessly with rains or asphyxiated under masses of snow. Travel could be paralyzed for weeks. In the early Camino years, there must have been a handful of pilgrims each winter who tried to get over the pass from Rabanal to Molinaseca, good souls naively making their way up into the deepening snows, growing concerned and cold, not at all sure how far the next hostel was, finally no longer even sure where under all this maddening snow lay the trail. Their bodies would be found in the spring, a melancholy discovery for the locals who had to identify them and get them a decent Christian burial. Eventually, lookouts were established to keep track of the pass conditions. To prevent pilgrims from wandering off the track to a death by refrigeration, both Foncebadón and Manjarín were granted tax exemptions for placing eight hundred tall stakes along the route. Today there are dozens of modern, red and white snow poles by the highway, each standing like a memorial to a snow-blind, bone-cold traveller clutching his crucifix as he slumped for the last time into the snow.

Mount Irago was an irascible place, with its wretched little populace, its pitiful soils, its interminable winters, its demonic snows. But like the meseta, Irago had wilderness appeal, and a singular advantage: height. Mount Irago was the ultimate mystical landscape, calling to mind the temptation of Jesus on the "exceedingly high mountain," the transfiguration high on Mount Tabor, the crucifixion on Golgotha. The pass from Foncebadón and Manjarín came with its metaphors built in: on the holy road to St. James' shrine, hanging above the world and apart from its folly, offering purgative suffering in its snows and visionary rapture in the sun-pierced clouds that floated over the hills cresting off to the south.

So Irago attracted those rare orchids of the holy life, the kin of Anthony and all those spiritual adventurers who centuries before had gone off to the Egyptian desert to rid their souls of earthly evil. But it is almost certain that without all the Camino pilgrims making their way over Irago, neither the devout Juan Estefaniz nor the anchorite known only as Gaucelmo would have built their hermitages in the vicinity of Foncebadón.

The two men lived during the heady years of church and monastic reform. Charity, Christianity's greatest and all but forgotten ideal, had made a comeback. The goods of the Church, it was remembered, were the right of the poor. Remembered too were the loveliness of simple living, which is poverty only to those on the outside, and the equally lovely notion of Christian hospitality. In the minds of men like Gaucelmo, Juan Estefaniz and others who ran hostels all along the Camino, the religious life was to be lived apart from the world, but always in response to the world's needs.

Both Juan Estefaniz and Gaucelmo, whose name is remembered in the English-run Gaucelmo hostel at Rabanal del Camino, had their pilgrim hospices up and running by the turn of the 12th Century. Of the two, Gaucelmo's is the more famous, though Juan's story is perhaps more interesting. Juan had already made a pilgrimage to the Holy Land. He knew firsthand the trials that bedeviled pilgrims anywhere and he applied what he knew to the management of his own hospice. But Gaucelmo's hermitage, which included a church, an inn and a hospital, was the more influential of the two, and perhaps the longer lasting. In 1103 (the document still exists in the Archives of the Cathedral at Astorga) Gaucelmo obtained rights from Alfonso VI over the land for his hermitage. Both his and Juan's hermitages were later ceded to the jurisdiction of the Church of Astorga, Gaucelmo's at least on condition that the hospital be maintained in perpetuity.

Anyone wanting to join either order was welcome. But the cost was high: submission in faith to a life of poverty, austerity and charity. Christian humility is written all over the documents from the time. Juan never mentions his hermit status, referring to himself only as "an unworthy priest, not fit to be called a servant of the servants of God." Gaucelmo allows himself the luxury of being "a servant of the servants of God" but refers to himself only as a hermit, never a priest. It sounds like a sugary, morbidly self-effacing Christianity until you look at how it was actually practised. Meekness and humility may have described their state before God, but Gaucelmo and Juan knew how to stare down a thousand earthly obstacles: physical cold, punishing loneliness, windy chinks and leaky roofs, hard days on the road on hospice business, politicking with the Astorga Church. Then there was the human side of communal living, the snorers and the holier than thou's, the cooking and washing up, and all those exhausted pilgrims, sick souls, dead bodies, whining mendicants and perfectly healthy freeloaders. Men like Gaucelmo and Juan Estafaniz, with uncommon talents and a will made fierce by faith, managed for a time to subdue the Irago landscape.

In the end however, the weather took over. After Gaucelmo's death around 1123 his staff tried to keep the hospice going; but in 1222, someone was hired for two hundred *aureos* to dismantle the holdings of the centre and distribute them from Astorga to the Bierzo for the benefit of the poor. By the 14th Century, Foncebadón was in ruins. No confraternity has revived Gaucelmo's dream the way the Italians had at San Nicolás. There is no shelter at all at Foncebadón, though in an emergency you could wait out the night with stray dogs and the occasional cow in a wind-cracked manure-strewn stone shed. If you need a sleep before descending into the Bierzo, you continue along the road to the one hostel on the pass, the friendly, messy little shack at Manjarín, where they ring the bell when they see you coming.

To get to Manjarín, you pass the Cruz de Hierro, a small cross erected, they say by Gaucelmo, high on a crude oak pole. At the foot of the pole is a heap of stones that have been laid down, one by one, by pilgrims over the centuries. The cross sits at 1,500 meters; at one time it marked the boundary between the Maragateria and the Bierzo.

The scene here is even more desolate than at Foncebadón. Winds hurtle around the faceless landscape like so many demons while the cross tilts over all, disproportionately high on its over-long wood spike, too thin to be troubled by the rushing air. There are car tourists and pilgrims here. They mill about a nearby hut, or stumble awkwardly up the stone heap to the cross, or they stand by the road with cameras planted to their faces, trying hopelessly for a wide enough angle. The place speaks only of emptiness. Not the glorious emptiness of the meseta but the emptiness of abandonment, as if God, finally deciding to forget the whole thing, had simply turned his back and walked away.

Perhaps that is why, for pilgrims drawn to an operatic spirituality, the Cruz de Hierro has become an image of the crucifixion. The whole hilltop, especially under lowering clouds and more brutally during the winter snows, has the face of Golgotha. But for those who see the gaunt wood pole with its iron cross through a less refracting lens, these are moments of satisfaction. The long road from Rabanal has been *done*, either by trudging on foot or by driving legs and lungs on a bicycle. Even in the summer air, the journey leaves you a little dazed. Stopping by the mound of stones, you reflect that even in this isolated spot you are not alone in time. You have done exactly what centuries of pilgrims have also done: stopped at the top of a long hill, listened to your heart thumping into the road, looked up with relief at an old thin cross and wondered about something to drink.

The descent from the Montes de León into the flatlands of the Bierzo around Molinaseca is best done by bike on the highway and by foot on the Camino trail through the woods. The bicycle ride is a thrill. There is almost no traffic. The road swoops from one hairpin curve to the next, ricochets slowly off the graded shoulders, glides down the mountainside smooth as a ribbon. Your fingers play the brakes as you lean around the turns, swinging in gravity's net. You can go fast on your bike, but it is better if you slow down and let the scent of wild thyme caress your face. When you pause after the turns and rest one leg on the roadguard, you can savour the blue sky hanging in the gaps between tree-laden peaks.

Near Acebo, where highway and trail become one, the road suddenly becomes teeth-clenchingly steep. No one knows what happened on that day in 1987 when a pilgrim named Heinrich Krause was found dead by his bicycle in the road near the town. Some say he had a heart attack. Today a rough spokey sculpture of an up-ended bicycle stands at the spot where the German cyclist died. After the easy pleasures of a twenty-five kilometre descent, it is an eerie modern echo of the gaunt, metallic Cruz de Hierro hanging high on Mount Irago over a fallen world. The German's death monument is a reminder of our utter vulnerability to nature's indifferent gestures, a defencelessness that every pilgrim seeking to walk in faith must eventually come to recognize and even embrace.

In 1998, I walked alone from Manjarín to Acebo, following the uneven Camino trail across eroded patches of clear cut and old fires. The path went down steep slopes, criss-crossed the highway, climbed through stony rain gullies and across corrugated plates of gray rock. I was glad to have my walking stick. By mid-afternoon, I found myself once again in Acebo, walking between flower-loaded balconies down the main street.

Acebo lies on a shallow platform of land that spreads like a step off the mountainside and looks down into the Bierzo plain. Nearby are Roman mines, Las Medullas, and a medieval forge at Compludo that still runs. In the 1400s, this town, like Foncebadón and Manjarín, received tax exemptions for marking the Camino when avalanches blocked the road. They used eighty stakes.

Those avalanche slopes end some six hundred meters down from Cruz de Hierro on the sudden, horizontal edge of the Bierzo. The forty-three kilometers that lie ahead, from Molinaseca to Vega de Valcarce, must have seemed blissfully uncomplicated for those battered medieval pilgrims still dazed from their labour up and over Irago. The Bierzo undulated in a damped, low amplitude way that made it seem almost flat; the Camino led through rich forests of oak and loped across cheerful plains patched with vineyards and grain fields. A boat took you across the Rio Baeza until the 11th Century, when an iron bridge was installed, famous for its construction when most bridges were of stone. The bridge gave the nearby town its name, *Pons ferratus*, or Ponferrada. The streams that emptied from every which way into the Rio Baeza and the nearby Rio Sil danced with trout; there were plenty of hospices and a good deal of excellent wine. The thick, clay soil erupted not only with cereals and

)ut with vegetables, orchards, groves of pistachio trees, and, most delightful, the comely chestnut, with its shady, leafy limbs, its fruit and gorgeous wood. Today there is a grove of chestnuts on the way to Vega de Valcarce that pilgrims are still talking about when they get to Santiago.

The Bierzo is known for its moist Mediterranean climate. But the morning I left the hostel at Molinaseca, where I had slept in a tent behind the stone refectory, the rain refused to fall even as the clouds glowered petulantly above me. Lightning darted through the ill-tempered air, and thunder rolled in flatulent bursts, irritable about the unwilling rain. I took shelter in a metal hut by the road where bags of cement were stored, thinking that any moment now the clouds would open. But they never did. I walked on, watching thick sunbeams shoot through ghastly gaps in the towering cumuli, then back off as the clouds insolently folded in again. I felt thirsty, but it was merely a misplaced longing for the rain to break.

Perhaps it was a more complicated response to the Bierzo that made my mouth dry. If there is an anti-pilgrimage in Spain, its landscape shrines are the clearcut hillsides of the northwest. There was much that was pretty here but the valley often seemed inert, dull in spirit, exploited. The slopes had a weak, scratched out texture. The trees had been taken away and the earth, still looking shocked, was only just beginning to recover with a few tentative shrubs that seemed to be testing to see if it was safe.

Few medieval pilgrims would have seen this landscape with either my rapture or my despair. Today, our cherishing regard for nature almost passes for religious faith. But until the 15th Century, almost nobody came to northern Spain for the scenery. Certainly the Romans never did; they were here for the salt, the gold, the iron, the stone, the wood. The pilgrims were here for St. James. It was only towards the end of the Middle Ages that people arrived looking for beautiful views.

I had met a few pilgrims who believed that walking in the serenity of the Camino landscapes would help them find higher, guiding truths that would give solace and new hope to their lives. I do not know how successful they were, but the idea is common that pilgrimage imprints on its landscapes the presence of an approachable "Other." Nature is a "Thou" who answers our longing for the Reality beyond the walls of our inward-turned minds.

Perhaps this is the modern inflection of the medieval idea that nature held "signs" (to use Augustine's word) that pointed to God the Creator. In the Biblical traditions, Nature's gifts were to be used for the material benefit of man. But nature was also to be treasured for its transcendent value as a sign of God's abundant, eternal love. To see things - such as these Bierzo forests - only to use them was *cupiditas*, which flowed not outward through the language of symbols toward the Creator, but inward to the self, with its desire to possess things for the grossly utilitarian purposes of the fallen world.

There have always been people who look at a forest with greedy eyes. The appearance, the poetry, of trees is unimportant; to cut a forest down means only one thing: Wood for Sale. But if we look at a forest as part of an endlessly intricate chain of being serving other interests than our own, or if we can grasp an eternal beauty in the sight of treetops floating freely in the wind, the mind will expand, even if for just a moment, beyond itself. Our narcissism breaks up a little, and in the gap we see the translucent shimmer of another order. What is so offending about the clear cut is not the use of nature for material ends so much as the frightening evidence in the abandoned eroding slopes of our aesthetic amnesia. With the unrepaired loss of beauty goes a spiritual loss; we forget how to send our consciousness away from ourselves, to relieve ourselves of our relentless egos.

The clearcut lay before me today like the remains of a Spanish martyr after an inquisition by the priests of an industrial *Ecclesia*. That priesthood unnerved me. For in the traces of its work etched into the hills, I saw only our *cupiditas*, our small greedy minds, our selves without our spirits. The landscape would evolve, I knew, one way or another. Another kind of beauty would grow in, a new ecology. Perhaps, like the human martyrs, the clearcut would leave its own legacy, a reminder of our greed and the possibility of healing.

According to one of my guidebooks, Ponferrada today is notable for its "industrial vigour and uncontrolled expansion." This is code for something none too pretty. The afternoon I arrived on foot from Molinaseca, the highways into town vibrated in the discharge of truck engines. It was a complicated city to get out of too. I trudged through a maze of bleak city boulevards for hours it seemed, only to have covered five kilometers.

After the slag heaps and the electrical plant, I felt better; I had escaped Ponferrada, City of Cars. The air was still clogged with heat. The walk was a long one, past a wine-growers co-op where the samples were not bad, then along a dusty road where trucks were laying gravel. After vineyards and fields came the one-road town of Cacabelos, rebuilt after the 1108 earthquake. Then came Pieros, then Villafranca del Bierzo.

At Villafranca, I headed for the *refugio* on a hill overlooking the town. Partway there, I met Victor and José enjoying another picnic on the grass. They told me they were staying at a less popular hostel and gestured behind them to a rough building, part shack, part tent. Its main attraction: no curfew. They smiled at me, and I surmised that their pilgrimage wasn't all picnics in the grass. But I was worn out so I headed for the other hostel, the one with rules. I must have been more tired even than I felt. When I got to the hostel steps, Duncan was standing on the porch. He greeted me with a smile, then gazed at me in wonder. "Your face looks terrible."

I ate dinner with my admirer in the hostel's big tinny refectory. Afterwards I cleaned up the table and went outside for some yoga in the yard. My intentions were good, but before long I was back inside wearily climbing onto my top bunk in the upstairs hall. Three or four other pilgrims were already snoring. Someone nearby was being sick. I heard noise and the banging of dishes from the kitchen, where a few Spanish speed cyclists were having supper. An English voice beside me said, "Spaniards are *so* goddamn loud." But I was too exhausted to care and was asleep as soon as the sick pilgrim, who had fumbled back through the darkness from the toilets, had turned off the last light.

I was on the road late the next morning after dawdling over breakfast with Duncan. Villafranca del Bierzo lies in a pretty groove of land where the Rio Burbia meet the Rio Valcarce. I soon crossed the stone bridge over the Burbia and headed for Vega Valcarce, a little town lying at the foot of the Ancares Pass. Unfortunately I missed a turn-off to a new branch of the Camino that avoided the highway. Before I realized what I had done, I was doomed to the road, which was under major construction. I grew filthier by the minute as work trucks rumbled past me, the dust from their loads of dirt and stones swirling like a genie's vapour around them.

The pass through the Ancares rises sharply out of the Valcarce Valley through the villages of Ruitelan and La Faba to El Cebreiro. On our bikes, Scott and I had taken the alternate paved road all the way, up past Pedrafita and then across the long crest of the mountain to El Cebreiro. It had been very hard work getting up there by bike. But it was no easier this year to trek up the rocky, mountainside trail.

I walked alone, full of a new exuberance that had come after nearly three weeks of walking and the realization today that my leg was feeling better. The air was thick and moist. I discovered how to blow the sweat trickling off my nose into a wide, sparkling spray. The trail was choked with boulders and I used my walking stick for support as I scrambled around them, climbing ever higher along the valley wall amid poplar and oak trees and thick, leafy shrubs.

Where the trail widened slightly, I sat on an embankment and pulled some water and my diary out of my pack. I wrote for a while, then looked up to see eight or nine huge cows waddling benignly toward me. Behind them strode a wiry old lady dressed entirely in black. Lightly she touched their rumps with a stick as they plodded along. Their heavy heads swung blankly; the calmness of a Buddha was in their faces. The lady wore a gray apron around her thin waist. Wiping her hand on it as she walked by, she bestowed a warm, toothless smile upon me like a blessing.

I climbed through more shady forests, feeling a power in my legs as though I was being pushed from behind. After two hours, the path opened onto a mountainside meadow that tilted dizzily over a valley. A sweat-dissolving breeze rushed over my skin. Below me were fields and hedge fences and little angled plateaus. I could see El Cebreiro on a crest in the distance.

I arrived there late in the afternoon along a path lined with a stone wall high on the edge of the valley. El Cebreiro was as lovely as Scott and I had found it last year, with its pleasant walkways curving around neat, rotund *pallozas*. The *pallozas* were all in stone and thatch like the Celts of old had designed them, but now they served as hotels, bars and little shops. Walking through the door of the big, newly refurbished *refugio*, I met Victor and José again. They greeted me affectionately, offered me red wine and some cheese. I felt jubilant, I told them. It had been one of the best hikes of my life.

Elias Valiña Sampedro had lived here at El Cebreiro, another kind of mountain hero, not a mystic, not even a hermit, but certainly the greatest 20th-century patron of the Camino. His body lies in the north apse of the Church of Santa Maria Real. I visited his tomb in the early evening. The church is a stocky pre-Romanesque building in flat stones of steel-gray granite; a bell tower stands at one corner with a see-through iron cross on top. The modest front archway invites the pilgrim inside in a casual, "just folks" kind of way. The restful interior with its triple arches separating three short aisles is simple; as soon as I sat down in a pew close to the aisle, the feeling came over me of being, somehow, at home. Later I walked through the nave to Valiña's tomb, where I stood reading over and over the loving Latin epitaph carved into the stone that marked his resting place. I was startled by the emotion I felt towards this gentleman - friend and brother of all pilgrims, as the epitaph said - whose book I had been reading daily and whose personal stewardship of the Camino had brought it to life again and made it possible for me to walk its trails.

El Cebreiro lies on a crest overlooking, from thirteen hundred meters, one of the Camino's most exhilarating landscapes. Sitting on a stone wall behind the Church, I looked back to the east where I had walked just a few hours before. The path to La Faba slithered away along the high meadows, bent around vertical humps in the valley wall, then disappeared for good among slopes that fell like bottle-green waterfalls into the shadowed strip of valley floor.

Even now, that view was filtered through the lens of memory. Looking at it, my mind oscillated between the sensation of being here in this present moment and a longing for those recent hours on the way up from La Faba. I saw once again (I never get used to this) that there is no point in time that can be held or replayed just as it was. No matter how many more times I did it, the first experience of climbing on foot to El Cebreiro was the only one I would ever have. I could never repeat those moments exactly as they were; already the memory of them was distorted and molded to the shape of my mind.

To the west of El Cebreiro is Galicia. The view is best from the hostel. The land heaves and drops towards the setting sun in careless waves; dark forests stain taut sheets of pasture land. Dirt paths and low stone fences trickle over the meadow slopes. In late spring and summer, the hills are innocently green and spattered with flowers. But the view is deceptive; in the winter the flowers and grass are gone. The cold can be deadly, and of course there is all that wretched snow again. In the winter of 1488, two pilgrims, Jean de Tournai and his friend Guillaume, ventured over Alto de Poyo, trudging through waist-deep packed snow. Guillaume wept in despair. But, reports Valiña, who tells the story briefly in his Guide, "helped by God and Santiago," the friends survived the journey.

Over the centuries, a thousand dangers have shadowed the Camino landscape. I had escaped them all. The bridges were sturdy and beautiful, the passes magnificent, even the rain had been easy. It was unutterably pleasant now to sit in the summer sunshine with my legs dangling over the stone fence by the pilgrim hostel and gaze into the western hills of Galicia.

The Gothic cathedral at Leon, on the site of an old Romanesque church, itself on the site of a Roman bath.

6

CHURCHES

The world doesn't crumble apart.
The general, and rewarding, illusion
Prevents it.
        Margaret Avison. <u>Watershed</u>

Why do we people in churches seem like cheerful,
brainless tourists on a packaged tour of the
absolute?.... On the whole, I do not find Christians,
outside of the catacombs, sufficiently sensible of
conditions. Does anyone have the foggiest idea what
sort of power we so blithely invoke?
        Annie Dillard. <u>An Expedition to the Pole</u>

Gargoyles on the Church of San Martín at Frómista.

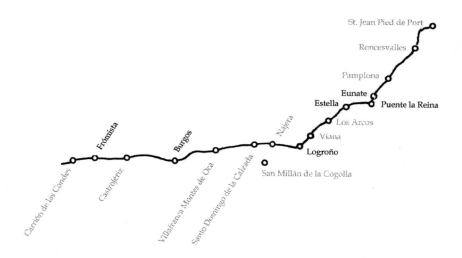

Seen from above, *El Camino de Santiago* hangs in a shallow loop like a necklace across northern Spain from the Pyrenees to Galicia. You can also imagine in this aereal view a dozen cathedrals conspicuously fastened along its length like old jewels. All are beautiful, though each one differs in its composition of shapes and shadows. Several, like Pamplona Cathedral and the Church of San Miguel in Estella, look like lop-sided crystals of solid stone with intersecting, shallow-pointed roofs. In Logroño on the other hand, the tawny Baroque towers of Santa Maria de la Redonda rise into the sky like a pair of elongated wedding cakes. The cathedral in Santo Domingo de la Calzada has a similar, single spire, free-standing above walls the colour of darkened sand. On the high, bright balustrades and Gothic spires of Burgos Cathedral, carved filigree and traceries shine against the patterns of their own shadows. Frómista's Church of San Martín, gold-toned in the sunshine, is smooth and heavy, with rotund walls that curve slowly under its mottled tile roofs. The brick-faced Mozarabic Church of San Tirso in Sahagún seems boxy from the front, though it too is voluptuously rounded behind. On its roof is an oblong belfry with three layers of arched, deeply shaded windows. In León, the long, low Basilica of San Isidore is, in contrast to the peaks and planes of other churches, more like a jewel box than a jewel itself. The gray, military Church of San Juan in Portomarín is even boxier, but high on the straight, severe west façade glows a delicate rose window. Finally, at the far end of the Camino chain, its nine spires gleaming in the Galician mist, Santiago Cathedral rises with imperial confidence above city roofs, a queen's jewel, the showpiece of the Spanish Romanesque.

As you approach them from the road, the Camino cathedrals begin to appear not so much as jewels on an imagined necklace, but as old creatures living in a private, slowed down universe. Like grandparents patiently waiting for nothing in particular, they lean over the streets and plazas of Spain's northern cities encircled by pavement, shops, paradors, outdoor cafes and a galactic swirl of human beings. Some churches are plump and stooped, others tower rangily; the Baroque harridans preen, while a few atrophied geezers hunker by the sidewalks, inward and alone. At night, the churches seem to exhale and settle slightly under the black sky. The introverts withdraw discreetly into their own shadows. If an evening service is underway, light streams graciously through windows high on the balustrade to anoint the dark street air. In León, under floodlights that come on at dusk, the Gothic cathedral becomes an opalescent deity hovering tenderly over lovers dallying in the square.

Many of the big Camino cathedrals were built between the 11th and 12th Centuries over the foundations of earlier churches. These were Visigothic mostly, stocky edifices with sturdy, angular walls and no-nonsense arches. The new churches domed up over the old Visigothic ones, their modern vaults and intersecting planes showing off the latest technical advances. But in time even these new churches deteriorated or went out of style. Some were torn down. Others were remodelled. León and Burgos Cathedrals were reincarnated as Gothic skyscrapers. The monastic cathedral at Samos, already old in the 11th Century, was given a Baroque facelift, then tailored along the sexless academic lines of the neo-classical in the 18th. Just past Trobajo del Camino near the city of León is the Church of the Virgin of the Camino, on the site of a hermitage where in 1502, Our Lady, now patron of the area, appeared to a shepherd named Alvar Simon. A shrine was erected and the place became a pilgrimage centre famous for miracles. The church was rebuilt several times, most recently in 1961, which makes it one of the youngest on the Camino. It has a dull, blocky, Sixties shape, but I liked the thirteen tall bronze statues lined up like kindly wraiths across the stained glass façade. My Everest guide said these are a good example of modernist religious sculpture in Spain.

Of all of these churches on the road to Santiago, it is the ones from the peak Camino years, the churches of what we now call the Romanesque, that I loved the best. The style appeared in Europe sometime after the end of the 10th Century, as the Empire of the Franks was whimpering its last and a revitalized Europe, innovative and technologically advanced, was beginning to stir. In a way, the Romanesque was not new, nor was it easily defined. Its roots ran far into the past, and though they are often lumped together as one style, Romanesque churches really had only a small number of features in common. They were often large, but not always; the classical lines of Rome were inherent in the design, but wherever it appeared, the style grew out of local traditions and made use of local materials. Inspired by Greek Byzantium and Moorish Spain, architects of the Romanesque were picking up, in the cross-currents of art and technology of the 11th Century, models that went back to Sumer, the ancient East, Celtic and Germanic parts of Europe, classical Antiquity and even Armenia.

As religious reforms swept through 11th-century Europe, Romanesque architecture reflected a fresh faith and a new vigour in Christian life. Church interiors, their altars, sculptures and even their paintings, were updated so that even the commonest men and women could grasp God's gift of salvation. Pilgrimage churches changed too, but for a different reason. These had always bulged with pilgrims, but on saints' days they were absolutely jammed. The hazards were obvious - fire mainly, but also crime, trampling, anything that interfered with the solemn services of the church. So architects got busy redesigning pilgrimage churches - the location of chapels, the size of columns and walkways, the number of portals and exits - to absorb the waves of visitors that swelled continually up and down the aisles.

In Spain, Romanesque construction peaked in the brief century between 1050 and 1150. It was as if a pair of almighty hands had grasped the Camino necklace at both ends and conjured up ornaments of carved stone and translucent glass along its length. At the east end of the Camino, the town of Jaca was chartered in 1063, and by 1094, Jaca Cathedral was on its way to completion. The church of San Martín at Frómista went up sometime between 1035 and 1066. León's San Isidore was built in a neo-Asturian style over an earlier church that had been demolished by the Moors. The cathedrals at Santiago de Compostela and Burgos were both begun in 1075, commissioned by Alfonso VI. About ten years later came Astorga's cathedral, a Romanesque treasure obliterated after 1471 in favour of a more modern style. The Cathedral at Pamplona started to go up around 1097 under the supervision of Estaban, the same master builder who had handled Jaca and Santiago Cathedrals. The Church of Santiago in Carrión began late, around 1160; San Miguel at Estella, 1195. By now, the Romanesque was falling out of favour. It had always been an expensive a way to build a church. Now it was becoming old-fashioned, as tastes eased into the Gothic. Work on the new León Cathedral began around 1200 on the site of the Romanesque church that had gone up not a hundred and fifty years earlier, over an old Roman bath.

Many of these cathedrals are scarred and cracked today, weary witnesses of a not especially faithful age. But at the start of the 12th Century, they are brand new dazzlers, a prime attraction for pilgrims. Many are still under construction. Turning into a town square after hours on the road, you might be surprised to see stone walls lined with wooden scaffolds, and hear the echoes of hammers and the thwack of the adze. You dodge an ox-drawn cart loaded with stones (already carved to save weight) from a nearby quarry. Leather-faced serfs with knotted biceps emerge from behind a wall hefting ropes and toting wheel-barrows spilling with mortar. Beady-eyed brats get under foot near the carpenters until a foreman or a monk gives them a holler. Depending on the stage of construction, you might run into smiths or tile workers, or plasterers mixing mortar and dyeing exterior stones walls with lime and pigment. If you ask, they tell you that this concoction is both a preservative and a paint and it gives a nice even colour to the walls. Some workers speak an odd language and wear strange clothes: Moorish prisoners of war, forced to labour on the church maybe they themselves had earlier wanted to destroy.

As soon as they were built, some of the early Romanesque churches had plunged to the ground, squirting dust and rubble as their huge roofs shattered. Defective vaulting was often the culprit; the earliest solution, a timber ceiling, had worried the fire department. Groin vaulting was one answer, which gave way to rib vaulting, which in turn prepared the way for the familiar arches of the Gothic. In a happy mix of engineering and metaphysics, Romanesque innovations in safe vaulting reinforced the spiritual program of the revived Church: an eight-sided dome resting on the square where the nave and the transept met became the technical expression of a divine design: the four corners of the world meet the circular perfection of heaven at the centre of the cross.

Inset among the large jewels of the Camino necklace are many smaller gems, churches and chapels that sit quietly in village squares or beside the Camino in open country: the octagonal Church of the Holy Sepulchre at Torres del Rio, where Scott and I listened to a German pilgrim playing medieval melodies on a recorder; the tiny, box-like Ermita de San Miguel at Población de Campos, where we sat against a shaded 13th-century wall one afternoon eating bananas; Santa Maria at Melide, with its faded frescoes lit by a single window in the apse. In the silence and soft light of these modest churches, the mysterious and contradictory spirituality of the Romanesque hangs like the smell of old roses.

The Church of Santa Maria at Eunate near Puente La Reina was built, likely by the Templars, in the 12th

Century. In the spring of 1997, this church was my introduction to the Spanish Romanesque. It was our second day of cycling. The Pyrenees and Roncesvalles were behind us and we were heading in top gear to Puente la Reina with the wind at our back and a smooth, swift surface under our tires. In the distance, a tawny stone church came into view, its circular tower rising like a bee-hive from a glinting light green field. It stood averted from us, but that very aloofness seemed to both slow our approach and draw us in, as if we were entering a new gravitational field. Sunshine fell from its walls and bell tower as we came close. In the driveway, the crunch of our tires seemed abnormally loud.

We left our bikes in a grassy enclosure where a workman was repairing the arcade that ran around the church. Scott and the man fell into conversation. I stepped away to the church, aware of the throb of recent exertion in my arms and legs. As I entered the modest doorway, the sunshine and wind, the bright greens and blues of a midday landscape vanished behind me. I felt an abrupt hollowness as if someone had switched off a radio. My breathing, at first laboured and disruptive, fused slowly into the dusky stillness around me. I waited inside the doorway, seeing stone walls the colour of maple syrup and stained by time with watery patches of light and dark. Gauzy ribbons of light floated from small hexagonal windows in the vault. Gradually the silence came to life, became a force that magnified the eyes of the Virgin gazing through me from the altar, and bent strips of shadow and light into odd angles through the sanctuary.

Scott joined me. We sat in a wooden pew and listened for a long while to an uncommon, expectant silence. It seemed to listen back, a gentle witness, impersonal yet absolutely present. Over the centuries, pilgrims had entered this God-haunted space beneath the arched portal of a simple doorway, faced this illuminated altar and felt at the same time, knowing no distinction, a divinity throbbing with life and a magical, material earth. For a few moments, I could almost grasp the oneness of the medieval cosmos, feel what it was like to know, without any doubt, that the universe was a living union of the material in the supernatural. I could almost believe that God was still at play here, hidden in the shadows, then revealing himself on an issue of light. The Virgin and Child stared from the altar, absorbing all the space, then bestowing it once again in a gesture of austerity and tenderness on two souls from a far off, data-mad world who sat near the centre aisle, straining across the chasm of time for something forgotten.

In its three soft syllables, the word "Romanesque" dallies between restraint and ebullient flourish, hints at an impudent energy lurking on the margins of a classical, perfectly proportioned whole. In the cave-like interior of Eunate, I felt that energy, a careless vitality among the shafts of light held in check by a sterner composition of domes and arches and squared, reliable angles. It is said that Gothic churches, with their pointed vaults and filigreed, spiked towers, tell of the human soul reaching upward to God. But in the Romanesque, God comes down to be with men and women on earth, makes himself present to share with us the pleasures of his mysteries. This lovely medieval image comes from the Book of Exodus, where the Israelites are commanded to pitch a tent in the wilderness, so that the Lord might dwell among his people as they journeyed to the Promised Land. Eunate and the Romanesque churches on the Camino recall that tent, are places of encounter with the God who helps his pilgrims on their way.

Burial sites have been found in the vicinity of Eunate for people who only with the greatest difficulty had gotten themselves over the Pyrenees. Malnourished, sick with infected blisters or pneumonia, their resistance low after weeks of walking through France, they straggled slowly down toward Puente la Reina, only to collapse on the open plain and be carried by friends or a kind stranger to this church. The walls at Eunate had heard many requiems, intoned perhaps with a routine, here we go again weariness, while the sorrow of the bereaved - mothers, husbands, daughters, best friends - would rise into a hymn of mourning and dread, and of an almost too exquisite hope.

Eunate holds that hope in its very stones, in its images, even in the symbolism of its numbers. As in all hurches, the apse faces east, towards the ~~lise~~, birth and eternal life. The altar is ~~sepulchre~~. Light streams down upon it from three cₗₒₙ₉ₐₜₑₐ windows high in the apse wall: the Trinity hovering over the scene of resurrection. The church's octagonal design gives it a roundedness like the circular shape of the celestial mansion, while the number eight announces regeneration, baptism, the new life of the spirit. Above is the vault, an image of the firmament, with its central point marking God's unchanging existence.

I have read that the Romanesque period was invented by art historians between the two world wars of the 20th Century, around the same time that the cave paintings at Lascaux were first discovered. Eunate has the hypnotic subterranean aura of a cave, a spookiness that inhabits many Romanesque churches, the chthonic energy of the womb, the appetites, death, things that must be mastered and controlled with ritual and chant. Eunate was a place still dense with mystery, shaded in chiaroscuro bands that rippled like a divine ether. Even against the barriers of time, of science, of different beliefs, it was mystifying in an oddly satisfying way, as if something that we don't know how to think about was being awakened.

One week after Eunate, we were cycling from Castrojeriz to Frómista on a flat track beside the Canal de Castilla, which the Everest guide calls "an important feat of 18th Century engineering … [with] a triple function: the transport of cereals, irrigation and grinding corn." To us, as we pedalled easily by its reed-lined banks, it was simply a happy companion, a cheerful strip of blue at our side on a beautiful sunny day. After twenty-six kilometers of pure pleasure, we hauled our bikes over the locks of the Canal and down onto the road that led into town.

Frómista originated in Celtic times, had been occupied by the Romans, and later been a Visigothic town of some importance. It was laid low by the Moors in the 8th Century and languished until the 10th when it began to be resettled. In the 12th Century, Doña Mayor, widow of Sancho the Great of Navarra, brought more settlers to the town and established a monastery and church here. Only the church remains now, sitting like a museum piece at one end of a rather ordinary rectangular plaza, near the Marisa Hotel and across from the Cheese Museum where, strangely enough, we saw more local modern art than cheese.

The Church of San Martín was large but not gigantic, with sand-coloured walls rising under a flat blue sky. Over the centuries, wind and ice damage, humidity, and cracks caused by the vibration of its bells have ravaged the church. In the 19th Century, it was restored in such minute detail that now, despite its round heaviness, it seems unnaturally pristine.

Usually, the superintendent of a Camino church was an elderly man in a sweater who could be identified moving like a shadow along the walls of his church. These shabby old duffers sometimes seemed to be the only working part in an otherwise inert building, the one essential, slightly creaky gear, still running adequately enough. I had trouble understanding them; they muttered to us about their churches in marbly, distant voices, squinting into the pews as if they were talking about an eccentric aunt.

But at Frómista we were greeted by a pretty blond graduate student who smiled beatifically at us as we entered the church. On a desk near the door she had arranged pamphlets and books about the church, some of very high quality. Politely she asked us to sign the guest book. As she gestured us into the sanctuary, she seemed to want us to experience something sacred in this church, as if she was taking care of something she believed to be religious within us.

We spent a long time at San Martín that afternoon. In the evening, after a good peasant's supper of soup and meat, wine and bread at the Marisa Hotel, we came back to sit some more.

San Martín had not so much been restored to perfection as stripped to its barest Romanesque essentials. It was far from bleak, but without the paintings that had once covered its walls, it seemed like a golden

Adonis, a ravishing nude on whom clothes would have looked just as wonderful. A crucifix from the early 13th Century hung in the apse over the altar; to one side was a naive wooden image of San Martín; on the other stood a statue of James as a pilgrim. A soft evening light suffused the stone vaults, something like a consciousness floated among the walls. The church had a poise and order that contained but never denied the free play of the mind. It was impossible not to be contemplative.

I was distracted by the crucifix, rather an attractive one as crucifixes go, not overly gushy, impersonal enough not to offend Protestant tastes. Along with tedious, hopeless prayers and hard-backed pews, this image had been part of my religious inheritance. I recalled how as a child I had stared up at this terrible, bewildering icon of salvation from where I sat between the big bodies of my parents. I felt the old wrestling match begin again between that childhood Christianity so uneasily embedded within me and my rebellion against all the mistakes and pain that it had created in my spirit. I looked away from the cross to the deeply shadowed arches above me and felt, in that small movement, an uneasy emancipation. It would not be until the following year, when I returned on foot to Frómista, that I would see more clearly the darker side of the Romanesque and the traces of its terrors that had made their way down the centuries to inhabit my own memory.

The following day, we had a rain-soaked ride out of Frómista along flat, puddly red gravel roads. After fifty kilometers, we cut across to the highway that led down into the valley of the Rio Cea. Before long, the town of Sahagún greeted us laconically through grimy, drizzle-streaked windows. It was hard to find the pilgrim hostel, which turned out to be closed until later in the day. We ate lunch in the only open restaurant and when the rain cleared we went back once more to the hostel. An American woman was sitting on the steps bent over the sole of one foot in an unmistakable pilgrim posture. We chatted. No, the *refugio* was closed until four. She had stayed there last night, and wanted another night if she could get it. She had twisted an ankle. Her blisters were terrible. I asked if she needed anything, but she said no. The hostel, she said, was great, with room for sixty-four pilgrims in bunks, a really high wooden ceiling and good showers.

The Sahagún hostel had been built into the restored Church of La Trinidad and was thus a tangible link with the city's illustrious history during the pilgrimage era. That history was now hazed behind a ramshackle array of dull buildings and half-empty shops windows. As we walked the streets in the clearing rain, I saw a poster stuck with tape to the wall in the doorway of a little shop:

> Domnos Sanctos
> Sanctus Facundus
> Sancto Facundo
> Sant Facund
> San Fagun
> Safagun
> Sahagún

Sahagún is named for one of two saints executed in one of the stomach-turning ways made famous during the persecutions of the 4th Century. Where San Facundus and his fellow martyr San Primitivo, or what was left of them, were buried, a monastery was erected in the early 9th Century. It was replaced in 872, destroyed by the Moors a year later, and rebuilt once more. By the 11th Century, it was in the hands of the Benedictines from Cluny and had been joined by Alfonso VI's royal palace and a pilgrim hospice that could house, like its modern counterpart, sixty pilgrims.

Sahagún's little history is embedded in the great movement of Church reform that unfolded in Europe in the late 10th Century. Charlemagne's Frankish Empire had pretty well petered out by the start of that century, and hopes for renewal of any imperial glory were destroyed by Viking and Magyar invasions. Europe had never been more than a collection of competing clan interests at the best of times; now it faltered, then collapsed into chaos. The struggle to survive became mere violence; farm lands were abandoned; populations shrank. The ragged, unhappy souls who made up the towns and villages were politically rudderless, exploited by nobles and bishops alike. They were also hungry. Driven by the crude indignation of the famished peasant in terror of being enslaved to loveless, privileged nobles, they rose up in one rough rebellion after another. Meanwhile the Roman church busied itself like a spider in a network of money interests. Arrogantly casual, churchmen and aristocrats schemed in the complacent, conniving way of local politics to keep their power and privilege.

Then, over the wheezes of an age at a moral dead end came the voices of a few men and women for whom the Christian vision still meant what Jesus had said it meant. They were first heard in isolated monasteries in England, Germany and the Low Countries, faint but persistent protests against a Church, a whole society, adrift in sin. Monastics like themselves, they said, were the only beacon of Christian perfection in a fallen world. And if they, the servants of God, could not reform, then what hope was there for folk beyond the monastery walls. They would straighten out their own houses, the monks resolved, then beam their restored sanctity into a world yearning to be healed.

In time, the voices of reform were coming from France too, and from the great Benedictine monastery at Cluny. Here they swelled until, in a mighty chorus, they rang into the startled palaces and indolent monasteries and churches of Europe. Simony and nepotism were wrong, they cried; selling high offices was wrong (Pope Benedict IX had himself bought the Papacy); slackers in the monasteries should be brought into line; the rule of discipline and divine service must be restored; charity, the pinnacle of virtues, was to be practised without cease. And (while we are at it) the Roman Church, God's divine agent operating in a sinful world, must govern itself independently, with the Pope as absolute head of the Christian world.

The struggle was long, complex, a tug of war among monks, the Papacy, the nobility, and the crowns of

Europe. But by the late 11th Century, Europe's various secular powers found themselves subject to a unified, highly sophisticated Papal governance. The Roman Church had made itself Europe's religious and political authority.

To some it seemed repressive and totalitarian; to others it was liberating. Overall, spirits lightened as Europe crept away from the dregs of the old Roman Empire. The rule of law stabilized. More wealth was available. Contacts - artistic and commercial - opened with Italy and later with Byzantium. New ideas and techniques in art and architecture began to circulate along Europe's still porous borders. In the 12th Century, with France dominating European affairs, the monks of Cluny, flush with prestige, were taking their reforming message abroad. It was an expansive, inclusive world, a cradle in time for three crucial developments in western history: a reformed church with a unifying vision, new avenues for the trader, the artist and the scholar, and a renovated pilgrimage route to the shrine of St. James.

The kings of Spain were right on board, promoting church reform, mercantile expansion, and pilgrimage. Sancho Ramirez of Aragon and Alfonso VI of Castile were both opportunistic visionaries, God-fearing, pragmatic men with a country to govern and a reputation to uphold. They were contemporaries, and they shared a goal: to attract pilgrims to the roads between France and Compostela. They were also rivals in their greed for Camino glory: each endowed one property after another for monastic and church construction. To pay for it all, they exacted huge tributes from the failing Moorish cities in the south, drew on custom's duties and pilgrims' donations. With all this funding, they could invest in the best of craftsmen, many of whom were brought in from France.

The kings looked to France not just for craftsmen, but also for spiritual prestige. The monastery at Cluny was by far the largest and most esteemed in Europe. From its founding in 963, the order had grown in influence until at its peak it had nearly 2,000 houses throughout Europe. In 1025, Sancho the Great of Navarra sent the Abbot of an Aragonese monastery to Cluny to study the monastic way of life there. The Abbot returned with a few monks to pass on what he had learned. That mission had no major effects but it marked the beginning of a rapport between Spain and Cluny that was built as much on family and dynastic interests as on religious ones. Around 1055, Sancho's son, Ferdinand of Castile, began making annual payments in the egregious amount of a thousand gold pieces to Cluny. Cluniac monasteries were established throughout northern Spain on lands endowed by kings and nobles; with them came pilgrimage churches and hospices.

Cluny's biggest royal supporter would be Ferdinand's son, Alfonso VI. Alfonso doubled his father's annual donation to the Burgundian mother house. In 1079, to tighten ties even more, he took as the fourth of his six wives, Constance, the niece of Cluny's Abbot Hugh. One day during a conversation with Hugh in Burgos, Alfonso requested that monks from Cluny be sent to the monastery of Facundus in Sahagún to promote church reforms. Two monks arrived; their success was not remarkable. People were defensive about the arrival of the high-flown French with their new-fangled ways. Worse was to come, in the person of the energetic and bossy Bernard de Sidriac, armed with a letter from the Pope no less, naming him abbot of the Sahagún monastery.

Bernardo took charge, cleaned house, expanded the monastery's holdings, promoted its interests. In doing so, he attracted merchants and colonists from all over France. His pilgrim hospices were well known and well run. The area flourished. But his style was not popular; ill will developed. The French were feudal, refined, sophisticated. The casual Spaniards deeply resented these outsiders moving in for profit, fine, superior folks from Gascony, Brittany, Burgundy, Normandy, Toulouse, from Germany, England and Lombardy. There were skirmishes. In the long run, the strife was too much. Sahagún lost its glamour. The proud, roughneck locals won back their gritty, plain existence. Sahagún still bears a defiantly unadorned look, with its hodgepodge of Sixties' brick buildings and broken sidewalks and its shop windows thoughtlessly scattered with a few dusty items. People in the main square, where we had an exceptionally good fish chowder, were stolid and, it appeared, perfectly satisfied thank you very much with their dowdy town.

We cycled late the next afternoon over the Rio Torio into León. The city was undergoing street repairs, and the noise tore around our ears: the raucous vibration of steel on cement, electrical equipment whirring like the drill of hell's dentist, the chunky grate of pick-axes and shovels. We walked our bikes along the pavement, over cement blocks and around manholes. A young mother, her mouth clamped in determination, awkwardly forced a stroller up over a broken sidewalk while her child, eyes wide, gripped the little front rail. Old ladies with thin legs and handbags trenched gingerly through gutters of gravel and mud past men in hard hats muscling jackhammers.

We found a hotel near the downtown, on the third floor of a rickety building from the Fifties. I had picked it from a tourist brochure because it was cheap. The room was tiny and dark, vibrated slightly with the streetworks, had a sink with two glasses, one clean, and a sagging double bed with a mothy comforter. That night I fretted about bed bugs, needlessly as it turned out.

Next morning we left our bikes at the hotel and walked in old León. Even through the dust of repairs, I found the city very classy, with its long pedestrian mall and its bright streets running off the plazas at just the right slant to show their Baroque façades. In the square, we stood amazed, staring at León cathedral as it reared over us with benevolent majesty. Beneath stone carvings of Christ and the saints, the big wooden doors opened to us like a welcoming smile. But I was still in my Romanesque craze, and I wanted to see the Basilica of San Isidore first, so we left the square and continued a short distance to the older church.

Isidore's relics are on the must-see list in Aimery's *Pilgrim's Guide*. Most of his other favourites are in France of course. But of those saintly remains on Spanish soil, Aimery singles out St. James, Santo Domingo, at Santo Domingo de la Calzada, Saints Facundo and Primitivo at

Sahagún, and in León, the most venerable San Isidore, "bishop, confessor and doctor.... [who] decorated the entire holy Church with the flower of his writings." Today, I am told, San Isidore is a contender for patron saint of internet users.

The Basilica of San Isidore stands low on the edge of a wide square. Its doorway is stuck like a brown postage stamp to a long side wall. Above the door is a serene Romanesque portal that seems about to be squished from above by an impertinent Baroque coat of arms. King Ferdinand had Isidore's relics brought from Sevilla to León and this church was consecrated in 1063 to house them. Ferdinand renounced his throne in this same basilica the day after Christmas two years later and died there dressed as a penitent on December 29.

The Royal Pantheon is underground; its arches rise around you like the ribs of an animal. Its vivid walls and ceilings, with saints and other worthies slung across in dark reds and blues and green, make it one of the greatest marvels of Romanesque painting. Here too are Isidore's bony remains, a relic adored over the centuries by visitors on their way to Santiago.

One fact that is not always obvious to modern Camino travellers as they savour the Spanish countryside is that more than anything else it was the cult of relics that drove the Santiago pilgrimage. Relics, the great antidote for life's ills, lay at the centre of Romanesque spirituality, providing the synapse between earthly sinners and God on his heavenly throne.

High in the vault of most Romanesque churches, the figure of Almighty God looked out over his sinful world with impassive, inaccessible eyes. In the words of the Mass for the consecration of a church: "Terribilis est locus iste. Vere est aula Dei et porta coeli". This is the place of dread; indeed it is the court of God and the gate of Heaven. The Lord's authority was absolute, his Judgment severe and irrevocable, his gaze, like his judgment, inescapable. He had a dooming, suffocating presence that fed the paranoia of the age and could turn ordinary awe into teeth-chattering terror.

The awful radiance of such a God made trying to get through to him an intimidating process. Faith therefore had a political angle; for a word in God's ear, you had to solicit his more accessible agents, the gentle saints who kept an earthly home in the tombs and reliquaries of His temples. What most sanctified a church was not the land on which it stood, though many churches were built on pagan worship sites, but the relics it contained, the remains of those spiritual adepts who knew the secrets of successful petition. At best, the relic was all or some of the body of a saint-apostle like James. On the second string, but no less efficacious for everyday matters, was the body or a knuckled finger or a scrap of linen belonging to a local saint, someone who (preferably) had been martyred on that very spot. Inside these walls, in the presence of holy men and women (or parts of them), you could avert your eyes before God's ominous splendour and turn to his saintly couriers to intervene for your sick child, your failing crop, your shuddering temptations.

To get to the sanctuary of the Church of San Isidore, we had to leave the Pantheon and go back outside and through the square. No one was about and the plain door to the church was closed. The square looked like an empty stage-set. But I could just imagine the bustle here in the 12th Century when, on Isidore's feast day, outsiders and locals alike would troop into town prepared to make a day of it.

Rows of stalls would have been set up, for a saint's feast was always a good market day. You could mingle with friends, catch news from the next village, meet other pilgrims, haggle with peddlers, and jockey with the riff-raff. You might stop to watch Italian jugglers or jeer at a well-known huckster. The place was noisy with hawkers and gossips, and on the breeze danced the scent of vegetables and donkey droppings, ripe meat, and perhaps a streak of perfume from the Moorish south.

Once you passed the vendors and hustlers and had elbowed your way into the church, your senses were assaulted again. It is hard to know the location of the first attack: nose or ears. It was very warm, and a motley of reeks arrived steadily on the clothes and boots and armpits of God's supplicants - the odours of cooking, of disease, of manure, of garlic. The incoming smells bonded with incense fumes and acrid candle smoke and the tangy sweat of hard-worked priests, until the air rippled with a thick stench, a pungent, perhaps comforting mantle of olfactory truth closing around your head like a rough scarf.

But when the relics were on display or the prayers were at their climax, the noise would make your head spin: howls of supplication and lamentation; moans of physical torment as the infirm were lifted to the front of the church; ejaculations of penitential regret; outbursts of joy over favours and miracles; the squalling of sick babes and the sobbing of mothers. Nor was it all lamentation or devotion. The clergy at Santiago, it is said, were infuriated by the singing of rustic songs in the basilica. In great churches like Santiago and San Isidore, things could escalate to a freakish pitch that the priests must have come to dread. Fights and riots. The occasional murder. Accidents and fires. Over-excited kids threw up, men arrived drunk and quarrelsome from the taverns near the market, women became hysterical and were trampled in the frenzy to view the relics.

When the service came to an exhausted finish and the worshippers had flushed out into the streets, local auxiliaries arrived to scrub out the mess and return the church to a temporary dignity. You might be glad to be one of these humble souls, sweeping the floor with your twig broom. You could contemplate the colours leaping from the paintings of God's saints, or watch wands of candlelight waver in the chandeliers over the altar. You could stand near a column and study the stories carved into the capitals above your head. But before long, another rush of pilgrims, another service. More hullabaloo, more boots, more shawls and kids, more of God's sick and smelly world after a saving glimpse of the blessed, stone-cold saint.

To sit now inside the eerily hushed, stone-straddled sanctuary of San Isidore, with its vaulted ceiling and cool, musty air, was like being in a hockey arena when the brawling match is over and a few good figure skaters have come out to practise; you know you are enjoying the skaters more, but you wish you had caught the third period. Scott and I sat at the back of the dimly lit church and watched while the priest, operating under a

cloud of incense, ended the Mass. After he le
people remained in their seats to contemplate tn.
which was kept constantly on display on the altar under a
weak, weird light. People were true believers here, local
folks, old women, the odd youth with the priesthood in his
future, a few young women. An elderly couple sat together
a few pews ahead of us, at perfect ease with one another
and perfectly assured in their religion. I watched their
backs and the way their heads sat straight and parallel. It
was a kind of communion I would probably never know.
For a few moments, I wished I could believe.

Absolute faith in relics, and in God's plan for the
salvation of his people lay behind the church-building
frenzy of the 11th and 12th Centuries. But that faith was
stitched tightly into politics and personal ambition. Senior
churchmen were skillful jugglers of both earthly and
divine interests. Camino churches were the children of a
marriage between religious certainty and pragmatic
ambition.

Two men stand out in the cross-currents of
politics, art, personal desire, religious zeal and technical
know-how that fed the rich waters of the Spanish
Romanesque. As it happened, both held positions of rank
at Santiago de Compostela; both exercised political and
feudal as well as religious authority. Both, like most clergy
of the time, participated in the pleasures of their class,
lived full, worldly lives of feasting, hunting, and feuding.
Their names were Don Diego Pelaez and Don Diego
Gelmirez.

I first read about the two Diegos in a curious book
entitled *Compostela*, written in Franco's Spain by a certain
Gonzalo Torrente Ballester to commemorate the Jubilee
Year of 1948. Ballester is sentimental and romantic, often
openly contemptuous of historians. What intrigued me in
Compostela was his belief that the Camino is an object
lesson in faith and unity for the torn shreds of post-war
Europe. His book is a nostalgic call for a return to the
creeds of the past and to the road of virtue, symbolized in

the *Camino de Santiago.* Christendom had followed this path during her formative years - the years of the Romanesque - when the Church Universal held Europe in a common faith and a common worship. In Ballester's eyes, the Camino had been the means to that unity, had even, during the great pilgrimage days, led the Western Church to an apogee of spiritual beauty. Chill northern winds (read: Protestants) had blown apart that world and the Camino had withered. Ballester pleads for Catholic renewal in a ragged, post-war Europe rife with greed and an overabundance of reason. Now - the Jubilee of 1948 - is the hour of faith, of pilgrimage, of world unity, of one common word for all hearts. And so on in the same vein. Thirty-four years later, Pope John Paul II was calling for precisely the same thing in his Pro-Europe Act of Worship delivered in Santiago de Compostela.

What was also interesting was Ballester's idea - so typical of the Middle Ages - that history is the unfolding of God's will, and that Spain, Europe and Christianity are three words for the same thing. The Invention of James' tomb was both a local Spanish event and a major European one. Ballester wonders, and I don't know if he is merely being playful, whether James asked to be buried in Galicia because, though his spirit was called to God, his body still had work to do in Spain. In any case, from his little tomb in Galicia, Ballester tells us, the saint began the task of uniting Europe in a single religious vision, and of uniting Spain in her historical aspirations. Like the monk Prieto, Ballester is almost more medieval than a 12th-century cleric in how he reads Camino history. But for all its nationalism and religious fervour, and its odd fantasy of a Catholic Europe, Ballester's vivacious imagination wonderfully recreates the lives that are woven into the Camino. Some of his stories are from the *Liber Jacobi,* which he embellishes with clever and not completely improbable dramatizations. Among these biographies are those of Pelaez and Gelmirez.

Don Diego Pelaez seems to have been a well-intentioned bishop, though politically ill-advised, or just insensitive. In other sources, he is harsh, outspoken, not subtle in his official dealings. Like the resentful folks in Sahagún, he is eager to shed French influences from the city of Spain's patron saint. But in the 1070s, the bishop has an idea that would benefit Santiago beyond anything: a new cathedral for the worship of the Apostle.

The time is right. The old building is in a bad way. The Romanesque is hitting its stride. Technical problems - mainly the vaults - are being overcome. Reform and piety are in the wind. Pelaez recruits the best architects, master builders, masons and carpenters. It is possible that the overall design of the cathedral is his own. But his determination gets the tactless bishop into difficulties with local clergy. He also runs afoul of Alfonso VI. There are hints in the historical records of Compostela that he is suspected of trying to place Galicia under the rule of an English king. Perhaps this is his way of appeasing the Vikings who are harassing the Galician shoreline. But whatever his motives, Alfonso VI, intent on a unified front against the Vikings, is displeased. Pelaez is fired from his bishopric in Santiago and declared unfit for the episcopal hierarchy. During his time in exile in Aragon in the 1088s, work on the new cathedral is paralyzed.

The energetic, politically astute visionary, Don Diego Gelmirez is elected bishop of Santiago in 1100. Gelmirez personifies the spirit of the Romanesque. Unlike Pelaez, he is an out and out Francophile, a promoter of Cluniac reforms, a champion of the pilgrimage, and a relentless, well-connected wheeler-dealer for the pious new vision the church has of itself. He shows Machiavellian acumen from the start: in the election of 1100, he refuses to accept the bishop's position until the number of people who voted for him is doubled.

He has his accusers. He is called a separatist and a nationalist, at worst, an imperialist. It is whispered in Rome that he wants to turn Compostela into the head of the Church. That is probably the last thing on his mind, but Gelmirez recognizes a chance for glory when he sees one. When the deposed Pelaez schemes to prevent his trip to Rome for his consecration as bishop, Gelmirez simply has the ceremony performed by a legate in Compostela, on April 21, 1101.

Santiago de Compostela had traditionally overseen several churches in Braga, and for this reason, in 1102, Bishop Gelmirez makes a supposedly pastoral visit there.

He and his clergy are graciously received by Giraldo, the bishop of Braga. But Gelmirez is hatching a plan. How wonderful it would be, he thinks, to embellish James' holy corpse with a garland of other relics, namely those resting in Braga: Saints Cucufate, Fructuoso, Susana and Silvestre, not to mention the head of St. Victor and a number of objects that were touched by the hand of our Lord himself. Naturally, Giraldo will part with none of these. The citizens of Braga would revolt at the thought, and Gelmirez wastes no breath in asking. With the careless determination of a scholarly 19th-century thief after treasures from the tombs of Egypt, the bishop makes an easy decision: theft - pious theft for the betterment of Christians everywhere - is the only option.

There are plenty of precedents. Only a hundred years earlier, forty-seven merchants from the Italian town of Bari arrived in Asia Minor to pray at the monastery of San Nicolás at Myra. In their luggage they carried a large selection of crowbars. The saint was handily removed to Bari, and a good thing too, says the author of this story, for the saint was far better honoured in prosperous Bari than he could ever have been in the sleepy little town of Myra.

Gelmirez knows as well as those Bari merchants that such thefts are successful only if the saints themselves wish it. No doubt he has heard that in Castile, San Millán recently intervened in the removal of *his* relics from the monastery at Suso. But if a saint knows he can get a better audience, or honours more fitting in a new home, then theft is hardly to be blinked at. It is worth a try. Besides, robbery is preferable to purchase; with bought relics, you never know if you are being swindled, for relics dealers have shrewd ways of meeting a demand that far outstrips supply.

The way Ballester tells it, Gelmirez pulls off the crime with ease, assisted by men skilled in masonry who can hastily repair the excavated tombs and reliquaries. He orders the relics carried away before he himself departs; when he knows they are safely on their way, he takes leave of Giraldo who, saintly and unsuspecting, expresses the keenest *amistad* for his guest.

A league from Santiago, Gelmirez is met by townsfolk running to meet him, already rejoicing in the new acquisition. Giraldo must have found out what happened. What did he say? What did he do? Not even Ballester hazards a guess. What we do know is that Giraldo is later canonized, an honour no one probably ever dreamed of conferring on Gelmirez.

By mid-century, the bishop is hard at work creating and promoting the pilgrimage route. While Alfonso VI rebuilds every bridge between Logroño and Santiago, Gelmirez remodels towns and lines the Camino with pilgrim churches and hospices. He is the consummate impresario, busy in his office in Santiago, waited on and waited for by secretaries, architects, master masons, chancellors, VIPs and ordinary citizens. Message boys arrive constantly with news from Cluny, from the Pope, from Alfonso's court. Important pilgrims flock around the busy man, who is occupied here and there at once, talking business to one, church matters to another, Galician politics to another.

His pet project is the basilica begun by Pelaez. Here he pushes hard, both for the church and its cloister. While he is at it he renovates other churches in Santiago, replaces the episcopal palace with a fancier one, has an aqueduct put in, modernizes the Rua Nueva, and builds a new hospice.

Some church officials are put off by this pell-mell hustling. Gelmirez deftly placates them with a flattering new residence. One bone of contention is the humble old altar, out of place now, thinks Gelmirez, in all the rich new decor of the refurbished church. The traditionalist monks of Antealtares revolt: the apostle's altar is too sacred to replace. The bishop finds a compromise; tearing out the venerable old piece, he presents it, a sop but a worthy one, to the monastery at Antealtares, and has a new, sumptuously coloured, silver-encrusted one, resplendent in the Cluniac manner, installed in its place.

Gelmirez's most ambitious project is yet to come: the raising of Santiago de Compostela from a bishopric to an archbishopric, the highest status possible for a Christian city after the Apostolic city of Rome. In Spain, that plum had always belonged to Mérida, a city of religious importance since Roman times, some 500 kilometers south of Astorga. But driven by a thirst for glory both for himself and for Compostela, Gelmirez thinks it more fitting to locate the archbishopric in the city of the Spain's patron Apostle.

It will take him twenty years to bring it off, using strategies that are a deft mixture of smoke and mirrors, flagrant daring-do and cunning politics. He makes up Santiago to look like, even surpass, Rome. He refers to his canons as cardinals in the Roman manner, he gives them Roman-style surplices and copes and mitres. He makes them shave (canons had always gone to church with boots and spurs and three-days growth). Rome doesn't like it; since the time of Pelaez, the Holy See has been leery of Santiago, that upstart pilgrimage city on the fringe of Europe. Pope Pascal II refuses to grant the archbishopric to Santiago. But Pascal eventually dies, and a old friend of Gelmirez, Calixtus II, becomes the next Pope. Calixtus is fond of Compostela. He is also sympathetic to Alfonso VI, who is his relative by marriage.

Gelmirez's connections serve him well. But it is impossible to go to Rome to petition Pope Calixtus directly. A Moorish fleet blocks the Galician ports, and the belligerent Alfonso of Aragon, opponent of both Calixtus and Santiago, has closed the Aragonese passes into France. Gelmirez tries everything; he sends legates with rich gifts, legates disguised as pilgrims, legates disguised as beggars; nobody gets past Aragon. But his friends rally to the cause. Cardinals, magnates, the Abbot of Cluny, even relatives of the Pope join forces to bend his ear. In 1120, Calixtus takes the archbishopric from Mérida and bestows it upon Santiago. On the feast of St. James, July 25, 1120, a Papal Bull is read from the altar of the new Romanesque basilica; in the hypnotic tones of Church Latin, Gelmirez and his city of Santiago de Compostela soar to the height of their prestige.

But it is one of Gelmirez's last acts that is perhaps more far reaching than even the elevation of Santiago to the archbishopric. Alarmed by the Moorish and Norman marauders on Galicia's undefended coasts, he calls on experts from Pisa and Genoa, as well as on local know-how, to construct armed ships for coastal defense. He is considered the creator of the Castilian navy.

He died in 1140 and lies in an unknown tomb.

The city of Mérida had been the loser when Gelmirez won the archbishopric for Santiago, and it surely must have rankled. Although most modern guidebooks to Spain concentrate on its Roman heritage, Mérida was a flourishing and respected church centre in Gelmirez's day. Its Christian traditions date from the Roman period. Some of its churches and monasteries enjoyed the patronage of the Visigothic kings of the 6th Century. Mérida was also famous because it was an important city on the *Via de la Plata*, the pilgrimage route that ran from Sevilla to Astorga. Pilgrims on their way to Santiago from the south stopped here to venerate the relics of St. Eulalia, the virgin martyr of the early 4th Century. Then they carried on northward through thin forests and gently sloped plains to Salamanca and Astorga, where they turned west into Galicia.

For a brief few days in the spring of 1999, I walked on the *Via de la Plata*. The route was still not widely known. Although it had been waymarked with yellow arrows like those on the *Camino francés*, not much else had been done in the villages to prepare for pilgrims. Apart from my comfortable monastery bed at the Casa de Misericordia in Alcuéscar, my accommodations had been haphazard. I had one memorable night beside the pingpong table in a kids' games centre (fortunately minus the kids) and another on the tile floor of a town hall.

I found one exception to these awkward accommodations in a tiny village called Fuenterrobles, some two hundred and fifty kilometres north of Mérida. I arrived in Fuenterrobles in a light rain late one afternoon and, just as my guide book had indicated, it had a *refugio*. The building had once been the summer house of the local bishop. It was of whitewashed stone, had a roof of red tiles and a large line drawing of a pilgrim on the wall beside the front porch. Inside was a dark, wood-panelled hallway with coat racks and benches. I knocked on a partially open door off the hall through which I could see a fireplace and two tables littered with papers. No one answered, and thinking the room was probably the *refugio* office, I entered intending to sign the registration book.

With its low ceiling, off-white walls and dark trim, the room had a medieval air. On the table was a row of homemade candles lopsidedly stuck in a wooden holder. I saw among the books and scribbled notepads a well-used, copiously underlined copy of Prieto's *Tu Solus Peregrinus*. Someone had been working here recently, the fire was still smoking and the room had a warm, human scent. Off to one side was a small kitchen - a single man's kitchen, as evidenced by a head of garlic carelessly tossed into a big open box of cookies, and rockhard bread and old chorizo sausage strewn around the counter. The sink overflowed with dishes. I tidied the counter a little, then went to find the sleeping quarters. At the top of a flight of stairs, I found three rooms with sloped ceilings and skylights. In one, mattresses had been filed on their sides against the wall. In a corner were blankets, folded and piled like crepes. I threw a mattress on the floor, made up a bed, had a shower and went to find something to eat in town.

I returned in the rain an hour later and found the priest in his kitchen. Don Blas - his name according to my guidebook - was tall, heavy-set, and extremely handsome. He wore a Nike wind breaker and a pair of jeans. He told me to call him by his family name, Boyero. He lived in this *refugio*, he said, but his parish included several villages in the area. He grabbed a small fish from a plate in the refrigerator and began washing it under the tap. I commented on the books and papers on the table and told him I had liked Prieto's book. He said he had been preparing a talk to give this weekend at a conference in Sevilla on the spirituality of the Via de la Plata. He tossed his fish into a warm frying pan and we returned to the office.

Boyero spoke in quick, crisp Spanish. He told me about the Via de la Plata and the *refugio* here at Fuenterrobles. More and more pilgrims arrive every year, he said. In the month of April alone there had been over a hundred. He himself had organized group pilgrimages along local portions of the *Via*, one of which had included prisoners from the Central Penitentiary. As he spoke, rummaging around on the table for things to show me, Boyero struck me as a kind of country version of Diego Gelmirez, without, perhaps, the archbishop's self-inflating ambitions, but with the same drive and commitment to making a spiritual vision real for everyday people.

After he had eaten his fish, Boyero showed me through the *refugio*. On the wall behind a long table in the refectory was the same line drawing of a pilgrim I had seen on the front of the building. Across from it, a cross made of driftwood hung under an antique bell. We went outside to see an oratory that had just been completed, a tiny cave of a room intended for meditation and private Eucharist services. Ducking back out into fresh raindrops, we surveyed a small unfinished garden. Through the windows of a shed, I could see a pile of old furniture and a very old, decoratively painted cart. Boyero paused and, holding a toothpick to his mouth, nodded as he looked things over. The place was coming along.

When the rain cleared, he took me to see the church. It had been rebuilt recently from a ruin and had a vacant smell, like a new house. It also had the gentle light and tall, welcoming hollowness that I had come to love in the churches of the Romanesque along the *Camino francés*. I was struck by several modern wood statues in the apse, simple figures of the apostles. One was being added each year, Boyero told me, carved by someone local. The most surprising part of the church was behind the altar. Here, instead of a crucifix, a wood statue of the Risen Christ was suspended, a demanding, exultant figure with flat feet and outstretched arms. As we walked back to the *refugio*, I commented on the lack of traditional gore in the new church. "Si, si" said Boyero. "I've tried to get away from that. People here are too pessimistic. I want a more joyful spirituality. That's what I am working for." We passed an old man coming out of his house. Boyero stopped to chat, asked about something, told an in-joke that made the man smile.

A new spirituality. Listening to Boyero, I wondered if I was hearing voices from eight centuries ago. Had the people of the Church then not been working for the same thing? Would they not have gone about it in the same way, working pragmatically in the everyday world of the Camino to bring a refreshed faith into people's lives?

In the morning, I made another attempt at cleaning Boyero's kitchen. While I cut some fresh, sweet oranges for us to eat, the mayor of Fuenterrobles dropped in about some business. The two men invited me to sit at the table with them when I brought out a big place of orange slices. As they talked together over the fruit, I observed the process of Camino building unfold. After listening a while, I asked them how this all began.

The two men looked at each other. "Was it 94? 93?" asked Boyero. "93," put in the mayor. "What you see now," Boyero said, raising his voice a little, "was the result of a dream that came up one day in a conversation with Manolo here." He gestured toward the mayor. "And without thinking twice, we got the manpower together and started in on all this rubble. Because it had all fallen down, you see, it was all destroyed. The first thing we wanted to do was make a parish house for the community, but since there were more and more pilgrims coming through, we thought it would be a good idea to share it as a *refugio* too. And so now, since we had such a positive response from the town people, and above all, with the help of Manolo here, we have worked in stages little by little until..." he opened his arms to the room, "we have what we have."

I asked Boyero about his vision for the *refugio*. "Our idea is to keep on building so that this place can be an oasis for pilgrims. They can come here after a day on the road and find what they need. Nothing luxurious, only the essentials, like the good room you slept in last night."

I wanted to know how the community felt about this *refugio* and all the pilgrims coming through the town. The mayor answered. "The people worked hard here. Support is growing all the time. We have space - the whole lot is about 2000 square meters. We even want to put in a theme park and a fountain...."

Boyero broke in. "The most interesting thing is that the whole community worked on this because we have no official support or subsidies. The funds come from the people themselves."

"But it must have cost a fortune," I said.

"The people volunteered their manpower," said Boyero. "And it was the mayor here - he's a stonemason - who did the initial work and donated most of his time. And all the materials are recycled. That's the secret: voluntary manpower and materials that could be recuperated from elsewhere."

Boyero told me that the *Via* is promoted almost solely by word of mouth, though there are a few good guidebooks. "What most interests pilgrims who come here," he emphasized, "is the purity, the difficulty and the natural beauty of the *Via*. Above all, its spirituality. The *Via* must not become like the *Camino francés*, where there are so many people there for so many different reasons. It detracts from the pilgrim spirit. People come to the *Via* with a much clearer, more intense spirituality. There are hardly any facilities, and there are sections that are forty kilometers of nothing, real desert. This purifies the pilgrim spirit and this is what we are supporting here. That's what this conference on the weekend is about: raising the spiritual dimension of the *Via*."

Boyero would be leaving in a couple of days to give his talk at the conference in Sevilla. I think that if Gelmirez had been one of the participants, or the great master builder Estabon, or the 12th-century monks and priests of Eunate, San Martín, Sahagún, or San Isidore, they would have understood everything he was going to say.

The famous Cruz de Hierro on Mount Irago.
Tradition has each pilgrim add a stone
to the pile at the base.

7

A FALLEN WORLD

So now we flee the Garden
of Eden, steadfastly.
And still in our flight are ardent
For lost eternity.
        Margaret Avison. <u>The Mirrored Man</u>

He shall act with prudence and moderation as
concerns punishment, for if a pot is scoured too
vigorously to remove rust, it may break. Let him
remember his own frailty, for "the bruised reed must
not be broken. (Is. 42:3)
        <u>The Rule of St. Benedict</u>

Go a pilgrim, return a whore.
        Spanish proverb

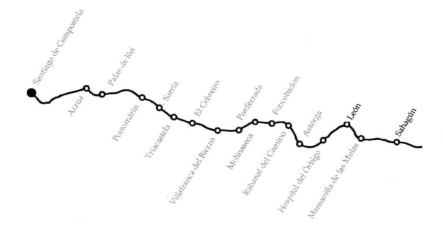

Pilgrims passing the Latin Lover's Club,
a local fleshpot in Léon.

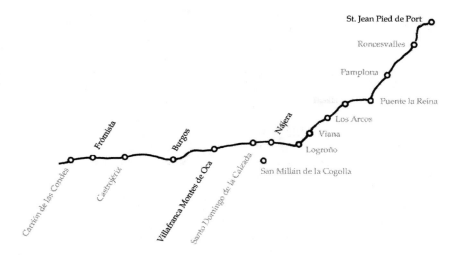

S ometime early in the 13th Century, two Italian ladies on pilgrimage to Santiago stopped halfway across Spain in the bustling town of Carrión de los Condes. Whether they were on their way to or from Santiago when they reached Carrión is not known; nor is it known whom they talked to, what they saw, or where they stayed. We do know that they were connected with the Italian religious order of Santa Clara of Assisi, sister order to the Friars Minor who had been organized in 1210 by Francis of Assisi. The Friars were penniless itinerant monks who travelled the roads of Europe preaching faith and repentance. The Poor Clares, as the nuns were also called, travelled less, but had no less determination than the men. Something in Carrión - maybe a spiritual need expressed by the women of the worldly meseta town - inspired the two ladies from Italy to establish a convent there. In time, it became known for its hospitality. In 1213, when Francis himself, age thirty-two, went as a pilgrim to Santiago, he stayed at the Carrión convent.

In May of 1997, after a day cycling on the meseta from Castrojeriz, Scott and I arrived in Carrión de los Condes at the restored convent of Santa Clara. The pilgrim's *refugio* was called *La Casa de Peregrinos*. We entered the small office only to say hello and have our pilgrim's passes stamped, for we planned to cycle a little further before day's end. We were greeted by a middle-aged couple with self-assured smiles and a wry, alert sense of humour. Scott bought a box of cookies, buttery confections made that very day by the Poor Clares. As well as their baking, the nuns supported themselves with a small museum and a modest book binding workshop. A few weeks later, when we returned through Carrión by car, I would buy an illustrated, hardbound book of recipes from convents in the region.

Cookies in hand, we left the custodians smiling in their office and stepped into the sun-drenched convent courtyard. Suddenly we heard loud voices coming from inside the dormitory walls. The accents grew distinct and raucous, then erupted through the doorway. Now we could make out the languages: a hoarse, desperate French and a blast of firecracker Spanish. Four slick and wiry cyclists wearing tight, black shorts and shirts with flaming logos shot like bees from the doorway. Furiously they swarmed around a lone, shabbily dressed French pilgrim, their tanned muscular arms angling in all directions. The pilgrim hung low under the abuse, cursing the Spaniards from beneath his beard. The air in the courtyard was paralyzed, the hot walls glared.

The señora came quietly to the porch behind us. We looked at her helplessly. Her soft face was stoic. There had been a quarrel a little earlier, she told us, when the bone-weary pilgrim had asked the cyclists, who were making noise in the kitchen, to be quiet. The issue apparently had not been resolved.

We felt the cyclists should not have been there in the first place. It was clear they were not pilgrims; their racing bikes were fit only for paved roads and they had no racks for gear. But it was not for us to tell the gentle señora whom to allow into her *refugio*. Eventually, two of the Spaniards returned inside. The others went to fiddle with their bikes, while the pilgrim, in a transparent mixture of fury and shame, shuffled jerkily through the courtyard on very sore feet and disappeared into the street.

You could say that the sport cyclists were the demons of the modern Camino. They sometimes streaked by us on N120, preened and wraithlike on their high-performance bikes. Their custom was to go on two- or three-day outings along the paved country roads of Castile. Some nights, they snuck into the hostels for a free bed. Ignoring Camino etiquette, they would lurk insolently by the door eyeing the female pilgrims. They hogged the kitchen facilities, smoked sullenly under the No Smoking signs, joked and guffawed in their bunks until late at night. They were harmless if you ignored them. But they took advantage in a proprietary, humourless way and gave nothing in return. What was worse, they gave the rest of us cyclists, grinding along dirt trails on bikes loaded with gear and good intentions, a very bad name. By 1998, the authorities had come down hard on them, and in their punitive clean-up took aim at even innocent bike pilgrims; no cyclists of any kind could get into the hostels before 8 p.m., and only then if there were enough beds.

On my foot journey across Spain the following year, there were no beds left for anyone when I arrived at Belorado just ahead of a violent afternoon thunderstorm. I had been walking on a twelve kilometer, black asphalt stretch of Camino that coincided with highway N120 from Redecilla del Camino. Transport trucks came roaring by only a few feet from my right shoulder. Ahead of me, ominous clouds oppressed the horizon. It was on this road that my leg had first begun to hurt.

The Belorado hostel was small and already overbooked; I was invited to sit out the storm and to wait with other latecomers to see if I could sleep in the cathedral. Medieval pilgrims had often done the same thing, hoping to eke out a night's rest curled over their bundles in the shelter of a church portico. But the 1998 priest did not welcome the idea. When the downpour ended, I decided my leg was too sore to walk further, and instead took a bus for ten kilometres to Villafranca Montes de Oca.

The original *refugio* at Villafranca, the Hospital de San Antonio Abad, had been founded late, in 1380, by

Doña Juana, wife of Enrique II. It was soon rated highly among pilgrims, had good food and an excellent resident doctor. I later learned that you can still see some of the doctor's old surgical instruments in the restored building. Valiña mentions with a touch of scepticism that the hostel reported 18,000 pilgrims a year during the 16th Century.

Restoration work was still being done on the old *refugio* in August 1998. I would stay in the temporary quarters nearby, in one of ten large tents spread over a small meadow just off the highway. I registered in a trailer across from makeshift shower and toilet buildings. Three smiling young Spaniards were in charge. They had prepared a table with first aid supplies, including loose needles lying helter skelter on a paper towel for breaking blisters. I had declined the needle treatment and was applying Betadine and bandaids when other pilgrims arrived: five German cyclists and Kjell, the Finn I had met at Santo Domingo de la Calzada, along with a couple of American foot pilgrims. The Germans were geared up on fancy bikes; they were fast and competitive but very congenial, and as they relaxed outside around the registration trailer they beamed with the breathy, expansive faces of people who have been happily exerting themselves for hours. They were politely hopeful about a place to stay. It was late in the afternoon; there were more than enough tents to go around. We were all bone tired. I slept in a tent between the Germans and the Finn.

We chatted the next morning on the grass in front of our tents. The Germans cheerfully brushed their teeth from their water bottles. Kjell prepared his bike, a chunky, modest affair he had named Rosinante, with faded packs fastened with leather straps and buckles that had belonged to his father. The Germans were openly amused.

A fleeting culinary discussion surfaced out of nowhere. One of the Americans, who was tall and dark, gave me a recipe for tofu marinated in beer, which I scribbled hastily into my diary. Before long, another tent flapped open and out crept a dour, bespectacled foot pilgrim, an older man with a long gray beard. He looked directly at me and scowled. Perhaps I had marked myself, hobnobbing with cyclists, and then trading recipes with good-looking American men under God's cool dawn sky. He marched off briskly with his gnarled walking stick, his canvas backpack, his scallop shell and his gourd, as if to say, apparently quite rightly, that *he* was a *serious* pilgrim. I never saw the man again, luckily, I suppose, for him.

The German cyclists navigated neatly down the short track to the highway and disappeared into the misty morning. Kjell lumbered after them on Rosinante. I patched up my blisters one more time and began the day's walk. I would head across the Montes de Oca, a ridge of land running south-west that, in the 11th Century, had divided Navarra from Old Castile. I had a steep, sweaty climb of about fifteen minutes before the track became a double farm road that rose gently onto a plateau. The walking was easy now, between open fields and forests of oak and pine. Ahead of me under a sky growing very blue, I could see other pilgrims, their orange and green backpacks tottering high above their thin, busy legs. People passed me, I passed others. Occasionally a cyclist or two crunched discreetly by, greeting me with a slow direct smile that said: "Please, I am friendly, I am not a speed cyclist."

The land was heating up like a griddle. I came to an optional detour down to Highway N120 and the Fountain de Carnero near the Ermita de Valdefuentes. There had once been a Cistercian hospice here. Last year Scott and I had followed the highway route on our bikes and had stopped at that fountain for a drink. After quenching our thirst, we began to fill our water bottles. A tourist with a camera came toward us. Giving us a significant look, he pointed to a sign: *Agua non potable.* We emptied our bottles, and I handed the tourist my camera for him to take our picture, joking that this might be our last living record. But the water had no ill effect, then or later.

We had been about to leave the fountain when two Portuguese pilgrims arrived. Their faces were resigned, but they leaned tensely into their walking sticks. She had inflamed shins, they told us, and he had infected blisters on both heels. They would walk along the highway today rather than follow the rough Camino track up on the plateau. We offered first aid, but what they really needed was to stop walking and let everything heal. Here on the faceless *carretera* between Villafranca Montes de Oca and Santovenia some fifteen kilometres away, they had no option but to continue. As they slowly limped away, I felt intensely sorry for them, and even now, a year later, standing on the plateau by the trail to the fountain, I wondered how they had managed that day.

Blisters, doubtful water, leg pains: these are the hazards of today's Camino. You could, if you wanted to dramatize, add storms, flat tires and sometimes, difficulty finding accommodation. With only these inconveniences, the medieval pilgrim would have considered herself in a traveller's paradise. A 12th-century pilgrim blessing lists the worst of the potential disasters:

> Oh Lord, heavenly father, let the angels watch over thy servants, that they may reach their destination in safety … that no enemy may attack them on the road, nor evil overcome them. Protect them from the perils of fast rivers, thieves, or wild beasts.

The Montes de Oca between Villafranca de Oca and San Juan de Ortega had been notoriously dangerous. Walking through here in the 17th Century, Domenico Laffi had come upon a wolf devouring a dead pilgrim. And if wolves, bears and the odd mountain lion were a menace, the situation was made worse by the criminal element that lurked in natural hide-outs by the trail.

In the early years, most Camino pilgrims were too poor to give a thief much return for his effort. Other much more promising victims were on the roads: immigrants, diplomats, clergymen, scholars, merchants with their goods, herders taking their animals from one pasture to another. The *Life of Santo Domingo de Silos* tells of a rogue named Stephen, who had grown up near the Monastery of San Millán at Nájera. "Prompted by the Devil, the root and author of all evils," we read, Stephen

> gathered round him a band of very wicked men, with whom he took to robbery in the

forests and hills and wherever he could, in his rapacious greed inflicting all the damage he could on the people who lived round about.... [On one occasion] they entered the forest near the aforesaid village and spotted a goatherd pasturing a great flock of goats. They seized him and kept him bound until nightfall, when they released him; but they drove off his flock to a certain town of the Saracens where they sold it.

Stephen's mistake was to let the goatherd go. The fellow later named his assailant, who was subsequently rounded up. Stephen protested his innocence, but was struck blind for his lies. A pilgrimage to the tomb of Santo Domingo de Silos restored his eyesight, and I assume, cured him of his marauding.

Not all hoodlums were caught; even fewer had the good luck to be healed and absolved by a local saint. Most criminals were little different than now: crafty, manipulative, sometimes sadistic; some were what we now call sociopathic. They used every conceivable strategy, from simple ambush to sophisticated trickery. Some posed as priests or pilgrims to freeload off the charitable, or to rob them. The *Liber Sancti Jacobi* tells of a man hanged for theft and murder. His ploy had been to call loudly, as pilgrims often did, at the town gates early in the morning for someone to walk with him. A guileless soul would join him, the two would walk for a while until, at a secluded spot, the man's partners in crime would leap out to rob and murder the pilgrim.

Certain nationalities were famous for their crimes. Norman travellers were considered arrogant and violent. In the 14th and 15th Centuries, many of the bandits hiding out along the Camino were English. In 1318, one John of London was finally captured by the provost of Estella after robbing pilgrims as they slept in a local hospice; a year later, a bunch of English hoodlums was rounded up at Pamplona. English prostitutes were well known. By the 12th Century, and even more by the 15th, a large number of travellers to Santiago were convicted criminals, men (mostly) - assassins, armed robbers, or just the town pests, sent packing by a local court on a pilgrimage to make amends for their crimes. Often, they were made to carry the instruments of their misdeeds on their bodies; some were fettered with chains or had iron collars around their necks. In ridding the towns of these miscreants, the courts of course added to the criminal element along the Camino. Some convicts must have been honestly penitential and resisted further crimes; others were true sociopaths, not easily deterred from their calling.

Improving the Camino roads reduced the dangers of weather and animals, but only worsened the risk of assault and robbery as opportunistic rogues had better access to the route. There were fast and hefty penalties for attacks on pilgrims: excommunication, physical punishment and mutilation, hanging. Safe conduct passes and certificates of individual pilgrimage - the ancestors of my photocopied Pilgrim's Pass - were common, but there were repeated pieces of legislation against Camino crime through the centuries, which means that harassment of pilgrims went on as long as the pilgrimage itself.

The road through the Montes de Oca had been improved by Sancho the Great of Navarra at the beginning of the 11th Century. The king's intention was to move his armies more efficiently between Nájera and Burgos, and as a secondary benefit, to make the route easier for pilgrims on their way to Santiago. But the traffic of soldiers brought with it disturbance and public mischief. These territories were awash with violence nine hundred years ago. While off to the south, Moors and Christians were pushing and shoving at the gates of Toledo, at Madrid, Guadalajara, and in Portugal at Santarem, here in the territories around the Montes de Oca, half a dozen aristocrats were driving their armies back and forth in a long and grisly competition for control of Castile.

1111. The daughter of Alfonso VI, the fearless Urraca, wants to govern Castile through her son by an early husband, Count Raymond of Burgundy. That son, Alfonso Raimundez, stands like a defiant toddler (which at the time he is) against another rival for the throne, Urraca's half-sister, the illegitimate and pregnant Teresa, soon to style herself queen in Portugal with Count Henry, her Burgundian husband.

Another contender for the throne of Castile was never even conceived. Urraca's current husband, Alfonso of Aragon, is either sterile or impotent. Without a child of his own to take over the throne of Castile, El Batallador, as he is called, is going to see to it that no upstart from the Burgundian side gets it either. Urraca leaves him to take up with her lover, Count Gomez Gonzalez of Lara, while her Burgundian child, Raimundez, is anointed king by none other than Gelmirez, in Santiago Cathedral. Alfonso of Aragon joins forces with Henry from Portugal, kills Urraca's lover Gomez in October, then tears on his own into León to defeat the Galicians who have just arrived to formally place the boy in power. Henry dies the following year in Astorga. Urraca, with her son and presumed heir, Raimundez, a lad no doubt receiving a graphic education, goes to war with her Aragonese ex-husband Alfonso. For five years, men and horses roam like the clouds of locusts that are also plaguing the meseta. Truces are arranged after 1117 on a three year renewal plan, so that both Urraca and Alfonso can go after the Moors to the south. But the fighting and feuding in these parts is nearly continuous. A document from Castrojeriz recalls a series of raids from around this time:

> In the time of King Alfonso [1065-1109] the *merino* of the *infanta* Urraca came and drove our cattle off to the *infanta's* residence at Villa Icinaz; and we went after him and wrecked the house and the estate, and drank all the wine we could find there and what we could not drink we tipped out on to the ground .... And another time we went with Salvador Mudarra after one Pedrero to Melgarejo; and he hid in the mansion of Gudesteo Rodríguez and we broke into the house and found him there, and we took him to the bridge at Fitero and forced him to jump into the water and there he was killed.

Today, walking in the Montes de Oca toward San Juan de Ortega, with peaceful fields planing off to the north and patches of shrub and trees lining the placid track into the distance ahead, I thought of the pilgrims of nine centuries ago, travelling in ragged groups, nervously, their capes flapping in the wind and their arms hammering their walking sticks into the road. How many were caught in the crossfire of battle is unknown. With so many terrorists roaming the Camino, there must have been more than the occasional assault, or rape, or butchery.

The towns saw their share of skirmishes too. When the bells of alarm sounded over the town square, the heavy stone churches changed from spiritual fortresses to earthly barricades. Pilgrims joined with exasperated merchants, weary clerics and frightened mothers and children to huddle with the walking wounded in the sanctuary, while mounted hooligans thundered in from the fields and rattled four-deep around the cobbled street corners.

Urraca the fierce and lusty died in 1126. But the wars went on between the bellicose Alfonso of Aragon and the now very adult Burgundian, Raimundez Alfonso VII, King of León and Castile. There was fighting at Burgos, Carrión de los Condes, Castrojeriz and Sahagún. Eventually, the young Burgundian began to get the upper hand over the grisled Batallador. But the old warrior would die instead in a skirmish with the Moors in 1134. Raimundez Alfonso VII, who had learned his war lessons well, went on to reign for almost thirty more blood-smeared years.

A few kilometres before San Juan de Ortega, I sat to rest in the stark shadow of an oak tree. The late morning sky was a heavy, windless blue, hazed almost to white at the horizon. A cross made of two sticks stood at a tilt on the other side of the trail. From where I sat, it seemed to soar inordinately high into the sky above a long grove of trees that stood like a big green wave. To the north was an open plain where, over the centuries, cattle and sheep and farmers, thugs and soldiers had roamed. The landscape bore an open, poised silence, calm but wary, as if it half believed that even after all these years, the terror of those days might return.

I leaned back against the tough, crimped bark of the oak tree, with its many branches and its little leaves spread like a green-specked quilt above me. An emptiness enveloped me like air wafting around a clothesline without its sheets. I had the sensation of being completely without fear. But as I rested longer, I began to hear my own interior bandits. There is always something on my mind, I thought, a phrase someone said, or one I should have said, a tiny drama repeating itself, a twitch of angst, distractions so persistent and yet so small you don't notice them until you have nothing else to listen to. It is something all humans share, the restlessness of fear erupting in the mind's automatic chatter. In the tranquil hours of this long morning walk, I glimpsed the discomfort that remains within, even when the evil outside us is as distant as another millenium.

In the area between Nájera and San Juan de Ortega, locusts have always been a problem. When I first read about them, I thought of my Northern Ontario childhood summers: the August shadfly plague, the years the poplar trees crawled with caterpillars, the evening clouds of black flies and mosquitoes, and those wretched horse-flies with their stinging bite. But on the Spanish meseta in the summer of 1040, it was locusts, villainous bugs, gobbling the crops and invading everybody's garden and barn and shirts.

Domingo de la Calzada was a young man of about twenty at the time. He was born into a successful Castilian family, but twice had failed to qualify for monastic vows, once at Valvanera and later at San Millán de Cógolla. Badly disappointed, Domingo decided to go it alone and embark on the life of a hermit. A few years later, he was in Logroño for some reason and chanced to meet a newcomer to town, Bishop Gregory of Ostia. Gregory had come to Navarra to help with the locust problem. Immediately, Domingo and Gregory became good friends.

They worked together for five years, on locusts mainly, and who knows what else. During this time too, Domingo finally succeeded in becoming a priest.

After Gregory's death, Domingo went on to several decades' worth of astonishing, some say miraculous, projects to improve the roads for pilgrims west of Nájera. He cleared forest paths, built roads and bridges, established a hospice in the town that later bore his name: Santo Domingo de la Calzada.

This was the man whom Juan de Ortega would run into in Burgos in 1094. Domingo was now close to sixty. Juan, a lad from a town just north of Burgos on the banks of the Ubierna River, was only fourteen. As had Gregory and Domingo many years earlier, the hard-working priest and the young Juan began a long friendship at that chance meeting. For the next fifteen years they toiled side by side on Domingo's building and road projects. When Domingo died in 1109, Juan, now twenty-nine, went into seclusion in his home village.

According to one source, the battles between the Aragonese and Castilians disgusted him, and he undertook a pilgrimage not to Santiago but to Jerusalem. On the return trip, his ship was nearly wrecked in a storm. Without the intervention of San Nicolás of Bari, he would surely have perished.

Safely back in Spain, Juan set about to fulfill the vow he had made in the fury of that gale. He built a pilgrims' hospice and a Romanesque church dedicated to San Nicolás in the town now called San Juan de Ortega. He founded an order of Augustinian monks that would survive for nearly three hundred years. In 1142, Alfonso VII granted rights over the Montes de Oca region to Juan's order "that you and your people in the service of God might possess it in perpetuity." To give the full benefit of the land to pilgrims and the poor, Alfonso exempted the Montes from royal tolls and granted free pasture rights for the animals raised by the order, namely, its cows, sheep, pigs and donkeys.

In his later years, Juan de Ortega had a reputation not only as a holy man but as an architect and engineer of great skill. A few years before his death in Nájera in 1163, he made his will. He wished it known, he wrote, that with his brother (or perhaps his nephew) Martín, he had erected the Church of San Nicolás and a hospice for the service of the poor. At his own expense, he went on, he had made safe the area where bandits had day and night robbed and murdered so many pilgrims to Santiago. When he died, his body was placed in the church at San Juan de Ortega. It is still there, under an incongruously ornate baldachino carved along its sides with images from his life. In 1971, he was named the patron of the College of Surveyors and Technical Architects of Spain.

There were no locusts the day of my walk across the Montes de Oca, only Juan's dry, straight road and around me, a well-meaning dome of blue air embracing me, almost crushing me with heat. When I arrived at San Juan de Ortega around lunch time, I found not a monastic centre busy with monks and merchants and herders and hired help, but a row of sleepy buildings on one side of the road, and a line of scrappy bush on the other. Pilgrims sat under umbrellas outside the one bar in town, looking from a distance like colourful cartoon figures. I soaked my towel in the fountain and splashed my face and arms, then wandered inside the monastic church, drawn as much by the prospect of cool air as anything else. The church was Romanesque, though it had been enlarged and given a new facade in the 15th Century. Queen Isabel had come here in 1477 to petition Juan de Ortega (now a saint) for a child. Adept at this type of miracle, Juan responded favourably to the queen and in gratitude, she commissioned the Church of San Nicolás, which stood near the monastic church and is now the pilgrim *refugio*.

Juan's religious order housed and fed thousands of Santiago pilgrims over the years, until its vitality waned in the latter days of the medieval pilgrimage. Now, once again, the *refugio* in this quiet little village is well known and liked. Several pilgrims I had met on my walk today were planning to stay the night. We talked outside over cheese and beer, sitting on white plastic chairs with our feet propped up on our backpacks and our elbows resting on white plastic tables. Inside, the bar was rowdy, crowded with locals watching television and playing cards.

I saw Kjell, the Finnish cyclist, having a beer, and went to sit with him. We wondered together how wise it was to walk in such flagrant sunshine. But I had to cover more distance today, sun or no. When I told him about the pain in my leg, he offered to strap my pack onto Rosinante and walk with me to Atapuerca.

The land was sweltering as we set out. We pushed through the air as if it was hot gelatin. Beside the track, scorched grasses stood like spears in Lilliputian armies. My boots felt heavy, my leg dragged miserably, my red pants were gray with the day's grime. The great Rosinante was piled high with our gear, a gypsy's heap of bags, purple and green, faded orange and red, lashed on with frayed shock cords that also held our water bottles, my running shoes, a map, and my towel, dried crisp after ten minutes in the sun. We were the only moving souls in the world. Time receded into the thin line on the horizon between yellow prairie and blue sky. We talked when we felt like it and stopped often to drink, tipping our bottles up high and gulping voraciously, letting the water dribble down over our chins.

At Atapuerca, we discovered, there was no *refugio* after all. We continued a couple of kilometres further on a slick strip of pavement that curved north over a rise and down into the little village of Olmos de Atapuerca. A lifeless street led to the hostel, a rectangular building plunked on a corner, looking out over low, almost imperceptible hills and the railway line to Burgos.

In the hostel kitchen we were greeted by two Spanish pilgrims who had just hung their laundry in the yard beyond the back door. One was the physical education teacher from Valencia I had met at Los Arcos. His girlfriend of the expensive face cream had by now abandoned him for Valencia, and he was with another friend, a short, round fellow with a calm expression, who "did philosophy." We sat at the long kitchen table chatting. Behind us, dirty plates still piled with old food sat by the sink. After a while, I cleaned the counter tops and sink and threw away the food that had gone off. Then I took a nap on my low, narrow cot in the dormitory.

That evening we went to the town's only bar for a lengthy and animated dinner: a Canadian, a Finn and two Spaniards working our way through plates of seafood and glasses of red Rioja wine and a multi-lingual maze of bad jokes, while behind us in the smoke-hazed bar, a crowd of townsmen roared over the games table and knocked back hefty glasses of the local intoxicant.

The hostel custodian had come to register us before we left for dinner. He was a sturdy, pear-shaped man in his sixties, a man inspired to do something good for the love of God and his pilgrims. He was well-intentioned and small-minded and he worried about sex in his hostel. The fact that I might sleep in the same dormitory alone with three other men bothered him. The next morning, after the Spaniards had disappeared and I had waved Kjell away on his bike for Burgos, he stopped me in the doorway and asked the question that had apparently consumed him since yesterday: "Did anything happen last night?" The question took me by surprise. He eyed me at first, sceptical of what he was hearing. He was a clean living man, but a little lust flickered in his eye. Perhaps at some level he worried that the Spaniards and the Finn were men like himself.

I changed the subject to the attractiveness of his hostel. He brightened and replied proudly that it was his responsibility to look after it for the pilgrims, to keep it clean and, he said, gesturing behind him towards a table littered with breakfast bread, to wash the kitchen. "Of course," he added, suddenly nervous and serious, "I would never clean up like this in my home. My wife...."

"Of course not," I assured him, implying, truthfully, that the idea of his cleaning his wife's kitchen had never crossed my mind.

Months later, after I had returned home, I read the story of a miracle that happened in the Montes de Oca. It was a sad tale with subtle insight, one that gave some texture to the crude picture we often have of good and evil in the Middle Ages. It was not about brazen wickedness like murder and adultery, but about the fine strands of selfishness and attachment and anxiety that are woven into our lives.

The story is told in the *Liber Sancti Jacobi*. It concerns a Frenchman who is healthy, wealthy and childless. Afraid that his legacy will end up in the hands of unworthy relatives, he makes a pilgrimage to Santiago to petition the saint for a son. There a priest tells him that in addition to his pilgrimage he must, on his return home, remain in prayer and fasting for three days and nights and abstain from relations with his wife. When he arrives home, his wife meets him dressed in her most seductive finery, ready to devour him with love in the expectation of conceiving a child. The husband resists, locks himself in his oratory for three days. The wife has agreed to respect his seclusion, but she (in her feminine weakness) is impatient and spends most of the three days looking for the key to the oratory. St. James overlooks her frailty however, and the man's sacrifices are accepted. His wife bears a son.

When the lad is fifteen, the family joins a company of pilgrims for another trip to Santiago. In the heart of the Montes de Oca, the boy falls ill and dies. The mother wails dreadfully. Over and over, she begs James to return her son. The boy remains cold and still. She threatens the saint: if her son does not come back to life, she will join him in death herself. Suicide is a terrible sin, but that does not matter; her spirit is mangled with grief.

The time arrives for the boy to be buried. To the amazement of all, he opens his eyes. Everyone exults; the mother is as mad with joy as she had been with woe. Then the boy tells his story.

Dying, he says, speaking sadly, was like the sudden gleam of a glorious light. For hours that seemed only moments, he had rested in ineffable pleasure before God's splendour. Even as his body lay in his mother arms, his soul had yearned to remain in God's light. St. James had come to his side, dressed in a white tunic. The boy struggled to go to God, but James restrained him. "Do you not hear the wailing of your parents?" he asked. The boy was torn. Yes, he said, he could hear his mother's laments, but a far stronger love was drawing him to heaven. James prevailed upon him. "Your parents are appealing to me. I want to help them." The lad answered that he too wished to help, but his desire for God was unbearable. Thus saying, he turned to walk into the light. James followed, reached out with his hand, reminded him that it was God's will for him to return. Sorrowing, the boy stopped, turned once more, away from the light, and came back to his parents on earth.

There is a hush among the boy's listeners. Then his mother speaks. "Do you mean to tell me," she says, in a voice that cracked the air, "*do you mean to tell me* that you preferred to stay dead than return to your own mother who loves you more than anything? Is *this* the love you have for me? Ingrate!! Probably you would abandon me for the first mother you came to on the road!" Her fury ruins the moment. Stunned, silent with embarrassment and pity, the group continues to Santiago. Later they return to France.

When he is older, the boy enters a monastery. But his mother never recovers from her bitterness, takes it with her to the grave. She spends eternity, we are told, in purgatory.

Of all the big churches that Scott and I had visited, the Church of San Martín at Frómista was among the most lovely. And since that morning a few weeks ago when I had walked west out of Pamplona, I had looked forward to seeing it again.

I arrived in Frómista at mid-afternoon. Walking toward the church, I relished once again its rotund, voluptuous solidity, its light stone walls leaning into the blue sky, the intricate gargoyles that lined its eaves. Inside, the nave was just as I remembered it, pristine to the point of frailty. I thought of how Scott and I had sat together here in San Martín's soft sunset of a silence. Light still floated under arches the colour of honey and roses. The Romanesque was gentle, embracing, something I remembered as pink even when its walls were beige, a womb of living space protected by the male sturdiness of hewn stone.

Sitting once again in the same pew, I turn my head up. On the two capitals that face each other across the nave of San Martín, the Biblical story of original sin is carved in exquisite detail. On the left capital, the tree of the knowledge of good and evil, the serpent, the fruit. Eve stands to one side, her hand over her disgraced vulva. Behind her, an animal head with a grotesque tongue signifies the serpent's lie. Adam has swallowed the fruit. He clutches his throat, stricken, knowing all too well what he has done. Next to him, an animal head devours a man. Touching the animal is a man in a robe carrying a book, the Word of God, the offer of hope and pardon to a sinner caught in the guts of animal desire. On the other side stands the good shepherd with his staff.

I turn my head to look at the capital across the aisle. I see the tree of paradise, Adam and Eve, hands covering their genitals, the serpent. Adam gestures, accuses Eve to God: the woman that you gave me for a companion gave me the fruit and I did eat. Above the couple, an animal head represents the devil and the sin just committed. To the right of the tree stands God, with a halo. He holds a book, beckons to Adam and Eve. Two angels are nearby. One carries a cross, the other an open book, the Bible maybe, or the Ten Commandments.

The symmetry is lovely: transgression and hope, fall and redemption. The reality of sin and the sweet, alluring hope of salvation. In San Martín, the mystical light of morning streams through windows in the apse to bathe the altar. In the vault above are Christ in Majesty and the Evangelists, bringers of good news. I see images of the Holy Spirit as a dove, of Jesus Christ (or is it St. John?) as an eagle. On another capital is a cock, described in the 5th Century by the Spanish Prudentius as "the winged messenger of the day, the symbol of Christ who awakes men from the stupor of night, which is sin and death."

Doña Mayor, wife of Sancho of Navarra, commissioned the Frómista monastery and the Church of San Martín in the 11th Century. Her husband had died in 1035; later that year, she retired to Frómista. She died here 31 years later, in 1066. These buildings had a single purpose: intercessory prayers for Doña Mayor's soul, that on her death she might escape the worst of her punishments in purgatory and fly with the greatest haste to heaven.

As I thought about Doña Mayor, the dark side of the Romanesque began to creep over me. Even as I loved these warm spaces, with their gentle unearthly peace, I had sensed, remotely, that they were too lush, too safe. Something else lurked under these stone vaults. It was fear. Doña Mayor was frightened. So were many people. Terrified in fact, of God, of demons, of death, of damnation, of hell's ruthless heat.

Man was a mixture of matter and spirit, taught the Church, slipped into creation just under the angels and just above the animals. We were supposed to look, not down into our animal nature for carnal delights, but upward, through our spiritual one to God. It was generally agreed that we hardly ever succeeded. Many felt we were doomed from the start, and that for the ordinary sinner, salvation was simply not possible.

A sermon in the *Liber Sancti Jacobi*, the *Veneranda Dies* starts this way: "The way of St. James is fine but narrow, as narrow as the path to salvation itself. That path is the shunning of vice, the mortification of the flesh, and the increasing of virtue." The preacher leaves us no room to move. Pilgrimage is to be conducted, he goes on, with the most abject humility. "The pilgrim may bring with him no money at all, except perhaps to distribute it to the poor on the road." The pilgrim who dies with money in his pocket is permanently excluded from the kingdom of heaven. "For what benefit can a man possibly derive from a pilgrimage undertaken in a spirit of sin?"

Rather to my dismay, I understood this; it sounded like the Calvinism of my Scottish forebears. Calvin had at least constructed out of the general doom a belief in salvation by faith, so that no matter how wretched you were, and no matter how hard you tried to do right and failed, which you always did, Jesus would save you if you only believed that he died for you. But what child, I wondered even now, can figure that out and still grow up sane.

Every Calvinist is alone in his faith; hope in Christ is personal, and nobody can do your praying for you. But in the Middle Ages, where the salvation of the whole community was at stake, it was the monasteries that gave the world hope. Only within their walls, in the presence of monks and nuns who prayed day in and out, was the perfect Christian life possible. And that holiness, it was believed, would unfurl like a mantle over all the rest of us wayward souls living outside the monastery gates.

So kings and nobles took great care of their relations with the monasteries. Governing was an iniquitous business. Supporting those who prayed professionally was a matter of spiritual self-defense. Like Doña Mayor, Alfonso VI, his daughter Urraca, and countless other aristocrats compulsively donated lands, built monasteries, and filled churches with treasure, all with a mind to extracting from God's throne a shard of mercy for their sin-soaked souls. We do not know the outcome for Doña Mayor, but not long after Alfonso VI died in 1109, an old monk from Nájera had a dream about the whereabouts of the king's not altogether pure soul. He reported that the prayers of the king's much endowed Cluniac congregation had been enough to get him out of the worst torments, but it was still unclear where he had finally ended up.

I had loved how Romanesque churches embraced and unified opposites. But opposites are still opposed, and unified or not, they lie in tension, often in struggle. In the Middle Ages, that struggle took the shape of a gaping ethical divide, an abyss, between good and evil. Looking around, I could see how adversarial the world of San Martín was, with its images of fallen humanity languishing in the struggle between vices and virtues. Christ is our saviour, but also our Judge; Creation is unrolling across time to the Last Judgment. Good and evil will be split apart one last time, and each shuddering man and woman will meet a doom deserved.

The Romanesque may have been comforting, but it was not the comfort of repose in unity. It was the cautious comfort of relationship, a negotiation in which faith in God's mercy was countered by an ominous sense of responsibility. Fear drove the quest for salvation. In *The Canterbury Tales*, Geoffrey Chaucer had written: "The .... cause that oghte moeve a man to contrition is drede of the daye of dome and of the horrible peynes of hell." As the Middle Ages wore on, fear of eternal doom began to border on the neurotic. Pilgrimage itself became an act of dread, supplication, petition, a frantic attempt to avoid the everlasting flames of hell.

I wandered through the Church of San Martín with my binoculars, looking up into the hundreds of sculpted figures on the capitals of its columns. Outside, in the corbels under the eaves of the tile roof I had seen hundreds more. Few were reassuring. Demons in the form of wolves, he-goats, even a dragon. Toothy dogs with balls in their mouths, a symbol of the divine perfection of the circle crunched in the jaws of the animal. A dual theme kept appearing like a repetition compulsion: the sins of men and the punishments of the damned, and the slim, poignantly alluring hope of redemption.

Evil was all around and everyone knew it. The world danced with malignant spirits. Demons could be lurking anywhere, upon a tile glinting on a palace roof, in the folds of an empty grain sac sagging by the miller's door. Floods, eclipses, miscarriages, a nightmare, shipwrecks, gusts of air, accidents, a large spider stick-legging across a pot lid, lightning bolts, the howl of a black dog, a deformed sheep, such things were never neutral acts of indifferent nature. In the 6th Century, Pope Gregory had advised making the sign of the cross over a salad, lest a demon was perched on a lettuce leaf. Six centuries later, Peter the Venerable, Abbot of Cluny, had at his disposal considerable evidence for the animal forms in which Satan went after sinners: a vulture in the sky, a black pig, a bear seen in the woods near Cluny.

The Church was the only defense. In a time when most houses were made of wood, churches were an image of safety, an unyielding fortress for both body and soul. The very stones of San Martín were a bulwark against evil. Inside its walls, in a crescendo of sound - the recitation of prayers, the intonations of the Mass, the cries of the supplicant - men invoked God's power against evil forces. According to Honorius of Autun, a French scholar of the 12th Century, the Mass was a battle with the devil. Even the church belfry was a sentinel; at the clang of its bells, flocks of blackened fiends would scatter into the air.

Like all Romanesque churches, San Martín used animal images for moral teaching. Some are positive and encouraging. The ox represents the force that ploughs the furrows of the mind to receive the fertile rain of heaven. The deer is prudence, or a human soul patiently seeking the divine waters. The pelican is Jesus Christ. In the church façade, I had seen the vulture, purifier and holy recycler. Scavenging through the compost, it regenerates vital forces and brings new life.

But sinners held in the grip of their animal instincts vainly try to force the flesh over the spirit. Of the hundred and fifty animals on the outside walls of San Martín, ninety-six are demonic, seven represent vices and only five represent virtues. The monkey is man, ridden with vice and lust, bathed in malice; pigs are gluttony; owl are the fiends of night, unable to support the light of the sun. Cats are demonic. The he-goat is the devil himself.

Lust is a woman, nude, with serpents sucking from her breasts. The liar is a man with his mouth stretched grotesquely wide. Everyone knows that if you stay in any position long enough, it will begin to feel like a punishment. The religious twist on this is originally Islamic, but its graphic sadism caught on in Christian circles: in hell, the body is contorted to mirror its sin. The wide mouth is the liar's doom: a permanent visit to the dentist.

Were people back then really that sinful? That guilty? Camino towns probably saw their share of the usual wrong-doers, but no more. Fishmongers had heavy thumbs, local kids swiped bird whistles from the market, young men masturbated in the woods, jealous wives gossiped and preened, men drank and flew into rages, young women got pregnant after a dance, self-righteous nobles spurned the poor, and priests debauched lonely women, and probably boys. Not much has changed. The Church saw itself as a counterforce to sin, tried to show, in its moral Disneyland of carvings and paintings, a way to salvation for anxious men and women. It came down with fearsome weight, or tried to, on human frailty, using all the usual psychological tricks - terror, shame, threats, a little compassion, a little indulgence, more threats.

If there is one thing modern pilgrims are not enthusiastic about hearing, it is what terrible sinners they are and what gruesome punishments await their unabsolved souls. We respond to the beauty of the churches, their maternal domes and arches and lilting streaks of sunlight and colour. But we rebel against the authoritarian and cruel, the threats of doom, and the guilt that seems, after all, too discouraging, too much to bear. Now, a year after my first pilgrimage, and nearly halfway through my second, I was feeling the dark Romanesque, the neurotic, unfriendly religion of fear. I was feeling my revulsion, as much from the stern and lonely Calvinism of my youth as from this depressing side of medieval Christianity. Both were hopeful in the abstract, but could be grotesque in the application.

My leg was hurting badly as I stepped from the Church of San Martín. To save a few kilometers, I decided to hitchhike from Frómista to Calzadilla de la Cueza. I walked slowly for about an hour along a pilgrims' path lined with short pillars that separated it from a strip of highway nearly devoid of cars. At Población, I ate a snack near the *Ermita de San Miguel*. A few minutes later, two Spanish men out for a weekend drive picked me up and took me as far as Carrión de los Condes, where last year Scott and I had witnessed the fight between the Spanish cyclists and the French pilgrim. My luck for hitch-hiking in Spain was never strong, and it ran out altogether at the highway leaving Carrión. Alone and on foot once more, I set out for Calzadilla knowing I would not likely be picked up again. The air was hot; pain shot through my leg like a dart from the sun. I tried not to limp, knowing that to do so would only hurt other joints. I took a step at a time, a step and a burning jolt, a step and a jolt. The road was flat and apart from a few vague curves, ended in the horizon.

I came to Benevivere. Last year, Scott and I had sat on a small stone bridge here eating the Carrión nuns' cookies. We had watched an immense flock of sheep bob and waddle down the road, driven by a solemn farmer on a horse and three maniacal dogs. Scott had picked a bouquet of wildflowers for me which I had stuck in my bike handle.

This year, I descended from the bridge to the river to soak my tired feet. I tried a mud cure for my leg, guaranteed by the massage therapist from Madrid whom I had met at the roadside bar near Logroño. For nearly an hour, I lay in the sun-dappled shade of the cool stream, my leg coated with thick clay. I listened to the water tumbling incessantly beside me, tried to make out each gurgle, each hiss, each brassy tinkle. Five pilgrims I had seen earlier at a rest area went by along the road above without seeing me. Drowsy, I let them pass, heard the dimming of their voices and the fading crunch of their boots on the road. Later, when my legs were cleaned and dried and dressed with tensor bandages and socks, I set out again. I was refreshed, but the mud cure had done nothing.

According to my Everest guide, a poplar grove stood near the road within three kilometres of Benevivere. It took almost an hour to get there along a stretch of crumbly pavement separating identical grain fields. Far ahead were the five pilgrims. I could tell they were tired from the way they straggled back and forth down the middle of the road, tottering under their packs.

I felt the inflammation in my leg expand. At each step, my foot flapped without strength. I thought of how medieval pilgrims had walked *because* of their pain, not in spite of it, had walked because they believed that James would take away their agony and make their bodies whole. Bent over their crutches, emaciated, their skin itchy and raw, their stomachs hollow, their cheeks and eye sockets sunken, they had crept, fevered and wheezing, toward the Santiago with more faith than I had when I applied the therapists' mud plaster, but with no less hope.

I was healthier than those poor pilgrims of long ago mainly because I was better fed. They had lived most of their lives on starch; fruits and vegetables were hard to come by, meat was expensive. A bad diet left many people with deficiency diseases, one reason for all the skin disorders reported from the time. Many others suffered from a general malaise aggravated by headaches, persistent constipation, parasites, menstrual agonies, runny eyes, and chronic bronchitis. Bladder and kidney stones, always ten plus on the pain scale, were common.

So was leprosy. Then there were injuries and congenital disorders, hunchbacks, withered limbs, fractures that never healed right, implanted bits of wood and metal, tumours, and mutilations inflicted as punishment.

In the medieval view, disease put a physical form on religious guilt, and the Church was often hostile to physicians who attended the mere physical body. The *Veneranda Dies* states that Jesus Christ is the ultimate physician: better to study the divine medicine by which he saved men than to waste your time finding mere physical cures. So the practice of medicine remained for centuries crude beyond believing. Visiting Arab doctors were appalled at the useless tortures European physicians inflicted on their patients. True, local herbalists and monks often practised medicine; many monasteries had medical libraries. Sahagún was known for its pharmacy. But except in areas with a Muslim or Jewish doctor, medical treatment was usually primitive.

Since pilgrimage was often a penitential exercise, the physical pain involved was taken for granted as the price for one's misdeeds. But as I limped along the crunchy road to Calzadilla, I wondered about whether my pain could be understood as penance. I thought of all the times I had let people down, been selfish, dishonest. But walking in pain across a flat strip of road in northern Spain did not feel like the payment of a moral debt. I knew how destructive chronic guilt could be, how close it ran to both masochism and narcissism, to a morbid attachment to the fantasy of how terrible one was. It bred a pointless asceticism or else a rebound flurry of self-indulgence, and neither one of these did any real good.

My pilgrimage to Santiago was supposed to be disciplined, but not punitive. Walking to Calzadilla, I gave up trying to find any meaning at all for my pain and returned to the Buddhist practice of simply observing my body feeling pain and the response of my nervous mind to something unpleasant. My shin burned with every step, and a torrent of emotions and rationalizations swept through me as a form of resistance. I saw how much I fear pain and how protective I am of my physical body. I worried that my leg would be permanently damaged by this day's walk. When I expressed this to a French

Canadian pilgrim I met a couple of days later, he scoffed. "Oh, don't be silly," he said, "it'll heal." Something in his dismissive laugh made me see how I was dramatizing my body, trying to control it against the very risks that would take me out of my attachment to myself. I saw how little I trusted that imperative in life that exists in our every cell and is so much stronger than any evil: the inherent, relentless compulsion to heal. On the road to Santiago, in a few off-hand words from someone from my own country, I would learn a brief but crucial lesson in faith.

The poplar grove eventually appeared; after a time, it too was behind me. Six more kilometres to Calzadilla. The road went up long, straight hills, each of which disappeared into the hazy horizon where I vainly imagined the town would appear. It was hours more before I finally saw the church tower at the cemetery just outside Calzadilla. A cemetery, I thought with a flicker of humour. What an appropriate destination.

At last, in a daze of exhaustion, I looked down a final hill upon the miserable one street village of Calzadilla de la Cueza. From Boadilla I had walked only twenty-seven kilometres today, but the last seventeen had taken me nearly seven hours. The plain hostel building fronted on the road; I walked distractedly through the door into an awkwardly small entrance hall, and was suddenly in a great deal more pain. Kjell was just emerging from the shower room looking clean and refreshed. As I leaned toward him with a sigh, he partly hugged me, partly held me up. I turned to see the five pilgrims who had been ahead of me, flopped on benches in the reception area, staring into the middle distance, as depleted as I was. I staggered up some rough stairs to the dormitory and collapsed onto an unutterably dirty mattress on the floor. I had trouble realising I no longer had to walk, felt almost as if I were still walking, a permanent sojourner in a purgatorial no-man's land.

Later I had a hard, cold shower. Kjell took me out for some bread and garlic soup and a bottle of red wine, and I began to feel better. After walking very slowly back from the bar, I prepared my sleeping bag on the grimy mattress to which I had earlier staked a claim. A dishevelled man in his late twenties came in whom we had seen loitering by the bar, obviously drunk. He had asked us for money, and I had given him a few pesetas. He turned out to be a pilgrim too. He planted himself on the bottom bunk in the room next to mine. A troop of Spanish cyclists thundered up the stairs and began to settle on the beds by his, but driven by the combined odour of alcohol and old sweat, they returned to my room. One sat against the wall across from me on his mattress and proceeded to fill out a form for something. He read out loud: "En caso de urgencia, llama..." In case of emergency, contact.... There was a pause. "... Pamela Anderson!" he quipped. Guffaws of laughter.

I awoke in the night with a start. The cyclists had all eaten something explosive during the day and their farts were piercing the night like bugles blown in hell. The room bulged with fumes. The drunken pilgrim muttered loudly and heaved in his sleep. The foot pilgrims, who had been forced by default to bed down in his room, were making a mass exodus out through my room. Out of one eye, I watched their five shadowy figures move in a slow row, bearing blankets, stepping over the wind-racking bodies of the unconscious cyclists. Every male in the room but one was snoring. That one was beside me, a curly-haired student from England, who was instead grinding his teeth. The squeaky crunch became too much, and I gave him a nudge. "Excuse me, but you are grinding your teeth," I said. "Oh, sorry," he replied. He rolled over. In a few moments, he was snoring. My sleeping bag was twisted and I shuddered as my shoulder touched the metallically cold mattress. It occurred to me that the drunken pilgrim was a serial killer or a pyromaniac. I fell asleep planning my escape.

In the morning, I scrambled from my sleeping bag, found my toothbrush, and crept stiffly out to the stairwell. The foot pilgrims had found their way there during the night and now lay in inert heaps under their blankets. Outside, where I stepped for a breath of fresh air, I discovered more cyclists, crawling half frozen from their bags. I had seen the *hospitalero* the evening before, but had not had the spirit to chat. He was an old man who seemed to dodder a little, and he did not appear this morning. Standing in the yard, I ate some yogurt and fruit, then went inside, gritted my teeth over the sink to splash icy water on my face and under my arms, and packed up. I left for Sahagún, walking slowly, scarcely believing the previous night.

When Scott and I had arrived in Sahagún the previous year, the hostel had been closed. I was luckier this time; the restored Church of La Trinidad was open to all. I hobbled up the stone stairway and entered the building, leaving the bright sunshine standing behind me in the doorway like an eager pet that wants to come in but isn't allowed. The reception area was a very long, wide hall, with a high looming ceiling. There was a great deal of brick and wood trim. On one side, through doors beneath a glass panel, was the sanctuary, completely stripped now of its medieval paraphernalia and looking more like an auditorium. Across from the doors, a fine wooden staircase led up to the dormitory. At the far end of the hall a solitary woman at a dimly lit desk waited like an interrogator. As I approached, she greeted me with a sudden, welcoming smile, as if she had been expecting me. I registered and hauled my pack upstairs, past a surprisingly small eating area and into a cavernous dormitory with a high ceiling and aisles lined with three-tiered bunk beds. The showers, I discovered, were spotless and the water was warm. My body was exhausted. I lay down on my bunk, relieved to simply relax into the ache of my leg, now that I no longer had to cope with walking on it.

It was hushed and safe here; pilgrims chatted quietly, occasionally I heard an outburst of laughter. Some people were writing their diaries. Others privately sorted their gear; I could hear the disembodied swoosh of plastic bags. The showers went on intermittently. I wondered how this hostel would have sounded nine hundred years ago. No shower sounds, but maybe the splash of a rain barrel from outside. People would have been resting their limbs as I was, while monks quietly attended to the sick. There would be the usual smells; sweat mostly, but also leather, animal feed, food cooking somewhere, maybe some vomit over in one corner, occasionally a breeze through the window from the latrines.

There are two ways in which the Santiago pilgrimage has changed from earlier times, and those changes have created a distance, some would say an abyss, between the experience then and now. The first is waymarking. In the Middle Ages, the route was sometimes obvious, but often you had to ask. In remote areas, you took your chances and made a guess at the right route. A mistake could be dangerous, leading to encounters with wild animals at night, or injuries in places where no one would find you. Someone with evil intent might give you wrong directions and send you to a meeting with thieves. At best you would simply waste time and exhaust yourself finding your way back. Bad weather made everything worse.

Today, yellow arrows mark the entire Camino all the way from Roncesvalles to Santiago. When you round a corner in a town, or come to a crossroad, or when the route veers from the highway to a foot path, the yellow arrow is there, eliminating all decision making. You have barely to hesitate before carrying on. This is a luxury that makes pilgrimage almost idiotically passive in some ways, but it is highly practical. You don't have to bother the locals for directions, and nobody has to come and rescue you.

Camino accommodations are the other big change. Nowadays the heaviest pilgrimage traffic is in July and August. In these months, the hostels are sometimes full and you might have to camp somewhere, or find a hotel, or make your way to the next town. During the rest of the year, you are almost always assured of a place to stay.

But it is not the availability of places that makes the modern experience different from the medieval one. In fact, at its peak, the medieval Camino had, if anything, more hostels than now. After Sancho the Great had the road put in across the Montes de Oca, kings and monks and local layfolk built hospices by the dozens from Navarra and Castile all the way into Galicia. Burgos, once called the City of Hospitals, is said to have had thirty-five.

"I have often seen this city praised for its charity," exclaimed St. Teresa when she stayed there in the 16th Century, "but I did not think it went this far!" At Carrión de los Condes there were at one time seven hostels, which, in addition to the large hospital at the monastery of San Zoilo, now a fancy hotel, included one built by the Templars next to the Church of Santiago, and another in the square of Santa Maria. Down the road was the White Hospital, and the important 13th-century hostel built by a Castilian noble, Don Gonzalo. At Benevivere, the Augustinian canons had a monastery and a *refugio*. León of course had many hostels. But Astorga, a much smaller town with a population of only about 1,500, was the most outstanding of all, outdoing even Burgos. Over the years, Astorga saw no fewer than twenty-five hospitals come and go, all dedicated to care of the poor, the sick and the pilgriming. It is estimated that thirty-four percent of the population of Astorga was directly involved in maintaining and running the hostels.

The hostels were simple but inviting places founded in faithfulness to the Gospel, where Christian hospitality was extended to all. Here too, hostel workers themselves could work off their sin, for charity of any kind had the power to erase evil deeds. Even to work on the pilgrimage roads and bridges was an act equal to the giving of alms.

In one story making the rounds in the Camino years, a pilgrim asked a local woman for food. The lady had loaves of fresh bread still warm under the cinders of her oven, but she was hardhearted and refused the pilgrim. He was not fooled and walking away, he upbraided her: "Let the bread you have be turned to stone!" Later, when the woman opened her oven, she found that her fresh bread had indeed turned to stone. Hastily, full of remorse, she went after the pilgrim but never found him.

There were lapses in the hostels too, and here lies the biggest difference between then and now, not in the absence of problems, but in the number and kind. Theft was common, and sometimes even pilgrims were the culprits. In the 18th Century in Santiago, a man caught robbing a pilgrim was chained up and left all night with a lamp burning by him to increase his shame. Even clerics sometimes robbed pilgrims. But punishments were not light. A 13th-century document from Castile reports that at the urging of his brother the abbot, a cleric named Andrés robbed a pilgrim's bag. Andrés was hanged and the abbot deprived of his office and sentenced to two penitential pilgrimages to Rome.

The situation was far worse in the inns where many pilgrims stayed. One risk was that a better paying customer might come along and a poor pilgrim be thrown out for the sake of a little more cash. The *Veneranda Dies* decries innkeepers who abuse pilgrims with promises of food, drink and good treatment, only to extract excessive cash from them for a third-rate dive with filthy beds, bad fish, and a selection of whores and fleas as companions. The preacher lists the wrongdoings, pointing to wicked men who cheat on money exchange, use incorrect weights, collude with thieves, and rough up innocent pilgrims, even poisoning or murdering them to get at their goods. Evildoers might lace syrups and foods with drugs to cause sleep or death. Thieving innkeepers might take a pilgrim's belongings for safe keeping, only to conveniently forget about them in the morning; sometimes they would go through a sleeping pilgrim's bag and steal what they fancied, or hide things that a pilgrim had lost, or hang on to goods belonging to the estate of a pilgrim who had died. One innkeeper took a dead pilgrim's money and his children's donkey. In this instance however, St. James arranged personally for the innkeeper to break his neck in a fall, and the same threat was apparently, according to the *Liber* at least, made plain to other "wicked innkeepers plying their trade on my road." There were other offences too, lesser but still annoying. Bad food, or food that had been cooked again. Diluted wine. The stables were dubious places; an innkeeper might tie his donkey close enough to eat the pilgrim's donkey's food; another might simply steal the pilgrim's extra barley and hay.

Outside the inns and taverns were other dangers: merchants who sold things to pilgrims at inflated prices; candle sellers who substituted goat fat for tallow; herbalists peddling quack cures at high prices to sick pilgrims; men who posed as churchmen to confess pilgrims and then made off with their money. Then too, pilgrims themselves were not always honest. There are reports of them stealing chickens and damaging fields, forgetful that St. James' eyes were upon them.

Still, for all the dangers and sorrows of the medieval Camino, there were men and women at every hospice along the way who were waiting for you with a smile, a beaker of water and a bed. And there still are. If there is one thing that impressed me above all else on my journeys to Santiago, it was finding myself on the receiving side of selfless service, and realizing that pilgrimage, the act of travelling in quest of some kind of personal salvation, is absolutely dependent on the willingness of others to stay in one place and serve. At Burgos, I had talked to three young Germans who were looking after the big *refugio* there. They told me they wanted to help people with their journey; they admitted they were getting tired but their dedication was holding firm. They were as human as any of us. To me at times they seemed naïve. But in their commitment to the spiritual growth of others, they reminded me a little of the Boddhisatvas in the Buddhist tradition, who forego their own enlightenment until others have reached theirs.

Camino hospitality, says Prieto, honours the divinity that inhabits the stranger, the mystical otherness of the one from away. This Christian ideal recalls the Old Testament, where Abraham entertains three strangers in his tent on the plains of Mamre. The life of Jesus, Prieto goes on, was a constant request for lodging. The sanctity of the visitor is implicit in the phrases of Matthew:

> I was a stranger and you took me in... inasmuch as ye have done it unto one of the least of these my brethren, ye have done it unto me.

Prieto tells the pilgrim to receive such hospitality in the spirit in which it is offered, with gratitude and humility, for thus do we learn the truth of our dependence on one another and on the world around us. This became ever clearer to me as I walked from hostel to hostel: Logroño, where I had been given water and helped by the smiling *hospitalero* to my top bunk; Los Arcos, where I waited a long time in a long line-up to register, finally to discover a wizened old man at a small desk trying his hardest to keep us straight and make sure we all had the right place to sleep. At Carrión de los Condes, the señora had laughed with us at her husband's jokes and wished us well as she handed us our nuns' cookies. Boadilla, where the organic farmer shared his whole grain cookies and his laundry shelter; Astorga, where the staff were as relaxed as jazz musicians, and someone had put in an electric clothes dryer for us.

For all the devotion lavished upon James in the Middle Ages, all the obsessions with guilt and fear that were laid down at his tomb, it was curious to me how remote the saint seemed here on the late edge on the 20th Century. What struck me instead was how the hospitable spirits of Santo Domingo de la Calzada, San Juan de Ortega, and the charitable ladies from Italy inhabited the hearts of our hostel custodians. I was moved beyond words by the outpouring of their charity, a love tempered with humour, and an ability to organize and maintain places that sometimes sheltered seventy pilgrims. In our fallen world, this is a kind of redemption: meeting people who in ministering to your body and your spirit, make you want to be more like them.

In Sárria, the tomb of an unknown Templar knight,
mouldering in the grass.

8

THE WHEEL OF FORTUNE

The Bodhisattva's way is called "the single-minded way," or "one railway track thousands of miles long." ... Sincerity itself is the railway track. The sights we see from the train will change, but we are always running on the same track. And there is no beginning or end to the track. There is no starting point nor goal. Nothing to attain. Just to run on the track is our way.
    Shunryu Suzuki. Zen Mind, Beginner's Mind

I walk in emptiness; I hear my breath. I see my hand and compass, see the ice so wide it arcs, see the planet's peak curving and its low atmosphere held fast on the dive. The years are passing here.
    Annie Dillard. An Expedition to the Pole

*The modernist station for pilgrim tour busses, built
for Pope Jean Paul's visit to Santiago.*

A fter spending the night in Olmos de Atapuerca during my 1998 pilgrimage, I had decided to take the noon train for the short distance from there to Burgos. My leg was still too painful to walk more than a couple of kilometers, and since I needed to be in Compostela by early September, I couldn't spend extra time in one place waiting for it to heal.

I spent the morning at the hostel with my leg up, writing my journal and reading. Close to noon, I said good-bye to the custodian and slowly walked along the road to the train station. Apart from the heat, which bellied in the air, the only sensation was my boots landing with an uneven thunk *thunk* on the tarmac. A single car crunched past me; the driver caught my eye and waved solemnly. In the southwest, low pale hills were smothering under a haze of heat that floated along the horizon.

The station, a plain, white building, appeared to be closed. But rounding a corner, I found a door marked "Tickets" that opened into a room piled with cartons and junk. Two faded posters hung on the wall like rags up to dry. The ticket master was a cheerful fellow in a half-hearted uniform that made him look as if he was down on his luck. When his ticket dispenser failed to work, he led me around more boxes to a cluttered desk where he made out my ticket by hand. I paid, and he came outside with me for conversation before the train arrived. Past him, I saw bags of cement sagging by a wall. Masonry tools leaned against them at odd angles as if repairs had been intended, but on thinking about it, nobody could see the point. Five ragged pilgrims with dreadlocks - perhaps they were just late season backpackers - sat cross-legged in a circle near the tracks, playing cards. This station might be closed down, the ticket master told me. He wasn't sure. Yes, his job was at stake. He shrugged resignedly. I asked what he would do without work, and he shrugged again.

Precisely on time, a Cadillac of a train glided into the dusty little station. The ticket master waved to the trainman. Having noticed my limp, he helped me across the track, then hoisted my pack into the train and took my arm as I got aboard. Nodding formally, he waved me off. The train began to move without a sound. My car was so solidly air conditioned that I felt I had to cut my way to a seat. I settled beside a graying man from the southern city of Jaen. As we cruised toward Burgos, I asked him about Andalusia. It had once had beautiful forests, he said with a bored look, but now it was nothing but olive groves.

My seatmate had taken this train to Burgos many times and clearly preferred napping to talking. I looked out on the passing fields, thinking of the late spring day over a year ago when Scott and I had pedaled into Burgos on the asphalt shoulder of the dreaded N120. The highway had taken us deep into the flat grassy lands of the Province of Burgos, past little towns with odd names: Zalduendo, Ibeas de Juarros, San Medel. Thick, moist clouds had hung like avalanches in the sky. The landscape shrank into the horizon as if blown back by the sounds of the road. Cars of tourists cruised past us with a zooming drone; children waved from the back seats, grinning with superiority. Local drivers rattled by with their windows open and the radio turned up. There were fewer trucks than on the bigger highways, but they came dinning at us just the same. I had watched them in my mirror, gaining on us, rumbling at first, then sucking the wind and making our bikes wobble as they missiled past our shoulders with a gargling squeal that, had trucks been living creatures, you would have thought was a cry of pain under torture.

Burgos rises off the Camino solemnly, the archetype of a city. Its glinting spires, which you can see from a distance, are as glamorous as the slim, white-gold towers of paradise that twinkle in the landscape of Gothic manuscript illustrations. But the howling, growling highway turned those silhouettes into a demonic caricature of heaven. As we drew near the city, the traffic had slowed. The air got dense with grinding gears and throbbing motors. Dark sprays of exhaust carried us along the main arteries into town. Then the trucks had turned off, leaving us stranded in a maze of car-filled capillaries.

We had gone immediately that day to the Cathedral. Santa Maria is a mighty swoosh of stone crammed into an impossible square, two squares actually, that have odd angles and distracting buildings. Its whale's interior is held up with osseous pillars, and it heaves with statues and over-sized sarcophagi. I found the monuments tediously egotistical, felt almost offended by El Cid lying like the hero he wasn't under the central vault. I had felt depressed and suffocated, as if my heart was leaving me, so we left the church to wander through the old city and the park by the river. In the morning we abandoned Burgos altogether, half visited and under-appreciated. I had not wanted to linger; the noise was tiresome. To me, the city was an image of self-inflated Catholic Spain, magnificent, conceited, inflexible as the stays in a prim old lady's corset.

In the year or so since then, I had chanced to read about Burgos' treasures, its ambitious history, and the repairs that were brightening the old cathedral. And so today, as my train coasted into the city, I felt as if I was dropping in on a rather unlikeable aunt about whom I might try to change my attitude.

Walking from the train station along the streets that led to the Cathedral Square, I discovered a city of sun-warmed stone, a mineral world of towers, staircases, gates, bridges and roadways. Through them flowed the people of Burgos: busy, unconscious urbanites entering shops and coming out of shops, clutching cell phones and briefcases, flinging big purses onto their shoulders, tossing their hair. They streamed across intersections; they came round street corners with blank determination; ceramic faces with city clothes, trench-coats, high heels, high hair, their shadows slipping and bobbing, tidy as a manicure, against the straight walls of buildings. In the long arcade of trees that lines the Arlanzón River, they slowed down: arm in arm, they strolled in and out of the sidewalk shadows, or lay alone on the grass reading books. Stout, well-dressed old people perched like figurines on the benches under canopies of leaves.

In the square, I sat down at a café table and tried to study the cathedral spires. But my eyes were overcome, faltered on the way up and fell too soon from the towers, landing on the dark doorway to the church, the beggar lady on the steps, tourists standing over their guide maps, the loaded bicycle leaning against a stone wall. You can't get off the ground in Burgos. Its stones seem to hold you down like a magnet.

The waitress brought me a plate of warm red peppers and a glass of anise, and I relaxed into the sunny urban afternoon. I got out my binoculars, tried again to look up. The cathedral spires had a hectic laciness, like that unlikeable aunt's doilies, starched and rolled into tall cylinders. But I saw how fine the carving really was. I could even see the blue sky through their interstices.

I set down my binoculars and looked up once more, tipping my head back until my neck crunched. I recalled a phrase I had come across, used by a certain Gundisalvo in the 12th Century, when the Gothic was on the rise. Architecture, he had said, was applied geometry. The Gothic cathedral thrust itself up into space like a long crystal, a likeness - in the perfection of angles and lines of light - of God's heaven.

This is an old idea, traceable at least to Plato and Pythagorus: the intellectual unity of mathematics joined to the rational beauty of perfect music, the music of the spheres. Even now it made sense: the cosmos as an infinity of unities held together in a harmony made discordant only by human folly. The Gothic architect tried to make visible once again, in a scurry of stone vectors and shafts of light, an image of that original perfection of number and harmony.

From my café table in the square, I could see a musical composition in the lines of Burgos Cathedral: its buttresses rose and fell in melodic phrases and the peaks of its spires pierced the air like a soprano. I also sensed a yearning in that upward reach; the two tallest spires over the south portal seemed to be scanning the sky in search of extra-terrestrial life. Not the science fiction fantasy of jointless creatures with antennae, but the *truly* extra-terrestrial quest for that which is absolutely beyond this mundane world: God himself, the mystical divine, surrounded by his orders of angels and saints. The spires stretched towards the invisible clouds of that unknowable place, poised in an eternal longing.

I sipped my sweet anise, watched people old and young, stylish and forlorn, foreign and local, as they came and went on errands unknown to me under the massive walls and long spires of the cathedral. I thought back to a discussion with Bernardo, the architectural historian from Madrid, during our taxi ride to San Millán de Cogolla, about the shift from the Romanesque to the Gothic in architecture.

Historians often emphasize the political aspects of the Gothic, Bernardo had told me. By the 13th Century, the Roman Church had lost much of its power and credibility. A new idea of monarchy was taking shape, one that downplayed the control of the Church. The feudal system was wearing out, the social hierarchy was evolving. Towns and cities were becoming commercial centres, and as the economic bases of the culture moved there, a new middle class began to take up positions of influence in the royal courts. Art and architecture are a response to culture, Bernardo had said, and you can relate these social changes in various ways to the rise of the Gothic. Churches became mirrors, reflecting the whole community and its activities and achievements. You could see your own world as an image in the house of God.

"So many pictures in the stained glass windows and the carvings - especially in France - represented everyday people of the community," Bernardo had said. "Even the architects 'wrote themselves in'. It was a very inclusive architecture, you could even almost call it democratic, though that's a tricky word to apply to that period."

It is often said that the Gothic was part of the new spirituality that would transform 12th-century Europe. The concept of God became more intellectual, more abstract, and found expression now in metaphors of number and harmonic balance, metaphors that before long made their way into architecture. At the same time, personal faith became more naturalistic and humanized, more rational and explicit, as the dark mysteries that had haunted the Romanesque receded. Romanesque churches had placed you at the heart of the struggle between good and evil. But Gothic churches were a sort of virtual paradise where you could see the bright, rational order of God's universe.

"But you know," Bernardo went on, and I remember him dragging on his cigarette and exhaling the smoke as he said it, "none of it would have made a lot of difference to architecture without innovations in engineering and technology. In fact you can explain the Gothic very nicely in terms of the economics of church construction. Take the vaults for instance: Romanesque vaults had enormous vertical and lateral thrust. You needed big, thick walls to resist the tonnage from above. They were really expensive, hard to put up. But with the Gothic you get two innovations: ribbed vaulting, which they picked up from the Arabs, and flying buttresses, those supporting arches like bridges you see on the outside of the cathedrals, that take the weight of the vaults off the walls. With these advances, you could build thinner walls - cheaper and needing less manpower to put up. You also got more interior height that way. But you never really know," he added emphatically, "which came first, the theological idea of God as the divine architect, or the technology that made that kind of idea - which wasn't completely new anyway - take off."

"More height meant more window space," Bernardo continued, "and when you got more light into the church interior, you got a good physical example of the spirit of God. Light was the perfect symbol of a transcendent and immanent God: intangible, but always present and visible. There was plain white light, like at Cluny, and then there was coloured light. They got the idea for stained glass from the illuminated manuscripts that were becoming popular, and when they perfected the technology to make the windows, the churches were filled with colour."

We talked about the timing of the Gothic, for there seemed to be no clear division between it and the Romanesque. The 12th Century is often called the Golden Age of the Romanesque, said Bernardo, although even before half of that century was over, St. Denis was going up in Paris. It was dedicated in 1144, and marked the so-called "Birth of the Gothic.' But the Romanesque and the Gothic both came up together on the curve of history, "like two seats on the top of a Ferris wheel, one just behind the other," as Bernardo put it. Romanesque churches were still being built - in Italy up until the end of the 13th Century - when the new Gothic style was reaching its height in northern Europe.

What Bernardo had explained to me about the Gothic being a play with light and numerical harmony was immediately challenged when I crossed the threshold of Burgos Cathedral under the heavy tympanum of the east door. Just as I had the year before, I found myself enclosed in an elephantine darkness that left me breathless. Tourists walked past me, rising out of the floor like ants on their hind legs beside impossibly tall walls and pillars. I walked around the cathedral, feeling that for all the sublime height of the eight-pointed, Arab-influenced vault in the crossing, I was being buried amid sculpture and hulking tombs and ironwork. I read in Valiña's *Guide* that an unused tomb in the family burial chapel of Constable Don Pedro is a block of jasper marble weighing in at thirty-four tons.

Burgos Cathedral is dedicated to Santa Maria, but the rotund femininity of an earlier faith was now angular and tall to the point of gauntness. The luminous emptiness under Romanesque arches had been forced upward, made tight and strained, and fixed into glass windows like a specimen of colourful insect wings. I couldn't deny that the cathedral was beautiful but I found to my great surprise that I missed the sense of doom I had found so disturbing in the Romanesque. Cosmic dread had been reduced to the merely authoritarian; the terror that always accompanies an interior quest was gone.

Everywhere I looked, I was directed outward to the powers and forces of the human world around me, and never inward to the still, scary places of the soul.

In the Chapel of Santa Tecla, under a tiny Gothic porch above the altar, is a statue of St. James in the attire of a well-to-do pilgrim: an elegant cloak lies in folds around his robe, his rounded hat bears a scallop shell; a staff is tucked under his right arm, and a purse hangs by his thigh against the cloak's border. He holds a book, the Word of God, in his two hands and appears to be flipping the pages. His face is wise, picks up golden hues from the sculptures around it. The beard is thick, the mouth is slightly open and the wide, oriental eyes look with interest upon the book. I watched him through my binoculars; perhaps it was his pleasure in words on a page that held me such a long time.

There are other reminders of the Santiago pilgrimage in Santa Maria. A carving in the choir shows the Virgin appearing before the Apostle at Saragoza. James Matamoros is on his horse in the Chapel of Santiago. The museum, which I liked much more than the church, also contained statues of James. But Santa Maria didn't have the feel of a pilgrimage church. In fact by the time it was finished in the 16th Century, James had receded from the religious panorama of Spain. Some were beginning to doubt he had ever evangelized here, much less been buried in Compostela. By the 17th Century, proposals were being put forward that St. Teresa be made the patron of Spain, though this was hotly resisted by such people as a certain Francisco de Quevedo. Santiago is not the patron of Spain because he was picked from other saints, wrote the cleric, but because when there was no Spain at all, Christ chose him to win the land and create the kingdom of Spain.

Before leaving Santa Maria, I sat in the chapel of Santo Cristo of Burgos, a place reserved for true believers and people who wished not to gawk the way you felt you had to everywhere else, but to pray. It was fresh and bright in here. A dozen people were scattered through the pews. Above the altar, I saw a Gothic, 14th-century crucifix brought to the cathedral from an Augustinian monastery in 1835 when the religious communities of Spain were being closed. I looked at the cross and saw the antithesis of that Christ in Majesty who lorded it over the faithful from the vaults of the Romanesque basilicas. Here was a meager Jesus wearing nothing but a womanish skirt. His skin, made of oxhide to resemble human skin, was bloodsmeared and cracked with sores; the thin, articulated arms stretched at a gawky angle, and the head, also articulated and racked with thick thorns, sagged awkwardly down on one shoulder. The Cristo de Burgos, Laffi had written, "would move the very stones to compassion, were they capable of feeling." According to old pilgrim songs, the body sweated and bled, had to be shaved weekly, and needed a regular manicure and pedicure.

The Romanesque had been concerned with exorcising the forces of evil, and it had taken a deity's power to do it. But from the look of this wasted Christ, done in by man's sin and bearing all his guilt, the wrestling match with darkness had petered out, and in its place was an almost masochistically sentimental Christ who inspired no dread, nor even Laffi's compassion. At least not in me.

How odd that this despondent Christ appeared just as the church was entering its most feverishly intolerant era. Heresies and counter-heresies were making the authorities nervous. Books would soon be cast to the bonfires; before long, human beings would go too. Jews were about to be persecuted with a vigour unseen since Visigothic times. I sensed an eerie connection between the suffering Cristo de Burgos and the loveless machine of Church management. It was a paradox I found far more distressing than the shuddering Romanesque obsession with salvation in a demon-soaked world.

I left Santa Maria, relieved by the sight of plain blue sky over the square. Across from the Cathedral was a posh hotel and as I walked past, I recalled something that happened last year. Scott and I had been looking for a hotel, but this one, we found, was too expensive. We were about to leave through the lobby when we ran into Tommy, an Scottish pilgrim we had met on the way to Sahagún, whose sore feet and German walking sticks had been the subject of a brief but lively discussion. It was a pleasure to see him again, and we had chatted for a few minutes on the stone steps of the hotel. We asked him how his walk into Burgos had gone.

"It was hell," he said, "utter hell. My feet were killing me, the trucks left me deaf, and when I finally got here, I didn't even bother to look at where the hostel was. I just headed for this place and said to the laddie at the desk, 'give us a room!'."

"Rich pilgrim!" he added with a laugh. "I brought the means for a little luxury just in case."

Tommy's joke was scarcely new. A comic character in a play by the 16th-century playwright Tirso de Molina tells us: "I made a vow to visit the sacred tomb of our Apostle; walking on foot and asking for alms. However," he adds, his voice dropping slyly, "I bring my servants behind me on a litter."

On this day, Scott and I, Tommy, and Tirso's character were all behaving like the richer pilgrims of the late Middle Ages. In the 13th Century, the preacher Jacques de Vitry had complained about "light-minded and inquisitive persons [who] go on pilgrimages [to Jerusalem] not out of devotion, but out of mere curiosity and love of novelty. All they want to do," fumed Jacques, "is travel through unknown lands to investigate the absurd, exaggerated stories they have heard about the east.

The trend got even worse than Jacques could imagine. One of Chaucer's most famous characters in *The Canterbury Tales* is the Wife of Bath, a blousy, red-cheeked, high-living (or pretending to be) woman of fashion, five times married and with very definite views on who should dominate whom in marriage. The Wife knows the remedies of love, can "dance the old dance," and counsels multiple husbands if you're lucky enough to get them. Chaucer gives her a gap between her front teeth, a sure sign of a vain and lascivious nature. The Wife fits to a tee the image of the "light-minded" pilgrim so reviled a century earlier by Jacques de Vitry. She travels to Canterbury on a horse, wearing fine scarlet stockings and a hat the size of a shield. It's a good picture of the carelessness of the times, and when we learn that the Wife has been to *Seint-Jame* in Galicia, (as well as Jerusalem, three times, and to Rome, Boulogne, and Cologne) we understand Chaucer's slur on both the too well-travelled wife, intent on picking up men and showing herself off, and on the pilgrimage routes of the day, where such things could happen more easily than ever before.

By the 15th Century, throngs of visitors were arriving on the Spanish Camino from France and Germany whose principal interests were culture and tourism. These were aristocrats usually, out for some sight-seeing or adventure. A companion to the court of Henry of Saxony remarked cynically that "on a trip like this, what could be better than a few succulent meals... the best devotion and indulgence." To the purists such travellers were only slightly less repugnant than those enterprising pilgrims who kept a constant look-out for business contacts.

Nowadays the lowest caste on the Camino is reserved for precisely the same folks. A little booklet I picked up in Santiago called *St. James the Apostle and his place in history. 10 Study Themes*, calls them "bogus pilgrims." These are "the hikers" who merely want exercise and to get to know the country, "the initiatory groups" who use the Camino to support bizarre gnostic and esoteric doctrines; and finally, those who live for a few weeks off the Camino, using Christian hospitality for a cheap tourist trip.

I found my way to the Burgos *refugio*, arriving just as an afternoon rainshower began. A torrent of water slammed at the windows as I climbed onto my assigned bunk at the far end of a crowded, dimly lit room. I sat with my sore leg stretched out and completed my ritual: peel off my socks, examine my feet, sort out my backpack, make a laundry pile, organize my food supplies, get out my shower stuff. Anya arrived, veiled like a colour-blind nun in a shiny red poncho. I hadn't seen her in days. She looked wonderful. Her feet had healed, she had lost weight, and in her face was the exuberance of renewed health and optimism.

I talked a while with the English Martha and Virginia. Martha had also lost weight, but she was finding pilgrimage very hard. She felt that Virginia was a little bored with her. Virginia told me that Duncan had mailed a load of unnecessary clothes back to Valencia and had carried on alone to Santiago, leaving her with his mother. She rolled her eyes. "He's going really fast," she added with a tone of disgust, "and as usual he's getting very competitive about it."

When I had last talked to Duncan, he said, "I haven't mentioned this before, but I have to tell somebody how much my shoulder hurts. I can never get comfortable with this pack. Sometimes I think I'll go crazy, when the pain shoots into my back on the downhill." Duncan had always been so jolly; I'd had no idea he was in pain. That must have been one reason he had sent some of his things back to Valencia. I had caught a glimpse of him walking into Burgos, almost bouncing along the road as if he were feather-light inside.

"How's Duncan's shoulder?" I asked Virginia.

"Shoulder?" she replied. He really hadn't told another soul. I have often wondered why he chose to tell me.

I talked to a young American who was resting his feet on a bunk near mine. He studied art in Barcelona and on a whim had decided to walk the Camino before going home to the States. I liked his friendly American face, and he seemed to think that, by being twenty-five years older than he was, I was exotic, though it did not feel that way to me.

A Mexican pilgrim had the bunk below me. He had already been to Santiago and was making his way west again to León. He was also good-looking, but in a different way from the fair, clear-eyed American. He reminded me of the romanticized St. James. His beard was thick and dark, and his sympathetic eyes looked out at you as if from a deep cave.

I watched him from the corner of my eye as he prepared his bunk. No doubt about it, he was attractive.

Well, you can't leave your hormones at home, I thought. The Wife of Bath would have been in her element here.

I took the bus for the last few miles into León to spare my leg, which was starting to heal. On this bright August Saturday in 1998, I recalled the street noise and dust from a thousand jackhammers that had dogged Scott and me as we searched León for a hotel. Now the streets were fixed and flowing with traffic. The outdoor cafés were crowded, the buskers were drawing audiences in wide circles. Local gents shuffled along the sidewalk among tourists, shoppers, even a few nuns. In the square, you could sit in front of the Tourist Office gazing at the facade of the cathedral, the gleam of its towers, and the Apostles standing still over its doors while human figures walked to and fro in the striped shadows of its tall railing.

Saturday was wedding day; inside the cathedral the bonds of matrimony were being welded with assembly line efficiency. I stood beneath the visceral colours of the León's stained glass windows listening to the organ's sugary diapason. The church seemed to float on the sound, listing like a boat on a musical sea. As the service ended, I walked up and down the aisles, my head back, staring in wonder at the torrent of colours that gushed through the church from the windows. I looked at them through my binoculars. The detail of their design astonished me: a bruise of purple on a liverish green, scarlet hearts flattened against a fatty yellow, bright, lake-like patches of azure trimmed with black, all illuminated by a wash of white light that I couldn't quite see. In some windows, the colours simply coalesced into a huge balloon of yellow sunshine.

It was barely fifteen minutes from the time the first wedding party departed through the north exit and a new one had stepped into position under the main vault. I watched the cast. Men wearing black suits with shirts like bottles of milk stood before the altar with their hands folded obediently over their crotches. The women were in elegant dresses with three-quarter coats. The mother of the bride wore a black skirt with a slit up the side. The

mother of the groom was in salmon brocade. A cumulus
bride stepped with her father to her serious groom and a
patient priest. It was folk music this time, sung by a
quartet of old hippies lurking near the choir. They looked
as if they had been coralled off the street for a quick song
when the soprano failed to show. But they were highly
trained, and their music was a delight; as they sang, the
stained glass saints in the windows of León Cathedral
seemed to smile and tap their feet.

I watched a little longer, then wandered in the
aisles until a final organ fanfare exploded through the
vaults, signaling two more families united. I turned down
the central aisle to leave. High on the back wall of León
Cathedral was the rose window: a cyclone of flower petals
in every colour, blowing straight at me down a tunnel.

I left the church to sit once more in the square, my
back against a pillar by the Tourist Office. Idly I watched
people traverse the square, locals with shopping bags,
tourists with cameras and kids, a few pilgrims in light
hiking boots swinging their walking sticks and pausing to
peer through the church railing. More brides and mothers
of brides dawdled near the doors, puffs of white beside
balloons of hot pink, bright orange, magenta and lime
green. A bride walked with her groom below the church
railing, a froth of white foam billowing from her jet hair to
the pavement. He was in regulation black, looking slick
and slightly effaced. They paused and turned toward each
other, huddled for a moment, then straightened and
walked determinedly forward again toward the other side
of the square. The bride held her dress in front like a
wheelbarrow. Sticking horizontally out of both their
mouths like thick milkshake straws, in perfect silhouette
against the stone church wall, were two long, white
cigarettes.

The road across the meseta between León and
Astorga runs through La Virgen del Camino, with its
Sixties church, and across the meseta to Villadangos del
Páramo. Villadangos is a small place that had once been a
Roman town. In 1111, Doña Urraca ran her army near
here against her despised Aragonese husband Alfonso El

Batallador. The Church is a small compendium of Santiago lore, with a scene of La Virgen del Pilar appearing at Saragoza, three images from the Battle of Clavijo, and James Matamoros on a horse, about to leap directly into the nave from the main altar.

After another ten kilometres came the bridge over the flood-prone Órbigo River, with Puente del Órbigo on the east bank and Hospital de Órbigo on the west. This is one of the oldest bridges in León, also one of the longest. On its stones you can see the original masons' marks - their signature graffiti. Scott and I had stood on this bridge last year eating apples and cheese and looking over the floodbanks of the Órbigo and its army of swooshing poplars. I paused here again, remembering the voices of children who were playing in the park that day.

In 452, Swabians and Visigoths had fought near this bridge. Moorish troops had done battle with Christians under Alfonso III around 900. The Hospitalers of St. John ran a pilgrim hostel in Hospital de Órbigo in the 13th Century. But Órbigo is most famous for an event that took place in the later years of the Santiago pilgrimage.

It is the 15th Century. Heading to Santiago amid the usual Camino traffic are a special kind of traveller: pilgrim knights, veterans of the Crusades, on their way to offer thanks to James for their lives, for a battle won, or perhaps for an escape from a Moorish prison. On the way, the knights like to keep up their skills - and their image - with a little jousting. Tournaments are held at particular seasons along the Camino, and if you are a fit knight and you time it right, you can have a good couple of months of combined pilgrimage and competition.

Sometime before the turn of the year 1434, a Leonese knight from Palas de Rei, Don Suero de Quiñones, finds himself imprisoned not by Moors but by love. Since the 12th Century, this has been the traditional troubadour's obsession, though at this late date, there is an element of self-consciousness in the tale, even of self-parody. Still, Don Suero seems serious enough. The lady herself is absent from the story - she may have been a certain Leonor de Tovar. In honour of his captivity by this ravishing damsel, Don Suero wears, every Thursday, an iron ring around his neck. His desire is, of course, unfulfilled, and the only appropriate response to the situation is the performance of a mighty deed in honour of the lady.

On a January day in 1434, - a Holy Year in Santiago de Compostela - King Juan II presides over festivities in Castile. Don Suero is in attendance. Rising from his seat, he makes the following declaration with the Apostle James as his witness: he will compete by jousting with as many knights as care to accept his challenge, at the bridge over the Órbigo River, for two weeks on either side of the Feast of St. James on July 25. Suero will be accompanied by nine of his men. Together, he vows, they will break three hundred lances. Juan gives his approval to the competition, though the Bishop of León frowns upon these shenanigans.

Word goes out. Knights from France, Germany, Italy, Portugal and Spain declare their intention to travel to Santiago and play at the Órbigo Bridge on the way.

July 10. On the west bank of the Rio Órbigo, a large area is fenced off from the road so that those pilgrims foolish enough to pass up the excitement can carry on to Santiago unimpeded. Flags and pennants snap at the sky. The officials are present: tournament judges, heralds, arms bearers, priests, and tonsured monks with their cowls hanging in great loops down their backs. Already the scribes are taking notes, like good reporters anywhere. Bands of musicians entertain the gathering crowd.

The ladies are in attendance too. Their dresses (a little behind Paris) shimmer in the warm sunshine: vermilion, indigo and magenta, silks and linens, here a wide collar starched upright, there a little red cape like a bed jacket, and over there a cloak that falls in rust and green panels. The ladies are demure. Their heads bob as they gossip. Some heads are bare but for a circlet, and jet-black hair drops to the waist in a braid like a mink's tail. On other heads are ornate and colourful hats created by whimsical milliners. Here and there a veil floats high above the other heads, strung out like a white bat. The ladies' faces are plucked and polished; their shoes are dainty, but prone to mud, as are the hems of their dresses. They stand back from the *hoi polloi*, who are here in droves of course, along with buskers, hawkers, and pick-pockets. But this is a classy event, and the real rowdies are permanently sidelined by a team of hefty bouncers. Keeping a little apart from the beauties and the rogues, pilgrims watch the goings-on, leaning on their staffs.

A solemn Mass is held today and every morning for the next twenty-nine days. Then the trumpets crack the air. The competition is on. The crowd hushes. Two knights ride towards each other, their long lances horizontal, their shields held tight on their arms. Under the sun, their helmets shine softly like pewter. Horses' hooves knock the ground. The knights nearly collide, veer off, come back and run at it again. The crowd erupts in cheers, the hats bob as a lance flies up in the air, broken in two; a man is down. The judges make their call and a new competitor comes forward. Again and again, day after day. Each night there are celebrations. A daily message is sent to Don Suero's mother, who is in a constant fret and prays without ceasing at his home in Laguna de Negrillos.

The play is stopped for just one day: July 25, Feast of St. James. On the 26th, it's jousting as usual. Only one man is killed, an Aragonese knight named Esberte de Claramonte, caught in the eye by a badly aimed lance. He may have belonged in the company of nine knights competing under a certain Gutierre de Quijada. Gutierre is himself defeated by Don Suero, fairly, mind you, but he takes it badly.

On the evening of the final day, with his last competitor down, Don Suero tosses himself from his inexhaustible horse, bows to the crowd, and makes his way amid a trumpet fanfare through a tunnel of torchlight to the judges. Solemnly he removes the iron shackle from his neck and is pronounced free at last from his prison of love - whatever that meant. How the lady liked losing her prisoner is, of course, not recorded.

The event made front page news in Europe as one of the most ambitious and certainly one of the longest jousting competitions ever. Purists complained that the old religious values of courtly love had degenerated. The Bishop of León, thoroughly disgusted, denied any knight killed in the competition a burial on consecrated ground. There was a time, he grumbled, when the deeds inspired by adoration of an unattainable woman had been a battle for virtue in the interior self and on the battlefield for Christ and the Virgin; now that love was just a flimsy excuse for a sensationalized contest of brutes.

In later centuries, the exploits of Don Suero would be variously interpreted. To some, he was the last member of a heroic caste that had begun with Roland in his battles with Ferragut and the Moors. Others saw him as an anti-romantic who tried to play a note of realism in the fanciful mystique of the knight errant. It has been argued recently that Don Suero wanted to restore the prestige of León, and to unite, in the image of the knight, Leonese imperialism with the universal concept of Christianity as it was represented in the Camino. After the tournament, Don Suero did in fact go first to León to pay his respects to San Isidore, the patron of León. He also attended a ceremony commemorating the Battle of Clavijo. Then he went with his nine men to Santiago as the modest pilgrim he always intended to be. There he offered a gold bracelet to the saint - some say it had belonged to his lady. This bracelet, Valiña tells us, is the one that now encircles the neck of the processional bust of St. James the Lesser.

Twenty-four years later, Don Suero is exiled from León for rebellion in connection, surprisingly, with Santiago de Compostela. In Navarra, he meets up with Gutierre de Quijada, who is still smarting from his defeat in 1434. Suero is killed by Gutierre in hand-to-hand combat. Gutierre's name closely resembles that of the great-uncle of the wife of Miguel de Cervantes. Some say Don Suero was his inspiration for *Don Quixote*; Cervantes mentions the tournament of 1434 in his famous novel.

When Scott and I were cycling into Astorga in May 1997, I had a flat tire. We pumped it up enough to get up the last hill, past the Cathedral with its overdone facade, and into a narrow park that ran between the Bishop's Palace and the Gaudi Hotel. We checked into the Gaudi, then took my bike and the patch kit into the park, where

Scott, with a man's endearing alacrity, busied himself with the repair. "It's an act of love," he said.

An elderly Astorgan gentleman had observed us from a bench on the other side of the fountain. Now, on bowed, arthritic legs, he walked over to us. Excusing himself, he suggested we use the fountain to find the hole in the tire. By now the thing was nearly fixed, but we invited him to stay and talk. He was curious about our bicycles, told us he too had been a cyclist in his younger days. It was clear that he missed those times. Listening to him, I felt it wasn't his physical decline that bothered him as much as the pain of being excluded and forgotten, or, worse still, ridiculed. He seemed to want us to know that like us, he had also pushed his bike at full throttle across the meseta flats, and swooped down the hills with the wind jetting past his ears. Our interest in him now, and in his memories, gave him back a place in that carefree eager world. I liked him very much, and after we had talked about his cycling past, I asked him about Astorga.

"Famous for hostels during the pilgrimage years," was all he said about the Camino.

I commented on Astorga's religious heritage. From the 3rd Century, it had been an important Christian city. Priscillian's heresy had flourished here, along with who knows how many other cults. Later there were Visigothic monasteries here too.

"They say St. James and St. Paul both preached here," said our new friend, "but personally" - he frowned and made an erasing motion with a gnarled index finger - "I have doubts about that."

He switched to a topic he thought much more interesting: the ethnic heritage of Astorga. I had read about the Maragatos, the mysterious people of the lands between Astorga and Ponferrada. The Maragatos may have been among the earliest inhabitants of the region. One theory claims they were Phoenicians who arrived from the Atlantic coast and were later enslaved by the Romans to work the local mines. Perhaps they were Berbers, or Moors, or Jews, or Mozarabs, or what have you. "They have wonderful food," our new friend said. "You should try the pastries." He pursed his lips and his face crinkled in delight at the thought.

I asked the man if he was a Maragato.

"Yes," he replied with a smile. "But many in my family have left the area. They drive taxis now, things like that, in Madrid, Sevilla."

"You should visit the Gaudi Museum," the man said, poking his thumb backwards to the white granite confection across the road. "It was to be the Bishop's Palace but the bishop died before it was finished. No one liked it anyway." He shrugged. "In the Sixties, when I was still a young man, it was made into a museum."

"It's worth seeing then?" asked Scott.

"Sí, sí!" he answered, sticking out his lower lip indignantly and frowning, as if we had just asked him whether there were any good Spanish wines.

The Bishop's Palace stands just inside the Roman walls that overlook the valley of the Rio Tuerga. It is said to be neo-Gothic, but from the outside, it is closer to a Gothic caricature, more a fairy castle than the palace of a 19th-century bishop. It had everything you expected of a fairies: a moat, thin circular turrets drooling with windows of blue stained glass, a collection of peaks like a box of witches' hats, steep slate roofs and a spider's web of white granite in a brickwork facade.

In 1887 the Bishop of Astorga, Juan Bautista Grau I Villespinós, asked his old friend from Catalonia, a promising young architect named Antonio Gaudi, to draw up plans for a new palace on the site where his old one had burned down. The design was, to say the least, unusual; the Bishop liked it, but everyone else hated it, as the man in the park had said, including the regulatory Academia de San Fernand in Madrid. The construction ran into difficulties. The bishop died. Gaudi abandoned the thing in disgust in 1893, and it sat half-built until around 1913, when Ricardo Guereta finished it. In 1963 it was opened as the "Museum of the Ways," dedicated to the history of all the roads that ran in and out of Astorga.

If the outside of Gaudi's palace creates whimsically Gothic expectations, once inside you quickly discover that a crucial ingredient is missing: height. The palace was a Gothic midget laid out in the rough shape of a Latin cross. The low vaults, their ribs painted in geometrical designs, arched over us like a cup from a child's tea set.

We walked through softly lit rooms decorated with fine paintings and sculptures. Gaudi's inspiration, if not his personal touch, infused the whole place. He himself had designed the stained glass windows. In the room dedicated to St. James, where the vaults unfolded into little nooks with panes of coloured glass, the light seemed to come from somewhere other than the windows and the air was infused ever so slightly with nameless shades of pink and blue, yellow and green.

The palace had reassuringly human proportions. I felt like a participant - or more, an inhabitant - of each room we entered. The Gothic architect had striven to represent God's paradise in a colossus of stone, but in Gaudi's little Gothic comedy of a palace, you could expand your heart into all the spaces and in doing so discover a heaven within yourself.

Our friend in the park had mentioned the Roman origins of Astorga. The Celts had been here before the Romans, but he had been right: it was the Romans who had turned Asturica Augustus into a nerve centre of commercial activity. At one time, nine important roads led to and from Astorga, of which the most famous were the one that would become the Camino, running west from the military post at León to the mines of Galicia and the Atlantic coast, and the one that connected that east-west route to Mérida, or Emerita Augustus, on the route from Sevilla. The man had also told us that every August, a festival commemorated the day in AD 31 when Caesar Augustus came to town.

By sheer chance, I was in Astorga on that anniversary day in August 1998. After registering at the *refugio* and taking a short rest, I went for a walk to the large square by the town hall. It was nearly dark, and the square was strung with coloured lights that made it look like Christmas. A stage had been set up and a live band was lurching self-consciously through something by the Rolling Stones. People were gathering on cordoned off sidewalks.

Abruptly, as if silenced by a peace-loving parent, the band stopped before its song was over. There was a brief lull. Then from a side street came a blast of trumpets and a noisy shudder of drums. I turned to a woman standing beside me with a young child in her arms. "*Que pasa?*" I inquired.

She regarded me with a mischievous smile and said, as if it was a secret: "Caesar is coming!" Her husband, who was holding another child, turned his head to me and laughed.

Line after line of drummers marched into the square, wearing tunics of shiny white polyester with green sashes on the diagonal. Behind them came the trumpeters and a bevy of young women wearing white robes, with thick blue bands over one shoulder. A squadron of Roman centurions rattled in, holding their spears vertical and grinning in a very un-Roman manner at the kids who leaned eagerly against the wood barriers on the sidewalk. Caught for a few seconds in the street lights, each soldier, especially the ones wearing glasses, had a glaring, brassy look, as in a surreal dream, each with his shiny helmet and tall plume like a punk rocker's hair, and a flashing plate of armour. All around me, people cheered and waved. Fair ladies were being carried to the stage on palanquins by slaves in red capes and Birkenstock sandals. The girls reclined like Playboy centrefolds under the canopy of their litters, their dark hair streaming over the pillows and their tunics hitched to the thighs. There was clapping and more cheering, and teenaged boys whistled huskily.

Augustus Caesar entered the square, announced by trumpets, flanked by centurions. He mounted the stage, now unlit except by the lights that blazed in the darkness like a sign from the gods. Walking back and forth, his left arm swinging in a grand, Shakespearean arc, he read us his speech, expounded on Rome's legacy in Astorga. When he officially opened the coming week of festivities, the crowd hailed him exultantly, and the trumpets and drums made the neon lights quiver.

His oration complete, Augustus paraded with his men off the stage and out of the plaza. The entourage of ladies and slaves and drummers and trumpeters began a slow, ragged exit, which eventually dribbled out altogether as one after another stopped to chat with friends in the crowd. Everyone was waiting for the dance to start. I knew we were in for more would-be Stones, so I returned to the hostel. But I wouldn't have missed the coming of Caesar Augustus to Astorga on a warm (August!) night for the world.

The Templar Castle at Ponferrada was closed the morning that Scott and I had wheeled into town from Molinaseca in May 1997. We decided to look for a place to buy food before carrying on to Villafranca del Bierzo. We walked our bikes through the old town with the traffic winding around us like a boa constrictor. After fifteen minutes, we found a small store across the road from the Castle. A few white plastic chairs were set outside the door beside a confusion of wooden crates and boxes of produce. Inside the shop was the usual scattering of candy, cold meats, yogurts and flans, soft drinks, batteries, pens and toilet paper. We bought peach juice and went to sit outside. Across from us, the Castle perched like a giant stone and mortar nest over the passing traffic: a realist's version of Gaudi's fairy pavilions at Astorga. I almost expected to see Don Suero walk down the ramp from the castle gate.

Three pilgrims strode past us toward a bar that leaned onto the road next to the store. An Irish voice called in our direction: "God in heaven! You wouldn't be after drinkin' juice now wdj'a, when there's beer next door?" The man reappeared in a few minutes with his friends and a couple of pints. "Never let it be said that an Irishman said hello and never stopped to visit." He pulled up a chair and plunked it and himself down beside us. The store owner came out immediately, brought tables (white plastic) over from somewhere and wiped them clean, then collected a few wooden boxes for us to put our feet on. The two companions disappeared into the shop, and returned carrying big bocadillos - long breads with meat flopping out along their edges like a row of thin red tongues. The Irishman, whose name was Keith, bought chocolate. We went back inside for yogurt and fruit.

Keith was walking that day with two pilgrims, one Dutch, the other Australian. The arrangement was friendly but apparently temporary. The three had met the evening before at a convent in Astorga that offered a hostel to pilgrims. "The nuns were a tough lot," said Keith. "Real sticklers for the rules. We had to be in bed - such as it was - before ten, and then they locked us in this morning while they went to Mass. Just left us alone in there! We weren't sure if they were planning to come back to let us out!" He broke off some chocolate and handed it to me. "You didn't happen to see my friend Tommy back the way now did you?" he asked.

"Why yes!" I said, "you mean Tommy from Scotland, with the sore feet and the German walking sticks?"

"That's the lad," said Keith.

"We talked to him near Sahagún, and then ran into him at the big hotel in Burgos," said Scott. "Quite a character."

Keith and Tommy had started the trip together, but when Tommy's feet had slowed him down, they had decided to separate. They communicated by calling Tommy's wife in Scotland every couple of days, and were hoping to meet up to walk into Santiago together. We gave our latest report on Tommy from Burgos. "Fine lad," said Keith of his friend. "Don't know what the hell he's doin' on the Camino though."

I said he had told us he was trying to sort out where to go next in his life. "Ha!" said Keith. "Did he tell you he's figured it out? The man's been doin' that all his bloody life!"

I asked Keith why *he* was on the Camino. He thought a moment, then said, "I've had a good time of it. I'm doing this pilgrimage out of gratitude. I was raised by the nuns, you see, and I survived."

The Australian offered that he liked to travel on foot and wanted to see the world. He'd always heard about the Camino and the idea of a pilgrimage appealed to him. He was a pleasant, attractive man in his early thirties, soft spoken, quietly sure of himself. He stood up and began to stretch his legs, spreading them wide and bending from the waist. "It's good to stretch," he said, exhaling, "when you're walking so much." The Dutch pilgrim hung back, looking painfully shy.

We talked nearly an hour in the sunshine. I felt very relaxed, but this was partly from pure fatigue. I had not slept well in several nights, had been tormented with dreams, as if I was trying to work out some confusion in my mind that refused to reveal itself completely. I fervently wished we didn't have another twenty kilometres to go before we stopped at Villafranca del Bierzo.

We had kept the shopkeeper busy with many rounds of food and drink. Before I left the store for the last time, he handed me a postcard with a picture of the Castle. "Un recuerdo," he smiled, and shook my hand. I tucked this souvenir into my diary before we left. I thought of his gentleness and quiet generosity as we pulled out around the Templar Castle to leave Ponferrada along the old N-VI highway to Villafranca. I was too tired to miss not seeing the Templar Castle, and besides, the experience of the good man's warmth was better than any tour of an old stone building.

The following year, I arrived on foot in Ponferrada almost exactly on time for a Castle tour. The day was belligerently bright. I walked up the stone ramp to the gate off the street where the shopkeeper still had his place. Restoration work had moved quickly over the past year. About ten people waited with me for the tour to begin, inside freshly scoured stone walls. Our guide was a nervous, dark-haired woman who seemed tentatively to enjoy what she was doing. She spoke in such rapid Spanish that I had to ask her to slow down. But this gave her some trouble; she hesitated a few times in her talk and then confessed to the rest of the group, all Spaniards and French, that when she goes slow, she forgets her speech. Everybody laughed and a couple of people looked at me sympathetically.

The town that would later be known as Ponferrada had begun as a little Asturian settlement in a womb-like loop of land lying between the Rio Baeza and its tributary the Sil. There was gold in the hills around the settlement, and when the Romans arrived, bringing with them their technology, their machine-like greed and their superb organization, they exploited the area without the slightest reservation. They erected a fortress, turned the place into a local hub in their road system. A bridge built over the Sil only improved the situation.

Over the centuries, the place saw its share of violence. It was destroyed by the Visigoths in the 5th Century and again by the Moors in the 9th. It was rebuilt by Alfonso III. By the late 11th Century, the old Roman bridge, a wooden construction, looked to be in danger of collapsing. Osmundo, bishop of Astorga, was alarmed by the danger it posed to pilgrims and had it fortified with iron. This won for the town its present name, Ponferrada, for *Pons ferratus*, Ironbridge. In the 12th Century, the town was handed over to the Knights Templar, who put up the Castle.

Our guide soldiered through her speech. I stared out from where we stood on the parapet across the Rio Sil to the hill opposite. It was clear cut and scarred with roads and erosion. To the east, irregular farmlands stretched back toward Molinaseca. Beyond them, dusted by a haze of heat, were the mountain slopes descending out of Irago Pass.

The builders of the Ponferrada Castle - the Order of the Knights of the Temple - first entered history in Jerusalem. The idea for the order was conceived around 1118 by Hugh of Payens, a knight from Champagne, as a way of protecting pilgrims against the perils of the roads to the Holy Land. The knights were serious fellows, poor to begin with (Hugh had to share his horse with one of his supporters), and filled with "a horror of chess and dice." They despised hunting, mimes, jugglers, story-tellers, dirty songs, and the performances of buffoons, all of which they regarded as vanities and inane follies. They lived in community under a severe rule based on monastic vows of poverty, chastity and obedience.

The rule of the Order is said to have been devised by Bernard of Clairvaux, the great monastic champion of the Crusades. But there was a crucial difference between the monk and the knight. Monks could not bear arms and were forbidden to commit murder. The practical matter at hand was that Christian lands were in peril, and killing the enemy seemed the only way out. The Knights were created to get around the problem, their fourth vow, after poverty, chastity and obedience, being armed defense of the Holy Land. The Order's headquarters in Jerusalem was a former mosque near the enclosure where Solomon's temple had once stood, and from which the order took its name.

There was a pilgrim hospital in Jerusalem around this same time. Run by the Hospitalers, it could hold 2,000 patients and even had an obstetrical ward. It was not long after the Templars were founded that this group too, on the initiative of another French noble, formed its own order of knights. Their headquarters were near the Church of St. John the Baptist. Here the Hospitalers (they were also called Knights of St. John of Jerusalem or the Sanjuanistas) continued to care for the sick and poor while working with the Templars to defend Christian territory.

The Templars and the Hospitalers received rich support from church and secular donations throughout Europe. Within a few decades, they had created an international network of religious houses using land grants handed out by heads of states in return for successful campaigns. The Grand Master of the order was eventually responsible directly to the Pope.

Only a few years after their founding in Jerusalem, the Templars and the Hospitalers arrived in Spain. Their role in helping and defending pilgrims was easily transferred to the Camino, where the Moors were still a threat, but their land holdings here, which were enormous, also contributed to their work in the Holy Land.

From their castles, such as the one here at Ponferrada, the knights managed large tracts of fertile land, often renting them out to local farmers. They made huge profits from grain, livestock, wine and orchards, and used the money for religious observances, to pay monks who prayed for the souls of departed knights, to finance military campaigns both in the Holy Land and in southern Spain, and to provide hospitality for pilgrims.

The Sanjuanistas eventually ran estates and hospices all along the Camino from Logroño to Carrion de los Condes and Calzadilla de la Cueza. From a peace-keeper's point of view, they were an attractive addition to the area; they were international and non-partisan, and they helped create a buffer between the warring factions of royalty tearing back and forth between the Cea and the Pisuerga Rivers.

The Templar Order was also firmly established in Spain by the late 12th Century, though the number of their holdings was smaller than those of the Sanjuanistas. Villalcazar de Sirga was its primary location. There were interests too at Eunate (it is thought), Puente la Reina, Carrión de los Condes, Rabanal del Camino, and here at Ponferrada.

The Templars may have had an ulterior purpose in taking over Ponferrada. Along with looking after pilgrims and protecting the Camino, especially along the two passes, Irago and Cebreiro, they may have been after the gold remaining in the hills mined by the Romans. The story carries, if nothing else, a certain metaphoric truth. Both the Templars and the Sanjuanistas were becoming rich as kings. By the 13th Century, they were treasurers for the French kings, and had developed a system of money-transfer that earned them the sobriquet "the bankers of Europe." They invested in shipping, even established one of the few reliable Holy Land pilgrim travel agencies. The Grand Masters of both Orders were advisors to royalty and at the peak of their power, they controlled almost forty percent of Europe's frontiers.

Like multi-national corporations now, of which they are rough medieval analogue, the Templars drew both grudging respect and violent criticism. With wealth and power came competition and jealousy. The Orders began to vie with each other and to quarrel with royal courts and feudal aristocracies. A kind of hubris set in, a creeping arrogance and moral carelessness that attracted even more resentment. William of Tyre criticised the Templars' "neglect of humility." They looked too greedy, too insidiously powerful, too self-serving to be trusted. By the 14th Century, they were over the crest: their very power was about to make them vulnerable.

The Hospitalers were able to duck most of the controversies, but the Templars were caught, partly by their own intemperate money-mongering, on the flywheel of French politics. King Philip the Fair was close to broke, having borrowed and taxed to the limit. The Templars were, conveniently, filthy rich and openly resented. In 1307, every Templar in France but twelve was rounded up by Philip's henchmen. It took forty-eight hours. The men were imprisoned and accused of heresy, homosexuality, blasphemy, and the worship of idols. Torture was liberally applied and confessions extracted. In 1310, fifty-four Templars were burned at the stake. In 1312, Pope Clement officially repressed the Order. In 1314, Jacques de Molay, the Grand Master of the Templars was himself put to the stake, recanting his confession made under torture and maintaining his own innocence and that of his Order.

The Templars' archives in Spain were mostly destroyed and their patrimony dispersed. By 1340, Ponferrada belonged to the Counts of Lemos. When Isabella and Ferdinand came to the throne of a united Spain in 1492, the Castle became theirs. New controversies and claims over its possession began, involving various bastard granddaughters, upstarts and usurpers. It was at this time, during the 15th Century said our guide, most of whose speech about this castle I had missed, that new courtrooms were added, along with a drawbridge, a few towers and a gate. In the 19th Century, Napoleon toyed with the idea of blowing it up, but decided instead to blast other parts of the old town to rubble.

I scanned the Castle walls as the guide sped away to the end of her speech. From certain angles, a hint of something romantic flickered in the spaces between the towers; it did look vaguely like a fairy tale castle, I decided, but without any slimness or gleam. It was hard to imagine a courtly, or even a monastic life here. The stones were mottled and weathered, and the place had the grizzled look of a worldweary warrior. Its tall, pock-marked turrets made me think of Rapunzel, with her long, long hair gone gray and in need of a brush.

Before leaving Ponferrada, I dropped in to see the nice shopkeeper across the street from the castle. I bought a couple of things. He didn't recognize me, but I reminded him that we had visited his shop last year, and that I still had the card he gave me. His face lit up and he seized my hand to shake it warmly. Then he kissed it. "Que placer!" he cried, "What a pleasure! Thank you for coming to see me again." As I left he waved from the door. "Adios, mi amor," he smiled, "y buen viaje a Santiago !"

Only a few years after the fall of the Templars in 1312, and around the same time that Ponferrada was being handed over to the Counts of Lemos, William Langland was at a desk in his home in the English countryside writing line after line of the long - the very long - dream poem, *The Vision of Piers Plowman*. William wrote of the diseases that were running like a plague among his fellow Christians all around Europe. Not diseases of the flesh, though God knows there were enough of those, but diseases of the spirit. His poem was, first of all, a diagnosis: fashion and comfort, bribery and vice had infected God's Church. The love of Truth that had kept the early church (or the memory of it) clean and clear had, amid the heavings of social and economic change, cooled like a tub of old dishwater. Pilgrimage, that great devotional discipline, had unravelled into mere frivolity. Unlike Geoffrey Chaucer, his urban, and more urbane, compatriot a few decades later, William was never coy or amusing in *Piers Plowman*. Instead, his words cut like a knife into the moral cancer that was bringing the church, and with it the pilgrimage to Santiago, to near ruin in the later Middle Ages. The problem William described had many facets, and he raged against most of them. But they all stemmed from one foul practice: the traffic in indulgences.

The indulgence problem had already been around a long time when it cropped up innocently enough at the Church of Santiago, near Villafranca del Bierzo, in the 15th Century. Today this plain, right-angled church looks utterly forlorn in its gravelly, unkempt yard. Scott and I arrived here late one afternoon after a gruelling ride on N-

VI from Ponferrada. I felt utterly spent as we approached the church up a hill on a street lined with low, boxy houses. We plunked ourselves onto the steps of the north portal and drank the last of our water, looking down into the town of Villafranca del Bierzo and beyond it to the Ancares mountains into Galicia.

The name of the Romanesque north portal of the Church of Santiago is *La Puerta del Perdon*, or the Door of Pardon or Remission, after an edict issued by the Spanish Pope, Calixto III in the 1450s. In the chipped sculptures on the piers and the archivolt around the portal you can make out paired figures of the apostles, along with a Crucifixion and scenes from the Adoration of the Magi.

Calixto was responding to a long-standing difficulty with the Santiago pilgrimage. Villafranca del Bierzo is, at a leisurely rate, only nine or ten days from Santiago, but for pilgrims who had barely made it to the Bierzo on the dregs of their endurance, the steep pass ahead to El Cebreiro and the long descent through Galicia was going to be impossible. Calixto therefore granted that pilgrims whose lives would surely be up before their journey to Compostela was over could kneel here in the north doorway of the Church of Santiago to receive their absolution and a plenary indulgence. La Puerta del Perdon became a kind of stand-in or surrogate for the Holy Door, the Puerta Santa, at Santiago Cathedral. Even today, every Jubilee Year, the Puerta at Villafranca is opened just like the one in Santiago.

Sitting here in the portal, tired but healthy, I felt a sudden wave of tenderness for all the pilgrims who had hobbled onto these steps knowing that their lives were nearly over, but that they were blessed and forgiven here even as if they had gone on to Santiago. This was such a modest little church, yet the emotions expressed on these steps must have broken the hearts of the kind priests who stood waiting with their sacraments.

La Puerta del Perdon was a sensible idea. But like many good ideas in bad times, it had floated to the surface of a dubious brew that had boiled like an evil potion for centuries. The practice of granting indulgences began in the 10th Century. The sacrament of penance was not a light matter; punishments, often physical, prescribed by the church for the humble penitent could be severe. There were always a few people who couldn't take it. Thus the indulgence came about as a payment made to the church by the sinner that excused her from going through the physical motions of penance. It was never to be confused with the removal of guilt for the sins committed, though of course it was.

In the beginning, the indulgence was carefully considered; it was common to make only a partial pay-off of the penance. But the practice slackened, becoming first an easy substitute for the sacrament of penance, and then a psychological substitute for guilt and contrition; you could soothe your conscience with a payment, but you didn't actually have to change your ways. The new habit of indulgences cleared the path for a new occupation: the pardoner, a travelling indulgence salesman who went round preaching and collecting money from semi-repentant sinners. The job had obvious loopholes and it attracted just the kind of low-lifes crafty enough to make the most of them. In *Piers Plowman*, William's pardoner preaches like a priest, but hands out indulgences to any gullible wretch who will pay him. How much of the money got back to the Church was another story. The pardoner, the epitome of debased Christian values, became a lightning rod for public cynicism about a money-grubbing church and its corrupted officials. Chaucer puts a pardoner in his troop of pilgrims to Canterbury. He's a dandy from Rouncivale, on the edge of London (where there was, interestingly, a branch of the Spanish convent of Our Lady of Roncesvalles, whose mother house was on the Camino). The pardoner is tarted up in the latest fashion; his stringy blonde hair is splayed over his shoulders. His mincing mannerisms suggest the usual homosexual stereotypes. He carries a bag of indulgences "hot from Rome" and a packet of good relics: a pillowcase that was Our Lady's veil, a piece of the sail from St. Peter's boat.

Towards the end of the 11th Century, pilgrimage itself began to shift from being a form of penance to being a form of indulgence. "In order to help the sinner to achieve his salvation" pronounced Pope Urban II on his visit to France to preach the first Crusade in 1095,

> [we] recommend ... that the Church of St. Nicholas of Angers be honoured, protected, and visited by the faithful..., and we accordingly remit a seventh part of the penance imposed for any sins, for all those who visit the church in a devout frame of a mind on the anniversary of its dedication.

Like their relics, indulgences became a staple product of pilgrimage churches, attracting those sinners anxious to lop off as many days in Purgatory as they could, and in as brief and convenient a way as possible. The competition was fierce. The large churches vied with each other for pilgrims, while smaller ones often forged indulgences for themselves if the Pope wouldn't grant them one. Pilgrim guidebooks started carrying indulgence information, to save you time and energy as you dashed from one shrine to the next. A Sicilian woman who expected to get her dead son out of purgatory through indulgences granted at Santiago de Compostela was given a vision from her son. "Dear mother," he pleaded,

> the pilgrimage which you are about to make is a fine and worthy act, but it will not do much for me. If you wish to liberate me from my sins you must go not only to Santiago but also to the church of Maria de Angelis at the Portiuncula. Only then shall I be released from Purgatory.

The Camino's indulgence business had much to do with the Crusades. In 1095 Pope Urban II proclaimed that every crusader was a full-fledged pilgrim, for each one was fulfilling a personal act of penance by fighting for God's cause. In return for their brave exploits for Christendom, the pilgrim-fighters would receive a plenary indulgence. This meant a lifetime of sins would be wiped clean off the knight's slate. Even better, if he died in battle, heaven was automatically his. This emphasis on paying a spiritual debt rather than on personal reform paved the way for the vicarious crusade: by the 12th Century, crusaders who were themselves unable to fight could pay someone else to fight for them, and still get a plenary indulgence.

Before long, pilgrimage itself came to be done vicariously: you could get yourself an indulgence merely by paying the cost of a trip to the pilgrimage church of your choice. In April 1330, a certain Agnes de Rocquefort paid 133 gold lambs and five shillings to get herself out of a long walk to Santiago. By 1400, the practice was common. Alternatively, you could pay somebody to go in your place. In Scandinavia, many of the contracts for professional pilgrims and for their services still survive.

By the 15th Century, when Calixto made what seemed the perfectly reasonable grant of a plenary indulgence here at Villafranca del Bierzo for people who couldn't make it to Santiago, most pilgrimage churches had become hopelessly dependent on revenues from indulgences to stay financially afloat. A spiritual disaster had occurred.

Thinking people could see it coming. As far back as 813, the Council of Chalons had spoken out against "the simple-minded notion that sinners need only catch sight of a shrine of the saints and their sins will be absolved." In the 12th Century, the *Veneranda Dies* made it very clear that pilgrimage minus contrition was worthless, and admonished pilgrims to make a sincere confession in a state of true regret for their sins. By the 14th Century, the abuse of indulgences was causing great public cynicism. A French contemporary of William Langland observed icily, "he who goes to St. James and then kills his father commits no mortal sin." And as Langland's dreamer says in *Piers Plowman*:

> Pilgrims pledge themselves together to go to seek St. James or the saints at Rome, go out on their way with many wise tales, and come back and lie for the rest of their lives about the wonders they had seen at the tombs of the saints.

The allegorical Lady Reason says she will have no mercy on men until they visit St. James, not at his Galician tomb, but in his teachings. Will makes a pun on the idea of visiting by quoting from the only Epistle actually written by the Apostle James: "Pure religion and undefiled before God and the Father is this, to visit the fatherless and widows in their affliction, and to keep himself unspotted from the world."

But the world was not yet ready for Lady Reason's corrections. It would take the earthquake of the Protestant Reformation to cure, or at least palliate, the Church's sick fondness for indulgences.

Tired and ready for a bite to eat, we left the steps of the Church of Santiago and cruised down the long hill into Villafranca del Bierzo. We checked into a modest hotel - Casa Mendez - and took a room overlooking the burbling Rio Burbia. We had a fine dinner - soup, pork, bread, fruit, cheese and wine - served without a trace of finesse. That night, I slept better than I had in days. Next morning, the hotel credit card machine broke down; we paid in cash, but the señora reduced the price for us, in case, she said, we were short on cash later when we really needed it.

Two days later, we were on our way from El Cebreiro to Triacastela and then Sarria. The Camino followed the highway a short distance along the spine of a long, graceful hill towards Alto de San Roque. We stopped on the ridge to linger by a larger than life bronze statue of a traditional pilgrim. The man seemed to be in motion, pressing westward against the wind as if shouldering sideways through a door, one arm crooked up holding his hat to his head and the other gripping his staff, with its gourd and cross on top. Whatever forces of history and faith had moulded the Santiago pilgrimage over the centuries, this image has remained constant. Here was the eternal pilgrim, with the wind plastering his tunic to his legs and lifting the flap of his cape as he pushed through the elements towards the western horizon.

From Triacastela we headed to Sarria by way of Samos. The distance is considerably longer than the direct route from Triacastela, but many pilgrims in the past had chosen this longer road because they had heard of the hospitality in the Benedictine monastery there. The road to Samos descended a curved hill toward the slender Ouribio River. The monastery sat on its banks, a collection of dark grey, stone buildings of three or four stories, with shallow roofs and the occasional spike of a cross.

There had been a monastery here in the 7th Century, which in the 8th was occupied by monks from Toledo and Córdoba who were fleeing the Moors. A mixed monastery, it was run by Abbot Areginas and his sister Sarra, and had been placed under the spiritual protection of a parallel couple, St. Julian and his virgin wife Basilisa, of Antioch, who had died as martyrs in 309 during the persecutions of Diocletian. Statues of Julian and Basilisa look down from the front facade of the monastery church, just above one of St. Benedict.

In the 10th Century, the place had to be reconsecrated due to "evil deeds" committed by certain of its monks. You might think first of all of sexual indiscretions in this monastery of men and women, but the problem was likely more serious, having to do yet again with the heresies of Priscillian, which blew like fluffy bullrush seeds through the hamlets of Galicia during the Middle Ages.

The Benedictine Rule came to Samos at the end of the 10th Century, and the monastery underwent the Cluniac Reforms of the 12th. In the 16th, it was rebuilt in a mixture of styles, few of which I was moved by during our tour. Samos remained in Benedictine hands over the years, and in keeping with Benedictine tradition, offered ample hospitality for pilgrims and wayfarers. Though its facilities were probably not as developed as those at Nájera or Sahagún, the records show that there were separate lodgings for rich and for poor pilgrims, and probably an infirmary.

We were shown through the monastery by a monk in a creaseless black habit. Despite the Benedictine enthusiasm for hospitality, his tour had an air of perfunctory resignation. But while we stood in the oversized cloister, an older monk waddled cheerfully down the corridor and greeted us as if he was thoroughly glad to see us. We chatted, and Scott asked him how many monks lived in the community here.

He lifted his head slightly and looked straight at us. "We are eight," he said. That seemed pitifully few. "We are eight," he repeated, "but we are good." A delightful smile wrinkled his face.

Heading back into the sunshine after the monastery tour, we were happily surprised to find Else and Heinrich leaning their bicycles just behind ours against the wall.

"We thought these were yours!" they said, pointing to our red bike packs. "We're so pleased to see you again! We've been wondering about you ever since our dinner in Logroño." Else's smile was radiant and Heinrich, as always, wore the expression of an alert, friendly businessman. The next tour wasn't starting for another hour, so we invited them to share a late-day snack. We sat on park benches facing the long, lugubrious wall of the monastery, with the big leaves of shady trees at our backs.

"How did you like Samos?" asked Else.

"Fine," said Scott, "but we're not wild about the Renaissance or the Baroque. Mary thinks it's too worldly."

"The cloister is the biggest in Spain," said Else.

"Yes, but too big for me," I said. "It seemed less like a cloister and more like a park."

"When they are too big, they lose their intimacy, it's true," Else replied.

Else and Heinrich's pilgrimage was a true spiritual exercise. They were on clumsy old three-speed bikes; they had few of the gadgets or gear that other pilgrims, including us, were carrying. No fleece, no gortex. They restricted their diet, had sworn off chocolate and wine until they got home. And not to lose weight.

Scott and I had been wondering how Protestant believers responded to the Catholic iconography of the Camino. "How do you make a pilgrimage through this kind of foreign theology," I asked Else and Heinrich, "when every day you see imagery that doesn't always fit, even aesthetically, with how you see your Christian faith?"

Heinrich thought a minute. "The Camino is almost all that is available to us as Christian pilgrims. Of course we don't believe in the idea of relics and indulgences or the intercession of saints. But our faith still has its roots in those old traditions; Luther had to start somewhere, and a flower never looks like its seed. We think the Holy Spirit works through history to provide people what they need at the time. If you believe the flow of history is divinely guided, you have to believe that the forms of the Spirit evolve - not God himself, but the way He shows himself and the rituals he asks of you - those things change to fit the changes in our human situation."

"So why is the Camino attractive to Protestants?" asked Scott, "when there is so little that reflects a Protestant way of thinking?"

"It *isn't* that attractive to Protestants, but it should be," answered Heinrich. "The rise of Protestantism was in a way the end of pilgrimage. Many people at the time predicted that the Camino to Santiago would be forgotten after the Reformation. And the Catholic Church blamed the Protestants for the decline of the big pilgrimage sites when that prediction almost came true."

I recalled reading about someone from the time referring to the Protestants as "that evil knave Luther and his band of accomplices like Erasmus."

"Yes, the reformers upset the Catholics because they were against indulgences and the worship of relics. But in my opinion," Heinrich went on, "by getting rid of those things, they accidently threw out pilgrimage too. You see, indulgences and all that are just trends in theology that come and go, but pilgrimage itself has many legitimate styles, and there is no reason, I don't think, why being a Protestant means you don't go on pilgrimages. Look at that English pilgrim's story, for instance. I can't remember the author."

"Bunyan? The Pilgrim's Progress?"

"Ach, yes, that's it. We have a German translation at home."

"But that's really just an allegory, an inner journey in an allegorical landscape."

"Of course, but the idea is there, that just by being in the world, you can travel towards the Holy Spirit. There's no reason why you can't act that out literally, as a sort of spiritual lesson for your body. We feel we are rebuilding a connection that shouldn't have been broken in the first place, between travelling in the world and seeking God's presence in your life."

"What kind of a relationship do you feel you have with St. James?" I asked.

"James was Christ's disciple and whether he is there in the tomb in Santiago or not, you are still walking there to honour him as someone who knew the Lord. It's a symbol for us more than a reality. We don't need to have James in Spain the way the Spaniards do, but by going to a place where he was traditionally honoured, you honour him too, wherever he is.

Else spoke. "You refresh your own faith by the memory that Christ lived in this world and had men like James as his friends."

Scott asked if they had any special hopes or expectations for when they arrived in Santiago .

Heinrich pondered a while, looking at Else. "I really don't know," he replied. "Just the trip itself is a blessing, seeing this beautiful land of Spain, being with Else all the time, feeling physically better every day from the good exercise, and of course we are following a traditional route of Christian devotion. Compostela, I think, will be like a celebration of what we've been feeling all along."

We had asked Heinrich and Else questions that were extremely personal, and I was grateful to them for revealing so much to us. I thought about Heinrich's ideas, and liked them. He was right that theological and religious history is unique to its culture, but pilgrimage is an activity that every human soul understands. I thought too that even though some of the means of pilgrimage would change, and even the expressed reasons for undertaking one, the act of pilgrimage itself was a constant: an instinct toward the sacred that is tucked into human nature like a muscle in a leg.

Many months after leaving the Camino, Scott and I were travelling in South America. One evening, we ate dinner in a Montevideo restaurant with, as it happened, a marine archeologist from Canada. Robert Grenier was attending a meeting of the Basque Association of Montevideo. He himself had Basque ancestors. The conversation began with the Basque heritage of northern Spain but later moved to the Camino, and then to the religious changes in Spain in the later years of the Santiago pilgrimage.

"Nobody could get through to Spain after the Reformation because the religious wars had left so much of France in Protestant and Hugenot hands," Scott had been saying. "Add to this the tense relations between France and the Hapsburgs at the beginning of the 16th Century, and all the wars that resulted. After the 1650s, you get a forty-year civil war in France and an eighty-year war in the Low countries. So things only got worse for pilgrimage, right up until the middle of the 17th Century. And in addition to the wars, poverty and crime reduced the number of people who were willing to risk a pilgrimage even more."

Robert had been listening carefully as Scott talked about the Camino. There was a pause. He hesitated, looked puzzled, as if trying to recall something. Then he leaned forward. "Some time ago," he said thoughtfully, "I saw a document in the archives of the Canadian Government about a group of Basque fishermen. It was in 1566, I think. Yes, late fall. They were heading home to Spain from Newfoundland, where they had been fishing. Apparently it was a terrible crossing. The ship nearly went down several times in the storms. They finally put in at Lisbon, and because they had lost so much cargo, they filed an insurance claim. And in that claim they included the cost of a pilgrimage to Santiago de Compostela to thank St. James for getting them back home safely."

"You're kidding," I said.

"*That*," said Scott, "is the best footnote to history I've heard in a long time."

By the 16th Century, the Reconquest was over and Islam exterminated in Spain. James Matamoros, Slayer of Moors, might have had time on his hands. But the Conquest of the New World was gearing up, and the Spaniards were still in need of their saint. Juan de Contreras, author of *Santiago Apostol*, writes of Spain in America with an oblivious chauvinism that I found both amusing and disconcerting. So enormous was the accumulated wealth of Spain after 1492, Contreras states, that Providence created a means for them to go forth on that adventure [the conquest of the New World] which was "the greatest thing since the world's creation, except for the Incarnation and the Death of Christ." Nobody other than the Virgin could compete with James for glory in the New World. Contreras lovingly details James' appearance in 1520 on the plains of Mexico when Cortez fights Guatemoc at the Battle of Otumba. (There has never been anything like it in the military history of any country.) James was with Pizarro in Peru (as he betrayed and butchered the Incas, I remembered, the goal ostensibly being to eliminate the practice of human sacrifice among the Indians). And, reports Contreras, the booty that appeared in the wake of Pizarro's humanitarian deed sent shock waves back to a Spain.

Interestingly, in a strange detour from war and defeat to myth-making, the Incas themselves eventually adopted James as one of their own. As if calling the Spanish missionaries' bluff, the Incas turned the saint, whom Jesus had once called a son of thunder, into a thunder god.

Travelling in Bolivia the summer after my Camino trip, I met a Kallewaya shaman who began fortune-telling sessions by invoking St. James Matamoros. On a shelf in the darkened room where he sat cross-legged throwing coco leaves on a blanket, was a small ceramic statue of the saint, a perfect copy of the figure from the Camino paintings, complete with white horse, flying robe, sword and standard. The shaman told me I would eventually finish this book.

In 1545, a Church council had been held in the Italian city of Trent to confront the Protestant heresy head-on and to take a hard look at abuses within the Church that could no longer escape the notice of any thoughtful person. Over the next few decades, the moral tide of Europe turned enough that by the start of the 17th Century - a hundred years after Grenier's fishermen had made their insurance claim - ordinary pilgrimage was once again thriving. This time around, it was a modest, serious affair that harked back to the idealized pilgrims of the early Middle Ages.

Domenico Laffi made his pilgrimage in 1673. His diary reveals a man for whom pilgrimage was an expression of a living faith embedded in deep emotion. Many religious refugees who fled Ireland during the time of Cromwell found their way to Santiago. In 1717 there were not enough confessors to handle the number of pilgrims arriving in Santiago, but there was enough cash coming into the city that between 1738 and 1750, they could redo the facade of the Cathedral in the flamboyant style of the new Baroque.

But the Wars of Succession in Poland and Austria between 1733 and 1748 once again made travel difficult. In 1756, the Seven Years War began between France and Britain. This was something we had learned about in high school. I had had no idea, as I studied for my Canadian history exam, that while Wolfe and Montcalm were fighting it out on the Plains of Abraham near Quebec, a parallel conflict between France and Britain on the other side of the Atlantic was forcing pilgrims to cancel their plans to go to Santiago, especially those who were taking the sea route down the French coast, where British ships were thickening the waters.

As the century wore on, European politics stabilized enough for the pulse of the Camino to quicken yet again. Records from this time show an influx into Santiago of wealthy pilgrims from Italy, Portugal, England, Poland, Lithuania, and Hungary. By the eve of the French Revolution, pilgrim traffic was steady, though the proportion of vagrants and vagabonds, and of young men avoiding military service, was increasing, which taxed the charitability of the hospices just as it had at the end of the Middle Ages.

In 1789, the Bastille fell in Paris. The world, including Carlos IV and the Spanish Bourbon court, watched as revolutionary propaganda coursed through France on a tide of blood. When Louis XVI went to the guillotine in 1793, Spain declared war on France. A year later, France invaded northern Spain. By 1804, Napoleon was emperor of France, and before long he held most of Europe as well. Reassessing the situation, Spain switched allegiance to become a French ally against Britain. This was an easy ticket for France: Napoleon's men quickly began to occupy more and more of Spain. In 1807 they moved into Portugal, packing the Portuguese royal family off to Brazil. It dawned on Madrid that the peninsula would soon be nothing more than a French pawn, and the old griping tension between the French and the Spanish revived once again.

In April 1808, Napoleon pronounced his brother, Joseph, king of Spain. On May 2, the Madrid mob went wild. The Madrid Uprising, as it came to be called, was the start of a thorough-going, but thoroughly disorganized revolt against the French. On May 4, Asturias joined the fray. Guerrilla bands began to emerge throughout the north. When Wellington arrived in Portugal in August, the long war began in earnest. It would end only in the final defeat of Napoleon in 1814.

The Camino was in shambles, buried in the rubble of fighting between the organized French and the enraged and scrappy Spanish. Napoleon's men had occupied northern Spain for over a decade, had looted and desecrated every Camino treasure they cared to. But with the war over, Spanish unity against the French fell apart. Conservatives, mostly from the north, defended the old regime while the mostly southern liberals, who had caught on to the ideals of the Revolution, alternated between exile and open rebellion. The conservatives called these people atheists, puppets of the French, "los afrancesados" - the Frenchified ones. A six-year civil war tore an already battered country to shreds. There were droughts and floods and a plague of yellow fever. Pilgrimage was in its death throes.

It wasn't until the 1830s that liberal leadership was consolidated in a new constitution. But the public purse was empty. In a harsh anti-clerical stroke, the government went after the monasteries, making them state property. In Burgos alone, twenty-seven were closed and their treasures sold on the open market.

This was the all but fatal blow to the Camino. Without the support of the monasteries, pilgrimage had little chance of recovery. To make matters worse, northern Spain began to fall on hard economic times. Land shortages in Galicia were forcing people to pack up and sail away to Argentina and Brazil. The region turned into a backwater. There were few tourists and fewer pilgrims, though the Spanish Queen Isabella II visited Santiago in 1858. But by now, even the saint himself had been effaced. The patron of the battles with France in 1808 was the Virgin Mary and in 1822, the Feast of St. James was observed in Santiago rather casually and without any trace of the old hoopla.

As the 19th Century rolled over into the 20th, the pilgrims' road to Santiago across the sun-bright fields of Navarra, the high meseta desert and sweet-smelling forests of Galicia, had reverted to a geographical line on a map. St. James had all but vanished into the emptiness of the mythless present.

But not quite. When emigrants from Galicia went to the New World, they took with them the memory of the saint that had kept Galicia on the front page of European history for so many centuries. Santiago, who had already seen battle on the fields of Mexico and Peru in the 16th Century, made a return trip to the New World in the 19th. Except that this time, he wore his pilgrim's tunic.

In Argentina's southernmost city, Ushuaia, where the winds howl in off the Beagle Canal and the last vertebrae of the Andes curl across the sacrum of South America onto Antarctic ice, there stands, at the centre of a bleak little crossroad, a stone cross on a pillar. It is almost identical to the 14th-century *cruceros* we had seen throughout Galicia. Jesus Christ hangs as usual on the cross. On the pillar just below him is St. James the Pilgrim, robed and carrying his walking staff and purse. The date on the stone is 1996.

Village fair in Galicia.

9

Songs

The Indian mystics speak perpetually of the visible universe as the Lila or Sport of God: the Infinite deliberately expressing Himself in finite form, the musical manifestation of His creative Joy.
Evelyn Underhill. <u>Practical Mysticism</u>

Physicists have broken through; some are dismayed to find
The new air they inhabit
They share with poets.
Margaret Avison. <u>Apocalyptics III</u>

Street musicians in Santiago.

There are four or five major cities on the *Camino francés*, but no matter where you are in your pilgrimage to Santiago, the city of Burgos remains a geographical point of reference. If the city of St. James, located in the west as if on the far shore of space and time, is the paradisal city of the pilgrim's dream, Burgos is the city in the middle of the here and now, the busy nucleus of worldly culture in northern Spain. For centuries, Burgos has pulled prestigious and influential people into the swirl of its politics, controversies, feuds, and artistic movements.

One day in the spring of 1081, a bustle of official activity occurred in Burgos as an entourage of carts made its way slowly through the streets. One cart bore the Papal Delegate, Cardinal Roberto. Behind him came advisors and courtiers. Bodyguards were everywhere. In the most majestic cart of all sat Alfonso VI. The king had come to Burgos with Roberto to pursue a mission whose significance might not be obvious nowadays: the replacement, throughout Spain, of the old Mozarab liturgy of the Mass with the new Roman one. This was much more than a simple change of clothes for the Mass; it was a powerful emblem of a shift in the political balance of western Christendom. For if he succeeded, Alfonso would see all those church reforms that had swept into Spain from France take a huge step to completion, and his own kingdom become part of a prestigious royal in-crowd in a united Europe. In the end, the king got his wish: final approval, once and for all, for the switch to new Roman ways in the music of the Mass.

If Burgos was the city where the old Spanish liturgy was officially silenced, it was also the city where, a century or so later, a new music, complex and elegant as a crystal, would lift into the bright Castilian air. For the changes to the Mass had brought a rush of creativity to the musical life of the new Europe. Much of it was concentrated in the nearby monastery of Las Huelgas de Burgos, right on the Camino, close to Moorish influences, full of up and coming clerics with talent, and connected with the best music schools both in France and in Santiago.

On our cycling trip, Scott and I made a detour to see this birthplace of Spanish music. Las Huelgas is only a few minutes from downtown Burgos, an easy ride among the trees by the Rio Arlanzón and past the site of a 12th-century leper colony. It was, and still is, a Cistercian nunnery, founded in 1187 by Alfonso VIII - son of the young Blanca of Navarra - and his Aquitainian-English wife, Eleanor. In this opulent monastery, high-born nuns had, over the centuries, offered prayers round the clock for the safety of the monarchy and the well-being of royal souls.

The nuns were generously supported by Alfonso and Eleanor. They owned vast tracts of land, held jurisdiction over hundreds of villages around Burgos. Their sheep grazed in royal pastures, their firewood was cut from the king's forests. They coined their own currency, collected their own taxes.

Las Huelgas - the name comes from the Spanish *holgar* to rest or be idle - was also a summer palace. Kings and queens were crowned here, also buried. Their tombs were said to contain the richest of silks and muslins from the workshops of North Africa and southern Spain, bought, plundered, or received in payment from the

Moors. A great many were ransacked for their treasure by Napoleon's troops during the 19th-century Peninsular War.

Scott and I rolled into Las Huelgas along a narrow street lined on one side with shops. The monastery stood beyond an iron fence that gleamed in the morning sun. The buildings looked prim and confident under their sturdy buttresses and red tiled roofs. A parapet railed in stone sat like a square crown atop the straight-sided bell tower. Just below it hung a small, moon-white clock.

Las Huelgas has been called a fortified city, but today it looked, if not exactly inviting, at least not defensive. Near the entrance to the courtyard, a queue of white tree trunks held up a long banner of dark green leaves. Once inside the courtyard, I could almost hear the hollow rattle of 12th-century horseshoes over the cobblestones, the rustle of nuns' habits and faintly from behind the doorway, the voices of a choir and the giggles of young royal daughters on a break from their studies.

Behind us, tourists were stepping from a convoy of busses; stout bellies, polyester pants and baseball caps drifted across the courtyard. We leaned our bikes on a wall and followed them inside for the tour.

Our guide was a slim, blonde, rather business-like woman. She had likely repeated this tour a hundred times but she seemed to find it satisfying. Her talk had scientific precision, as if she was explaining the circuitry of a large radio-telescope. We followed our group from one polished room to another. Las Huelgas was as poised and efficient as our guide, and unabashedly prosperous. It had an air of quality: things were done well here.

We were shown the sarcophagi of Eleanor and Alfonso where they lay under the high vaults of the chapel, their sides touching like two little semi-detached houses. The guide pointed to a carving on Alfonso's tomb that showed the king officially founding Las Huelgas. His wife Eleanor, she said, was the daughter of Eleanor of Aquitaine and the Plantagenet king, Henry II of England. One of her brothers was Richard the Lionheart.

I dawdled beside Eleanor's tomb. This was a surprise: I had no idea she was here, nor known she had been married off to this, or any, Alfonso. I thought back to my high school history classes. I had loved the name

Plantagenet. But I never dreamed, sitting almost exactly thirty years ago in that high-ceilinged wooden classroom hazy with chalk dust, that I would be standing now by the tomb of the daughter of the priest-despising Henry. That Henry, I imagined then and still do, looked like Peter O'Toole in the movie, *Becket,* and I pictured his daughter Eleanor too with blond hair and those fiercely questioning blue eyes.

She had been born in Gascony. She loved music and had many friends among the troubadors of southern France. When she came to Spain for her wedding to Alfonso, she was only fifteen years old. But she was accustomed to power, and she must have had an uncommonly clear idea of what she was on this earth for. The greatest achievement of her monastery would be its *schola cantorum,* the singing school. One of Europe's finest, it would influence musical trends for centuries.

By 1257, with Eleanor and Alfonso in their tombs and their son Alfonso X on the throne, Las Huelgas had in residence - in addition to administrators, gardeners, Jewish surgeons, Mudejar stonemasons, forty noble girls in the convent school, and a community of priests - dozens of music teachers and a hundred choir members, all nuns from the upper classes, with forty lay sisters to attend them. The monastery had close ties with the musical elite at Notre Dame de Paris. French and Spanish musicians arrived regularly in Burgos, having traversed the Camino humming new melodies and nervously keeping an eye on their manuscripts. One of the most important polyphonic codices of the Middle Ages, copied in the 14th Century, rests in the library of Las Huelgas: a parchment manuscript with a hundred and seventy folios of music.

In the 1990s - seven hundred and fifty years later! - Vox Iberica produced a three-volume set of CDs of the music of medieval Spain; the second in the series was the music of Las Huelgas. Scott had given me this CD for my birthday. I had listened to it often, loving the cadences of limpid, unhurried notes, the rise of melody and tone before a downward cascade that never fell too far, as if an elastic net was catching note after note. Some pieces had sounded almost too abstract to be called melodies. Others were a little like modern songs I already knew, pleasingly estranged by time in their themes and inflections: songs in praise of the Virgin, a *conductus* in her honour with parts to be sung "in the French manner" or "in the Spanish manner;" motets for Santa Catarina, San Nicolás, Thomas á Becket; a *planctus* on the death of Sancho III in 1158 (Lament, O sorrowing Castile...) and of Alfonso VIII in 1214 (The King has fallen, and Castile's glory totters.....); warning songs about the Last Judgment (that hated day, that bitter day.... O wretched man, why do you pursue false joy?).

I looked up. The guide had an assistant, who frowned as he beckoned me to follow. No lagging! There were other tours behind us and we might get mixed up. At Las Huelgas, order and obedience were assumed.

We arrived at the cloister, with its interior quadrangle of rosebushes and hedges. Slowly we walked under ribbed vaults down one corridor. The floor had been laid in big rectangles of rough stone. Streaming from my feet was a bold middle runway of contrasting stone that was plaqued today with sharp squares of morning sunshine. My eye followed the bright squares until they vanished as if through a time tunnel in a shadowed wall at the far end of the corridor.

Over the centuries, thousands of nuns had walked upon these stones, meditating with their missals and rosaries. I turned to see the fountain in the centre of the garden: paradisal waters, source of life. Around it were the flowerbeds, contained by hedges pruned to reflect God's divine order on earth. I looked again the leaping roses that had been left to find their own place in the sun-drenched beds: songbird yellow, blood red, pink like a doll's cheeks.

The Chapel of Santiago was next, entered from the outside through a brick and marble entrance. Moorish craftsmen had built this chapel - that was obvious from the arched doorway alone. Moorish captives had also been imprisoned inside its rectangular walls by Ferdinand III. And a Moor had carved the statue of a seated Santiago that looked out from a ledge on the sanctuary wall. Our eyes looked more or less at his knees. Looking up, I immediately noticed the thick, low hair and the stylishly braided beard, then the Garbo eyebrows and clear, kind eyes. The Santiago of Las Huelgas, who was neither a pilgrim nor a killer of Moors, wore a knight's simple tunic.

This chapel was "the heart of Castilian knighthood," said our guide, standing straight and surveying the scene before us with satisfaction. She produced a pointer and directed our attention to the saint's right arm. The hand held a sword and the arm was articulated at the elbow. This contraption, the invention of a mechanically minded Moor with a taste for gimmicks (or perhaps it was Ferdinand's idea) was used to dub knights. If you were one of the many high-born men who came here for their knighthood, explained the guide, you could say you were inducted into the order by St. James himself. People in the group giggled. Someone said "That's ridiculous." For the first and only time, I saw our guide smile. Edward, King of England, she said, had himself dubbed here in 1254 when he came to marry Eleanor's daughter.

I asked the guide whether a pilgrim hospice had been connected with this monastery. Not on the site of Las Huelgas, she replied, but the nuns had had one built a little further west. The Hospital del Rey was big and famous, with confessors fluent in enough languages to hear confessions from practically anyone. Later, reading my Everest *Guide*, I came across a comment from Laffi's diary of 1673. Although it was on the edge of Burgos, he had written, the Hospital del Rey seemed a city in itself. It accommodated two thousand pilgrims with great charity, and had excellent food and beds. He doubted there was anything else like it in Spain.

Later that afternoon, we cycled over more meseta, explored the ruins of the Monastery of San Antón, then followed a line of trees along a pretty road until we spotted a ruined castle high on a crown of land. Just below it, pasted to the side of the hill, was the town of Castrojeriz. We wanted to see the castle in daylight, so we left our bikes in town and went there at once along a well-used track winding up the south side of the hill.

"This is my favourite place so far," Scott mused, as we stood together staring out from a parapet above a ruined wall. The wind bellowed in our ears. In every direction, cultivated valleys stretched wide and long between brown and sage-green hills.

"I sure like these open spaces," shouted Scott over the wind. "See how strategic this place was? Nobody could get here without being seen. They had the whole area covered, just from this one hilltop."

The Everest *Guide* said Castrojeriz was founded at least in the Visigothic time. According to one theory, it was first named Castrum Caesaris, after Julius Caesar, who built it for war against the Cantabrians. But even in pre-historic days, anybody passing by would have recognized the site as the perfect lookout.

We looked down over the town. "It's a micro-history of the Camino right here!" said Scott. "We're standing in a castle that was occupied by the Moors. The town has three churches full of medieval art, and the whole place has hardly changed from the time of the Camino." That wasn't quite true: Castrojeriz had a few spiritless modern buildings and an enormous public swimming pool. But from high on this hill you could see the features of a typical Camino town: a main street running from end to end, little buildings with tile roofs, and churches rising chunkily into the air just above.

To escape the wind, we sat together on a steep stairway in what was left of the castle's interior. The steps were chipped and cold. The wind slammed into the walls, making the long stairwell hum. It was easy to imagine old sounds from a man's world: husky voices at the bottom of the stairway, a sword slipping icily into its sheath, hoarse laughter, someone spitting in the lull of an evening's watch. A little later, we left the castle and returned down the road as the wind whipped around us like a rush of Moorish horses.

There were no vacant bunks at the *refugio*, so we took a room in a no-star but perfectly adequate hotel overlooking a skinny Castrojeriz alley. There was a bar on the ground floor, and after a rest we went down in search of supper.

It is always a little unnerving for foreigners to enter a small-town Spanish bar. The floor crawls with peanut shells and cigarette butts. On the television screen is a bullfight: rows of human busts squinting in the stands, a matador with a goofy hat and an insolent cape, and a gracefully hulking bull, too stupid to be puzzled, but acting with a bull's intelligence, which is never to be slighted. Your heart sinks at the blood drooling from the long darts stuck into the skin along his spine.

Except for the reds and yellows on the television, the bar is shadowy. It smells a little off. The customers, old-timers hunched over their drinks, legs braced against their barstools, are either indifferent or slightly mocking when they see you. But this particular bar had a restaurant downstairs, and once we had crunched across the filthy floor past the kid just starting with his broom and gone down a few narrow steps, we found ourselves in an immaculate dining room with white tablecloths and a waitress in a black uniform standing at the ready.

Eight or nine pilgrims had already pulled up extra tables and chairs and crowded together, so we sat apart and invited one leftover man to join us. This was Ken, who was from England, middle-aged, not tall, with a tight, academic face and glasses that sat like a windshield on his nose. He said he was an apprentice stonemason, which I believed, but found hard to.

"I'll have one of those," Scott told the waitress, pointing to something on a plate at the next table.

"Me too," said Ken. I ordered soup, always a good bet, and beef stew. The Rioja red was excellent. The conversation turned to church masonry and architecture. Ken and Scott debated the engineering design behind flying buttresses, an argument I began to have trouble following. Burgos Cathedral was mentioned, and between sips, I expressed my distaste for that pompous church.

"Structurally, it's in terrible condition," said Ken, "which is a great pity. Been to Silos?"

"We plan to see it on the way back," said Scott.

"Well worth it," said Ken. "It's of course where all the Christmas chant was recorded on CD a few years back." Ken poured me more wine. He was a medieval music buff, he told us, raised a Catholic in England. He had studied a few years of music and theology before taking up stonemasonry.

Though even more dubious about Ken, I was intrigued by this turn in the discussion. "I think," I said, reaching for my wine, "I think the chant was one of the best things the Roman Church ever produced. Even the name, Gregorian chant, sounds so elegant and dignified." Privately, I thought back to the stolid little hymns I had heard sung so threadily, week after week, in Calvin Presbyterian Church.

"Ah," said Ken abruptly, as if hitting back a tennis ball, "but actually Gregory didn't write the chant himself, you know, though he did, it is now agreed, bring the *schola cantorum* back to life."

I said I was aware of this, feeling animated now by the tone of challenge. "But his name has always been linked to the new chants that appeared in the 8th Century." I said. "Everybody at the time thought he had written them."

"What did they sing before?" asked Scott.

"Chant, of course," said Ken. "They've always chanted. The early Christians got it from the Jews. But Rome couldn't really control how the chant sounded once it got out of Italy. Each region developed its own liturgical style: there was the Gallican in France, the Celtic in Britain, the Ambrosian in Italy...."

"And the Visigothic in Spain," I contributed.

"But of course," answered Ken, "*that* came to be called the Mozarab rite after the Arabs invaded in the 8th Century."

"Of course." I poured us the last of the wine.

Ken paused to order another bottle. "The Visigothic rite had a lot of Byzantine embellishments because, you see, it had come with the Visigoths when they came to Spain from the East in 5th Century. Over time, it got more ornate than the liturgy in France. Then in England we had our Celtic rites, which were also rather fancified."

"But the Franks were bloody imperialists," he went on, a little louder, "and they wanted to make their own church practices the gold standard. They got in consultants from Rome to help, but they changed a lot just to fit their own likes and dislikes. The result was actually more of a French liturgy than a Roman one."

"That was during the Carolingian Renaissance," I said. "I understand Charlemagne worked on the liturgy himself, with Alcuin helping him."

"I rather doubt that," snorted Ken. A triumph was coming. He peered at me confidentially: "Charlemagne couldn't read or write, you know." He laughed loud enough for the room to hear, pouring our wine with one hand while he pushed his glasses up on his nose with the other. "Actually it was his father who started the whole reform thing off," he shrugged.

I began to feel muddled, both attracted and repelled by this kind of intellectual one-upmanship. I could see Scott was amused by the show. He winked at me. I looked at Ken: was he a show-off or just an enthusiast who didn't know when to quit? Or was I?

Scott urged the conversation on. "So the French started importing the Roman rite into Spain - "

"The changes caused a lot of turmoil." I said.

"It was a hard sell," Ken said. "The Spaniards didn't like it."

"It would have sounded odd for the Spanish to hear the new liturgy in their churches." I said. "And for the French too, to come to Spain and hear the old rites, or the new rites with a Spanish accent." .... Or something like that, I thought.

Ken took a long sip of wine and put down his glass. Leaning forward on his elbows, he said, "What's so interesting about the Camino is that it was a kind of a -"

"A conduit," put in Scott.

"Right, for all the innovations of the 11th Century - polyphony, new notation, all the new musical forms like tropes and sequences that were coming into vogue. The *Codex Calixtinus* at Compostela has one of the first pieces of polyphony ever written down! There are a few more pieces from around the same time in Limoges. But of course, the *Codex Calixtinus* was written at Limoges."

"At Vezelay, to be exact," I said.

"Ah, yes," said Ken, pointing at me magisterially.

"Which shows you," said Scott, "how important the Camino was to getting culture and innovation from one place to another."

"Did you see Las Huelgas? That's where musical styles began to cross over into the *ars nova* of the 14th Century."

Ars nova was beaten out by the arrival of dessert, which allowed, mercifully, for a change of subject. I asked Ken how he was travelling. "Believe it or not, I'm on a motorbike."

"A motorbike!"

"I have a bad back, you see, and I can really only do this on a motorbike."

Scott asked, "Do they let you into the *refugios*?"

"Not a chance. I'm a pariah. Someone told me I'm not a real pilgrim, travelling this way." He looked at me with a pariah's eyes from behind his big lenses. I saw the shadow of sadness there, and it wasn't just from being excluded from the pilgrims' in-crowd.

"What do you think?" he asked, looking from Scott to me. "Am I any less a pilgrim for going to Santiago by motorbike?"

I said I didn't think so. "It's funny that they won't let you into the hostels, but they'll let a bunch of speed cyclists in, just because they're on bikes."

"Yes, it is strange," he agreed. He reached for the dinner bill. "I'd like to pay for your dinner, you two, to thank you for letting me blabber on. I haven't had a good conversation in days."

In the end, I had liked the conversation and even liked Ken. The evening, wine-soaked as it was, had enlivened me. As Scott and I got ready for bed, I was still thinking about how music informs a nation's identity, and how jarring a change might be in such a profound ritual as the Mass. Even Laffi remarked, after hearing Mass at Pamplona in the 1670s, that "it is all very different from the way we do it in Italy."

Two years later, during my walk on the Via de la Plata, I would be reminded of our dinner discussion with Ken. I happened to spend one night at Alcuéscar, where that day I had visited the old Visigothic Church of Santa

Lucia. My accommodation was an active monastery that was also a pilgrim hospice and, interestingly, a home for mentally disabled adults.

My little cell of a room was on the second floor. Just down the hall were the bathrooms. To my surprise, the showers there were shared by monks and pilgrims. I went to bed early that night after attending vespers. As I lay in my cot, I heard, from the shower nearby, one of the monks idly singing bits and pieces of Gregorian chant. His voice sailed like a boat around splashes of water and the gurgling drain. That chant was as familiar to him as his own skin. How long would it have taken, I wondered, for someone like him, a simple Spanish monk whose very body breathed in praise of God, to get used to humming a new chant dictated by the powerful country nextdoor, whose customs were not his own?

To clear our heads of the previous evening's wine, Scott and I had a swim in the Castrojeriz swimming pool. Then we visited two of the town's three churches. We sat first in the high, slender, very Gothic nave of the Church of San Juan. I stared into the spaces that hung between its still walls and soaring roof. I did not think, deeply or otherwise. I questioned nothing. A soft light streamed over the delicate ribs of the vault and dropped down the pillars in thin bands of white gold. It was one of the most restful churches I had seen.

Later, we ambled in the soft sunshine over to the Collegiate Church of Santa Maria del Manzano. Its doors were still locked, but three women were standing outside. They turned out to be graduate students from León, who had driven out this morning to see a few Camino churches. They had made prior arrangements with the church custodian and were expecting him soon.

The custodian eventually arrived, a stooped, dazed priest wearing a cardigan and leather bedroom slippers. His Spanish, which was impenetrable, erupted in spurts and hums. There was something the matter with his upper lip. He settled a fee with the women and when they entered the church, we followed.

I stopped near the group to admire a statue of St. James dressed as a pilgrim in a soft blue cloak and a big hat with scallop shells. His handsome face looked out over us, kindly and animated. I became aware of the priest beside me, telling the women something about this statue. The women were expectant and attentive at first, but when he appeared to bungle his story, they began to steal glances at each other and to smirk with feigned, amused alarm. By the time he had finished, they were giggling uncontrollably. He seemed not to notice and when he had finished his recitation, he shuffled away along the aisle towards the Flemish and Italian *tablas*, his large head leaning out over his chest as if it felt heavy.

Scott was absorbed in the retable behind the altar. I wandered towards the tombs of some local nobles, past baroque ornaments and *cajonerias*. But it was that priest who interested me. From the corner of my eye, I watched him mutter vaguely into the air above the women, oblivious as their amusement turned to restlessness. They shifted and look around. One studied her fingernails.

I came to a statue of the Virgin, Santa Maria del Manzano. We had already looked up the word *manzano* in our dictionary. "St. Mary of the Apple Tree?" Scott had asked quzzically. The story goes that this Virgin appeared in Castrojeriz one day by an apple tree. On seeing her from the castle on the hill, James' horse lept down through the air to the tree, thus confirming her wishes that a church be built for her on this spot. In later years, Alfonso X composed a few songs in honour of miracles she had performed.

I looked at the Virgin carefully. She was poised on a long crescent moon, wore a lovely blue dress with a cape and, on her head, a sturdy, simple crown. Her face was gentle and intelligent. I gazed at Santa Maria del Manzano, silently begging her to help a poor priest blundering his way through a guided tour for three mocking women.

Later that day we pedalled to the small village of Villalcázar de Sirga. The going was easy on the flat, straight Camino track beside C980. A translucent shield of cloud covered the sky. Now and then, huge flocks of birds would spring like an explosion of cinders from the grass beside us. Birdsong was everywhere. In Villalcázar de Sirga, each little street had its chorus of chirpers. At the Church of Santa Maria la Blanca, we watched swallows disappear into cracks in the masonry.

We leaned our bikes on the church steps. No one was about. The angular, flat-roofed building with its one high, round window and its tall porch stood under the sky like a lone warrior. Under the porch, the air was cool; bars of shadows angled over our heads. There were two doors to the church. A pair of large panels sat over the first door, with Jesus and the Apostles on the panel above and the three wise men below. Five deeply receding arches curved over the main door, and three over the second door. Every arch was carved with heavenly minstrels bearing harps and wind instruments. It was as if a welcoming party had come from the courts of paradise to meet us.

The church doors, as it turned out, were locked. Villalcázar de Sirga was dry and deserted and apart from the porch, shadowless. Scott went round the back to look for someone. I wandered into the street. A thin old woman in black came creeping toward the church. Seeing me, she squeaked fiercely and with an arm like a stick scratched the air in the direction of the bar. At the bar, which was empty of customers, a gray-haired lady who was plump and used to managing pilgrims sent me to the house of Señor Juan. At Señor Juan's house, a woman in an apron came to the door. She held it slightly ajar and smiled, looking into my eyes with the placid confidence of a born priest's housekeeper. Infinitely satisfied, she informed me that Señor Juan was shaving and would come to open the church as soon as he was finished. She was still smiling as she closed the door. This, I could see, was life in Villalcázar de Sirga: public, untroubled, run by irreproachable women.

A German tour bus had glided into town and come to rest by the church steps. It looked like a silver space station.

"They sleep in that thing?" I exclaimed to Scott, looking at the hieroglyphic list of amenities pictured on the side of the bus. But the tourists turned out to be earthly creatures in polyester shirts and silly sunhats.

They milled around the church expectantly. Something had been planned.

Señor Juan was a short, discrete, very clean-shaven man in a sweater, who carried a large key. He greeted us all cheerfully, then unlocked the church. Once inside, he busied himself in its recesses with tasks known only to himself, and did not speak to any of us again.

I loved this church. The rose window hung like a shining wheel on one wall, sieving the daylight into three long naves. Streaks of sunshine fell through smaller windows, skimmed over the squared stones in the walls and darted mischievously through the vaults. Reds, yellows and golds gleamed from the retable behind the altar. Like the portico with its sculpted figures, the church seemed to vibrate with the spirits of real people. On one of the carved capitals, a lady bids adieu to her knight. Under her headdress, her face is solemn but not despondent; the knight, perched on his horse, is downcast, but acknowledges his sacred duty. Only the horse wants to break free of the moment.

According to Valiña, the church's Chapel of Santiago is "a museum of medieval sculpture." There are three tombs here. One belongs to an unnamed knight. Another holds Doña Leonor Ruiz de Castro, the second wife of the occupant of the third tomb, Don Felipe, brother of King Alfonso X and a strong supporter of the Knights Templar. On the lids of the tombs, the effigies of Leonor and Felipe lie with studied composure, like actors at the end of a death scene. Their impeccable carvings bear traces of their original colour. The master carver has shown Felipe's funeral: a crowd of mourners under Gothic arches, and the knight's horse, dumbly forlorn without his rider.

This Felipe had an interesting life. He was educated in Toledo in the early 1300s, then went to Paris, where he studied theology with Thomas Aquinas and Bonaventura. He returned to Spain, first to Toledo, then Sevilla, where he was made Bishop. Meanwhile, his older brother, Alfonso X, was preparing to marry the princess Christina of Norway, who arrived in Spain only to be repudiated by him. Not surprisingly, there was a crisis, both diplomatic and personal. To patch up the business, the king summoned Felipe from Sevilla, defrocked him and forced him to marry the rejected bride. The poor girl never got over it and died of melancholy sometime after her wedding to Felipe. She was buried at Covarrubias. Felipe later married Leonor Ruiz de Castro. It is said that he never forgave Alfonso for the terrible humiliation of his Norwegian bride.

The Germans had come quietly into the Chapel of Santiago and were standing near us as we looked at the statue for whom this church is named: Santa Maria la Blanca. After the beautiful virgins we had seen all along the Camino, the White Virgin of Villalcázar de Sirga was something of a shock.

"She looks a little dumpy," I said to Scott, keeping my voice low.

"She looks like a gnome," he muttered back.

The Christ child was on her lap, missing his head and an arm. Mary herself was short her right hand. The amputations looked too clean to have been accidental and they made the head of the Blessed Virgin all the more puzzling: her face was long and rather horsey; a thin veil flopped down the sides of her head to her shoulders; the eyebrows were lifted and she had the bright, slightly crinkled eyes of an opera singer; below her too-large nose, the mouth was parted in a slight smile. "She looks like she's just heard a really good joke," I said, too loud. A German tourist behind me, who I suppose understood English, made a disgusted sound.

I hadn't meant to sound irreverent. I thought of the Mother of God we had seen in Roncesvalles, holding her child and gazing at him with such love in her young face. I remembered the all-seeing stare of Santa Maria la Real in Nájera, whose eyes had the piercing clarity of a Zen master. Just this morning in Castrojeriz, I had seen the luminous, prim, young Apple-tree Queen of Heaven, standing on her crescent moon. Her eyes had been more inward, like those of the Buddha or one of his adepts. But this slightly bosomy Virgin of Villalcázar de Sirga reminded me of a laughing Buddha. Rising above her mutilations, beyond coy motherhood or limpid serenity, she had gotten the joke in the divine comedy, and was eternally on the verge of a wise woman's grin.

The Germans were listening with strict attention to their guide. Scott moved closer and tried to pick up some of what he was saying, thereby breaking the etiquette about listening to tour guides that other people had paid good money for.

Alfonso X had written over four hundred songs in honour of the Virgin Mary, to whom he was very devoted. His songs belong to the troubadour tradition of love poetry.

"Not bad for a guy who treated at least one real-life woman rather badly," Scott remarked.

"There may have been more to the story," I replied.

I had read some of Alfonso's tales before our trip, and one in particular had fascinated me with its subtle insights. A German merchant suffers from an incapacitating paralyses; his wrists and ankles are twisted and useless. His sickness has cost him his business. Frustrated, despairing, hopeful for a miracle, he begs his friends to carry him on a litter to Santiago. It is a difficult journey. After months on the road, he is taken into Santiago Cathedral and down the aisle to the altar amid a chorus of prayers. The company waits, lips parted, eyes lifted imploringly to the saint. The man closes his eyes and holds his breath. To his unspeakable disillusion, nothing happens. The clubbed hands lie obstinately at his sides; the obscene feet contort the cloth that drapes his litter. It is his unconfessed sins, his friends say knowingly, looking down at him now and shaking their heads.

On the return trip, the disease progresses: the merchant goes blind. The friends, seeing the hopelessness of his condition, decide to leave him here at Villalcázar de Sirga at the foot of this White Virgin. Terribly sick, and now abandoned, the man cries out to Mary from his litter; perhaps it is not even a petition, but a last howl of rage and despair. The Virgin sees his agony and bestows upon him her healing gifts: his sight returns, his phalanges uncurl, his ankles lengthen. The merchant walks home to Germany.

This was Story 218 in Alfonso's Canticles to Mary. Many of the songs in the collection are about the miracles of this particular Virgin at Villalcázar de Sirga, and a surprising number have to do with blindness cured. If, in the language of metaphor, loss of eyesight suggests the gaining of inner vision, then perhaps the friends were right: the German merchant was blind to the illness of his own soul until physical blindness forced him to look inward to the heart of his human anguish.

Alfonso's Canticles to the Virgin blended Hebrew and Arabic rhythms, religious melodies, and local folk tunes. The king had been born in Galicia, but in later years had some kind of falling out with the Santiago Church. It is said that you can feel his hostility to Compostela in his Canticles. Only seven of the Virgin's miracles take place in Galicia. Many, on the other hand, take place at Villalcázar de Sirga, as if Alfonso didn't think you needed to go all the way to Santiago to be healed. In one Canticle, a formerly sightless man tells a blind friend not to go to Santiago, for he had been healed at Villalcázar de Sirga. In another, a French lady, tired of going to useless shrines to be healed, starts off for Santiago but finds her cure at Villalcázar de Sirga. Then there is the man on a penitential pilgrimage with an iron fetter around his waist, which is removed here by the White Virgin before he goes on to Santiago.

Alfonso X was a mediocre king in matters of politics and war. His genius was in cultural pursuits: music, ethics, political theory, chess, astronomy, and literature. He was on intimate terms with Spain's intellectual elite: Jewish diplomats and translators, Moorish philosophers, Christian scholars. He is considered the father of the Castilian language for his Chronicles and for the translations he ordered of important Arabic texts into Castilian. But he is best known now, at least outside Spain, for his musical interests. And as the German tour guide had said, he liked to think of himself as the Virgin's troubadour. He once wrote:

> I wish from this day forth to be Her troubadour, and I pray that She will have me for Her Troubadour and accept my songs, for through them I seek to reveal the miracles She performed.

In saying this, Alfonso was placing himself within a musical tradition that had begun in southern France some hundred years before his reign. It is believed that the music of the troubadours was born in familiar phrases of church music. Making popular songs out of the Mass was simply not done, but lifting a few of the new musical decorations - tropes and sequences - and making your own tunes from them might be. The troubadours' topics were sometimes satirical, but most often they sang of the chaste, idealized love of a knight for a highborn lady, usually already married.

Travelling west along the Camino to Santiago, pilgrims and minstrels brought the music of the troubadours from France into Spain. On the way, they heard the Moorish *zejel* from Andalusia, a musical form used for ring dances. In Galicia, the French songs of Platonic love met the Galician-Portuguese *cantos de amigo*. These were simple ditties of longing and loss, whose "voice" was that of a young girl. The *cantos* had modest lines, just enough to build a melody and a little picture of innocent rural life in western Spain: a girl dallies by the fountain, another washes her hair in the river, one awaits her lover by the seashore and catches her skirt on a branch, tearing it. A girl asks the trees and flowers for news of her lover, another pretends to dance with her lover in the chestnut grove. The birds sing, the sea waves lap the shore. A maiden rises at dawn and goes to wash her blouses in a hillside stream. The wind catches the clothing as it dries and blows the blouses about, to her annoyance. The songs are full of such charming images, though they "lack intellectual and rhetorical content," as historian Gerald Brennan gently remarks.

When French troubadour music arrived in Galicia, it blended nicely with the soft pathos and occasional gaity of the Spanish *cantos de amigo*. But Galicia was a different social world, much earthier than the refined courtly spheres of southern France. As children, many Galician poets had been sent to be raised by nannies in the countryside, and their later compositions were filled with the unpretentious lyricism of the natural world. The marriage of French musical intellect with the nuances of

Galician emotion and imagery gave birth to a simple, melodious, highly pleasing tradition of lyric poetry. By the 13th Century, the Gallo-Portuguese love-lyric had become one of the most sophisticated musical forms in Christian Spain.

In addition to his own musical achievements, Alfonso founded a music school at the University of Salamanca. Among his court musicians were Paro Gómez Chariño, remembered for his song of a young girl who begs St. James to help her lover as he fights the Moors in Jaen; and the broad-bodied Airas de Corpancho, who sang of a girl who goes to Santiago to find her lover. Then there was Pedro Amigo de Sevilla, composer of a song about a Knight who falls in love with a Shepherdess on the way to Compostela. When he died, Pedro left his viol to the minstrel Pedro Lozano, so that the instrument, whenever it was played, would pray for his soul.

At the very end of August 1998, I was about to begin the final portion of my foot pilgrimage, from El Cebreiro through Galicia to Santiago. The day was brilliant but it was going to be humid; a feathery haze was already settling over the distant hills.

I felt strong as I set off down the road. I was more fit than I had ever been in my life, and possibly happier too, though that is hard to measure. My leg was healing nicely. I had established a unhurried rhythm of walking and resting. I could sleep pretty well all night in a room with snoring men and I had mastered the art of organizing my backpack so that the things I needed were no longer always on the bottom.

The Camino from El Cebreiro to Triacastela followed forest paths. This was new territory for me. Scott and I had taken the highway the previous year because the path was not recommended for bikes. The route was stony and blocked with boulders; the final descent into Triacastela was long and rough.

When I arrived in the wide yard of the Triacastela *refugio*, I spotted Anne and Alan sitting on a blanket in the grass. I had met this cheerful, middle-aged English couple only briefly in Burgos, but had liked them at once. She was a social worker in Liverpool, he taught trades at a technical school. This was their second pilgrimage to Santiago. Alan's feet were giving him trouble so they had been going slowly. But somehow they had gotten to Triacastela before me. I was glad to see their smiling faces and eager to hear how Alan was coping with his feet.

Sitting beside Anne and Alan in the shadow of a tree was Kjell. He had been taking his time along the Camino, dawdling in the towns talking to whomever he could find who spoke a language he did. I was glad to see him again too. He handed me a can of pineapple juice, and I stretched out under the trees to enjoy the fading day.

Anne was dressing the blisters on Alan's feet. I rolled over and took a peak. His soles looked like partly peeled tomatoes; flaps of ragged skin lay limply over tender new flesh. With tiny, sharp scissors, Anne carefully cut gauze and tape. Then with a sly smile she took a piece of cotton and dabbed red iodine on her husband's foot. Alan yelped. "I love this part," she cooed.

Later we half-carried Alan like a wounded soldier to an outdoor restaurant in what would pass for Triacastela's downtown. Our dinner was served with an almost charming indifference. You got what you got in Galicia, and nobody - neither waiter nor diners - felt the need to bother with any etiquette whatsoever.

In the morning I left Triacastela for Sarria while the others took the more southerly route that went through Samos. My forest path went uphill; I could feel the weight of my pack and the rhythm of my walking stick. Though I relished the solitude, I was still in a mental conversation with the wonderful people I had just left. But gradually I became aware of my striding, of my breathing. I noticed the masses of trees and shrubs reeling slowly by on either side, and the blue sky that split the forest wall in front of me. With only a little mental effort, I started to collect the details of this day's walk - a white flap of birch bark curling on the edge of the trail, a twitch of leaves where a small rodent burrowed beneath a tree root, the chit-chit of a bird darting in front of me, the sting of a new blister where my walking stick touched my thumb.

The forest trail opened onto a paved country road. There were almost no cars. In the villages, all dusty, the high-pitched stink of manure burned in my nose. I passed little herds of goats and sheep, watching them munch the grass with mute, urgent familiarity.

For much of my trip, I had walked alone. But each evening at the *refugios*, I was meeting more and more familiar faces: Anne and Alan, the Italian Martino, now without his friend from Paris, Anya the German social worker, Victor and José, still picnicking under the trees, Errol, whose book about Buddhism I had nearly finished, the Spanish physical education teacher and his philosopher friend, and Luis and his daughter Ana.

Luis was a purist; he had walked the Camino five times. He knew a lot of good Camino stories. He was also a fervent believer, and when I told him about Prieto's book, he vowed to find a copy in Madrid. This year, he told me, he was introducing his nineteen year-old daughter, Ana, to pilgrimage.

Luis also liked to plan feasts in the hostels: he got people to chip in whatever they could, then busily directed the cooking. After all was prepared, he would sit everyone down around the big table to share food and friendship. "La vida del peregrino!" he would say expansively. "The pilgrim's life." I liked Luis very much, although by sheer coincidence, he and Ana often slept near me in the hostels, and he snored dreadfully.

I had chatted with Luis while we washed our laundry back at Triacastela. I told him Scott and I had cycled to Santiago de Compostela the previous year. "And now," he replied, wringing out his socks with plump, strong fingers, "you have come back to do it the proper way." That remark came back to me as I walked to Sarria.

I registered at the Sarria hostel, a homey building with balconies overlooking a cobbled street. Anne and Alan arrived a few hours later. They wanted something to take Alan's mind off his feet; the movie *Titanic* was playing in town, dubbed in Spanish, and they invited me to go with them in the evening. I debated their offer as I sat in my bunk to write some diary notes. But Luis' comment about the "proper way" was still on my mind. I wanted to mull it over first.

I should have asked him what he thought the proper way was. I wasn't so sure there even *was* a proper way. I thought that if there were, it wasn't necessarily the traditional one. I guessed that Luis would have said something about pilgrimage being a communal affair, something you shared with like-minded people. Fellowship was important to him and he would have been correct, I think, if he had said that pilgrims on a bicycle feel less sense of belonging to a pilgrims' community.

I started my diary entry by noting that the way you think when you walk alone is different from when you walk with a companion, and that both ways have their risks. The monk Prieto, in his solitary pilgrimage, had busied himself with interpreting what he saw along the Camino, as if nature was God's loudspeaker and his job was to heed the announcements. To me this seemed an isolating and reductive approach, a little unbalanced and anachronistic. I am sure Prieto would have said that *my* so-called objective way of thinking is also just as arbitrary a way of looking at the world - and, he would have added, morally not a very useful one. To some degree, this was true: when I look out at the world, I habitually see it through a lens of curiosity. I seek information, not allegory, and certainly not moral lessons, at least not right away.

But on my walk to Santiago this year, I had chosen a third way of using my mind, which had nothing to do with either religious lessons or curiosity. Walking meditation had seemed impossibly difficult when I first attempted it during my retreat in Massachusetts in 1990. But here in Spain, alone on the Camino, if I wasn't going to impose a private fiction on what I saw, or exercise my superficial curiosity on it, there was no other option for me than to simply pay attention to the experience of putting one foot in front of the other and walk west to Santiago.

That act of noticing sensations as they emerge into awareness - the feet on the ground, the smells of manure and sweat, the clouds bulging in the blue disk at the end of a tunnel of trees - is extremely difficult, in fact impossible, to do hour after hour. But it is the effort itself that makes the difference. After three weeks of working at it every day, one way or another, floundering, trying to relax about it, getting it and then immediately forgetting it, I was starting to perceive more clearly not just the world - like a twig snapping in two as I stepped on it - but how I related to what I perceived, what my mind did with its sense of the world. I saw how quick I was to judge and repress certain thoughts, or to latch onto an idea as an escape from what the world was really telling me. Sometimes my mind simply wandered off into its own thickets, as if on a clandestine pilgrimage. This was fine, except that I wasn't there with it. I found too that a significant portion of what my mind did was not especially interesting. None of it was bad, but a lot of it was unnecessary, and sometimes made a barrier between myself and the life around me.

During our laundry discussion, Luis had remarked that pilgrimage helps you find the important things in life. A true pilgrim, he had said, can easily list the things you really need on the back of an envelope: water and air, some food, a few warm, dry clothes, a place to sleep, good companionship, faith. Nothing wrong with that list, I had thought: The Ascetic's Guide to Life on Earth. But for me, the important things were relationship and response. Walking to Sarria, I realized that the *most* unnecessary things were the ones we carry in our heads: our habitual responses to a world we assume we understand. I made my own tentative list of the mind's necessities: calmness, attentiveness, a caring response to what is happening now. And humour: the capacity to be surprised.

Neither my list nor Luis' excluded other people from the practice of pilgrimage. When he had named his three bad reasons for pilgrimage, the monk Prieto claimed that the social life of the Camino could undermine its spiritual value. I understood what he was getting at. I thought back to the day I walked with Evy, Alfredo, and Errol to Nájera. It had been a wonderful walk, though not a mindful one. I had been caught up in my social persona, which seemed all right, but I felt by the end of the day as if I had missed an opportunity. Things had gotten crowded and busy inside my head. I had forgotten to just walk and see what was there. It didn't set me back, but it hadn't pushed me forward either.

But Prieto was only partly right. Like so many "serious pilgrims," he felt that the solution to distraction was to avoid, as much as possible, social contact with other people on the Camino, or at least to choose whom you talked to with meticulous care. What *I* learned, though, was just how seductive solitude is, how easily it becomes an end in itself. And the craving for solitude can make you judgmental and irritable. I thought of the pilgrim who, a couple of weeks ago at Villafranca de Oca, had scowled at me as I chatted with the Americans, and of another I met walking alone on the road one day who had snubbed me when I asked if she spoke English. I thought of the pilgrims who sneered at Ken, the books I had read by pilgrims who ranted about shallow tourists and sports cyclists. People with fixed ideas trying to define their pilgrimage beforehand, and to exclude what didn't fit their point of view.

Unlike Prieto, Luis had set a great deal of store on the social life of pilgrims. He had fixed ideas too, and some people thought he went overboard. Even I fled a few times to a quieter place for dinner. But I had been touched by his gregariousness and welcoming spirit. I started to take more risks meeting people, chose not to respond in my usual ways, tried to relax more when people annoyed me or, much more often and alarmingly, when they attracted me. In bringing the same attentiveness to my social relationships on the Camino that I did to the world when I was alone, I discovered my own version of the ordinary person's defenses, fears and hungers - things that nobody probably notices or cares about much, but that sap your energy and take up valuable space. And at the same time, I became more selective: some people were truly a negative influence, or pulled me too much from my purposes; some people probably saw me in the same way. But with any one of them missing, my whole Camino walk would have been diminished.

I finished writing and put away my diary. Then I took Anne and Alan up on their invitation to see *Titanic*. It was a mess of a movie, and, I found out too late, high on the list of unnecessary ways to spend your time.

The trail from Portomarín to Palas de Rei went by pastures where cows sat serenely staring into space in the shade of trees. It ran through hamlets where misanthropic dogs reared on the end of their leashes and bared their teeth, and past barnyards where pigs made daily donations of shit to the *pozos negros*, or black wells, where manure was kept for fertilizer. The *pozos* had a scream of a stink. Sometimes they made my eyes water half a kilometer away.

Leaving one village, I glanced sideways to see Kjell sauntering into my path from an unrecognizable bar, carrying an empenada in his hand. For company, he suggested that he push his bike and walk with me to Palas de Rei.

It was just after noon and the air was clotted with moisture. We had walked two or three kilometres when from up in the gray sky we heard what sounded like a volley of gunshot. Hunters or bird-startlers maybe. In a reeking village further on, we passed a group of men standing in the road. A little self-consciously, each wore a dark suit that had been pressed over and over for decades. The fabric shone, and the sleeves looked too short.

"I think we heard firecrackers," I said to Kjell. "Scott and I heard the same sounds when we cycled through here one afternoon last year."

Before long, we came to a small field lined on the far side with trees. A stage had been set up near the road and young men were stringing cables around the black boxes of an elaborate sound system. A big sign in front of the stage announced: *Las Silouetas*. I asked someone if we were to have music. "Ahora mismo!" he said brightly.

"He says it's starting right away," I told Kjell.

"What's starting?"

"Haven't a clue." But my words were drowned out. The band had trooped on stage and was already teasing its way into *In the Mood*. The thick air began to jiggle with the good-natured wheeze of saxophones.

Laughing, Kjell shook his head. "I can't believe this! I walk in the middle of Galicia and here's a jazz band out of *nowhere!*"

"Playing Glen Miller!" I added.

Old cars were pulling up. Folks who had been milling under the trees moved toward the stage: slim, young mothers holding toddlers; thick women past child-bearing, straight and sturdy in dresses from the city; their husbands, wearing their obligatory suits; old pear-shaped aunts. Game booths were set up across the field from the stage; in front of them stood clumps of teenage girls in short skirts and snug tops from Benetton and Calvin Klein. The boys, wearing white shirts and looking like daddy-longlegs or else half a head shorter than the girls, pretended not to notice them. A herd of little girls in bright dresses was taking a last run at being improper. Small boys darted among the crowd trailing balloons on long strings. Grown-ups were buying drinks in a tent that looked from the side like a white sand dune. Near the tent, a teenage boy with Down's Syndrome watched the stage with interest and worked at tapping his foot.

The band was swinging like crazy. *Las Siluetas* were nothing if not versatile: Spanish rock and roll, big band, lounge music, American pop, Beatles. Slick-haired musicians bent over their trombones and trumpets, the saxophones scooped the air, the percussionist whacked at his drums. After the band leader had introduced the musicians (lots of applause), a female singer let loose with a selection of heart-broken Spanish love songs. A man sang Frank Sinatra. Around us, people danced on the grass: husbands and wives, mothers and daughters, seven-year-old girls and their five-year-old brothers, grammas and grampas. In the centre of the crowd, a large, serious woman in a bright blue dress hooded over her wiry husband: a fancy moth dancing with a larger than average ant.

"Dance?" said Kjell. I took off my backpack and laid it by a tree, then rolled my t-shirt sleeves up over my shoulders. Kjell grabbed my arm and twirled me almost off my feet over a mass of roots. The spinning made me laugh. We danced, we jived, we twisted in the hot, moist air, until I was out of breath and the sweat ran down my legs into my boots. Nearby, a large girl with an orange hair-band and glasses stared at us as if we were from another planet.

The mayor got up on stage, welcomed us all, handed out awards (more cheers and applause) and announced that the big dance would start at nine that evening. People drifted from the centre of the field and the bar got busy. We bought drinks - gin, foolishly - and wandered around the booths. I thought fleetingly about coming back at nine, but knew it was impossible.

As we gathered our packs to leave, I looked over the field again. The stage sat now like an empty cardboard box beside the children with their dresses and balloons. Red and blue streamers hung windlessly on the booths. I looked at the big white wings of the tent and the line-up of folks curling back from the bar into the trees - a milky way of white shirts, shiny black suits, gleaming buttons and gray hair. Above us spread a timeless, warm, damp sky.

In medieval times, no matter where you came from, you would not have been surprised to round a turn on the Camino and come upon people dancing. Even the meanest pilgrim knew that music, dance and poetry were the trinity in the heart of any medieval town. In Galicia between the 11th and the 18th Centuries, you might watch people dancing to the melodies, not of Glen Miller, but of a *canto de amigo* accompanied by pipes and strings. Or a *danza prima*: two concentric circles of dancers face to face, one circle singing and moving to the "a" rhymes of the song and the other to the "i" rhymes. Then there was the long and dreamy ring dance called the *cossante*, which looked complicated even if it seemed natural enough for the locals. After a while you might start humming the tune, even if you couldn't figure out the steps.

Such dance songs, with their strict but endlessly inventive word patterns, are said to have evolved in Spain from fertility rituals in the centuries before the Camino, when Christianity was just a few threads on a pagan tapestry, and pilgrimages were made to rocks and trees more often than to holy bones. The earliest tunes were more incantation than love song; their very syllables hummed with magic potential. To dance was more compulsion than entertainment: it was to snuggle up to nature, worship her and, under the cover of charms, tease out her lucky, lively powers: longevity, a good crop, survival through the winter.

The Roman geographer Strabo mentioned these Galician vegetation rites in the 1st Century. A thousand years later, they had turned into the *danza prima* and the *cossante*, still part ritual, but now an amusement too, sharing the scene with hawkers in their booths, kids eating whatever passed for sweets in those days, blushing girls with clean blouses that smelled of the wind, men with jugs of ale in their hands, and a few pilgrims, one maybe with a flute, waiting his turn to play a tune from his part of the world for the locals.

Another thousand years later, I would happen upon a Galician fair in a tiny corner of the global village. I would see kids drinking Coca-Cola and Fanta, sip the same Beefeater's gin I had drunk on the plane out of Toronto, look at young girls in Calvin Klein tops, ladies' dresses I had seen on farmwives at country fairs in Alberta. And then there was all that familiar American music: Elvis and Frank and Ella. I couldn't imagine what Galician culture would evolve into from this.

But if the content had changed with the centuries, the old form seemed to be surviving almost intact, like the spinal column in eons of vertebrates. It was all there at that afternoon fair, the 20th-century version of a 10th-century version of a rite as old as humankind: a piece of land with trees, a tent, a row of booths, a stand for musicians, a community of human souls dancing under the sky, and a couple of wide-eyed strangers.

The earthen paths through the Galician forests have a light brown colour; when it rains, as Scott and I had found out the year before, they get thick and clotted, and snakes of water wriggle through their creases. This year it wasn't raining, at least not yet; the track was like buckwheat flour, and scattered with rocks and twigs and long, thin eucalyptus leaves. The forests were quiet but very rich in smells, as if any noise at all was immediately converted into scent. The resinous whiff of eucalyptus was everywhere, but there were other odours that vibrated on the eucalyptus like harmonics: moss, rain, your own sweat, a hint of manure, oak leaves drying to powder, and that other, nameless smell that makes things grow in moist earth.

I spent the night in the *refugio* at Palas de Rei, in a clean, crowded room overlooking the curved main street and a small municipal park. I ran into Errol here and returned his book about Buddhism to him. He was giving back rubs this evening, and he offered me one as I was climbing into my top bunk for a rest. Under his strong hands, my muscles oozed into the mattress. Later we cooked potatoes and canned beans and sardines for supper in the little kitchen.

Errol was a marvellous singer. He had studied music and belonged to a choir in South Africa. I wish I could sing, I told him. He had looked at me with quiet surprise. "You can," he said. "You shouldn't hold back, you just have to let it out. Go deep into your body and then let it fly."

I thought about that as we continued to cook, but decided I would try it in private first.

Over the next two days, I walked, sometimes with Errol, sometimes with Kjell, sometimes alone, to Melide and Arzúa, then to Santa Irene, which I had trouble finding. The hostel was some distance down a hill from a bleak crossroads. At the reception desk, a young woman with dark hair and friendly eyes welcomed me kindly. She seemed to find it miraculous that I was from Canada, as if I had walked over the ocean to get here. The hostel was half-empty. It was September now, and most summer pilgrims had gone home.

I met a French pilgrim named Pierre unpacking upstairs. He had seen two restaurants back up the hill at the crossroads, which, it turned out, was all there was to Santa Irene. At dusk we went up together with Errol. The first restaurant was openly hostile to the idea of serving us dinner. At the second, surprise was expressed that we wanted to eat, but not hostility, though the rule was made very clear that not even a salad or a bun could be served before the cook came at nine. We waited at a table outside the restaurant door, slouching on white plastic chairs and sipping mineral water. At nine fifteen the cook arrived, amiably shaking our hands as if he had been looking forward to seeing us. We made him take our order even before he entered the restaurant. He was cheerfully confident the meal he prepared for Pierre, Errol and Mary - he had asked our names - would be perfect.

Which it was: huge, hot potato tortillas, good fresh bread, salad. We shared a bottle of wine and talked about our pilgrimage. Pierre had walked all the way from Paris, a trip that had taken a little over two months. He was out of work, he told us, and was walking to Santiago de Compostela to get help in finding a job.

"You mean you're going to ask St. James for a job?" I asked.

He nodded, looking without expression from Errol to me and back. He had one eye permanently crossed. A large crucifix hung from his neck. He was extremely tall. Walking to the restaurant, I had barely kept up. He had a wild, intense gait, a long stagger with a leap in the middle like a hiccup. His face was always composed, but I could sense how desperate he was.

In the morning, Pierre had left the hostel before I even woke up. Errol was gone too. I walked alone in the dawn through redolent forests. It was like floating in an intoxicating vapour. After several kilometres, my attention was pulled to the middle of the path, where someone had used pistachio shells to make an arrow pointing in the direction of Compostela. A little further along was a little heart-shaped wreath of blue wildflowers. Rounding a corner, I came upon Errol sitting with his back against the embankment, eating pistachios. I sat down and pulled out some peanuts, and we made another arrow out of shells.

We walked on together, talking about places we wanted to travel, our families, world politics. We caught up with Pierre, who was eating a meager lunch from things he had scrounged at the hostel. He walked with us for a while, but we were not fast. At first, he tried to slow down, awkwardly changing his gait to a combination of tramping on grapes and the long jump. Finally, we gave him permission to go on ahead of us, and he bounded off like a deer released from a yard.

I asked Errol to sing for me. Soon we were both singing: Beatles tunes and old folk songs: Michael Row the

Boat Ashore, Kumbaya, Four Strong Winds; music "lacking intellectual and rhetorical content" and, in my case, out of pitch.

Pilgrims have always sung on the way to Santiago. Though you can imagine their gritty voices, and the tap of walking sticks keeping rhythm, it is almost impossible now to know what they actually sang. Pilgrim songbooks began to appear only in the 17th Century. The earliest to be written down is a French one from 1616. It contains a verse text about what to take on the trip to Santiago, a little information about the difficult terrain, and bits and pieces of advice. Tunes also exist from Scandinavia, Central Europe, Italy, Germany and England; the majority are French. In 1718 a songbook appeared entitled *Les Chansons des pélerins de Saint-Jacques*. Others like it appeared throughout the 19th Century. From such books we can guess at the earlier repertoire: songs of devotion to St. James, songs telling stories of Camino miracles and misadventures. In a Spanish collection, there are songs about pilgrims unjustly hanged and saved by the Apostle. Another song, appearing in several variations, tells of a highborn girl who is raped by a certain Count Miguel de Prado. The Count is caught and given the option of marrying the girl or hanging, both of which he refuses, though in one version the girl herself punches him to death.

In the 18th Century, the French *Grand Chanson* appeared, another advice song in a minor key taken from a Christmas carol. It blends religious and popular themes, and it captures the big emotions that still infused the pilgrimage to Santiago even at this late date in its history. The *Grand Chanson* tells of the sadness of departing from France, of leaving parents and friends, of the heart's deep desire to see St. James, and the need to abandon all pleasures to make the journey.

Santiago de Compostela itself had a lively popular music scene in the Camino years, and normally serious music students often cut loose on a free afternoon to play in the streets. The city had its share of wandering goliards too: clerics or vagabond monks who had taken up the minstrel's life, travelling - or sometimes chased - from town to town. Not all of their songs were monkish; a

Cistercian document from 1199 forbids monks to write goliards at all; if you were caught, you were sent to another monastery.

I told Errol about a story - more vignette than story - I had read in Ballester's book, *Compostela*. A knight from Provence, probably a heretic or, just as bad, a non-believer, hangs up his sword behind the door, throws his guitar on his back and heads off to see the world. He happens to arrive in Santiago, which he finds crude and overdone. He is about to leave when he finds himself in conversation with a clergyman who, it turns out, hosts a regular evening literary group. They are meeting at his house that very night in fact, and the man from Provence is invited along. For hours the club and the exotic visitor sing *cantigas de amigo*, laugh over satirical lyrics of the *cantigas de maldecir*, and argue about courtly love and the new flower dances. The knight, personally acquainted with the fashionable world of Provence and Catalonia, is pumped for news and gossip about famous musicians and poets that the Galicians have only heard of. The evening is a huge hit, the locals are delighted, and the knight goes off the next day immensely satisfied with his visit to Santiago de Compostela.

"Sounds like a story that could happen any time, anywhere," said Errol.

"That's why I like it," I said. "Stories like that make me trust that some things about human beings will never change."

We arrived at a bar in a small village. Across from the building, about a dozen pilgrims lolled on white plastic chairs lined up against a stone fence, with their bare feet hanging over their boots. A few more lay on the ground with their legs up on the chairs. Dirty white bandages were wrapped around various knees and ankles. Two pilgrims were busy giving foot massages. Business was roaring for the bar owner, who was not at all unhappy when two more customers entered his establishment. Errol and I bought drinks and returned to the group. We eagerly greeted Kjell, who looked exhausted. He had come down with the flu a couple of days ago. "It just keeps getting harder and harder," he said. "I know I'll get to Santiago, but I have to keep stopping because I feel so sick." Just as we sat down beside him, Anne and Alan emerged from the outdoor privies. Alan was hobbling, leaning on two sticks to take the pressure off his agonized feet. They sat down with us and pulled out their water bottles and chocolate. Errol produced more peanuts and I contributed some apples from my pack.

I do not know what became of Anya from Germany. I never saw Victor and José again either, or Martha or Virginia, or Luis and Ana. Martino was probably already in Santiago, along with the ever speedier Duncan. The fast-talking Arnoldo had disappeared early on; Evy the Brazilian was probably back in Italy by now. Bernardo was long gone back to Madrid. A year later I would get an email from him saying he was coming to Canada to see his son, but I heard nothing more after that.

I got up and took pictures of Anne, Alan, and Kjell squinting into the sun and smiling lamely. Then Alan began to examine his feet while Anne prepared her combination first aid and torture kit. Kjell seemed to be about to sleep sitting up. Beside him, Errol pulled out a book and put his hand over his eyes for shade.

I looked again at Kjell. Like all of us, he was tired and grimy. The flu had made his tanned skin pale but he still had the lean robustness of a handsome Scandinavian man. I thought of that hot afternoon only two weeks ago when he had carried my gear on Rosinante from San Juan de Ortega to Atapuerca, walking slowly beside me under a glaring sun. He had taken me for supper at Calzadilla de la Cueza after my terrible journey from Benevivere. Only last week, we had met again and danced at a country fair. A few days from now, I would give him my second scallop shell, the one I had taken from the restaurant in Ottawa, as a souvenir of our hours together and a thankful reminder of how he had helped me.

I took another picture of Anne and Alan. She had begun the iodine treatment and Alan was yelping before she even touched him. In such a short time, they had become good friends. I had gone to see *Titanic* with them at Sarria. Afterwards, we had gone to a bar for a drink, where we talked about our jobs. All three of us were what is called, awkwardly, "helping professionals." That meant we were paid to care for other people, but it was also true that each of us was defining some moral purpose for our own lives through the work that we did. In later years, every Christmas, I would hear from them. I would visit them in Liverpool too, admire their English garden, meet their children, talk more about the Camino, life, faith.

In the deepest text of one's pilgrimage, I wondered, what meaning do such encounters hold? Are they the heart of the story, or are they its sweet ephemeral gifts?

The Cathedral of Santiago in the Plaza Obradorio.

10

SANTIAGO

Yet I am grateful to those who have provided me with the benefit of their illusions. They have journeyed ... from so many distant places in order to share with me the purest of all deceptions - that of their own willingness to be entranced.... For each man, whether he wandered in the desert or tramped through the jungle, was able to change the nature of space for himself....
        James Cowan. *A Mapmaker's Dream*

Your arrows do not carry," observed the Master, "because they do not reach far enough spiritually. You must act as if the goal were infinitely far off."
        Eugen Herrigal. *Zen in the Art of Archery*

A few kilometeres past the city of Santago, Finisterre overlooks the Atlantic Ocean to the west, close to where legends say St. James's body arrived in a stone boat.

It is a curious fact that one of the earliest pilgrim's diaries in Europe was written not by a traveller *to* Santiago, but by someone who left Galicia to travel east. Four hundred and fifty years before Pelayo and Theodemir plied the woods near Iria Flavia, a local woman named Etheria, highborn and literate, probably Roman, turned her back without knowing it on James' tomb and went on pilgrimage to the Holy Land. Etheria carried with her a Bible, Eusebius' *Ecclesiastical History,* and various *Lives* of saints and martyrs. With "unconquerable bravery" she journeyed to Jerusalem, gazing as she went upon the very soil where Moses, the prophets, the saints, and Christ himself had walked. "Nothing could hold her back," wrote her Spanish biographer Valerius three centuries later. "Fearlessly," she travelled among "the perils of seas and rivers, the dread crags and fearsome mountains."

Etheria would walk sacred history right into the soles of her feet, feel it rise through her tissues like sap. Retracing the Israelites' journey out of Egypt, she stopped at a rock cleft on the side of Mount Horeb while her companion read from the Book of Exodus. Over these stones, Etheria heard, the Lord in his glory had passed by Moses, shielding him with his almighty hand that he might not die at the sight of him. *God Himself had passed by here!*

In Jerusalem, she made a practice of following processions along the Way of the Cross. On Good Friday, she writes, when the relics of the Passion were displayed at Golgotha and the story was read out, "everyone present was overwhelmed by emotion and the strongest men there could not contain their tears."

What amazed me about Etheria was her readiness for affirmation: she visited Melchizedek's palace and Job's tomb, stood on the banks of the River Jordan where John had baptized the multitudes, ducked reverentially into the Holy Sepulchre, and shouted "Yes! This is It!" to it all. The Via Positiva. Everything could and, it seems, did take Etheria home. In every desert, every mountain she crossed, every shrine and tomb she entered, lived an event in time and space, a fragment of history, that curled like the green stem of a morning glory across the border into God's eternity.

Why is it that we humans desire so ardently the stories that inhabit the mute, solid things we find on our path? I imagined Etheria travelling from Galicia to Jerusalem like an archeologist possessed, seeking the occurrences, the acts of God, the sparks of the divine, that inhabited material things.

One day as we paused for a rest on the crest of a hill not far from El Cebreiro, I had asked Scott why he liked so much to travel among the remnants of history.

"Back at Roncesvalles for instance, what was so compelling for you when we stood there on top of the Pyrenees?"

He paused. "I guess it's that my ancestor Sam Burgos had been there, and a thousand years before him, the pilgrims, and before that, the Moors and Charlemagne, the Visigoths, the Romans and everybody else. You look over the landscape now and you see how things change in time until history finally comes down to you." He grabbed his water bottle and flipped the lid. "Being there puts you in contact with the time dimension, makes it visible. That's the only way you can grasp the meaning of time - by looking at something in space and using your imagination to see what was here before." He paused to drink. "You have to participate: you add memory and the things you know from history to what you see, and you get a feel for the flow."

Etheria had participated too, and more: she had stretched out the tentacles of her Bible-fed imagination and taken *God's* history into her soul. Of course she knew that buildings fall down and paths grow over, but the prototype - the Eternally Real - still shone like the edge of a diamond in the grooves of the material world. Etheria didn't care about the changes and shifts that took place in earthly time; she blithely carried on as if not once since the days of Moses had history and space drifted apart. The only time she bothered with was locked into the surfaces of things touched by God. Divinity had entered history, was laced into the walls of palaces and the lintels of tombs. Look deeply enough at those solid things and the Alpha and the Omega would spear into your soul in one pinpoint flash.

Jonathan Sumption, in his book *Pilgrimage: An Image of Medieval Religion*, says that Etheria's passion for holy places was a compound of imagination and romanticism. But wasn't that what the Via Positiva required? How else to spy out God's eternity in all those solid walls and spacey places? *Seeing into* is what the imagination does best. Using her Bible and her books to keep herself on track, Etheria looked upon the rocks and roads of history as into a microscope, watched the Eternal shimmer along their borders as ageless Divinity suffused them without ceasing.

I admired Etheria's trust. Pilgrimage would take her precisely to the places where God had passed and she knew exactly what to do there: submit with a romantic's single-minded passion, curl and elongate that pliant soul of hers into the mold of salvation geography. By Valerius' time, she was a saint herself, the exemplary pilgrim who had perfected herself by travelling to Jerusalem, with the Bible in her hands for a map.

"Another thing," Scott said, "is that these historical sites are a testimony to people who used to exist and aren't here any more, and to their values. If you destroy the places, or the memory of what happened, you're denying them their just due, and you might as well deny yourself your own just due. I suppose it's the basis for some kind of morality. It's a connection of responsibility between yourself and a bigger family."

He paused thoughtfully and took another sip of water. "It's not really morality, it's more a kind of humility. The important thing is to know how relative your world is. You think you live in a World X, but you look around and you realize that the same place used to be part of World P, and a whole lot of potential things that *didn't* happen were in World N. Knowing that keeps you from being stuck in thinking you have all the answers or can imagine all the possibilities. The past gives you a chance to see if there are other ways of doing things, or of thinking about them. You can check what you're doing against it to see if we've gone in the right direction, or are just buzzing around the same place, or going backward."

That wasn't what history had been for in Etheria's day - to give us a measure of how we are doing. History was God's action in his world. It was a testament to human iniquity and the promise of salvation. Pilgrimage was more than an excursion through the world, it was to invite God's laws, told to you by the world, into your own will. You needed an especially confident pilgrim's spirit for that. You had to believe that landmarks, rivers and perilous mountain clefts, were synonyms for events in the history of man's salvation.

What a paradox it is that we know so much more of the world and how it works, and yet it is almost impossible for us to trust any kind of narrative about what happened before us. The Camino itself is a concoction of rabble-rousing propaganda, nationalistic fetishes, falsifications and forgeries, well-meaning moral tales, religious hoaxes. If medieval people knew about them, they don't seem to have cared. We, on the other hand, go for the ironic. We feed our scepticism, deconstruct what we see. Sometimes the habit gets out of hand, and we find only a grim satisfaction in the destruction of illusions.

It was early June. Scott and I would arrive in Santiago in a few days. Our Camino pilgrimage had always been confusing, and was getting more so. But I was learning to embrace confusion. And I was still asking: these days, what *does* a pilgrim *do*? Where is the pilgrim's transformation to happen on a journey so full of sceptical history, fractured meanings, and ironic contradiction? Affirmation of Etheria's sort seemed impossible; but to reject the idea completely that the world has, embedded within it, its own mystical significance seemed as pointless as asking my legs to stop wanting to move.

Modern pilgrimage, I still believed - I couldn't see how it might be otherwise - was a Via Negativa, a quest in learned ignorance through a landscape of theatre sets. As Zen teaches, "Not this! not this!"

Not likely, anyway. *But then what?*

Buddhists hold that beliefs and ideas are, like everything else, ephemeral phenomena that rise and fall in an ocean of ephemerality. In this view, scepticism is one such fragment, a bundle of thoughts and counter-thoughts bouncing around our pinball machine of a mind. Scepticism has its uses, can help us decide whether the sales clerk is honest or the odometer is accurate. But when scepticism is a habit of mind, a posture, a way of leaning into the world, we can miss seeing things as they are. Scepticism makes us doubt before we even see. Pilgrimage, it seemed to me, was to go out *doubtlessly* and see *first*. I recalled my father's voice as he led me into the woods that rainy day in Ontario; in the deepest sense, pilgrimage was about taking "a look around." It was to pay attention to the place where we come upon ourselves moving in time.

Galicia in June 1997 was beautiful, moist, glinting with sunbeams. The air was perfused with the scent of eucalyptus and the musty undercurrent of wet earth. When it rained, the forest leaves trembled behind streaky slits of silver.

The rain also thickened the trails with slick brown mud. On the hills it was tough going. "We're on the slippery slope," Scott quipped one morning as I skiddered down a mud-slicked track and nearly slid into a tree. When we walked our bikes, our feet got wet to the ankles. I could feel grit between my toes. Sometimes we took the roads, but they had their own rigours: long hills rounding upwards through dripping forests, until a last turn would bring us to a height of land. Then we would skim down through the drizzle into a valley, and the whole thing began again.

By Portomarín, I was extremely tired. We stopped for a rest on the church steps. Portomarín, I read in my Everest Guide, goes back to Roman times. Doña Urraca had destroyed the bridge here over the Rio Miño to keep her enemy-husband Alfonso the Battler from attacking the town. The Knights of St. John of Jerusalem ran a hospice nearby. In the 1950s, the entire town was moved to its present location when a new water reservoir flooded the old site.

I was still reading the Guide to Scott when a young woman in short shorts and a bright orange tanktop walked by. She looked startled when she heard me, and veered our way as if we were magnets.

"Oh my gawd!" she cried. "You speak English! Oh my gawd, what a relief!" She belonged to an American tour group travelling to Santiago in a van. While she had been out hunting down the English language, the rest of her group was enjoying the outdoor bar of Portomarín's best hotel.

Scott asked her how she found her trip so far. Despite the fact that Spaniards spoke Spanish, she was enthusiastic. They were staying in the best hotels, could make day trips along the Camino on foot whenever they felt like it, and were picked up when they got tired. And the food, which was prepared from a kitchenette in the van, was "absolutely fantastic."

We went with her to the hotel patio where we met her group, twelve youthful middle-agers lounged on white plastic chairs. The beer was going down easy. We declined an offer to join them, and after chatting a little longer, made ready to head to Palas de Rei and Arzúa. "Today's the Feast Day of Corpus Christi," someone called to us as we were pulling away. "Happy Corpus Christi!"

We arrived at Arzúa late in the afternoon. The rain had left the town's concrete buildings black with moisture. Although my body was exhausted, I was in a mood of peaceful endurance. We took a room in a seedy hotel on a street off the main square. Later we returned to the square to look around. A few young men were erecting bleachers near the road, and up on a hulking stage, others squatted over the wires of a sound system. The speakers reminded me of the monoliths in *2001: A Space Odyssey*.

The restaurants would not be open before eight-thirty, so we ate a picnic supper in the square from leftovers in our packs. By nine we were back in the hotel room lying in our narrow, single beds like two corpses. Through the drapes I could see the pale brightness of the solstice and the hazy shapes of low-rise apartments in the direction of the square.

At 9:45 sharp, the first twang of amplified strings raked the air by the window. The drums cracked, and we were off. Scott stirred and said, "It can't be." But it was. Arzúa was celebrating the Miracle of Transubstantiation with a rock concert. "Happy Corpus Christi," I said. My body was dead still; I was being carried into the spheres on a giant acoustic guitar.

I submitted, too weary to resist, grateful at least that nothing else was being asked of me than this. The night slowly darkened. I lay and listened while the hours passed. As a matter of fact, the music wasn't bad. I was ever more grateful that someone had managed to contract a decent band for the night. At three fifteen the show was abruptly over. Scott had somehow managed, he later told me, to go to sleep around two; I was kept awake by the silence and by his soft breathing until the first cars passed in the alley below our window.

An enormous woman with a shattering voice ruled our hotel. In the morning she stood over us at the breakfast table with her chest out wide as if rejoicing in her fatness. In barely understandable Gallego, she told us that we *must* see *las alfombras* before we left Arzúa. "*Las alfombras! Las alfombras!*" she cried, raising huge eyebrows into the shape of a tent, and hurtling her arms like footballs in the direction of the town square. We left after packing up to look for *las alfombras*, whatever they were, on our way out of town.

There were rainclouds in the sky. Turning into a shabby street, we asked a thin, baggy woman with a crooked nose where *las alfombras* were. She peered at us silently. We stood before her, feeling large and foreign. She made an awkward movement, then wandered away from us at an angle. A little dog trailed after her, stopping to scratch his fleas. The thunder muttered in the distance.

A young man had seen us with the woman and came over now to shepherd us back to the square. On the way, we saw the hotelier billowing like a tornado down the street. She had been looking for us, and when she saw us, she shouted and smiled fatly. We had taken the wrong street. *"Las alfombras! Alla, alla!"* She waved her arms to the right, her body rippling all the way to her ankles. We turned away from her to look.

Carpets! Carpets of red and yellow flower petals, nutshells, green chips and coloured stones, laid in designs on the sidewalks throughout the square. We stopped at a huge bed of green chips bordered in red chips, with the cross of St. James, a scallop shell of white pebbles, and a maroon church all outlined in black. On another, the image of a fish was surrounded by a yellow and orange mosaic. This *alfombra* lay before a four-tiered altar on which sat bouquets of flowers and religious statues. On the top rung under a tiny canopy was a space for the Blessed Virgin, though her figure was missing.

The most spectacular *alfombra* lay in the square beside the cathedral: a huge Crucifixion adapted from a painting by Salvador Dali, on a bed of green and yellow chips. The work was impeccably executed. Christ's arms stretched like the wings of a condor along a cross made with small pieces of bark. At the end of the wrists were limp hands that resembled an orchestra conductor's; the head, a oily stain of black hair in tiny chips, was sunk into the chest almost down to the loincloth; the rest of Jesus narrowed into a homunculus body. Two boys were putting the finishing touches on a red petal border while a couple of policemen watched from beside a temporary fence.

Las alfombras lay under the sky like little mirrors of divine moments, an earnest offering up of the imagination to God. The lot of them made a mini-pilgrimage through Arzúa, where the eternal could be tracked in space through the work of inspired human hands.

We bought lunch supplies at a café near the square. Coming out, we passed a pilgrim sitting on a chair by the sidewalk reading a book in English. She wore a red checked shirt and a blue scarf; her walking staff leaned against the wall and her boots were well muddied. We asked her how to get out of Arzúa. She saw we were on bikes, and her answer was hasty and rather disdainful. But I liked her confidence and her intensity. Pilgrimage was important, I could see that, and she wasn't going to waste much time on two perfectly well-off cyclists.

As we stepped away, I saw her look up when a man appeared around the corner and walked toward her. He was tall, with rimless glasses, gray hair and a gentle, bearded face. Gasping silently, her face suddenly alight, the woman rose from her chair and slowly, ecstatically lifted her arms to embrace him. The recognition of your own dreams in another traveller is a pilgrim's gift, I could see. I knew they would enter Santiago together.

We made our way out of Arzúa. The storm had swung around to the east and the rain, when it came, was merely a patter of drops. The trails were almost dry so we were able to take the Camino paths once again through Galicia's eucalyptus forests.

Today the woods were nearly deserted. We met only a few foot pilgrims. As we were crossing a road, two cyclists in glossy shirts whizzed by us. Back on the trail, we passed a lady who grinned at us sturdily as she prodded four cows with a stick. A herd of white sheep and a very small boy passed us the other way. The air tilted with the smell of shit and musky mud. The boy turned supercilious when he saw us; clearly he was in charge of his sheep, who he batted and scolded like a schoolmarm. Around them danced the boy's dog, maniacal lord of a universe of wool and brown earth.

At the foot of a steep hill not far from Santa Irene, we ran into a member of the American van tour group, an older man struggling with two walking sticks. We walked our bikes passed him and said hello again.

"Helluva hill," he said by way of reply as he stared up the narrow, mud-caked trail. He glanced at Scott. "You kids gonna ridyer bikes up there?"

"We'll give it a whirl," I answered, none too sure. The man was flushed and panting. I looked at him as we pulled away, nervously rehearsing CPR procedures in my head. He waved me off.

"You guys go on. I'm jes' gotta rest a little. Get my breath."

We left him and struggled up the hill. Before long, we came upon the rest of the tour group preparing to have lunch from the back of the van.

"One of your men is really working hard down there," said Scott to the guide. "He looks as if he could keel over any minute."

She nodded ruefully. "I know. We're worried about him but he won't quit."

Several of the Americans came to say hello, surrounding us with bright, well-rested faces and clothes that smelled of detergent. They were extremely friendly and full of questions; they also knew a lot about the Camino. A stout, red-haired woman with white legs was evidently something of an authority on Camino saints. She mentioned a chapel nearby that was dedicated to San Roque.

"San Roque," she said, as if reciting a catechism. "Feast Day on August 16. French hermit saint famous for taking pilgrimages. Looked after people in northern Italy during the plague. Got the plague himself but his dog cared for him. Brought him bread. French pilgrims brought the cult to Spain in the 1400s. Has an open wound on his leg and a dog and a walking stick."

I listened with interest to this, but had no reply.

The tour guides were all young American women with a background in tourism. One of them joined us, a travel writer who had walked the Camino many times. "I do it every few years," she told us. "This year I wanted to show it to people who can't do a foot pilgrimage. This isn't a traditional pilgrimage, but we try to point out the spirituality of the Camino. We want people to respect its traditions."

I asked if they were going to walk far today.

"Some of us are going to walk between Boente de Riba and Ribadixo de Baixo, through Castañeda."

"Castañeda," said the red-haired woman. "Site of the lime furnaces used when they were building Santiago Cathedral. Pilgrims would carry a stone from Triacastela to Castañeda to help with the work."

The man we had passed earlier hobbled into sight, sweating profusely. Relieved to see him, we all cheered as he came to the van.

"I had no idea it was like this," he said, wiping his forehead with a huge handkerchief. He turned to Scott. "You kids pilgrims? Or jes takin' yer bikes out? Didya really get up that whole hill without gettin' off?" He was a midwesterner; I recognized the accent, more attitude than accent.

"Almost," said Scott. "The mud ruts really slow you down."

"I quit halfway," I said.

"Whew! that was steep. But by golly, this is a great trip," he said, looking at a woman bringing platters of fruit and cheese from the van. "I couldn't do it on foot, and no way on a bike. This ole ticker o' mine ...." He wiped his handkerchief around the back of his neck. "I think my kids otta do sump'n like this. It'd be good for 'em to rough it a bit."

I could almost hear the whining.

Behind me the redhead was lecturing Scott. "San Lazarus. Has a chapel near Arzúa. Raised from the dead by Jesus. Brother of Mary and ...." I turned away, defeated by a volley of facts.

Throughout the day, we would continue to run into the Americans as our paths coincided. Each time, they offered us food from their stores - which *was* "absolutely fantastic." They were eager for us to share our experiences with the group. Once they waited for us to catch up, thinking we might be getting tired. After they had driven off to Santiago, waving out the windows at us, Scott commented, "I don't know why pilgrims get so upset about tourists on the Camino. People learn about the Camino in different ways. In the Middle Ages, that poor guy with the heart problem would have died here; now, he gets to see the Camino and what it means, and live to tell somebody else about it."

Late in the day, we stopped for a drink beside a low stone fence studded with shrubs. A solemn old cowherd came along the road. His cows were handsome, healthy creatures. I do not know cows well, but I noticed that some looked like Holsteins, some, the chocolate milk ones, like Guernseys, and others, with their big soft eyes and rusty hides, like Jerseys. The cowherd looked at us with narrow eyes, then asked in Gallego where we were from.

"Canada," I answered.

He had heard of it. "Very bad place," he said, "very bad." I was alarmed, wondered if news of Canada's codfish dispute with Spain had reached Galician cowherds.

"What's wrong with Canada?" Scott asked.

His reply was contemptuous. "They don't have any cows."

I was relieved to reassure him that we did have cows in Canada, huge herds of them where I came from. "Beautiful cows like yours," I added. "Why, my own father was raised on a farm."

What kind of cows did my father have, he wanted to know, frowning and lifting his chin to me as if in challenge. I described cows that looked like Holsteins and Guernseys and Jerseys. The man frowned at me. I told him (inanely, I later thought) about the time my father, as a young boy, had dashed from the farmhouse to the barn late one moonless night and had run head-on into the side of a big black cow that had been standing by the barn door. Even after hearing it a hundred times, we had always laughed at this story. The cowherd listened intently and did not laugh. After a few moments he gave me a withering look. "Why didn't your father turn on the light first?" he asked. I found myself explaining to an incredulous cowherd in the middle of Spain's poorest province, that eighty years ago, there had been no electricity on my father's farm in southern Ontario.

We had paused to check the map at a spot where the Camino ran alongside a quiet paved road when the speed cyclists appeared again. This time they stopped to talk to us. They were from Germany; one was lean, blond and loud, the other was stocky and a little quieter. Both were in good shape. They invited us to join them at a roadside bar they knew of just ahead. There they bought us some red wine and Spanish chorizo.

"I'm not sure I should drink wine while I'm cycling," I said.

"Makes you strong!" said the blond, shrugging in a muscular way and smiling by curling his mouth down and out.

The Germans' sole interest was to ride as fast as they could to Santiago. "Ve're trying to get zer before ze road!" said the blond, grinning. He had perfect teeth and sparkling blue eyes.

"Where's all your gear?" asked Scott. From the trail we had watched their light touring bikes skim like birds over the tarmac.

"Vee haff friends in a Volksvagon who meet us in Santiago," answered the blond. "Tomorrow vee go to Finisterre and zay vill follow us zayre."

The quiet one had worked in banking in Galicia some years earlier and spoke Gallego. The blond was in sales. They were happy, well educated men, thoroughly enjoying some leisure time in Spain. Pilgrimage seemed not to have occurred to either of them.

"Where will you stay tonight? I mean, which hotel?" I asked.

"Reyes Católicos," said the blond, munching hot sausage and bread.

Scott lifted his eyebrows over his wineglass. "That's very posh, I hear."

"It vas ze hostel built by Isabella in 1492. Ja, it's chic." He pronounced it "cheek."

"What are the rates like?"

"In ze sky."

Outside the restaurant we took photos of the friendly Germans, and they of us. We all got on our bikes together, but soon they had left us in the dust.

The Camino ran steadily westward beside fertile fields and eucalyptus forests, across small, empty roads and through nameless hamlets. At Lavacola the highway crossed the Camino, and we got confused by the road construction. My muscles felt as if they were sinking to the bottom of my bones.

At Monte de Gozo it began to rain. We stopped under a tree in a park to put on our raingear. Monte de Gozo means Mount of Joy - sometimes it is written as *Monxoi*. It was from this height of land that pilgrims looking west on a clear day were granted their first glimpse of Santiago de Compostela. Domenico Laffi was helpless with emotion when he arrived here in the 1670s. Like us, he and his companions had just come through Lavacola, "where we washed well and changed our clothes, for we knew we were close to Santiago." At Monte de Gozo, he wrote:

> we were rewarded with the longed-for site of the city of Santiago, some half a league away. On seeing it, we fell to our knees and began to weep for joy, and to sing the *Te Deum*, but we could not recite more than two or three lines, being unable to speak for the tears that streamed out of our eyes with such force that our hearts trembled, and our continuous sobs interrupted our singing. At last, our tears ceased and we resumed singing the *Te Deum....*

Now, three hundred fifty years later, Monte de Gozo is so profoundly ugly that when we saw it, we burst out laughing. The hostel complex is a cross between a third rate university campus and a Soviet resort. The sculpted structure commemorating the visit of John Paul II is an intellectual attempt at grandiosity by someone who, it appears, never felt grand.

But looking out from the top of Monte de Gozo, I caught a glimpse, the barest outline through the fog and drizzle, of the spires of Compostela. A dream just out of reach. Or an intimation of reality. I paused and stared for a silent moment, feeling my heart skip a beat.

We coasted our bikes down the long hill from Gozo, crossed the main thoroughfare and entered modern Santiago. We stopped at a small monument to pilgrims. Its message was unremarkable but as I read it, something brightened in my chest. Though my body still hung over my bicycle like a sack of lead pellets, that light felt like joy. It was an unfamiliar optimism, a streak of silver in the shadows of a room, a match unexpectedly lit.

The city where we entered it was not attractive; a galactic bus stop extended along the road beside us, a rain shelter apparently built for the Pope's visit. We rode on, made a wrong turn, found ourselves at the Convent of San Francisco and its big statue of the saint. On blind instinct we followed the Calle San Francisco, coasting slowly past formal stone buildings.

I *did* feel happy! It was unmistakable.

Suddenly, time and space seemed to flip, as if *we* had stopped, and it was the city that moved, reeling past us, revealing itself in a slow parade. The walls of the Monastery of San Pinario glided by on the left, the Hostal de los Reyes Católicos leaned away to the right. Then, ahead of us, the stone-floored Plaza de Obradorio appeared. On its far side, the Bishop's Palace materialized through the mist like a distant range of mountains. Almost modestly, Santiago Cathedral came into view on our left. Higher and higher it rose, as if inhaling, expanding until it towered over us like a sky goddess. We were in the middle of the square. My silvery lightness had turned to ecstatic amazement.

"Excuse me! Excuse me!" a voice called. "Is zis Santiago?"

I turned, startled. "How could anybody not know...." It was the Germans, laughing boisterously at their joke with their hands out to welcome us. Everyone took everyone's picture, and then we invited them into the church with us.

"Seen it," the blond said. "Vee are off to ze shower."

"Enjoy the expensive room!" Scott called after them as they waved and grinned.

We stood in the centre of the square straddling our bicycles, with the Baroque stairway and carved façade of Santiago Cathedral in front of us. Two busloads of old women in black dresses plodded up the stone steps and disappeared into the cathedral without taking the slightest look around. Behind us swirled a misted galaxy of buildings and people.

A few American tourists approached us, eager to gawk at a couple of sweaty cyclists just off the trail. They all talked at once. I was amazed by their amazement and by their enthusiasm for what we had done.

"Didya really bike all the way?"

"Uh-huh."

"How far was it?"

"About 800 kilo-"

"Where'dya start?"

"At St. Jean Pied de...."

"Ya tired?"

"Yeah, kind of, but...."

"Well, I just *have* to get a picture of *this*. Could you stand over there please?"

"Sure...."

"Congratulations! I want to shake your hand!"

We left our bikes on the west side of the plaza against the wall of the Colegio de San Jerónimo. Now it was our turn to climb the Baroque staircase of Santiago Cathedral. At the top, we entered the Portal of Glory, where the world's most beautiful apostles, carved into the walls by Mateo in the 12th Century, seemed to have been waiting just for us. Beyond them through the portal doors, I saw the cathedral's high, rounded vaults floating like canopies on billows of golden air.

We passed into the nave. I watched the light catch Scott's face as he looked into the arches and down over walls festooned with Baroque angels. "It's like a medieval Turkish bazaar," he said.

My gaze was pulled up the central aisle to the statue of St. James that stood behind the altar in a blaze of golden lights and silvery shadows. The great apostle pilgrim, friend of all pilgrims, seemed to fill the entire transept. He carried a walking stick, and his cape and robe were so finely worked with gold and colour that, looking at him, my mind drifted to Persian carpets and painted eggs. Above that robe, James' face was a serene orb, clearly visible even at a distance. The wide, lucid eyes were as innocent as a boy dreaming of greatness; the creaseless cheeks were a weatherbeaten bronze. A halo studded with plump jewels encircled that head; in the light of the nave, its gold rim reflected yellow like the small arc of a canary's flight.

I kept returning to that face as we walked up the central aisle. The crystalline eyes seemed fixed on the middle distance, but at the same time, they stared over me, out through the cathedral doors, past the Portal of Glory, and clear, without a blink or the slightest squint, into a nebula on the other side of the galaxy.

We walked through the ambulatory, past the chapels, past the door out to the gift shop and the museum. We stood in line and ducked down a narrow staircase into the crypt. The silver reliquary was there. There! I had not expected anything else, but its mute and utter tranquillity still astonished me. I felt I was staring into the motionless centre of a planet-sized wheel. Did the Via Negativa extend down even to this crypt with its casket of God knows whose bones? Not this! not this! *Not even this?* Not even I could resist this one. I stood in that cave, looking at the silver box as it gleamed serenely on its ledge in the wall, and felt, with a shocking snap of affirmation, goosebumps grazing the damp shirt on my back.

A few minutes later we were back in the sanctuary sitting under gold-spangled arches. I peered into their zenith; they bowed over us like the struts of a tent. A few people sat nearby, praying. I looked into the wood in the pew ahead of me and couldn't imagine what there was to say.

It was pouring rain when we returned to the Cathedral for a pilgrims' Mass. This time the church was crowded. The dampness of sweat and drenched clothes wafted in the light of the chandeliers. The organ was finishing a fanfare, and as we took our seats, the service began.

The metallic, amplified voice of the priest echoed hoarsely over our heads. It was indecipherable. Beside me, people were moving in the outside aisles as though in orbit through the heavens. I watched them, thinking how perfectly they illustrated the usefulness of an ambulatory in medieval pilgrimage churches: pilgrims could use them to visit the side chapels without interrupting the service.

Suddenly, the organ discharged another brilliant diapason, and the *botefumeiro* swung into view before the eyes of the congregation. Incense began to cloud the air.

The *botefumeiro* is an enormous censor that holds enough incense, it is said, to cover the stench of all the unwashed bodies in the church. The original one, made in 1544, had been swiped by Napoleon and was not replaced until 1851. Always something of a tourist attraction, the *botefumeiro* is handled by several nimble priests hopping among its ropes with their eyes on the pulleys. The thing acts as a pendulum, weighs about two hundred pounds, and at the given signal, drops like a science experiment from the ceiling into the transept, exhaling thick incense as it swings and twirls, almost out of control.

"It's a circus act," said Scott. I smiled at his candour.

During the Mass, the priest recited the places of origin of all the newly arrived pilgrims to Santiago. I managed to make out "France, seis peregrinos, Germany, ocho peregrinos, Brazil, ocho peregrinos, Canada, tres peregrinos, Russia, uno peregrino, Italy, seis peregrinos." In the *Codex Calixtinus*, there is a similar list of 12th-century pilgrims to Santiago: Franci, Normandi, Scoti, Hiri, Galli, Theutonici, Yberi, Wasconi, Baleari, Navarri impii (impious Navarrese! - I loved that one.) .... The list goes on for pages.

A few pilgrims had been asked to participate in the Mass today, and were now reading the lessons and prayers and saying a few words about their pilgrimage. In the Middle Ages, the Mass was sung in Latin, but a papal document from the 12th Century states that here in Santiago, between the readings of the epistle and the gospel, German pilgrims in the congregation were permitted to sing one small portion of the Mass, the *Dum Pater Familias*, in their own tongue. I had listened to this hymn at home on a compact disc from Polyphonia Antigua called *Ultreia! Sur la Route de Saint-Jacques-de-Compostelle*. It was part of the Mass, but it became a pilgrims' marching song too. Its refrain makes you think of confidence and great faith in the midst of difficulty: *Ultreia!! Suseia! Deus aia nos!!!* Onward!! Go up!! May God help us!!

In the *Veneranda Dies* sermon in the *Codex Calixtinus*, there is a depiction of Santiago Cathedral as it might have looked and sounded during the peak Camino years. In true medieval fashion, it is more rhetorical than descriptive, for its phrases mimic Old Testament lists of musical instruments. Still, it seemed to me a fairly believable portrait of a 12th-century pilgrim service in Compostela. And it contrasted sharply with the subdued congregation I saw on this, our last day on the Camino in the spring of 1997:

> One marvels with exceeding joy, who sees the chorus of pilgrims keeping watch around the venerable altar of St. James: Germans on one side, French on another, Italians on another standing in groups, holding burning tapers in their hands, which illuminate the whole church as the sun or rather the brightest day. Each one with his compatriots wisely performs the vigils by themselves. They keep awake, some by playing citharas, others lyres, others timpanies, others pipes, others trumpets, others harps, others viols, others Breton or Gallican rotas, others psalteries, others by singing various kinds of music, some lament their sins, others recite psalms, others give alms to the blind. There are heard diverse genera of tongues, diverse shouts of barbarous languages and the prattle of Germans, Angles, Greeks, and of all the other tribes and diverse races of all climes of the world. There are neither languages nor tongues whose voices do not resound. In this way vigils are observed there, some indeed advance and others retire and various people offer various gifts. If anyone approaches with sadness, he withdraws with happiness. Solemnities are continually celebrated there, feasts carefully conducted, magnificent throngs worship day and night, praise and jubilation, joy and exaltation, are sung together. Splendor pervades all days and nights, as though under

a continual joyful solemnity to the Lord and to the apostle. The doors of his same cathedral are seldom closed day or night, and it is ordained that night has no place in it, because the splendid light of the candles and tapers shines like mid-day.

Scott and I remained in our pew while the Mass ended and people began to leave the cathedral. The air was musty with sweat and vapour. I could hear the rain outside sloshing coldly over the stones. Beside me, Scott was still. I felt the edge of his arm against my shoulder, inhaled his damp male smell.

He took my hand as we walked out to the Portal of Glory. There we leaned together against the wall under the smiling eyes of Mateo's sculptured musicians. We studied their sedately cheerful faces, the instruments in their laps, their crossed legs, the soft folds of their garments. Oddly, it felt almost as if, without our even knowing it, they had been our companions on our journey across Spain.

We put our rain gear back on: red jackets with flourescent safety strips. From the cathedral doorway, we looked out upon the huge plaza, a celestial dance floor from one baroque facade to another, glinting with raindrops and bobbing with bright umbrellas and shiny yellow rain ponchos. We stepped slowly down the mighty staircase onto the pavement, like creatures from outer space arriving at a ball.

We walked our bikes through the rain until we found a hotel in a small square not far from the cathedral. As we waited to register, an English pilgrim came toward the desk, exhausted and dripping with rain. "You look like it's been a hard journey," I said.

"I've come up the hard way," he said, "through Portugal." I wasn't sure what he was implying by "the hard way," though it is true that the route through Portugal is not well marked, and the terrain is full of obstacles. He leaned on his walking stick, shifted his pack, and let out a huge sigh. I asked him about his journey, but he was too tired. "Sorry," he said, shaking his head as we let him jump the line. "I just have to lie down."

Our room was bright but it could barely contain its two twin beds and little table. I stood at the window holding the white lace curtain back like a wing. In the square below were a fountain and a flower garden surrounded by a low chain fence. A few people walked by, dodging raindrops. I looked again. Heinrich and Else were walking their bikes into the square, squinting through the drizzle for a place to stay. I squeezed onto our shoebox of a balcony and shouted down to them. Their arms flew up and their mouths opened into wide smiles when they saw me. "Come in *here*," I called through the rain. "They've still got rooms. It's fine and it's cheap!"

We went down to meet them in the hotel entrance. Else was radiant, and Heinrich had the look of a satisfied but dripping wet businessman who had just completed an excellent deal. "We are here at last!" said Else. "We can't believe it." They registered, and once again, just as in Logroño, we had adjacent rooms.

"We want to hear about your trip." said Scott. "Shall we have dinner together this evening? We're thinking about some Galician seafood."

"Good! See you at 8:30!"

After a rest, during which I had peculiar dreams of trains and tombstones, we went to the Pilgrim Office to receive our Compostelas. The office was near the cathedral, a stone building with a dark doorway and a flight of blackened steps ascending to a dim anteroom. We joined a collection of pilgrims facing every which way in a haphazard queue. Each one stood with a Camino-hardened posture and stared into the middle distance at some invisible thought. Attenuated emotion hung in the air. Once or twice, a pilgrim known to some of the others came in; arms rose in a flutter of warm hugs, the new arrival was teased a little, there was a short discussion, and then the hush crept in again, prodding everyone back to their private world.

Carnival spirit overtook the Pilgrim Office when a group of Brazilians clattered up the stairs into the waiting area. The tallest, loudest Brazilian was a fellow in his thirties with a dark beard, who announced to his friends that as soon as he received his Compostela, he was going to shave, go to confession and then Mass. He was ebullient, exuded irrepressible confidence and a flat out faith. His excitement rippled through the room, nudging other pilgrims to a state of indulgent amusement. But eventually, even he settled down, and the Brazilians, though they never stopped talking, were absorbed into the collective Camino reverie.

It was a long wait, but we had no wish to hurry. As we drew closer to the door into the office, I peered in. Pilgrims were being questioned at two desks by "officials" who sat opposite them like interrogators. One official was a priest in his sixties who wore Dalai Lama glasses, though his eyes were far from merry. With stony severity, he spoke to the gaunt pilgrim seated before him. It was clearly a serious business to place one's soul before the mercy of James. But a smile suddenly cracked across the priest's face as he handed the pilgrim his Compostela. The man reached for the sheet, then got up from his chair and hefted his pack over his shoulder. As he came through the doorway, Compostela in hand, he grinned at us. "Congratulations!" said Scott.

The office was a bright, pleasantly entropic room cluttered with tables and shelves holding pamphlets and books. Posters from former Holy Years were tacked on the walls. The atmosphere was busy and inefficient. Another official, a slim, pretty young woman, walked to and from her desk organizing people, carrying pencils and papers to pilgrims filling out forms at the tables. I picked up a booklet written for the Jubilee Year of 1993: *St. James the Apostle and his place in history: Ten Study Themes.* I read it while we waited:

> From the ninth century to the present day the Jacobean pilgrimage has sustained the reasoning behind the emphasis on the pilgrim already present in biblical and patristic records. See a place, a tomb, a relic. See an earthly, material goal in order to enter into spiritual realities. Ask and pray that revealed reality may become a means of going beyond the merely earthly, of attaining other, higher goals. The pilgrim to Santiago sets out on the

Way to obtain a foretaste of salvation through voluntary exile. The pilgrimage is a type of break with the world and one's native land; it reminds us of Abraham, our father in the faith, who set out for the land promised him by God....

The pilgrim who sets out motivated by faith and hope is beginning to discover that he is a "fellow citizen with the saints and member of the household of God".... He must go on further into our true country ... and thereby feel a deeper commitment to the Church.

We were summoned by the priest. He greeted us pleasantly but seemed to back off from a smile, as if he knew he was doing something for us that was far more important than we realized. He asked where we were from, wrote some statistics in a book, filled out our certificates. He asked us why we had come, and we gave the answer he had heard ten thousand times: cultural and spiritual reasons.

Scott asked him about the elderly Spanish pilgrims we had seen arriving by the busload in Santiago. He was interested in the priest's views on this kind of pilgrimage. "What inspires those people to come?"

The priest looked at us, amazed that we would even ask the question. "They come for their holy water," he said, as if it was the most obvious thing in the world. When we left, he gravely shook our hands and gave us some pamphlets about the Camino. I think he was tired of what he saw in us: another pair of self-assured non-believers making up their own pilgrimage, unable to grasp the obvious and simple faith of the bus people. Clutching our Compostelas, we made our way out through the crowd of pilgrims waiting their turn in the anteroom, down the stairs and into the street.

Else and Heinrich and Scott and I found a promising restaurant just off the main square and across from a pizza take-out joint. A flotilla of motor scooters was lined up along the sidewalk. From time to time, one would start up with a sudden cough, then emit a shatteringly loud, lazy buzz that gradually faded up the street.

We ordered plates of seafood and vegetables. "Are you drinking wine yet?" I asked.

"Not yet," said Else gaily. "Not until we get home again."

"Four mineral waters *con gaz*," Scott told the waiter.

"Well," I said, settling down for a good talk. "How was it?" There were so many things I wanted to ask them.

We compared notes, shared stories. We devoured Galician octopus and red peppers in oil. The delivery scooters zipped away and back.

"How did you find cycling in Galicia?" asked Scott.

"We stayed on the highway for most of the time after El Cebreiro," said Heinrich. "It was so rainy and our old bikes couldn't cope with the mud."

"You guys had three-speed bikes," said Scott, remembering. "That must have been hard work."

"Sometimes it was tough on those hills," said Heinrich.

"So, how did it feel, getting here finally?" I asked. It sounded like a poor question, too intrusive and too early.

"I don't know," said Else, unperturbed. "How does it feel for you?

I paused. Scott looked at me expectantly. "Surprised. I was going to say I felt it was worth it, but that was just a thought. The feeling was surprise. For one thing, I was surprised by the joy I felt when we got here."

Heinrich looked incredulous. "Did you think you wouldn't be happy? That it wouldn't be worthwhile?"

"I never thought it wasn't worthwhile. It's more a general discovery, a rediscovery, that making an effort at something is worth it. Before we left, I was starting to doubt that."

Heinrich kept staring at me. "And being on the Camino gave you back the belief that things are worthwhile?"

"I wouldn't call it a breakthrough. It didn't take guts or courage. I just kept going. That's what we were here to do, so I did. No choice. I never thought about quitting. And I thoroughly enjoyed so much of it. But when I got to Santiago and walked into that cathedral, I felt true astonishment. There *is* something at the end of things you do, which you don't know about until you have done them. That was the surprise. Like the sun suddenly reappearing out of the blue just when you thought it had gone down this time for good, and were starting to get on with things in the dark."

"Was it a renewal of religious faith for you?"

"No, not faith *in*, but faith *that*: faith that things matter and when they are done, they have a meaning, they become part of the life you exchange with the world. Is that religious faith? I don't know."

Pilgrims are said to be in search of something, a reality beyond the material world. But I wondered as I listened to our conversation whether something hadn't found me. It wasn't God, not a consciousness at all, nothing personal. We recognize it in our bodies, our breath, our muscles, in our silent place of pure knowing. It's an embrace like a grandmother's arms, that comes to wait with us, for us, around us. It has always been there, but the moment you know it, it feels like being found. Maybe faith is allowing yourself to know that wherever your pilgrimage takes you, no matter how lost you may feel, something always knows where you are.

"For me," said Else, "arriving in Santiago was very peaceful. It was raining when we got here and when I walked into the cathedral, there was no more rain, just light - as if the rain drops had turned to crystals of light - and everything was calm and quiet. I felt like praying, and I did. It was so beautiful."

"Very impressive church," said Heinrich. "I would like to have seen the *botefumeiro*. We'll go to Mass tomorrow. You don't go to church, you two?"

Scott and I looked at each other. "That's something I left behind a long time ago," I said.

"And I got kicked out of Sunday School when I was six."

"What for?" Else asked in surprise, giggling mischievously.

"General impertinence."

"So you do the Camino in what spirit then?" said Heinrich.

We had asked other people about this, but no one had ever asked us. "I came because I wanted to enjoy the cycling and the outdoors," said Scott. "It's also a pilgrimage into history, and a way of defining yourself against the past. I wanted Mary to write a book about the Camino so people would see how they could enjoy it, interact with it. She's gone off on her own tangent since then. But I think the concept of "eco-tourism" is important for reviving pilgrimage as a kind of dialogue with your cultural history and your values."

"So there was nothing religious in your purpose?" persisted Heinrich, looking at Scott. "Not even when you look back at it afterward?"

"Not for me. But that doesn't mean it didn't affect me. I think a lot of people who think of themselves as real pilgrims misunderstand the idea of going on the Camino to experience the outdoors. They don't believe it has a meaning. But movement isn't just exercise, it's an instinct. It's a form of communication with physical reality through your body. It's our physical nature to move. It's what we are designed to do. You feel the wind, you feel the ground, you see land change as you move through it. We have legs so we go places. Always have. How else do you get your bearings unless you walk around? I think our attraction to movement and landscape and our interest in our environment are a natural extension of that basic pattern."

"It's innate in people to make meaning out of what they do, but we all do that in different ways. Our bodies resonate with landscape. But it's not always conscious, and it isn't always expressed in the language of pilgrimage either."

Pilgrimage is a way of explaining the movement of the body in space. It gives a conscious form to a basic instinct, takes us into an awareness of the wonder of being able to move over the earth. But movement itself doesn't *need* explaining. If you want an explanation, you can set to work devising one, but that won't change either the physics or the imperative of movement. Scott was right. Maybe we try too hard at meaning. As far as the universe is concerned, the action contains enough meaning in itself. The action is the thing to keep your eye on.

"But if what you say is true," argued Heinrich, "then all we need to do is walk around like robots. We have the gift of consciousness. Shouldn't we use it to lift our ideas to a higher plane than merely our physical nature?"

"I like this trip because I like to move my body. I like being on a bike - it's fun, it's pretty and it's interesting. That's Level One. Then there's all the history and architecture. All the environmental aspects: geology, ecology. That's Level Two. Level Three is what you build onto the first two, some meaning. It's manufactured, sure, but it's authentic if it grows out of what you see, what you feel, how you respond. It's the meaning that can take you somewhere you haven't been, or make you do things better and differently afterward."

A group of about fifteen pilgrims came into the restaurant, bringing rainy smells and human vapour. A few of them greeted us as they passed, people Else and Heinrich had met in the hostels or on the road. Waiters arranged a table behind us, and the pilgrims piled noisily into their places, scraping their chairs, vigorous and tough and intent on a feast.

There was a pause in our conversation. The newcomers were nothing if not lively. Out of their chatter came bursts of boisterous laughter and song. I turned to get a better look and spotted the ringleader at once: the Brazilian we had seen in the Pilgrims' Office. His warmth spread along the table; even the waiters standing near the kitchen door kept an affectionate eye on him. More pilgrims entered the restaurant to join them; there was much rearranging of chairs and stumbling of boots and kissing. More platters of food arrived and the Brazilian made himself a full time job pouring wine.

"There's a happy group of people," said Else.

"I'm happy with my bunch," I said. And I was. I knew that being on bikes had cost us that kind of on-going companionship, but it didn't seem to matter. Having Scott with me had been enough. I looked at him as he poured water for us. His face was sun-burned and roughened. His beard had grown longer and grizzlier, and his eyes were very clear, almost shining.

I had heard of pilgrims who felt a great loss when they finally arrived at Santiago. I asked Else and Heinrich if they were at all sad about coming to the end of their pilgrimage. They were not, but they also knew of people who became depressed as the time to leave the Camino drew near, sometimes severely.

"We came to affirm our faith, Else and I," said Heinrich, "but a lot of people come to the Camino to be transformed or healed in some way. When the transformation doesn't happen the way they expect it to, it's depressing."

On pilgrimage, you try to let go of *things*, of worldly pretensions, of greed, even of yourself. But it occurred to me that the real pilgrimage, the one that is even more difficult, starts the moment you are off the Camino, when you begin your return to the everyday world. The last great task of the Santiago pilgrimage is to let go of the Camino itself. It's hard. Despite ourselves, we have romanticized it, identified with it, clung to it as the expression of who we are or want to be.

And even if transformation does happen, to go on to live healed in an unhealed world is another challenge. I recalled something I once read in *Zen in the Art of Archery*. The pupil has concluded his years of study with the Master and is about to return to Germany. The Master tells him:

> You have become a different person in the course of these years. For this is what the art of archery means: a profound and far-reaching contest of the archer with himself. Perhaps you have hardly noticed it yet, but you will feel it very strongly when you meet your friends and acquaintances again in your own country: things will no longer harmonize as before. You will see with other eyes and measure with other measures.

"Speaking of transformation," said Heinrich, "I read recently that James was the patron saint of alchemists.

Raymond Lull made a pilgrimage to Compostela in the 13th Century after he was refused by a woman he was infatuated with."

"Was Lull an alchemist?" asked Scott.

"They say so. And the Camino was seen by alchemists as an initiatory pathway. It was the geographical equivalent of the "Great Work" of purifying your heart, of transforming your spiritual lead into gold. Pilgrims purged themselves along the way so that when they got to Santiago they were an empty vessel, ready to receive the gifts of the spirit at James' shrine."

"You got the lead out on the Camino!" quipped Scott.

"What was the name of that Brazilian writer who wrote the novel about the Camino?"

"Paolo Coelho," I said. "He plays with the notion of the pilgrimage as a rite of inner transformation, and he brings in a lot of esoteric notions. I found it rather weird."

I thought more about this as the others talked. Santiago Cathedral was bedecked with thousands of pounds of gold, much of it stolen from the New World. I hadn't felt anything like gold in myself as I had sat looking at James' shining casket. But I could now say I knew a lot more about lead. It was the lead you needed to understand first, the dross that you had to start with. The alchemist had to understand every characteristic of that which he wanted to transform. What it would be transformed *into* was only a matter of recognition. Gold didn't require much analysis. Lead, on the other hand, was maddeningly complex.

"I would say that almost half the people we met on the Camino are non-believers," Heinrich was saying, "or at least skeptics. They equate that with being totally separated from the Christian symbols along the way. They observe them, appreciate the art, but they say they have no other kind of emotional or spiritual link with them. They say they are doing the Camino for personal growth. And they also deny that anything of the old religion still lives on in themselves or in their modern culture. They have no sense of responsibility for what they see on the Camino."

"What do you mean?" asked Scott.

"I mean, they have little sense of inheritance. We are almost all inheritors of the Judaeo-Christian tradition. It is our cultural foundation. We pretend it isn't, but it has shaped who we are from centuries back. I think of St. Augustine - "

"One of the world's great introspectors," I said.

"Yes, and I think he would understand the modern search for truth, and understand our narcissism, though he would still have argued for Christianity. That preoccupation with the self - you see it on the Camino - the obsession with whether we're ok, whether we're doing it right - all that belongs to the same tradition as the Protestant search for God in a spirit of individualism and independence. And the Catholic concern with the state of the soul belongs in this category too. I think we should recognize the habits of mind that link us to our tradition. Even if you discard the belief, you are still responsible for it. It's a huge denial to think we have no connection to the pilgrims of a thousand years ago. They are our cultural ancestors."

"So what you're saying is that people need to acknowledge their spiritual heritage, even if the beliefs are dissonant, and recognize their role in transforming it, and not try to pretend that they are on a journey in isolation from any other influence."

Heinrich helped himself to more octopus. "Yes. Yes, something like that."

"It seems to me," said Scott, "that there has always been a pilgrim's instinct in human beings, but it's always been expressed in a particular religious and cultural context. We must be the only people in history to set out on a journey that is important only to ourselves, outside a social framework. But pilgrimage is still, at least, a quest, something people are interested in, and still feel an urge to do. We are really back on the instinct level again, without any coordinates in a common culture. We go on pilgrimage and we're not quite sure why. We even go on pilgrimages to the shrine of a saint who isn't there!"

"Are you Buddhists?" Else asked, turning to me. "We heard you mention it once."

I said I didn't know, that the label bothered me. But plugging away on my bicycle over the Camino, I had discovered that the Buddhist practice of mindfulness was an essential pilgrim's tool, as useful as a walking stick for keeping you firmly on the trail, and as daring an act as wearing an open purse the way the early pilgrims did. It had taken me some time to grasp this, I told the others. At first I had looked for lofty reasons for making a pilgrimage, like getting a new grip on my life, if that could be called lofty. But after a while, those reasons had become only words rolling in my head. Introspection is good, but the mind wanders and it is easy to get lost.

"You need an anchor as you travel," I said, "a fixed point of reference for what you are doing, separate from your inner monologue, something that keeps your mind alert and attached to the present moment outside yourself. Pilgrimage is a trip from your own small mind into a larger reality, but it's difficult; it's hard to see things clearly, without fear or resistance. It's a good idea to have a practice, a disciplined meditation, to take with you. That way, you keep the pressure on to stay with things as they are, rather than floating off into all your little dreams about yourself."

Heinrich looked at me, challenging. "And after you get attentive to the present and seeing things clearly, then what?"

"Honestly, I don't know. I just do it anyway, on faith. It seems to work."

"How do you *know* it works?" said Heinrich, but Else, who had been listening quietly to the conversation, cut him off. "Do you know what I think?" she said. "It's other people. That is what follows seeing clearly through the eyes of faith. You can't do anything *else* then but reach out."

I looked at her smiling face and her blond hair messy from the rain. Was that what I had meant? It was something to think about, even if it wasn't.

"What are your plans now," asked Else.

"We spend tomorrow here. Next day, we rent a car and drive to Finisterre, then we head back to France," said Scott. "We'll stop at Silos and Vilar de Doñas, and a few other places where we can buy some books and see things we missed. We drop off the car in Irun, and call a cab to get us back to Biarritz." Scott turned to me. "Do we still have the guy's card?"

"Both of them," I answered. "And you?" I asked Else.

"We fly home in the morning from Santiago," said Else.

Before we left, we said goodnight to the pilgrim mob at the next table. They invited us to join them; the Brazilian grinned at us and held up a bottle of red Spanish wine. Else and Heinrich pulled up chairs and stayed to talk with their other pilgrim friends, but I was too exhausted and let Scott lead me back to the hotel.

In the morning, we spent a long time in the Cathedral, then toured the museum. After lunch, we rested in our room. I slept a long while, dreamed in broad strokes, and woke up not having the slightest idea where I was. Still in bed, with Scott sleeping beside me, I picked up the Study Themes book from the Pilgrims' Office and some tourist pamphlets I had taken from the museum.

In 1589, when Don Juan de San Clemente was Archbishop of Santiago, Sir Francis Drake arrived with his English fleet on the north coast of Spain to take the city of Coruña. Drake intended to go after Santiago de Compostela too, that "ultimate hotbed of papist superstition." The plan was never carried out, but Don Juan had a set of relics taken from the Cathedral for safekeeping. I found it odd that none of the records specified that James' bones were removed, but historians think they must have been.

By 1592, doubts were circulating about whether the story of James had any foundation in fact. A canon from Toledo, seeking to establish the primacy of his church over Santiago de Compostela, tried to discredit the claim that James had even set foot in Spain. A cardinal in Rome took the argument seriously and began to swing Vatican opinion to his side. The prospect of losing their patron saint ignited great protest, and for a while, a nation-wide wave of pro-James fervour overshadowed the age-old squabbling between Compostela and Toledo.

Involved in the authenticity debate was a certain Juan Roa Dávila, a Spanish theologian who had belonged to the Jesuits for some eighteen years before leaving the order over a doctrinal dispute. Regarded in Santiago as something of a scoundrel, he had once argued that the State had legitimate rights to punish abuses of power in the Church. He had also been accused, convicted, then acquitted of sodomy. Eventually he was exiled to Rome, where he spent the remainder of his days writing theological treatises which I for one would never read.

In one of these documents, Dávila outlined his argument that James had preached in Spain. His approach was more theological than historical, since like many religious historians, he believed that salvation history and worldly affairs were one and the same. Dávila made much of Biblical prophecies of James, even claimed that the conquest of the New World, largely completed in the 1590s, was the work of St. James as prophesied in the Old Testament. The argument was compelling. Reading about it, I observed uneasily that if you thought about it long enough it almost made sense.

In 1602, Rome conceded that the coming of James to Spain was authentic church tradition. By 1631, the story was declared a matter of historical fact.

Nobody bothered much with the whereabouts of James' bones for the next few centuries. Pilgrims came, fewer than before. James' life in Spain became a relatively minor piece of history, as was the presence or absence of bones.

1878, Astorga. The gnostic carving of the sun and moon over a temple facade with an open hand is discovered. *Eis Zeus Serapis Iaw.* Zeus, Serapis and Jahweh are One.

1879. The age of nation states. Sigmund Freud is twenty-three. Darwin's *Origin of Species* has been in print for twenty years. Mendel has been at work for almost fifteen years on the laws of heredity. Dynamite, reinforced concrete, wound antiseptics and the periodic table of elements are about ten years old. The bacilli for tuberculosis and diphtheria are three or four years away.

Siemans has put together the first electric locomotive engine and the motor car is only six years down the road. The Salvation Army is one year old. It is the age of "isms." Positivism, materialism, scepticism. German higher criticism has exposed the Gospels as myths, and even the existence of Jesus is in dispute. What hope does this leave for Spain's patron saint?

1879, Santiago. The "isms" are on Cardinal Payá's mind, as he looks over his cathedral in Compostela. Payá decides to excavate the floor over the place where James' body is said to be buried. It is nervous work. One slip and the whole thing comes undone; even if the story is true, few will believe it if the archeology isn't dead on.

They dig and find the tomb sealed by Gelmirez in the 12th Century. The grave is open and empty. But popular traditions say the bones may be behind the altar. Overnight on January 28, two canons uncover an urn holding three skeletons. Leo XIII is informed and a trained team of experts goes to work.

1879, Northern Spain. The year they find the paleolithic cave paintings in Altamira.

1884, Rome. It has taken six years "to clear up certain difficulties" about the bones in the urn behind the altar. When the results are in, Pope Leo proclaims to the world in a bull called *Deus Omnipotens* that the bones said to belong to James and his disciples are authentic. Leo makes much of the event, draws a line back in time to his own namesake, Leo III, who had declared in the 9th Century that James's body was in Galicia. Later, I read Ballester on this, who says that despite the most exacting scientific tests of the time, there was still no lack of detractors, enemies who wished to see in Galicia merely a regional myth.

I picked up a magazine called *Compostela*. Idly, I leafed through it until I came to the pages of statistics. If pilgrimage had nearly died out altogether in the early part of the 20th Century, there were enough graphs and pie charts here to show that it was making a triumphant comeback. In 1985, there were 2491 pilgrims on the Camino. In 1996, there were ten times that number: 23,218. Most were German and French. Three quarters, roughly, were on foot; a quarter were on bicycles, and an all but invisible .24% were on horseback.

I reached over and took my Compostela from the bedside table. Every word was in medieval Latin, including my name, Mariam. After seven lines of preamble full of genitive plurals and ablative absolutes, it said that on June 2, 1997, I visited this most holy temple out of pious devotion. Something like that, anyway. The text was enclosed in a rectangular frame decorated with ribbons and scallop shells. At the top of the frame was an inset picture of an 18th-century pilgrim dressed in robes and holding a staff. Earlier Compostelas, I knew, had had a picture of Santiago the Killer of Moors as well. He had been tactfully removed. I felt a streak of rebelliousness.

Why gloss over things we know? I recalled that day we were cycling across the meseta. I had marvelled then at the fierce force of my own muscles and bones. I had felt the resistance of the path as though, once it had my attention, it was playfully giving itself back to me. I had seen that pilgrimage required a submission to the moment, a release of illusion and a movement of body and soul, in trust, into the world as it was. *As it is.*

Scott was awake. I said I was annoyed with my Compostela. "It makes it look as if I came here because I believe something about James," I said. "I didn't. I was here to encounter *this* world, the one I live in because I can't help it, and this piece of paper doesn't honour that." I knew I sounded petulant.

"Pilgrimage should account for the world we experience *now* for it to be authentic," I went on, "and that includes accounting for the world we go home to. We can't put the Camino in a little nook of the world and play at being serenely in touch with things from the past. This kind of nostalgia is a frill; there is nothing that acknowledges the real, honest difficulties of being a modern pilgrim on a Camino - and in a world - that is full of dissonance for us. It's as if we are not supposed to act like the people we are!"

I couldn't stop. "It's a terrible strain, trying to maintain an illusion of what the Camino means. No wonder a lot of people feel depressed after they come off the trail: I think it's their head's way of telling them to get real!"

"I guess that's what I mean about a modern Via Negativa. We have to see the path clearly as it appears to us now, in all its contradictions and absurdity. Its instability is the reality that we have to work with in our search for truth!"

I paused for breath. "What do *you* think?" I said, feeling as if I had gotten something out of my system.

But Scott was breathing softly, asleep again, in another world. I waited.

I picked up the sheet again, looked at the photocopied pilgrim with his little bag-like gourd dangling at the top of his staff. We are all inheritors of the tradition, Heinrich had said. It dawned on me that we are still a community of seekers, even out here on the fringe of the millenium. Here was I, flat on my back, utterly worn out from eight hundred kilometres, holding the picture of a past pilgrim in my hands. I remembered Etheria. She had done her pilgrimage in the only way she knew how. I had done this, my first pilgrimage, the only way *I* knew how. I wondered whether the pilgrim's burden now is to carry Etheria's passion in trust, and seek in the "whatness" of things as we find them today, the responses that would lead us to the goal that all religions share: salvation from our own small sorrowful stories.

I heard buskers outside the window, a clarinet and guitar duo playing jazz. Evening was coming. Scott was still deeply asleep beside me. I listened to the music, thinking, watching the tulle curtains shiver in a draft from the window.

In *Zen in the Art of Archery*, the pupil diligently practises for years under great strain just to learn how to shoot an arrow. When he has finally succeeded, and is counting on hearing some words of praise, the master tells him: "He who has a hundred miles to walk should reckon ninety as half the journey. Our new exercise is shooting at a target."

My pilgrimage with Scott, wonderful, exhausting, confusing, on mountain bikes, on the margins of pilgrim society, was in one sense the most authentic one I would ever do. It was like the first singing lesson, when you hear with embarrassed recognition the raggedness and the tentative longing in your own voice, and your teacher tells you that you will have to learn to go deep into your body and then let it fly. I thought of the German merchant in King Alfonso's Canticle, come to Santiago for a cure, and so spiritually inept that he was all the way back to Villasirga before he opened his soul enough to be healed. I thought of that American tourist, slogging up the hill with his heart pounding. "I had no idea it was like this," he had said with such surprise. I hadn't either.

One way or another, we had all done our first ninety miles. Now we had to train for the longest distance.

"I think I'll come back again next year and walk the Camino," I told Scott when he woke up.

"I knew you would."

"I just got the hang of it this time. I think I know what I'm shooting for now."

NOTES

The personal names and biographical details of a few of the pilgrims I met on the Camino have been changed in *Among the Pilgrims* to respect their privacy.

With minor exceptions, the information about the Camino in *Among the Pilgrims* is accessible in a variety of books, from the scholarly to the touristic. Full bibliographies for the Camino, including many wonderful books and pilgrim accounts not mentioned here, are available on the web or from any of the Confraternities of St. James in England, Canada or the USA. There are plenty of Spanish books and articles on the Camino, many - even the popular works - of a high scholarly quality.

These notes acknowledge all the informational sources I used directly for *Among the Pilgrims*, and are intended as well to give a sense of what kind of material is available and where more information about specific topics might be found. Pages numbers are given for extended direct quotations only.

Chapter 1 - Pilgrimage

This chapter drew for factual material on Jonathan Sumption's invaluable *Pilgrimage: An Image of Mediaeval Religion* (Totowa: Rowman and Littlefield, 1975), and on William Melczer's Introduction to *The Pilgrim's Guide to Santiago de Compostela* (New York: Italica, 1993). This is a translation of Aimery Picaud's 12th-century *Pilgrim's Guide*. The boy's quotation is on p. 70 in *St. James the Apostle and his place in history: Ten Study Themes*, a partisan but informative book by José Antonio Gonzalez Garcia et al, published in Santiago by the Comisión Diocesana del Ano Santo, 1993 and translated by members of the English Confraternity of St. James. *The Seafarer* comes from *The Exeter Book* in *The Anglo-Saxon Poetic Record*, edited by G.P. Krapp and E. Van Kirk Dobbie (New York: Columbia, 1936). For Bede's *History of the English Church and*

People, I used the 1965 Penguin Classics edition. William Langland's *Piers Plowman* is most accessible in A. V. C. Schmidt's *The Vision of Piers Plowman* (London: Everyman's Library, 1984). As for Spanish works, I found Isidore G. Bango Torviso's *El Camino de Santiago* (Madrid: Espasa-Calpe, 1993) useful. I translated the pilgrim's blessing on p. 74 for quotation. Fray Juan Antonio Torres Prieto's *Tu Solus Peregrinus: Viaje interior por el Camino de Santiago* (Abadia de Silos, 1996) gives a medieval interpretation to his pilgrimage to Santiago; for anyone who reads Spanish and wishes to understand the medieval mind in a sophisticated modern expression, the book is a must. The guidebooks mentioned in this chapter provide most of the incidental touristic details throughout this entire book. The Everest *Guide* is Millan Bravo Lozano's *A Practical Guide for Pilgrims: The Road to Santiago* (Madrid: Everest, 1998). Alison Raju's *The Way of St. James* (Milnthorpe: Cicerone, 1999) is compact and handy. Finally, the observations in Elias Valiña's *The Pilgrim's Guide to the Camino de Santiago,* translated into English by Laurie Dennett (Vigo: Editorial Galaxia, 1992) make it one of the most accessible and enjoyable guidebooks for anyone on the road to Compostela.

Chapter 2 - The Time Before

William Melczer (for quotes from Aimery), Jonathan Sumption (for notes on Nicolás of Bari), and Prieto's comments about the Santiago pilgrimage provide some facts and a point of departure for this chapter on pre-Camino Spain. All the quotes from Domenico Laffi, in this chapter and elsewhere, come from the Everest *Guide*. The full text of Laffi's account is translated by James Hall in *A Journey to the West: the Diary of a 17th-century Pilgrim from Bologna to Santiago de Compostela* (Leiden and Santiago de Compostela: Primavera Press and the Xunta de Galicia, 1997). The section on the *Song of Roland* draws on the Introduction and text of the poem in *The Song of Roland,* translated with notes by Glyn Burgess (London: Penguin, 1990). Juan G. Atienza's *La Ruta Sagrada* (Barcelona: Robinbook, 1992) was helpful for the section on the Celts. The learned and well-written Spanish commentary on the Camino, Juan Ramón Corpas

Mauleón's *Curiosidades del Camino de Santiago* (Madrid: Ediciones El País, 1992) provided anecdotal material about the nymph Pirene, and the Celtiberians. The Camino's "goose" connections and the theory that Priscillian is buried in Santiago Cathedral come from Dana Facaros and Michael Pauls' amusing and off the cuff but more or less trustworthy travel guide, *Northern Spain* (London: Cadogan Books, 1996). From the first two chapters of Bernard F. Reilly's excellent history, *The Medieval Spains* (Cambridge: UP, 1993) come much of the factual material about the Roman and Visigothic presence in Spain. Information on the early Christian mission and the persecutions comes from *The Dawn of European Civilization*, edited by Ian Sutton (London: Thames and Hudson, 1965), in particular from Chapter 9, William Culican's "Spain under the Visigoths and the Moors." Accounts of James and his burial in Spain, available in many histories and guidebooks, are nicely summarized in Fernando López Alsina's "Genesis of the Road to Santiago," found in *El Camino de Santiago*, a well illustrated "coffee table" book with an excellent text, edited by Pablo Martínez Sáiz (Madrid: Lunwerg Editores, 1991). The selection, interpretation and "framing" of these bits of history within my experience of the Camino is, of course, my own. The Sam Keen quotation is from *Apology for Wonder* (New York: Harper and Row, 1973), p. 88.

Chapter 3 – Moors

Historical material on the Moors in Spain and the Reconquest is readily found in a variety of scholarly, popular, and even touristic sources, including the Everest *Guide* and Valiña's *Pilgrim's Guide*. For more details, I turned to two seasoned and accessible historians: Richard Fletcher, whose books *The Quest for El Cid* (Oxford: UP, 1989) and *Moorish Spain* (London: Phoenix, 1994) were a pleasure to read and reread; and Bernard F. Reilly, once again, in *The Medieval Spains*. More facts on the Basques and Francis Xavier came from the section on Pamplona in Torviso's *El Camino de Santiago*. Details on the Virgin Mary in Navarra and along the Camino are from Atienza's *La Ruta Sagrada*. Scholarly notes about Faray's chest in the Museum of Navarra are found in Marie Madeleine

Gauthier's *Highways of the Faith: Relics and Reliquaries from Jerusalem to Compostela*, translated by J. A. Underwood (Secaucus: Wellfleet, 1983). The Teodosio tale is mentioned in the Cadogan Guide and recounted more accurately in Arenas' *Los Caminos de Santiago: Arte, Cultura, Leyendas* (Barcelona: Anthropos, 1993). Further details on the Moorish invasion were taken from Mary Vincent and R. A. Stradling's *Cultural Atlas of Spain and Portugal* (Oxford: Andromeda, 1994). The Covadonga story is told in a wonderful treasury of Spanish epic tales called *Leyendas Épicas Espanolas*, edited by Rosa Castillo (Madrid: Castalia, 1971). The complicated theological controversies behind the Invention of James' tomb are described in several books, many of them Spanish. I relied mostly on Alberto Ferreiro's excellent essay "The Cult of Saints and Divine Patronage in *Gallaecia* before Santiago," in Maryjane Dunn and Linda Kay Davidson (Ed.) *The Pilgrimage to Compostela in the Middle Ages: A Book of Essays* (New York: Garland, 1996). Accounts of the Invention of James' tomb and the political and popular responses to it, including the Clavijo story, are also easy to find in every Camino guide, as well as in academic books. My sources were mainly Fernando Lópoez Alsina's "Genesis of the Road to Santiago"; Torviso's *El Camino de Santiago*; Paolo Caucci von Saucken's spectacular tome, *Santiago: La Europa del Peregrinage* (Barcelona: Lunwerg 1993); and Ferreiro's essay "The Cult of Saints." The quotation about the Moors in Masudi's *Kitab al-tanbih wa'l-ishraf* is from Bernard Lewis's *The Muslim Discovery of Europe* (New York: W. W. Norton, 1982) p. 139. The quotation on the Vow of Santiago is from Juan Contreras' *Santiago Apostol* (Madrid: Biblioteca Nueva, 1940) p. 155, and the 1064 story from the *Historia Silense* is from von Saucken, p. 89. The material on al-Mansur, the fall of Córdova, the taifa states, and Peter of Cluny at Nájera come mostly from Fletcher's *Moorish Spain*.

Chapter 4 – Stories

Richard Fletcher's *The Quest for El Cid* was the factual basis for the discussion of horses in Spain, and for the sections on El Cid. The quotation about El Cid's battles near Nájera is from p. 97. The story of Garcia and his wronged mother, "El Caballo del Rey Don Sancho" is from Castillo's *Leyendas Épicas Espanolas*. The *Song of Roland* quotations are from Glyn Burgess's Penquin edition: ll. 3723-7 and ll. 3307-8 and ll. 1006-16. The Roland and Ferragut story has many versions; I mainly used the one in Torviso's *El Camino de Santiago*. The section on the history of the *Liber Turini* drew on Colin Smith's essay, "The Geography and History of Iberia in the *Liber Sancti Jacobi*," in Dunn and Davidson's *Essays*. The quotation from Aimery's account of the lances at Sahagún is on p. 87 of Melczer's translation of Aimery's *Pilgrim's Guide*. The tale about Garcia and the Virgin is found in Valiña's *Pilgrim's Guide* and elsewhere. Reilly's *The Medieval Spains* provided some facts on Alfonso VIII and his exploits against the Moors. The tales connected with San Millán come from a guidebook I purchased at Suso: Juan B. Olarte, *The Monastery of San Millán de la Cogolla: Suso and Yuso* (León: EDILESA, 1995). The Fernán Gonzalez story is mentioned in Prieto's *Tu Solus Peregrinus*. The grizzly *Siete Infantes* tale is in Castillo's *Leyendas Épicas Espanolas* and also Olarte's *San Millán*. The passage on saints who stop people from moving their relics is amplified with details from Sumption's *Pilgrimage*. The Berceo stories are found in Connie L. Scarborough's "The Pilgrimage to Santiago de Compostela in the *Cantigas de Santa Maria*," in Dunn and Davidson's *Essays*, and in Gerald Brenan's *Literature of the Spanish people: From Roman Times to the Present Days* (Cambridge UP, 1951). I used the Spanish translation of Brenan's book, by Miguel de Amilibia, entitled *Historia de la Literatura Espanola*, (Barcelona: Editoriale Critica, 1984), where I also found some useful literary criticism about *El Cid* (p. 74). Torviso's *El Camino de Santiago* provided a few details about the bridge at Santo Domingo de la Calzada and about Grañon. The story of Bernard del Carpio is from Castillo's *Leyendas*.

Chapter 5 – Landscapes

Aimery's comments about water and river crossings are from pp. 88, 91 and 89 of Melczer's translation of his *Pilgrim's Guide*. The Asturian and Mozarab settlement of the Duero region is well documented; I kept mainly to Reilly's account in *The Medieval Spains*. Information about the Órbigo floods and other geographical details throughout this chapter are from José Manuel Rubio Recio's "Los Paisages Naturales y El Camino" in *Congreso International de Geografia: Los Caminos de Santiago y el territorio* (Junta de Galicia, 1993). The Rabé–Tardajos song is found in many Camino guidebooks; I took mine from the Everest *Guide*, p. 128. Quoted remarks about the meseta come from Prieto, pp. 297, 307, Valiña, p. 76, and, for Aimery, Melczer, p. 96. The Laffi quotations are collated from the Everest *Guide*. Information about medieval agriculture on the meseta comes from Recio's article, as does the 1846 flood story from Santa Catalina. Material on knights and hospices at Itero del Castillo is found in José Vicente Matellanes Merchán and Enrique Rodrígues-Picavea Matilla, "Las órdenes militares en las etapas castellanas del Camino de Santiago" in Horacio Santiago-Otero (Ed.) *El Camino de Santiago: La Hospitalidad Monástica and las Peregrinaciones* (Salamanca: Varona, 1992). Details of Galician geology are from Augusto Pérez Alberti, "Formas y processos geomorfológicos desarrollados a lo largo del Camino Francés en Galicia," in *Los Caminos de Santiago y el territorio*. Aimery's remarks about Galicia are from Melczer, p. 96. The accounts of Juan and Gaucelmo come from Gregoria Cavero Domínguez, "Fundaciones hospitalarias del clero secular en la diócesis de Astorga (Siglos XII-XV), in Santiago-Otero, *El Camino De Santiago*. The quotation about Jean de Tournai is from Valiña, p. 121.

Chapter 6 - Churches

There are many good general resources on the Romanesque period. I relied on R. W. Southern, *The Making of the Middle Ages* (New Haven: Yale, 1975), Friedrich Heer, *The Medieval World: Europe from 1100 to 1350* (London: Cardinal, 1961), Isidro G. Bango Torviso's *El Camino de Santiago*, Serafin Moralejo's excellent article "Art on the Road to Santiago" in Carandell et al, *El Camino de Santiago* (Consejo de Europa: Lunwerg, 1991), and Millán Bravo Lozano's beautiful book, *El Camino de Santiago: Inolvidable* (Madrid: Everest, n.d.) Several guides to the Camino provided detailed information about specific churches: the Everest *Guide* and Valiña's *Pilgrim's Guide* were always helpful. Atienza's *La Ruta Sagrada* discusses more arcane theories about the symbolism of Eunate and other locations on the Camino. Prieto's *Tu Solo Peregrinus* was useful for the symbolism of Eunate. I drew on Gonzalo Torrente Ballester's old-fashioned but still fascinating *Compostela* (Madrid: Afrodisio Aguado, 1948), on Sumption's *Pilgrimage*, and on James S. Stone's *The Cult of Santiago: Traditions, Myths and Pilgrimages* (London: Longmans, Green and Co., 1927) for stories about Pelaez and Gelmirez. If I have one regret about my sources for *Among the Pilgrims*, it is that Richard Fletcher's wonderful book about Bishop Gelmirez, entitled *St. James' Catapult*, was unavailable to me at the time of writing.

Chapter 7 – A Fallen World

For general historical content, including wars and crimes on the medieval Camino, inns and hostels, religious superstitions, and health and medicine, I used Sumption's *Pilgrimage*, Torviso's *El Camino de Santiago*, Arenas' *Los Caminos de Santiago,* the Everest *Guide*, Fletcher's *Quest for El Cid*, Reilly's *The Medieval Spains*, and Heer's *The Medieval World*. The story of the Carrión convent is from Torviso's *El Camino*. The prayer for protection comes from Sumption, p. 175. The quotation about the rogue Stephen is from Fletcher's *Quest for El Cid*, p. 63. The story of the criminal hanged is from Torviso, while other details about Camino crime are taken from Robert Plotz's article "Peregrinatio ad limina beati Jacobi," in Saucken, *Santiago: La Europa de las Peregrinaciones*; and José María Soto Rábanos's very useful article, "Picaresca en algunos puntos de la ruta asturiana," in Santiago-Otero, *El Camino de Santiago*. The quotation about the *merino* of the *infanta* Urraca is from Fletcher's *Quest for El Cid*, p. 62. The accounts of Domingo, Gregory and Juan de Ortega, and Queen Isabel come mainly from Torviso's *El Camino* and the Everest *Guide*. The tale from the Montes de Oca is in Ballester's *Compostela*. Information about San Martín is from a first-rate, hard-cover guide to the church, *Arquitectura y*

Simbolismo de San Martín de Frómista, by Jesus Herrero Marcos and Carlos Arroyo Puertas (Diputacion de Palencia: Ars Magns, 1995). The Prudentius quotation is on p. 130 of that work. The dire warning in the *Veneranda Dies* comes from Sumption, p. 124. The Chaucer quotation is from the Parson's prose sermon, quoted in Sumption, p. 16. Pope Gregory and the lettuce leaf is in William Dalrymple's fascinating book, *From the Holy Mountain* (London: Flamingo, 1998). The note on Peter of Cluny is from Sumption, p. 16, as is the remark from the *Veneranda Dies* about Christ as physician, p. 77. The moral tale of the lady with the loaves is in Torviso's *El Camino*. The story of Andrés and the abbott is from Rabanos' article on the Picaresque in Otero, *Hospitalidad*, as are more details about the perils of Camino inns. The innkeeper whose neck is broken is mentioned in Sumption's *Pilgrimage*. Prieto's comments on hospitality are from *Tu Solo Peregrinus*, p. 215ff.

Chapter 8 – The Wheel of Fortune

Friedrich Heer's *The Medieval World* was helpful for the rise of the Gothic; the Gundisalvo quotation is found on p. 396. For touristic details about Burgos Cathedral, Villadangos, and Órbigo, I used Valiña's *Pilgrim's Guide* and the Everest *Guide*. The Francisco de Quevedo allusion is taken from Prieto's *Tu Solus Peregrinus*, p. 212. The quotation from Laffi on the Cristo de Burgos is from the Hall translation, p. 137, as are a few incidental details. Tirso de Molina is quoted in Torviso's *El Camino*, p. 71. Tirso was in reality a Mercedarian friar named Bagriel Tellus, the first playwright to dramatise the legend of Don Juan. The quote from Jacques de Vitry is from Sumption's *Pilgrimage*, p. 257. Henry of Saxony is quoted on p. 31 of Robert Plotz's "Peregrinatio ad limina beati Jacobi," in von Saucken's *Santiago*. The Study Themes booklet is an earnest, badly edited, little Catholic treatise available at the Santiago Pilgrims' Office. The quote is from p. 74. The description of the tournament at Órbigo is my fantasy, but historical details are from Atienza's *La Ruta Sagrada*, and Luis Alonso Luengo's "El *Passo honroso* de Suero de Quinones y su significación para el Camino de Santiago," in Santiago-Otero, *Hospitalidad*. Details on Astorga, the

Gaudi Museum and the Maragatos, also on Ponferrada, are from the Everest *Guide*. The history of the knights is taken from Malcolm Billing's *The Cross and the Crescent: A History of the Crusades* (London: BBC, 1987), with the quotation from p. 79. Also useful were two articles in Santiago-Otero's *Hospitalidad*: "Las órdenes militares en las etapas castellana del Camino de Santiago," by José Vicente Matellanes Merchán and Enrique Rodríguez-Picavea Matilla; and "La Huella guerrera en el Camino: el apóstol Santiago y las órdenes de caballero," by Francisco Castrillo Mazeres. Information on the Church of Santiago, the history of indulgences and vicarious pilgrimage is from Lozano's *Camino de Santiago: Inolvidable,* Torviso's *El Camino,* Arenas' *Los Caminos de Santiago,* Sumption's *Pilgrimage,* and the Everest *Guide*. The Chaucer quotation is from ll. 669-714 of the Prologue to the *Canterbury Tales*. I used Albert Baugh's Edition (New York: Meredith, 1963). The quotations about Nicolás of Angers and the Sicilian mother are from Sumption, pp. 141 and 296 respectively. The Chalons quotation and the Frenchman's comment about mortal sin are from Sumption, pp. 144 and 289. The quote from *Piers Plowman* is from the Prologue, ll. 46-49. The Biblical quote used by Langland, incidently, is from James 1:27. Facts about the Samos monastery are from José M. Andreade Cernadas, "El monasterio de Samos y la hospitalidad Benedictine con el peregrino (siglos XI-XIII), in Santiago-Otero, *Hospitalidad*. The quotation about the "knave Luther" is from Sumption, p. 302. The demise of the Camino after the 16th Century is well described in von Saucken's *Santiago: La Europa del Peregrinage*. The Contreras quotations are from *Santiago Apostol*, p. 117.

Chapter 9 – Songs

My sources for factual information on music on the Camino are mainly Gerald Brenan's *Literature of the Spanish People* (the Spanish translation); von Saucken's *Santiago: La Europa del Peregrinage*; and a good article by Ismael Fernández de la Cuesta, "El canto de los peregrino," in a book of essays collected, I assume, at a conference in Santo Domingo de la Calzada in 1993, entitled *Vida y Peregrinación* (Madrid: Ministerio de

Cultura, 1993). Las Huelgas and the lives of Eleanor and Alfonso VIII are described in Arenas, *Los Caminos de Santiago*, with details taken too from the Everest *Guide*. The Las Huelgas CD, with its good liner notes, is *Vox Iberica II Codex Las Huelgas*, a Deutsche Harmonia Mundi recording, D-7800, Freiburg. The Silos compact disc is *Canto Gregoriano*, EMI Classics, CMB 5 65217 2. The story of Santa Maria del Manzano is well-known; I took my version from Arenas' book. The little quotation about the Chapel of Santiago is from Valiña, p. 193. The story of Felipe is in both Mauleón and Arenas. The German merchant story is from Scarborough's, "The Pilgrimage to Santiago de Compostela in the *Cantigas de Santa Maria*," in Dunn and Davidson's *Essays*. The material on love-lyrics, Galician dances, and vegetation rites is from Brenan's *Literature of the Spanish People*, as is the quotation (p. 14 of the Spanish edition). Alfonso X and his court musicians and Canticles are discussed in von Saucken's *Santiago*, as are the *Grand Chanson* and the traditional pilgrim songs.

Chapter 10 – Santiago

For information on Etheria, I drew from Sutton's *The Dawn of European Civilization*, where she is referred to as Egeria, from Sumption's *Pilgrimage*, and from Simon Coleman and John Elsner's informative *Pilgrimage : Past and Present in World Religions* (London: British Museum Press, 1995). Coleman and Elsner quote Valerius on p. 92. Etheria's Golgotha quotation is from Sumption, p. 90. The music on CD entitled *Ultreia! Sur la Route de Saint-Jacques-de-Compostelle* was made in 1982 by Ensemble de Musique Ancienne Polyphonia Antiqua, (Aix-en-Provence : Pierre Verany, 1990.) The *Veneranda Dies* quotation about Santiago Cathedral is from Vincent Corrigan's "Music and the Pilgrimage," in Dunn and Davidson's *Essays*, p. 62. The quotes from the *Ten Study Themes* booklet are on p. 58. *Zen in the Art of Archery* is by Eugen Herrigel (New York: Random House, 1999). The "hotbed" quote is from *Ten Study Themes*, p. 40. The story of Dávila is taken from Klaus Reinhardt and Horacio Santiago-Otero's article, "Juan Roa Dávila (1552 – ca. 1630) y las controversias sobre la venida y predicación de

Santiago en España" in Santiago-Otero, *Hospitalidad*. The final quotations from Eugen Herrigel, *Zen in the Art of Archery*, p. 61.

Quotations at the beginning of each chapter are taken as follows.

Carl Jung. *Modern Man in Search of A Soul*. New York: Harvest Books, 1955, p. 208.

Northrop Frye. *The Great Code: The Bible and Literature*. New York: Harcourt Brace Jovanovich, 1982, p. 50.

Annie Dillard. "In the Jungle," in *Teaching a Stone to Talk*. New York : HarperCollins, 1982, p. 73.

James Cowan. *A Mapmaker's Dream: The Meditations of Fra Mauro, Cartographer to the Court of Venice*. Boston: Shambala Publications, 1996, p. 101.

Bodhidharma is quoted in D. T. Suzuki. *An Introduction to Zen Buddhism*. New York: Grove Press, 1964, p. 50.

Steven Vogel. *Cats' Paws and Catapults : Mechanical Worlds of Nature and People*. New York : W.W. Norton, 1998, p. 181.

Nicholas of Cusa. "On Learned Ignorance." In *Late Medieval Mysticism*. Ed. Ray C. Petry. London: S.C.M. Press, 1957, p. 363.

James Cowan. *A Mapmaker's Dream*. p. 134.

Margaret Avison. "Unbroken Lineage," Winter Sun and Other Poems. Toronto: University Press, 1960. p. 18.

Robert Kroetsch. *Excerpts from the Real World: A Prose Poem in Ten Parts*. Lantzville: Oolichan Books, 1986.

Paul Rezendes. *Tracking and the Art of Seeing*. New York: HarperCollins, 1999, p. 22.

Pierre Hadot. *Philosophy as a Way of Life*. Oxford: Blackwell, 1995, p. 197.

Margaret Avison. "Watershed," *Winter Sun and Other Poems*. p. 18.

Annie Dillard. "An Expedition to the Pole." In *Teaching a Stone to Talk*. p. 52.

Margaret Avison. "The Mirrored Man," *Winter Sun and Other Poems*. p. 71.

Anthony C. Meiself and M. L. del Mastro (Transl.) *The Rule of St. Benedict*, New York: Image Books, Doubleday, 1975, p. 100.

Shunryu Suzuki, *Zen Mind, Beginner's Mind*, New York: Weatherhill, 1988, p. 54.

Annie Dillard. "An Expedition to the Pole." In *Teaching a Stone to Talk*. p. 60.

Evelyn Underhill. *Practical Mysticism*. New York: E. P. Dutton, 1915, p. 91.

Margaret Avison. "Apocalyptics III," *Winter Sun and Other Poems*. p. 54.

James Cowan. *A Mapmaker's Dream*. p. 132.

Eugen Herrigel. *Zen in the Art of Archery*. New York: Random House, 1999, p. 62.

ISBN 141200796-8